UNITED NATIONS REFORM

LOOKING AHEAD AFTER FIFTY YEARS

D1535084

Lester B. Pearson, President of the seventh regular session of the United Nations General Assembly, opening the General or "Steering" Committee meeting on 15 October 1952.

UNITED NATIONS REFORM

LOOKING AHEAD AFTER FIFTY YEARS

—————————— EDITED BY ——————————

ERIC FAWCETT AND HANNA NEWCOMBE

SCIENCE FOR PEACE

Printed and bound in Canada by Best Book Manufacturers

Canadian Cataloguing in Publication Data

Main entry under title:

United Nations reform : looking ahead after fifty years

Co-published by Science for Peace.
Includes bibliographical references.
ISBN 0-88866-953-4

1. United Nations. I. Fawcett, Eric, 1927- .
II. Newcombe, Hanna, 1922- . III. Science for Peace (Association).

JX1977.U55 1995   341.23   C95-930706-0

Includes bibliographical references and index

Science for Peace
University College
University of Toronto
Toronto, Ontario M5S 1A1

Distributed by

Dundurn Press Limited
2181 Queen Street East
Suite 301
Toronto, Canada
M4E 1E5

Dundurn Distribution
73 Lime Walk
Headington, Oxford
England
0X3 7AD

Dundurn Press Limited
1823 Maryland Avenue
P.O. Box 1000
Niagara Falls, N.Y.
U.S.A. 14302-1000

Science for Peace · Dundurn Series

Books submitted to Science for Peace for publication in the Dundurn Series are published on their merits with regard to the purposes of Science for Peace, and the timeliness of the subject matter. Generally a typescript is submitted to a process of peer review prior to acceptance. Authors wishing to publish through Science for Peace should write in the first instance to the Publishing Committee, Science for Peace, c/o Professor Veronica Dahl, Department of Computer Science, Simon Fraser University, Burnaby, B.C. V5A 1S6.

The present volume brings together great diversity of subject matter and many authors. We have tried to preserve the full range of individuality of their writings, even where this prevents uniformity of convention.

Views expressed in this book are those of the authors, and do not necessarily reflect those of the granting agencies who supported its publication, or of the members of the Publications Committee.

Derek Paul
President
Science for Peace

Contents

Acknowledgements

Thanks go to the following for significant assistance to the editors, or for opinions on one or other of the chapters: Newton Bowles, John Brenciaglia, Shirley Farlinger, Terry Gardner, Gerald Morris, Morris Miller, Derek Paul, Geoffrey Pearson, Cranford Pratt, and Fergus Watt.

We are grateful to Patricia Woodcock, without whose secretarial and word-processing services the book could hardly have been produced.

The publication of this book has been made possible by the financial support of the Franz Blumenfeld Fund, the Panicaro Foundation and the Walter and Duncan Gordon Foundation. We thank these organizations.

We are indebted to the Canadian Committee for the Fiftieth Anniversary of the United Nations for their endorsation and for permission to reproduce in Chapter 22 the Executive Summary of their document *Canadian Priorities for United Nations Reform*.

Foreword

Anatol Rapoport

All proposed reforms of the United Nations converge on one theme. An indispensable item on any reform agenda is restriction of nation state sovereignty. It is also the most important item, since without this restriction no other reforms designed to make the UN more effective in realizing its professed goals can be meaningful.

Yet restriction of sovereignty seems to subvert the very goal of the United Nations expressed in the *Preamble* to the *Charter:* "… to reaffirm faith in fundamental human rights, in the dignity and worth of the human person and in equal rights of men and women *and of nations large and small …*"

Thus, not only the human individuals but also the nation state is declared to be the possessor of rights. And if rights are to be understood in the juridical sense, in accord with the traditional recognition of the nation state as a juridical entity, then sovereignty is assumed to be among them.

To be sure, guarantee of sovereignty to a small, weak state can be regarded as protection against encroachment on its autonomy by a large, powerful state. But guarantee of sovereignty to a large, powerful state can be and is frequently interpreted as a freedom from interference with its own actions, and these frequently amount to encroachments on the autonomy of small states and violations of human rights within its own borders.

A way out of this dilemma might be to make a clear distinction between sovereignty and autonomy. The latter could be understood as an analogue of liberty as it pertains to an individual – that is, freedom limited by prohibitions of encroachment on the freedom of others. To extend this idea to states would mean the abrogation of the principal component of sovereignty – the right to make war. It may be pointed out that the *Charter of the United Nations* already abrogates the right to make war *except in self-defence,* but this essentially reasserts the right, since all wars are now claimed to be in self-defence.

Under the present *Charter,* the nearest approach to removing war making from the province of individual states is manifested in *Articles 42* and *43* dealing with actions aimed at stopping wars and other forms of organized violence.

> *Article 42:* Should the Security Council consider that measures provided for in *Article 41* [short of war] would be inadequate or have proved to be inadequate, it may take such actions by air, sea, or land forces as may be necessary to maintain or restore international peace and security ...

> *Article 43:* All members of the United Nations, in order to maintain the maintenance of international peace and security, undertake to make available to the Security Council, on its call ... armed forces ... necessary for the purpose of maintaining international peace and security.

Clearly these articles do not abrogate the right to make war. Instead they *accord* this right to the Security Council and, in a way, obligate members of the United Nations to participate in military actions authorized by the Council. Such authorized action (authorized by default as a result of the Soviet delegate's failure to attend a meeting) was actually taken in Korea (1950–53). Aside from this war, however, the hot wars during the forty-odd years of the Cold War were like any other wars, except that they were all called measures of self-defence (or police actions, or defence of the free world, or wars of national liberation, or nothing at all), and none were "declared," that is, given formal legitimacy.

After the collapse of the Soviet Union, "defence of the free world" could no longer be sold, and so military actions habitually undertaken by the militarily strongest member of the United Nations had to find another blanket justification. Here *Articles 42* and *43* of the *United Nations Charter* came in handy. Without the constant threat of the Soviet veto, practically an automatic response to any proposal of coercive action apparently in the interest of the USA, the latter could dominate the decisions of the Council. The Gulf War was the most outstanding evidence of this dominance.

Here we find the only hint of disagreement among the authors of this volume on the opportunities generated by the end of the Cold War.

The disagreement is on problems arising in connections with the use of violence to enforce peace. Some accept without reservation the Secretary General's 1992 *An Agenda for Peace,* in which "peacemaking" (by force, if necessary) is listed as an integral component of the United Nations' role in "addressing the hunger for peace with justice" (Chapter 8). Others have serious reservations about this development *in the present state of the UN.* The allusion is to interventions by major powers acting in their own interests unrelated to the preservation or restoration of peace (Chapter 7).

Returning to the common ground among the contributors, we see a unifying idea in the conception of the reformed United Nations as the "Third Generation" world organization, the successor to the League of Nations and its child, the UN, in its present form (Chapter 4). This view reflects a belief in so-called progress, a concept that has come to be viewed by many as a battered carry-over from nineteenth-century Eurocentric ideology. Indeed, comparison between the past and the present "human condition" by any number of criteria seems at times to make faith in "progress" untenable. Yet if we examine the projected image of the third-generation world organization, which presents itself in virtually every contribution to this volume, we see the one meaning of "progress" that may justify continued belief in its reality. We see a unidirectional evolution of ideas of *organization for global cooperation* and, moreover, impressive unanimity on most these ideas. We can say that simply the existence of the United Nations (powerless as it has been) has to a large extent shaped the direction of this evolution. Evidently, at least a portion of humanity has learned something from recent history and this learning has been facilitated by the existence of an organization *designed* to improve the human condition regardless of its actual record. The very failures of the United Nations fuelled the progress of ideas.

We have, for example, learned the following lessons from the at times disastrous Somalia "peacekeeping" operation (Chapter 9):

- cold warriors carry a continuing responsibility for bloody conflicts in many fragile states;

- conventional arms are killing people – the international arms trade continues uncontrolled, with the USA and Germany in the lead;
- humanitarian aid will go down the drain unless there is concomitant social and political healing and reconstruction;
- UN success depends on unconditional and sustained commitment and unconditional acceptance of UN leadership;
- etc.

The concept of universal human rights in a juridical (not just moral) sense arose in the process of formation of the United Nations. The document that emerged at the *World Conference on Human Rights* in Vienna reaffirmed (Chapter 13):

- the principle of universality and indivisibility of human rights;
- the important role of Non-Governmental Organizations active in human rights;
- the principle of the rights of the child to survival, protection, development and participation;
- etc.

Among the reforms proposed, the most far-reaching involve extensions of the role of the UN in providing a framework for protecting the environment and for sustainable development, issues that have forced themselves into our awareness during the past quarter century. Implementation of this programme must necessarily be based on considerable technical expertise (Part V); so here, too, there is a solid basis for consensus.

Finally, another direction of reform on which there is practical unanimity among the contributors is that of democratizing the UN as an institution with reference both to its internal structure (Chapter 5) and to the agenda of its activities (Chapters 17 and 18). In fact, this task largely overlaps that of abrogating the absolute sovereignty of the nation state while retaining its consolidating function. The problem is to separate sovereignty conceptually and concretely from autonomy. Sovereignty of an actor (whether that of an individual, for example, a monarch or an institution) implies the absence of an authority to which the actor is responsible, or else removing such an authority from the realm of the observable, for example, vesting it in a deity – recall the divine right of kings. Autonomy entails delineating the range of context in which the actor (an individual or an institution) is not controlled by an external authority. Ideally the boundaries of autonomy are defined by the range of actions that have no discernible adverse effects on other actors or on systems in which the actor in question is imbedded.

This principle governing the limits of autonomy can be formulated in terms of determining optimal levels of decision making. J. Tinbergen defined the optimal level of decision making as "(a) ... the lowest possible level in order that a maximum level of participation and maximum level of information be used, and (b) the level high enough to entail negligible external effects." Note that this principle amounts to a definition of democracy – a mode of social organization in which the boundaries of autonomy accorded to individuals and groups are optimal in some explicitly defined sense.

In sum, the present volume, appearing on the semi-centennial anniversary of the United Nations, represents a concerted effort to save this institution from the fate of the League of Nations. The League was an organization of states rather than of people. So-called collective security depended on the willingness of *states* to act in the collective interest of *people*. This volume represents an awareness that the assumptions underlying "collective security" are unrealistic. To the extent, therefore, that the *Charter of the United Nations* still reflects the assumption that states, as presently constituted and juridically recognized, can act otherwise than in their own interests as traditionally conceived, the UN is not viable. The proposals for reorganization, democratization and redefinition of goals all converge on turning the UN into a global organization of people rather than of states. The mot conspicuous manifestation of this change of focus is the virtually unanimous recognition of the three tightly interrelated global problems that the UN should be designed to face and to serve as the coordinating centre for efforts to solve them: the problem of abolishing war as an institution; the problem of ensuring the viability of the biosphere; the problem of reducing the disparity between the affluent and the destitute worlds.

Drawing of Boutros Boutros-Ghali by David Levine. Reprinted with permission from *The New York Review of Books* 41 No. 9 12 May 1994 29 (Brian E. Urquhart "Who Can Police the World?")

PART I

UNITED NATIONS REFORM:
PROLOGUE

CHAPTER 1

An Agenda for United Nations Reform

Geoffrey Grenville-Wood

*Great problems usually come to the United Nations because governments
have been unable to think of anything else to do about them. The United
Nations is a last-ditch, last resort affair, and it is not surprising that the
organization should often be blamed for failing to solve problems that have
already been found to be insoluble by governments.*

U Thant, 1978[1]

*Even as it stands the UN system is considerably more effective than the
impression given by many stringent criticisms, especially those emanating
from its most powerful members. It is, if anything astonishing that this
group of public-service international institutions, staffed from and gov-
erned by nearly every country in the world, have achieved so much of
enduring value in the last forty-nine years. It would, however, be surprising if, after such a period of time, they were not in need of radical overhaul, the more so as their mandates and critical responsibilities are rapidly
increasing in volume and complexity.*

Erskine Childers and Brian Urquhart, 1994[2]

These are two views expressed by knowledgeable people a quarter-century
apart. U Thant, after retirement showing the fatigue and frustration to be
expected from someone who had tried to run the United Nations during
some of its most difficult times. Childers and Urquhart exhibiting the
commitment and hope of those who have lived through the darkest hours
and who now see potential and possibility. Who is right? This book about
reforming the United Nations will not provide the full answer. It will at
least contribute to the discussion.

In truth, U Thant's opinion reflects a stark and uncomfortable reality,
as accurate today as it was then. Member States, especially the powerful,
do not accept that the UN is anything more than just a minor instrument
of foreign policy. An attitude which could be characterized as: "if it serves
our purpose to have the UN act, or if we can dump the problem in the

UN's lap, we will use the organization." There is as yet no firm commitment to the UN as the prime instrument for such states to conduct their foreign relations.

Thus, we see the UN constantly begging Member States to pay their dues; living a hand-to-mouth existence, while lacking the minimum funds to carry out the mandates demanded of it. At the same time, the organisation is under a constant barrage of criticism from many of the leading Member States for its "bureaucratic mess," its financial "chaos" and its "corruption and nepotism." The other truth is that the UN's total regular operational budget, including all the specialized agencies and excluding peacekeeping and the international financial institutions (who do not like to think of themselves a part of the UN system, anyway) is US $ 6.384 billion per year. As Childers and Urquhart point out, this is equivalent to the amount US citizens spend on cut flowers and potted plants in a year.[3]

The whole UN system employs a total of 51,484 persons, including all professional, support and general service staff. The UN Secretariat proper, based in New York, Geneva and Vienna, and including at the regional commissions, comprising a total of about 9,100 persons. This is fewer than the City of Winnipeg which employs around 9,900.[4] Yes, perhaps these are not the best people in the world, although many are. Most of the employees of the UN are highly talented and dedicated. I would guess that the proportion of vastly superior to deadwood probably exceeds that of Winnipeg or any other city or government department in Canada.

Lest there be any misunderstanding, there is also a great deal of truth in the quotation from Childers and Urquhart. The United Nations, after fifty years, has performed near miracles in many fields including health; but it is in need of major reform. The past fifty years have taught us that we need a better and more effective UN. The world, if it is to survive another fifty years, must reorganize its system of international and global governance. Perhaps we could call this requirement our Global Agenda for Change. Within this overarching Agenda, there are several components, each more daunting and challenging than the last, all interconnected, related and interdependent.

Sustainable Development and Agenda 21

Some of the changes needed have been outlined in a number of powerful documents emanating from the United Nations itself. For example, the *UN Conference on Environment and Development* (UNCED) approved its *Agenda 21*, a vast list of actions required of states, international organizations and citizens. What is most significant about *Agenda 21*, apart from its scope and reach, are the demands full and proper implementation of its recommendations will make of the international system. There is no historical precedent for the kind of global supervision of individual, private and public sector and nation state activity called for. There is also no precedent for the changes in day to day activity needed immediately. Thus, changes in the international system and the implementation of a truly global system of governance for the planet will be required to give real meaning to the concept of a shared environment and ecology, while still ensuring a decent life for the inhabitants of the planet.

The United Nations provided the occasion, in Rio de Janeiro in June 1992, for the governments of the Member States and for thousands of representatives of the peoples of those states, through Non-Governmental Organizations (NGOs), to meet and identify the environment and development problems facing the planet. As can be expected, that huge effort only served to start a complex process leading to: "measures which place environmental concerns at the centre of the development policies of all countries," to quote Maurice Williams, the President of the Society for International Development.[5] The international system itself needs to embark on the same path. The international financial institutions, the private lenders and international institutions need to change approaches and standards and governments must have some form of accountability for the undertakings made and received at UNCED and after.

UNCED took place more than two years ago. It is now clear that the impetus for real change in national and international institutions, called for by the scope of the issues identified there, is largely lost. The poor state of the world economy has had the effect of weakening the resolve of governments and of sapping the creative energy of the policy-makers. Furthermore, it is apparent that the weak compromise institution created at UNCED, the Commission for Sustainable Development (CSD) will never have the capacity or the power to be the overseer for the implementation of *Agenda 21*.

In May 1994, the InterAction Council, a group made up of former heads of state and government, in a report which was the result of meetings involving a wide range of experts as well as several members of the Council itself, said the following regarding the CSD: "The mandate of the CSD – covering virtually everything dealing with sustainable development – may turn out in practice to be a considerable bottleneck. Rather than speeding up, it may retard the adoption and implementation of meaningful measures."[6]

The Council went on to say: "Consideration should also be given to whether there is really a need for CSD to report to other intergovernmental bodies, such as ECOSOC or the General Assembly, inducing a proliferation of meaningless debates. Would it not be sufficient for CSD to report directly to governments and to the Secretary-General, suggesting particular areas for attention or initiatives?"[7]

In light of the lack of real authority around the CSD table, some of the ideas regarding institutional mechanisms, rejected at UNCED mainly because of the failure of governments to screw up the nerve to do something meaningful, have been resurrected. The InterAction Council said the following about the need for a stronger institution:

> Given deficiencies resulting from its genesis, mandate, composition and operating modalities, doubts have arisen whether CSD will be able to become the desired, effective fora to discuss, coordinate and cope with the cluster of global issues of environmental degradation, poverty and overpopulation. The suggestion has been made that it would be desirable to have in this area a body as powerful and efficient as the Security Council is in its field. Such a body should be empowered to pass binding resolutions and to seek enforcement of decisions (although, to be sure, the Security Council itself is lacking this very power to impose policies on national governments).[8]

Another aspect of the *Agenda 21* dilemma arises from the historic underpinnings of our system of international law. Common sense, we hope and sometimes even believe, will confirm that environmental concerns transcend national boundaries and therefore their solution must be addressed transnationally. Thus, it should be taken as a given that issues of national sovereignty should be made subservient to overriding environmental concerns. Not so – Professor Nicholas A. Robinson of the Centre for Environmental Legal Studies at Pace University School of Law and a noted international environmental legal scholar, in a paper delivered in advance of UNCED, set out the problem as follows:

> Existing international law has not served to protect the environment: globally, this system has allowed the acute deterioration now experienced. There are reasons for this. Classic international law since Hugo Grotius focused on

three key relations among nations:(1) that restitution be made when one state harms another; (2) that a state's promises must be observed (*pacta sunt servanda*); and (3) that freedom of the seas be assured. Under the United Nations Charter, three further elements were embraced: (1) collective security; (2) the protection of human rights; and (3) the duty of international cooperation. While this framework has conferred enormous benefits on the community of nations, worldwide environmental trends highlight inadequacies. The system presupposes that nations can each take care of their own affairs, largely as independent 'citizens' or subjects under international law. Environmental problems, however, obliged nations to deal with matters over which each state has little to no control alone. No single state can be self-sufficient in its environmental well-being.

Mere treaties do not protect nature. International law rarely concerns itself, however, with the measures a state takes to observe a treaty until the breach harms another state, and by then the environment is injured too.[9]

At UNCED, the most heated debates took place around specific environmental or development issues. Delegates and NGOs alike were mesmerized by the potential of words. Words which marked either progress in the way the issue was described or which effectively protected the status quo. In fact, the real debate and the strong lobbying should have been on institutions and legal instruments. Subsequent events have shown that words on an Agenda have no meaning unless there are laws, in the form of treaties and agreements, and that there is in place an institution to oversee and enforce those laws.

There is therefore an urgent requirement to reopen the discussions about the *Earth Charter*, the international treaty that would protect the sustainability of the planet in a meaningful and substantive way. Dr Parvez Hassan, a distinguished jurist from Pakistan and a leading international lawyer, put forward the case at The Hague in August 1991:

We ... believe that the time has come when the international community must acknowledge and accept environmental rights and obligations in the same manner as it has acknowledged and accepted the international protection of human rights. A few decades ago, it seemed revolutionary to assert that human rights could be protected at the international level. "Domestic Jurisdiction" and "sovereignty of states" were then pleaded as iron curtains that barred international efforts to promote and protect the human rights of individuals across state boundaries. But the collective voice of the international community which first manifested itself in the Universal Declaration of Human Rights adopted by the United Nations in 1948 brought about, "overnight," a virtual global acceptance of the internationalization of human rights. I believe that, today, we stand on the threshold of an equally promising era: an era where the international community should move to accept and acknowledge the basic and fundamental rights and states to be free from environmental degradation.[10]

Thus *Agenda 21* should be more than the list of actions required. More fundamental change at the institutional level is needed if we are to have meaningful results. The 50th Anniversary should provide a renewed impetus to examine the institution and the law that would make reality of the hopes and expectations that drove the UNCED process.

An Agenda for Peace

Shortly after UNCED, the Secretary-General of the United Nations, Boutros Boutros-Ghali published *An Agenda for Peace*.[11] This report, which was commissioned by the Security Council at its historic summit meeting of 31 January 1992, dealt with three key aspects of the role of the United Nations in the context of collective security. These were Preventive Diplomacy, Peacemaking and Peacekeeping. Events since 1992 have made it even more obvious than it then was that the report only scratched the surface of the international security challenge facing the UN.

The demands made on UN peacekeeping and peacemaking capacities by the crises in Somalia, Bosnia, Rwanda and Haiti show that there is a need for fundamental analysis of what precisely the UN ought to be expected to provide and on what basis should these demands be met. These issues are, in and of themselves, enough to keep reformers occupied well past the 50th Anniversary.

However, there are other equally pressing issues to address. The reform of the decision making process of the organization needs work. There are many ideas circulating about the membership, structure, powers and voting at the Security Council. The General Assembly, the Economic and Social Council, the other UN bodies and the agencies all need to be examined with a view to improving their operations and effectiveness.

The term *Agenda For Peace* referred only to those matters that related directly to the peacekeeping and peacemaking function as supervised by the Security Council. It is however important to broaden the concept of the *Agenda For Peace* terminology to include the whole issue of restructuring the United Nations system. The United Nations is the globe's main engine for peace; renewal in all its aspects is in fact the *Agenda for Peace.*

Childers and Urquhart begin the process by identifying what could be called the nuts and bolts of the system; the machinery for decision making, finance and management, the staff and the relationship to NGOs.[12] The process for renewal does not necessarily include *Charter* reform, although perhaps it should. There is much to be done in the context of making the existing design, as set out in the *Charter,* more effective, more responsive and accountable.

The InterAction Council, in May 1994, identified one of the major shortcomings of the existing system which has to be addressed in this context. They said:

> One of its major shortcomings is that it really does not operate as a system with common guidance, supervision or central direction. The main reason for this state of affairs is the system's polycentric nature, which by itself is due to a decentralization of institutional competence on functional or technical grounds dating back in some instances more than 50 years. Thus, a plethora of more or less independent organizations pursues largely uncoordinated economic and social policies and programmes. In spite of an abundance of coordination devices, which remain largely in effect, the activities of the UN system lack coherence.[13]

The InterAction Council has identified one of the major difficulties with the UN system, a difficulty that has to be addressed immediately and decisively. This is not a matter for *Charter* reform, nor is it an issue that can be addressed by the Secretary-General alone. Member States are represented in more or less pivotal roles in all of the agencies. Governments deal, on a daily basis, with each of the agencies and continue to perpetuate the lack of coherence referred to. An international effort led by the

Secretary-General and supported by the Member States and the non-governmental organizations must work towards bringing the United Nations system to order.

Erskine Childers, in a speech at the University of London in January 1993, gave an excellent example. He said, while addressing a British audience, thus alluding to British examples:

> Britain left Ghana with only 95 University graduates among 9 million citizens, a ratio to total population which, by the way, had it applied here would have meant that Britain in 1960 would have had only 600 graduates for all needs. But in only 20 years the UN Development Programme, with UNESCO, trained over one million teachers, more than half in Africa. I know since I helped in this work. The British government withdrew from UNESCO in the very year when this enormous achievement could be announced.
>
> Yet even as the million new teachers was reached and surpassed, the International Monetary Fund, supposedly a part of the system, was demanding that Third World governments dismiss tens of thousands of those very teachers, under its "structural adjustment" policies supported by the G-7 powers that control it. Whole portions, up to a third of the educational staffs so painstakingly built up by the rest of the system – and incidentally also with the G-7's own bilateral aid – have been wiped out in the last decade. This is an example of no-sense contradictions in the system that simply must now be confronted.[14]

Therefore, reform is needed to deal with the chronic lack of coordination in the system. This would mean far more accountability of the agencies to some central authority residing within the office of the Secretary-General. Of course, that office is still clearly accountable to the members of the United Nations. The problem to date seems to have been that each of the agencies, although accountable to member governments, through their governing bodies, is not accountable to the UN system *per se*. In this way, the supervision by member governments is divided between many sectors within those governments and dispersed through a lack of central coordination within the system. The challenges the world faces in the second fifty years of the United Nations' existence will not permit us the luxury of such practices and lack of accountability.

One major area that clearly needs reform is the office of the Secretary-General itself. It would seem that not enough attention has been paid to the role the Secretary-General is expected to play on the world scene. In the public's mind, he is seen as the world's foremost international civil servant. The office is the embodiment of the hopes of mankind for a peaceful and prosperous world. Unfortunately, the reality is that the office has no real independent authority and is severely circumscribed by budgetary and political considerations. In the new era this reality will have to change. At the same time, the office cannot be all things to all people and cannot be expected to perform all of the functions now required under the existing *UN Charter*.

Perhaps the first reform should be in the process for selection of the Secretary-General. No self-respecting organization would permit its executive head to be selected in such a highly inappropriate and Byzantine way. It cannot be denied that the office of the Secretary-General is a highly political one, and therefore the major powers in the United Nations will want to have a major say in the selection. However, such a selection should not take place merely upon the basis of whether certain individuals have the self-regard to put their names forward to their governments and others for consideration.

The United Nations has been lucky in its first fifty years in that the calibre of most of the persons who have held the high office has been of the highest order. There have been of course exceptions. In addition, one cannot help but wonder if there were not others available, from time to time, who could have been persuaded to accept the office had they been sought out and recruited. In fact a selection process based upon search and recruitment must be one of the first orders of business in the context of United Nations' reform. In the final analysis, the real selection will be made by the Security Council. The hope is that the range of candidates put before the Security Council will in fact represent the best available candidates at any time.

Erskine Childers and Brian Urquhart prepared a report in 1990 on the issue of leadership and the United Nations. With reference to the selection of the Secretary-General they stated that the existing process was haphazard, increasingly parochial, and predominantly political. In their report they propose a different and improved process, as follows:

> If the term of Secretary-General were to be limited to a seven-year single term, an improved process of appoint-

ment could be discussed by the General Assembly and the Security Council without any risks of possible embarrassment to the current Secretary-General.

The essential elements of an improved process are:

- serious consideration by governments of the necessary qualifications for the post, as indicated, among other things, by probable future demands on the UN;
- a single seven-year term;
- the cessation of the practice of individual campaigning for the Secretary-Generalship;
- agreed rules as to nominations and a timetable for the process;
- a well-organized search, in good time, for the best qualified candidates worldwide, thus taking the initiative away from self-perceived or nationally sponsored candidates;
- the inclusion of women candidates in the search in comparable numbers to men;
- a mechanism for the proper assembly of biographical material and for the assessment and checking of the qualifications, personal suitability, record, etc., of the candidates;
- high level consideration of candidates by governments, in consultation with parliamentary leaders and important non-governmental bodies, before a final decision.

A search group, to be established by the Security Council each time, should be representative of both its permanent and non-permanent members. It should be authorized to seek information and advice from any source, including the non-governmental sector and the international civil service. Its work should be carried out in the strictest confidentiality and well in advance of the date for a new appointment.[15]

It is also a matter of some concern to United Nations watchers that the office itself needs to become more focused and more closely identified with certain areas of the mandate of the organization. For example, it is highly questionable whether the office of the Secretary-General should be directly involved in actions authorized under *Chapter VII* of the *Charter*. Since it is always hoped that the Secretary-General of the United Nations will be available to provide good offices in the direction of resolving conflicts and attempting to avoid the use of arms, it seems appropriate that office should be removed from the day-to-day management of military operations, even if they are undertaken under the United Nations' flag. It is thus recommended by some that the *Chapter VII* operations should be managed and organized by the Security Council which should have answerable to it a command structure reflecting the United Nations' organization and system. This structure should be separate from the office of the Secretary-General which would thus be freed to act in a mediatory and conciliatory mode, as required.

Giandomenico Picco, a former United Nations Assistant Secretary-General for political affairs sets out the concept in some detail, referring to the difficulties the United Nations has endured since the heady days of 1990 and 1991:

> The Cold War actually ended for the United Nations more than two years before the Berlin Wall came tumbling down. The catalyst was Mikhail Gorbachev, the last Soviet president, with his new attitude towards the world body, and the occasion was the Iran-Iraq war, perhaps the first non-East-West conflict. The five permanent members of the Security Council began a new way of working together in early 1987, and a year later the Secretary-General brokered the end of the Iran-Iraq war, perhaps the most remarkable in a series of UN successes between 1987 and 1991. Among those, El Salvador's conflict was a civil war – whose resolution garnered a 1988 Nobel Peace Prize – and others had civil war characteristics. In addition, the United Nations helped broker the accords that led to the Soviet withdrawal from Afghanistan, shepherded Namibia to independence, extracted the hostages from Lebanon, and fashioned the agreement for the subsequent settlement in Cambodia.
>
> In all those cases, the office of the Secretary-General played a key role. Importantly, however, UN success was not secured by the use of force. The United Nations was engaged under the Secretary-General's direction solely in negotiations and peacekeeping.[16]

Picco refers to the Gulf War in which the military role under *Chapter VII* was subcontracted out to the US led military coalition. He alludes to situations such as Somalia and Bosnia, and indicates that management by the Office of the Secretary-General of these situations has not been particularly successful because the tools available to the Secretary-General are those more related to *Chapter VI* peacekeeping ventures.

Picco concludes that the confused chain of command we have witnessed in the Balkans and elsewhere has resulted in a loss of credibility for the United Nations itself and in a lessening of the effectiveness of the effort. Lewis McKenzie has made similar comments.

Picco thus argues that the Office of the Secretary-General should not be endowed with any of the military financial and intelligence tools of a state. He is against transforming that institution into what he calls "a pale imitation of a state." He claims that the institution of the Secretary-General is inherently inappropriate to manage the use of force and to involve itself in decisions on the use of force. In addition, this involvement compromises the institution of the office of the Secretary-General and the impartiality critical to its capacity as a negotiator. Picco relates a personal anecdote which highlights this distinction between the office of the Secretary-General and the Security Council, which represents more directly the Member States. Picco was of course the Secretary-General's representative in the process of negotiating the release of the hostages held in Lebanon. He describes his experience as follows:

> During the course of the Secretary-General's operation that led to the release of 11 Western and 91 Lebanese hostages, the recovery of the remains of 2 Americans and the identification of the remains of 2 Israelis, I met several times as the UN negotiator with the hostage-takers under unorthodox circumstances. One of the first questions asked me was whether I was an emissary of the Secretary-General or the Security Council. I gave the right answer. Had I said 'the Security Council' as I was subsequently informed, I would have been killed. The question demonstrated quite an understanding of the United Nations organization and a perception of the Security Council as supposedly representing the vested interests of its Member States. In this instance, the Secretary-General's office could do what the Security Council could not, just as the reverse was true in the war against Iraq.[17]

Picco identifies one issue which tips the balance in favor of a separation of duties:

> Finally, there is the importance of morality as an anchor for the Secretary-General. Even if the institution of the Secretary-General could manage a *Chapter VII* use-of-force operation, it would then be the decision of his office to authorize intentional killing. This power is quite another matter than the tragic but unintended deaths that may accompany peacekeeping operations. In carrying out an offensive use of force, UN soldiers, identified aggressors, and civilians might all be casualties in unexpectedly high numbers. The authority to order killing, far from strengthening the institution of the Secretary-General, would render it no different in the eyes of suspicious combatants than major nation states and their alliances.[18]

It would seem that reform of the United Nations, and more particularly the Security Council, requires a little more thought in terms of what powers the Council should exercise and whether the Secretary-General is independent of the Security Council in some aspects or merely a servant of it, as appears to have been the case to date. The issue of how the Council is to be restructured, whether or not the veto should be maintained and whether other states should be added as permanent members could almost be considered secondary to this more fundamental analysis of what precisely is the role of the Security Council in relation to its "management" of the Office of the Secretary-General. Does the world organization not require a more independent Office, able to act to preserve the peace using non-violent means, and to use its good offices where combatants may very well include members of the Security Council? We are in a new world, the ideals of the drafters of the *Charter* are being achieved, in many instances. However, it is very possible that their concept no longer applies in relation to this very important aspect of the operation of the United Nations.

An Agenda for Development

On another front, also aching for major reform and initiative, is the area of development. In May 1994, the Secretary-General published a report on *An Agenda For Development*. A final version is expected soon. In some ways the issue of international development has been a source of great disappointment for many in the world community. There have been spectacular successes: parts of South-East Asia come to mind. But there are also abject failures: Africa springs immediately into view. In addition, there are spectacular failures within the success stories and there are minor successes within the abject failures. Erskine Childers in his University of London speech in 1993 set the focus as follows:

> There are severe, potentially catastrophic economic inequities between the North and South which the G-7 powers have very largely ignored ever since the 1970s, which have not conveniently gone away, only become steadily worse. In 1960 the richest one-fifth of the world's population enjoyed thirty times the income of the poorest fifth; by 1989 the richest fifth was receiving sixty times the income of the poorest.
>
> The ratio of 20:80, or worse, dominates our world today. As the 1990s opened, the twenty per cent Northern minority of human kind had 82.7% of world gross national product; 81.2% of world trade; 94.6% of all commercial lending; 80.6% of all domestic saving; 80.5% of all domestic investment, and 94% of all research and development. The 80% majority of humanity in the South get the 20% or less scraps from the tables of the affluent.
>
> Among them, some 1.2 billion people now live in absolute poverty, on the very margins of survival itself and with more driven down into this condition every day, 40% more in the last twenty years. They include over 560 million rural women whose numbers in such misery are rising faster than men, with 75 million women the sole heads of rural households containing over 500 million children and older people.[19]

It is this truth that the UN must now reorganize and redouble its efforts to address. The *Agenda For Development* put forward by the Secretary-General, is only a beginning. There must be a major restructuring of the United Nations' instruments for achieving development and there must be, as mentioned earlier, a fundamental restructuring of all the organizations so that they work in a coherent way together towards the same objective.

The South Centre, established in 1990 following the report of the

South Commission, prepared a report in 1992 by the Working Group on Reform and the Future of the United Nations, that brought together many leading thinkers from developing countries. In relation to the institutions of the United Nations, the report had the following to say:

> These multilateral financial institutions [Bretton Woods institutions] are designed to reflect international economic power relationships; in a highly unequal world, they are therefore constitutionally and effectively under the control of major industrialized nations of the North. Under these circumstances the current concern for democracy and democratic control – if it is to apply even to a limited extent to international organizations and relations – has consequences. The arguments for institutional specialization become invalid when one set of institutions is based on 'the sovereign equality of nations', and the basis for the other is economic power. For it is not true that there are no competing views or interpretations of economic and social reality; on the contrary these matters appear very different from the North and from the South.
>
> Nonetheless, some Northern proposals for an institutional division of labour with respect to development-related functions assigned peace and social concerns to the UN, finance and macro-economic management to the IMF, development strategies to the World Bank and trade matters to GATT. If these proposals were to be accepted, the Northern vision of the world economy would be beyond effective challenge, intellectual pluralism would be threatened, and alternative views would have difficulty in attaining an institutional foot-hold for international visibility.[20]

The report goes on to conclude that too much emphasis on the Bretton Woods institutions would reinforce the current imbalance that Erskine Childers referred to. It concedes that the institutions themselves were created in order to avoid the economic and political injustices and distortions which had been the cause of the great depression and the Second World War. However, they note that it is important today for these institutions to adhere more closely to their founding principles and purposes. The report concludes as follows:

On the other hand, if the North-based world view rooted in realpolitik is allowed to proceed unchallenged, the basic moral, ethical and political premises of the United Nations will all be undermined. It is therefore vital and urgent that advantage be taken of the current 'window of opportunity'. A broad-based initiative must be initiated by the South aimed at protecting and promoting the basic principles of the UN; to that end it is necessary to insist upon a carefully considered process of change agreed through negotiation between different interests. Updating the mission and structure of the UN is a matter of concern for the whole of humankind. Changes in its mandate, functions and institutions must be determined in a democratic manner.[21]

Another aspect that is not receiving sufficient attention, but which United Nations reform should consider as a matter of priority, is the fact that financial behaviour at the international level is not subject to any international supervision. The InterAction Council spends some time in its report examining the relationship between new *ad hoc* arrangements, such as the G-7 and its various summit and ministerial meetings, the multilateral organizations, the Bretton Woods institutions and the United Nations *per se.*

The InterAction Council appears to throw up its hands in disgust and concludes as follows:

Neither the United Nations and its economic and social council (ECOSOC) nor the UN's specialized agencies have ever played any significant role in economic policy making and it seems unlikely that they ever will. Governments direct their energies only to institutions where cooperation is likely to be most fruitful. The real problem is that the United Nations system was never able to cope with the multidisciplinary character of interdependence. The organization of the system along functional lines led to a situation where international cooperation was approached only from a sectoral perspective (which in turn would have the effect of strengthening sectoral lobbies nationally). Instead it should have tried to balance the various sectoral interests for the sake of global progress and cooperation. This would require a determined and sustained coordination exercised at the highest level, which cannot be resolved by the executive heads of the agencies meeting from time-to-time under the chairmanship of the Secretary-General. One of the irritations encountered in the past was that the various agencies were operating at cross-purposes, engaging as they did in normative activities and in issuing policy directives which were at variance. Sovereign governments had adopted in different sectoral forms, contradictory decisions of a global nature.[22]

The InterAction Council recommends that a new representative reform commission should be set up with a view to preparing a package of proposals regarding reform of the UN system in this field, including a reduction in the number of organizations, the number of intergovernmental committees, the volume of paper reports and documents. Its despair and pessimism may be justified, but the scope of the problem and the challenge to the world organization cannot justify so minimalist an approach.

Erskine Childers' 1993 speech cited an essay written by the University of Sussex professor, Hans Singer, underlines the scope of the real challenge facing the international community: "The state has become too big for the small things and too small for the big things ... The small things call for delegation downwards to the local level ... The big things call for delegation upwards, for coordination between national policies, or for transnational institutions."[23]

An Agenda for People

The United Nations reform process must also address what I have chosen to call *An Agenda for People*. This aspect deals with the democratization of international institutions, including the establishment of some form representative assembly and the establishment of minimum norms of international humanitarian law applicable to all Member States of the United Nations and therefore to all the peoples of the world.

The major blockage to real progress in this whole area is the concept of the sovereign state. In the context of a representative assembly, the states fear diminution of their powers. In relation to the minimum standards issue, states claim immunity from international opprobrium for practices that fall below the international norm. The Independent Commission On International Humanitarian Issues stated the latter issue clearly, citing an article by Larry Minear as follows: "Many governments seem to take a rather relaxed view regarding compliance with humanitarian norms, as if by ratifying the Geneva Conventions they had been freed from all other obligations ... But as soon as they are directly or indirectly involved in an armed conflict, most states qualify, interpret or simply ignore the rules of humanity, evoking state interests and sovereign prerogatives. Political considerations prevail over humanitarian requirements and humanitarian concerns are used to further political aims."[24]

An Agenda for People requires reform of the United Nations and reform of international law in the sense that it is no longer acceptable to hide behind the concept of sovereignty while trampling on the rights of individuals and groups. International law is evolving. As David Matas stated in a presentation to the Federal Liberal Caucus: "According to international law, at least on one interpretation, it would be permissible to send in arms to aid the armed struggle of a national liberation movement combatting a colonial, racist or alien regime. The national liberation movement is an organization representative of a people ... This international law is controversial. It is not universally accepted, but at least, asserted by many. For those who accept it, the prototypical situation where it applied was the case of South Africa."[25]

Matas went on to talk about another evolutionary advance in international humanitarian law. He spoke of the actual armed intervention by one state against another in the name of human rights. There have already been many examples of this sort of action, in recent years. Matas makes the following point:

> This doctrine is, if anything, even more controversial than the doctrine of aiding arms struggle of national liberation movements. It is noteworthy that the United States, which is perhaps the most interventionist government in this century, and has produced many weird and wonderful justifications for its interventions, has never invoked the doctrine of humanitarian intervention. On the contrary, the US explicitly regrets the doctrine. The law offices of the US Department of State reject it as a matter of international law ... If there is to be humanitarian intervention, and I believe in some situations there should be, it is not enough for the human rights situation in the country of concern to be bad. A conclusion must be reached that with an indigenous successor regime it could not possibly be

worse. The level of human rights violations has to reach grotesque dimensions before armed intervention becomes justifiable. As well, no other course whether political or economic, must offer any hope. An example I would give is the Nazi holocaust, the murder of six million Jews in the attempt to exterminate the whole Jewish people. Where the level of human rights violations does reach those dimensions, I would argue that humanitarian intervention is justifiable and that individual rights must prevail over sovereign rights.[26]

As can be seen the whole issue of the inherent conflict between sovereignty and individual rights needs to be advanced beyond the scope described by Matas. Javier Pérez de Cuéllar the former Secretary-General of the United Nations, in an important speech at the end of his term in 1991 stated: "We are clearly witnessing what is probably an irresistible shift in public attitudes towards the belief that the defence of the oppressed in the name of morality should prevail over frontiers and legal documents."[27]

Pérez de Cuéllar was pointing the way to evolution in international law in the direction of the protection of individual rights when they are being violated in a gross way by the state. This is not to say that we are on the threshold of a new millennium in the context of human rights and fundamental freedoms.

Clearly, however, it is an essential element of United Nations reform to review the processes that are now available within the international system in order to make them more accessible and more responsive to individual representations. Furthermore, states that continually perpetrate violations of human rights must be brought to book on the international stage and there must be a process for doing this. Finally, the international system must prepare itself for a system of governance that is more in tune with the need of the peoples of the world to be represented in the decision making process in a more direct way.

The *United Nations Conference on Human Rights* made some significant progress in a number of these areas. However, it is apparent that the impetus of the 50th Anniversary must be used to achieve greater progress in this area. It cannot be argued that the individuals who make up the nation states, members of the United Nations, would be opposed to such progress. Only nation states stand in the way. To what extent can the people overcome the defiance of the states?

Conclusion

In a presentation I made to a *Symposium on The United Nations*, I put the broader questions we still face this way:

> The UN now has really to become an instrument for redressing the injustice that is lived every day by the vast majority of the world's people. In a very real sense, the UN must become, in the immediate future an organization for 'the peoples'. This is not some pious exhortation or an appeal to notions of charity. Not at all.
>
> The United Nations must become the instrument of first resort to address the peoples' issues. Since the beginning, the UN has been an organization by and for states whose territorial sovereignty and political integrity has been inviolate, in theory and for the most part, in practice. Article 2, Paragraph 7 of the Charter enshrines that principle.
>
> I am not suggesting that this principle is now to be set aside. But the UN must now turn its attention to addressing the issues of most immediate concern to the citizens of the Member States. We will all agree, I am sure, that the highest purpose of the nation state is to serve the needs of its peoples. The role of social organization throughout history has, in theory, been to ensure the protection and prosperity of its citizens.
>
> By the same token, the role of the UN, and its highest purpose, must be to reach beyond the strictures of inter state rivalry, and address the needs of the peoples of the world. It must now begin to bring real meaning to the concept, in the opening words of the Charter – "We, the Peoples ..."[28]

The current flurry of activity dealing with reform of the United Nations, triggered by the 50th Anniversary, must not be allowed to lead only to tinkering with administration and budgets. It is also not sufficient to add a few members to the Security Council and claim that is will thus become more accountable and representative.

It is simply not credible to ask the UN Secretary-General to keep adding to his tasks without some better definition of his role and authority.

We must not simply ignore the egregious lack of coordination within the UN system. We would be foolhardy to think that the North-South divide will go away with more of the international Reaganomics now practised by the international financial institutions.

Is it acceptable for the international community to continue to support blindly the nation-state idea without further questioning its ultimate usefulness to the advancement of humanity? Are we prepared to continue sanctioning, because of this essentially obsolete concept, massive intrusions on the fundamental rights of the people of the world?

These are all questions that this book and the process of reform address. The end result, I hope will be a better United Nations which is "a consummation devoutly to be wished."

Notes

1   Cited in Touval, Saadia "Why the UN Fails" *Foreign Affairs* 73 No. 5 September/October 1994 46.

2   Childers, Erskine, and Brian Urquhart 1994 *Renewing the United Nations System* (Dag Hammarskjold Foundation: Uppsala, Sweden) 21.

3   Cited in note 2, 28.

4   See note 2, 29.

5   Williams, Maurice "Guidelines to Strengthening the Institutional Response to Major Environmental Issues" *Development* 1992:2 (Society for International Development).

6   "The Future Role of the Global Multilateral Organisations" *InterAction Council Report on the Conclusions and Recommendations by a High-level Group* 1994 (The Hague, Netherlands) paragraph 73.

7   See note 6 paragraph 75.

8   See note 6 paragraph 76.

9   Robinson, Nicholas A. "The Legal Framework for Global Environmental Protection" *International Round-table on Environmental Law and Institutions* 1991 9.2 (Des Moines, Iowa) 8-9.

10   Hassan, Parvez "Moving Towards a Just International Environmental Law" *International Law Conference* 1991 (The Hague, Netherlands) 3.

11   Boutros-Ghali, Boutros 1992 *An Agenda for Peace* (United Nations: New York).

12   See note 2.

13   See note 5, paragraph 9.

14   Childers, Erskine "Strengthening The United Nations System in a
      Time Beyond Warnings" *Conference on Reforming the United Nations*
      1993 (University of London) 2.

15   Urquhart, Brian, and Erskine Childers 1990 *A World in Need of
      Leadership – Tomorrow's United Nations* (Dag Hammarskjold
      Foundation: Uppsala, Sweden) 29-30.

16   Picco, Giandomarico "The UN and the Use of Force" *Foreign Affairs*
      September/October 1994 14.

17   See note 16, 16.

18   See note 16, 18.

19   See note 14, 5.

20   South Centre 1992 *The United Nations at a Crossroads – Time for the
      South to Act* (Dar-es Salaam and Geneva) 17.

21   See note 20, 19.

22   See note 6, paragraph 55.

23   See note 14, 11.

24   As cited in Minear, Larry *Humanitarianism under Siege* (Red Sea
      Press: Trenton NJ) 99.

25   Matas, David "Sovereignty Rights *vs.* the Rights of the Individual"
      Federal Liberal Caucus June 1991 10.

26   See note 25, 12-15.

27   Pérez de Cuéllar, Javier *Address at University of Bordeaux* 25 April
      1991 United Nations Doc. No. SG/SM/4560 6.

28   Grenville-Wood, Geoffrey Presentation to *Federal Liberal Conference
      on the Future of the United Nations* Vancouver 1991.

PART II

THE UNITED NATIONS SYSTEM

Commentary on Part II
Michael Oliver

It is easy to get agreement on the need for the United Nations. It is even simpler to reach consensus on the proposition that the UN needs reforming. Ask *how* to reform the United Nations and the debate begins. But if we fail to engage in the debate, and postpone coming to grips with specific proposals for change, we risk letting a world that is difficult to manage deteriorate into an impossible world. The following chapters launch us on this debate.

Robert McLaren in Chapter 6 rightly insists that we should be clear on the objectives we set for the UN before we embark on any but the most superficial reforms; and Hanna Newcombe in Chapter 4 sensibly asks that we choose a time-frame (short-, medium- or long-term) for our reform efforts. But I doubt that these are the areas where it will be most difficult to find accord. There would probably be a substantial majority behind a programme of reform that called, over the next ten years, for greater UN effectiveness in assuring peace and common security, equitable and sustainable economic development, reliable protection for human rights, and a strong expansion of international law. Controversy intensifies when we ask: "How do we reach these goals? What UN system would be most likely to work well?"

Democratization

One pathway to change that is enjoying increasing support is the democratization of the UN. The famous "We the Peoples ... " phrase that opens the preamble to the *UN Charter* invites us to look forward to a time when states and their governments no longer monopolize the exercise of power within the UN, a time when decisions are reached by a more participatory process. No one expects the sovereign state to fade quickly away, but perhaps it can begin to share power.

Two lines of reform are usually advanced by those who seek to democratize. The first seeks to expand the role of Non-Governmental Organizations (NGOs); the second looks to the creation of a Parliamentary Assembly of the UN, where (democratically-elected?) members of national legislatures will select from amongst their ranks those who would sit in a new, second UN Assembly, initially endowed with advisory functions only. Hanna Newcombe assesses both these possibilities (as well as coming out for weighted voting in the General Assembly). For Dieter Heinrich in Chapter 5 the Parliamentary Assembly option is clearly preferable.

Equally strong voices can be heard that stress the importance of civil society and the direct involvement of peoples' organizations in the UN's affairs. These strategies are not, in the early stages of advocacy, contradictory, but each encounters quite distinctive obstacles. The parliamentary assembly strategy has to overcome the reluctance of national executive bodies to see their power diluted, the charge that the parliamentarians will simply constitute an expensive debating society, and the *fin de siècle* cynicism about politicians. The NGO strategy faces challenges to the representativeness of existing voluntary bodies, problems of consolidating international coalitions of NGOs, and great reluctance on the part of some governments to grant NGOs even minimal recognition. Unless Southern governments become much more hospitable to NGOs in United Nations councils and conferences, recognition of NGOs could begin to be perceived as just another device for having Northern concerns dominate the international agenda.

State Sovereignty – The Case of Human Rights

How are human rights most effectively assured on a global scale? Three lines of evolution stand out. The first centres on identifying existing abuses, giving early warning of potential human rights disasters, and directing a world spotlight upon them. The appointment of a new UN High Commissioner for Human Rights, following the *Vienna Conference* of 1993, is a measure of the success of this strategy. Dietrich Fischer's systems approach in Chapter 3 underlines the need to detect deviations from global human rights norms and to build appropriate corrective mechanisms that are triggered by violations.

The second strategy is exemplified by moves towards an International Criminal Court – moves which both Dietrich Fischer and Hanna Newcombe applaud. This approach is rooted in the liberal doctrine of individual autonomy and responsibility. It seeks to make it possible for persons to be brought before a recognized global tribunal to answer charges of violation of international law and to be punishable if found guilty. The War Crimes trials in Germany and Japan following World War

II are precedents for such a court, as is the new international tribunal of war crimes in the former Yugoslavia. Thus far, we find slow and cumulative action in developing international criminal law, rather than a general agreement by states to relinquish sovereign powers to a new international jurisdiction.

The third strategy is humanitarian intervention to protect human rights by a force representing the international community. The *Charter of the United Nations* focuses on UN interventionary powers and procedures when state sovereignty is violated by external attack. Only in recent years have precedents been set regarding intervention within the boundaries of a single state in defence of human rights. World acceptance for sending in UN troops in Somalia and in the former Yugoslavia expressed a growing unwillingness to tolerate massive violations of human rights on the grounds that state sovereignty is inviolable. Clearing our thoughts on the "dos and don'ts" of humanitarian intervention must obviously be a priority for those of us who want to see the UN become more effective. All the chapters in Part II touch on this problem.

As in the case of democratization, we are faced not so much with contradictory strategies as with the need to assign priorities to different approaches. Significantly, each approach requires that sovereignty be reinterpreted (and diluted). Rather than a new theoretical framework, trying to redefine sovereignty, the accumulation of precedent that is occurring almost month-by-month may hold out more prospect for success.

Coordination – The Case of Economic and Social Development

Three of the papers in Part II wrestle with the problem of conflicting and overlapping jurisdictions within the UN system and with the specially acute need for coordination in the international development field. Much of the disappointment that has been expressed in the *Agenda for Development* prepared by the Secretary-General derives from that document's failure to come to grips with the need to coordinate the specialized agencies, and especially the Bretton Woods institutions (the World Bank and the International Monetary Fund), with the UN bodies that fall under the jurisdiction of the Secretary-General. Robert McLaren stresses, quite rightly, that any attempt to achieve coherence in the development field goes to the heart of the North-South division within the UN. Northern countries do not want coordination if that means a reduction in their control over the key institutions that decide policy on loans, debt and the conditions of global trade and investment. Hanna Newcombe is surely right in insisting sustainable development demands better coordination. But the evidence accumulates that the South will insist that a commitment to equitable development must precede (or at least accompany) the acceptance of policies for the sustainability of that development. The kind of development coordination that developing countries believe is most needed is that which assures the South of a fairer share of the world's wealth.

Two lines of coordination reform are often put forward: strengthening ECOSOC and creating a new decision-making security council for the economic and social responsibilities of the UN. Neither can easily be accomplished: both require intensive debate.

Making a Beginning

Day-by-day, men and women are working away at making the UN a more effective instrument for fulfilling world aspirations. Newton Bowles in Chapter 2 gives a vivid picture of moves ahead, of blockages circumvented, and of energies devoted to reaching common ground within the UN itself during 1993/94. Whatever its faults, the United Nations is where we must begin, and learning how to work within its structures as well as how to circumvent them and change them, is the beginning of reformist wisdom.

A Year in the Life of the General Assembly: 1993 Session

Newton R. Bowles

Before Words

This is my third annual round-up on the UN. You will catch a whiff of arrogance in my disclaimer of omniscience. Here you are not likely to find the final word about anything. There are many layers of complexity in what goes on in and around the UN. There is the negotiating and legislative process: the General Assembly, the Security Council, ECOSOC and their many subdivisions. There is the hired help, the Secretary-General and all that bureaucratic machinery. Opening your lens a bit wider, you see not only the many mansions built by Mother UN (the General Assembly) – UNDP, UNICEF, UNFPA, *inter alia*; but also those other autonomous institutions – the Bretton Woods financial houses and the Specialized Agencies, with their separate governing bodies. It is one and the same set of governments that generated this amplitude, almost a mirror image of bureaucratic sprawl at home in Canada. There is no way that my little report could cover all that. What I have written is mostly about the 48th Session of the General Assembly. But I try, where I can, to set this Assembly's discussions and decisions in perspective and to link them to ongoing activities. I have also tried, in the first part of the report, to convey something of the general tenor of the gathering.

Those who know of my long years with UNICEF may wonder why I have made so little reference to children. That is because children and UNICEF did not have a prominent place at this year's Assembly. I should mention, however, that the Assembly has asked for a report on the impact of war on children. And President Bill Clinton, in his first appearance at the UN, singled out UNICEF and its Executive Director, Jim Grant, for special commendation, a refreshing change of appreciation.

I am the sole perpetrator of this report, yet I have been the lucky recipient of generous help from many friends and colleagues. My special thanks I extend to Ambassador Louise Frechette, to Ambassador David Malone and many members of the diligent and highly professional staff of our Canadian Mission to the UN. Canada played a major role in several important matters at this Assembly. Canada ranks high at the UN – we could do better, of course – but just being a Canadian has opened doors for me.

My own bias and interests must show up in the way I present this documentary. There is plenty of despond all about. "Worstward Ho!" said Samuel Beckett. Where lies the fault between illusion and hope? Watch your step!

Highlights

Security Council Reform:
* created an open-ended Working Group to review membership and procedures, and make recommendations to the next Assembly.

Peacekeeping:
* Security Council mandates must be clear;
* decisions to strengthen management, efficiency and professional quality;
* closer coordination with humanitarian assistance.

Protecting UN Personnel:
* Working Group established to prepare UN Convention.

South Africa:
* sanctions lifted.

Disarmament:
* complete ban on nuclear tests: Treaty negotiation approved by consensus;
* also consensus support to ban production of fissionables;
* land mines: suspending exports approved.

Agenda for Development:
* Secretary-General to prepare full report for important debate at next Assembly.

Human Rights:
* High Commissioner approved;
* universality affirmed;

- violence against women: Declaration approved.

Management:
- needs to be tidied and strengthened;
- decision on proposed Inspector-General postponed to next Assembly;
- Secretary-General: good head but disconcerting style.

Finances:
- arrears are $1.5 billion at 31 December 1993;
- Russia and USA main delinquents;
- budget total remains frozen.

Lowlight

More work for the UN but not the money to go with it!

The Opening Debate: Thoughts from the Top

The annual gathering of world leaders at the UN General Assembly goes largely unnoticed in our mass media. Millions around the globe are entranced by the sweaty Olympics; but wrestling and wrangling over war and wealth, over crime and punishment, over planetary power, this is a hard sell for the headlines. How could it be otherwise? This is a complex, violent and untidy world. At home political leaders struggle to gain or retain power; and having power, they hardly know what to do with it. Atop a smoldering volcano, who cares about the big world? And yet every year they come, an astonishing parade, to the one great theatre of the world, the United Nations.

This year's show had the regular three months' run beginning 21 September 1993, with member States now numbering 184, ranging from Monaco (population 30,000) to China (population 1.2 billion). The script, presented in six of the world's 5000 languages, was based on an agenda of 182 items. The Assembly began with the usual fortnight's exchange of views by government leaders.

On stage during this opening discussion were 175 speakers, most of them Heads of Government or Foreign Ministers. From South Africa came F.W. DeKlerk and Nelson Mandela. Exiled Aristide was there from Haiti. From Peru, the controversial Fujimori arrived to defend his record. The veteran Cheddi Jaggan was back, born again from the ashes of Guyana. From Canada came Kim Campbell, poised on the brink, and the USA was there in Bill Clinton, just to name a few.

At his ritual luncheon honouring government leaders, Secretary-General Boutros Boutros-Ghali reviewed the chiaroscuro UN landscape, its successes and failures, and set out five major tasks for the UN:

- establishing a more stable world order;
- advancing the cause of the poorest;
- delivering aid to those in danger;
- defending human and minority rights;
- overseeing repairs to the world environment.

To such challenges, everyone nods in rhetorical assent. Few agree on where to go and how to get there.

In South Africa official apartheid is dead, and UN sanctions were lifted by this Assembly. The PLO–Israeli accord put an end to years of sterile diatribe. After the success of Namibia came El Salvador and Cambodia, a bit shaky but moving away from war. Mozambique seems on the road to national reconciliation. The slaughter in Liberia is on hold. But evil rides high in the former Yugoslav heart of old Europe, in Angola and now in Zaire. Fear and the threat of violence reign in Haiti, in Somalia, in Afghanistan and in the spoor of extinct USSR. The UN hesitates: peacemaking is hard and its success uncertain. It is far cheaper than war but already it has doubled the UN budget. Will the UN turn away while the rivers run red? At this Assembly and ongoing meetings of the Security Council, the great powers have shrunk from biting the bullet.

Nevertheless, in a distraught and anxious world, it is reassuring that no one at this Assembly suggested that the UN should be torn down. Though reluctant to augment the authority or resources of an international regime, governments want to make the UN work better. Sweden's Foreign Minister, Margaretha Af Ugglas, recalled Dag Hammarskjold's statement: "The United Nations is, and should be, a living, evolving, experimental institution. If it should ever cease to be so, it should be revolutionized or swept aside for a new approach." At this session, the "North", the industrialized countries, pressed on with their campaign to rationalize UN governance, to modernize its management and to tighten its oversight. Their criticism of the Secretariat was balanced between exasperation with creaky old ways and praise for heroic service. While expectations and responsibilities grow, the UN remains a tiny establishment among the giants of the world: its regular budget is frozen, and still only a handful of governments pay their dues on time. The management of the Secretariat leaves a lot to be desired, but it in no way rivals the inefficiency and corruption of many important governments.

But nudging the Secretariat was only a footnote to the Assembly's policy overture. What is surprising and heartening is that the UN, despite old traditions of venal hypocrisy and unblinking power, remains a forum where most governments feel constrained to report on their legitimacy and their behaviour. Implicit or explicit as norms are the *Human Rights Convention* and the idea of participatory democracy. The recently elected President of Paraguay remarked that he was the first civilian to hold that office in 39 years, ushering in a new era for human rights. Bolivia's President spoke of his government's action to bring indigenous people into the democratic process. Guatemala reported its steps towards national reconciliation and democracy. Among African delegations, Chad, Lesotho, Malawi, Mali, Mauritania and Uganda made specific references to their establishment or strengthening of democratic governance. From Asia, Mongolia said democracy was on the way according to a specific timetable; while Nepal and Thailand spoke of their renewal of the democratic process. Azerbaijan affirmed its determination to promote a working democracy. In contrast, it was bizarre to hear the Foreign Minister of Myanmar (Burma) assert that in effect modern Burma is the military establishment: the Army does not covet power, it is above politics, it is the only disciplined organization in the country. Continuing, he warned against using an alien concept of human rights as a pretext for interfering in domestic affairs. Those who oppose the universality of human rights, as defined by the UN, gain scant legitimacy from Myanmar. Algeria, in the aftermath of subverted elections, was careful and subdued in making its case. No one defended military subversion of elections in Angola, Haiti or Nigeria.

Several delegates presented serious analyses of the nature of modern statehood. Uganda's Foreign Minister cautioned against basing a state on ethnicity or religion: the challenge in our time is to find democratic ways to achieve fair and peaceful coexistence in a heterogeneous society. Prime Minister Brundtland of Norway said that the doctrine of the ethnic state is a prescription for war. The world needs inclusive multi-ethnic communities where people live in enlightened diversity.

Syria claimed that the Western pursuit of Libyan and Sudanese terrorists and Western acquiescence in Israeli occupation of Southern Lebanon, was provoking groundless bias against Islam. Iran said the PLO–Israeli pact was a conspiracy against Islam and Palestine. The Prime Minister of Bangladesh, Begum Khaleda Zia, decried the arms embargo which deprived the Bosnian Muslims of the capacity to defend themselves. The crime of the Bosnian Muslims, she said, was their commitment to a non-Muslim heterogeneous state; and for this they were attacked by the Serbs so as to keep Europe Christian. Jordan's Prince El-Hassan Ben Talal struck a harmonizing note. There is extremism in the Muslim world, he said, just as there is in Christian, Jewish, Hindu and secular worlds. This has led to carnage in Bosnia. Don't demonize the one-fifth of humanity that is Muslim, he said, but look to the desperate conditions that breed fanatics. It fell to Kyrgystan to propose an international conference of religions to get at the cause of religious conflict.

Whereas the Secretary-General's *An Agenda for Peace* dominated Assembly discussions last year, the focus shifted this year to development. It is significant that the impetus for the peace agenda came from the Security Council, dominated by the big powers, whereas the demand for the *Agenda for Development* comes from the General Assembly, where the Third World sits. The mood has lifted from a tiresome replay of opaque *clichés* towards a serious exploration of a leadership role for the UN in development. The imprecision of the word "development" has its advantages: it accommodates the drive by the South for full participation in the modern economy, concerns about fair trade, debt, global and regional disparities, sustainability and the environment. More than ever, at this Assembly, human well-being was taken to be the measure of all development. Many delegates spoke of the precarious prospects for survival of countries dependent on one or a few prime exports to manipulated markets. The outlook for Africa remains bleak with things getting worse, and the Japanese initiative in convening a meeting on African development in October 1993 was welcomed. Regional free trade zones – Europe, NAFTA, MERCOSUR (South America), ASEAN, COMESA (Eastern and Southern Africa), and the Uruguay – GATT were hailed as the way of the future. Advancing countries stressed their need for access to scientific and technological resources. Many asked how participatory democracy can work in an impoverished nation. The outlook from the North, expressed by Prime Minister Brundtland of Norway, is that development without democracy cannot be sustained. But President Wasmosy of Paraguay, among many, said it would be difficult for democracy to survive in the face of poverty. Why had the Group of 7 refused to meet the Chairman of the Non-Aligned Movement at Tokyo last July, asked Morocco. The spectre of one billion people existing in absolute poverty (annual per capita income $370) hovered on the silent screen. Meanwhile, the economic predicament of the North, their export of capital and productivity along with structural recession and structural unemployment in the face of steady decline in social services, is forcing the richer nations to look for global solutions to domestic problems. Shared problems should make for a common search for shared solutions.

Coalescing around shared interests happens across the board these days, resulting in changing patterns and different groupings of States on particular issues. By far the most integrated and organized region is the European Community (EC) on whose behalf it was Belgium's turn to speak this year. Along with a concise oral statement, Belgium circulated a comprehensive 31-page memorandum setting out EC positions on most issues under consideration. In general, EC views support the UN. It is striking, however, that in reacting to Nigeria, the EC has gone ahead of the UN in deploring the flouting of elections by the military, and by suspending military and developmental aid. Still ambivalent about the EC, the Nordics maintain their tenacious drive towards a more integrated UN development system. The Non-Aligned Movement – the Group of 77 plus – still holds together on basic development issues; although the South Commission and the Group of 15 developing countries, for South–South Consultation, introduced a more professional and technical approach. India announced that, in December, it would host the Fourth Summit Meeting of the Group of 15. Economic association does not always carry over into specific political issues. The Group of 7 is not predictably the shadow power behind the Security Council's Perm-5 (the permanent members), as GATT and Bosnia show. On the other hand it was the West African Economic Association, ECOWAS, that first tackled Liberia when neither the OAU nor the UN would act. ASEAN (Brunei, Malaysia, the Philippines, Thailand and Singapore) by no means votes in a solid bloc and is only now talking about a free trade zone. Canada's participation in the Commonwealth and Francophonie plugs into important networks for consultation which facilitate cooperation at the UN. The *ad hoc* CANZ arrangement – Canada, Australia, New Zealand – is working well on specific issues. Although a handful of governments, great and small, are stuck in doctrinaire rigidity, many more are becoming more pragmatic and flexible in their toils around the UN.

But the big is writ small in living exemplars of fitful national pride. What's in a name? The Falkland Islands, says the UK. Malvinas, says the Argentine. Macedonia? The former Yugoslavia Republic of Macedonia, Greece insists. The great USA cannot let go of its unilateral embargo on Cuba. The annual Assembly resolution exhorting the USA to lift the embargo was adopted this year by 88 to 4, with 57 abstentions. The four opposed were Albania, Israel, Paraguay and the USA. Votes in favour included Australia and New Zealand. Canada joined in the brave ranks of abstainees. A footnote to symptomatic trivia. And who rewards the little heroes? Violetta Chamorro, struggling to hold Nicaragua together, reminds the Assembly that her country is receiving scant aid. Eritrea cries shame:

the UN ignored us during our 41 year struggle for independence, and now we get precious little attention from anyone.

Canada's main statement this year dealt mostly with peacekeeping, offering several ideas for its improvement that were later endorsed by the Assembly. President Clinton's appointment of Madeleine Albright as Ambassador to the UN was a harbinger of good things; and his speech to the General Assembly, while anything but a blank cheque for the UN, marked a major and positive advance: on financial support, on the nuclear test ban, on banning fissionables and on family planning. He was cautious on peacekeeping, saying that the UN can't take on every conflict in the world and that the US assessment for peacekeeping (nearly one-third of the total) is too high. Fair enough: but remember Somalia, Haiti and the Balkans! Yes, a good turn, Bill Clinton.

To what end this annual parade as the General Assembly opens? This year 175 governments participated. Who can hear and digest 175 speeches? The good professionals must do that. It is indeed important that a government has the opportunity, from time to time, to present its overall approach, policies, ideas and concerns. Without such a backdrop, the work of the Assembly would become more and more removed from political power. At best, many governments have great difficulty in making up their minds on critical international issues. But without political direction, government officials stall and equivocate. For heads of government and Foreign Ministers, coming to the UN and speaking is a political act, a confirmation of participation, and an occasion to meet many leaders face-to-face. For now, the ordering of our world is largely in the hands of national governments, and the UN is their only global parliament.

Whose Peace and Security?

It was the Security Council that set off the current UN advances towards a stronger system of collective security. In January 1992, with heads of government participating, the Council asked the Secretary-General to suggest how the UN's security functioning could be improved. That led to Boutros Boutros-Ghali's *An Agenda for Peace*. The Secretary-General's proposals, presented to the General Assembly and the Security Council, implied a major extension of the UN role, from peacekeeping to conflict prevention and the promotion of peace. The measures proposed, however, were pretty much within traditional diplomacy backed by force, although with greater attention to prevention and post-conflict reconstruction. Consideration of these proposals touched off a debate, not only on what governments want the UN to do, but also on who calls the shots: security for whom? The

1992 General Assembly worked hard and long on *An Agenda for Peace*, but it was regarded by the South (developing countries) as a view from the North. Threats to international security, the *Charter* frame of the UN, were sometimes seen as emanating from disorder within nations, from "failed states" and civil war. Would the strong now use security so defined as a pretext for intervening in the domestic affairs of the weak? And why was *An Agenda For Peace* couched in such narrow and discredited terms? Doesn't everyone know that social and economic deprivation and disparity breed strife? And so the South–North tension was manifest again as the UN burnished its weapons for peace.

An Agenda for Peace also served as a platform for interplay between the Security Council and the General Assembly. The Security Council held monthly reviews of the Secretary-General's agenda, culminating in June 1993 in a statement on what had so far been agreed and on specific issues outstanding. Once again, the Council asked the Secretary-General and the Assembly to have a fresh look at what can be done to implement this agenda.

Let us recall that, in December 1992, the 47th General Assembly gave its approval to six lines of action:

- enhanced preventive diplomacy;
- strengthened early warning of pending conflict;
- more responsive fact-finding in troubled situations;
- sustained confidence-building measures;
- assured humanitarian assistance;
- a peacekeeping reserve fund of $150 million.

But that was not all. The 48th General Assembly, on 20 September 1993, approved two more elements of *An Agenda For Peace*:

- preventive deployment of troops (already done in Macedonia);
- post-conflict peacebuilding.

For now, this seems as far as the Assembly is prepared to go. Its attention at the current session was focused on policy and operational issues encountered in giving effect to this agenda.

The key policy issue is where and when to intervene in domestic conflicts. The former Yugoslavia, Somalia and little Haiti each present problems with which the UN so far is unable or unwilling to cope. Major Western powers, who pressed for a broader agenda for peace, are now backing away from the commitment of funds and military resources – and the loss of life – that such interventions entail. This loss of nerve, even before the new rules have been given a serious try, weakens the authority and credibility of the Security Council, already haunted by ghosts of inconsistency, and flouters escaping unscathed. Will the UN in future only take on the easy ones, falling back to peacekeeping when conflicting parties are ready? This would leave the UN out of the worst savagery of our times, as in Angola, impending in Zaire, and in the shards of Afghanistan. Can nothing be done?

An ironic twist in this debate came from African delegates at this Assembly, who clearly wanted a strong international presence in their most troubled countries, especially Angola, Liberia and Somalia. They supported the UN presence in Mozambique, the Western Sahara, and in the electoral process in South Africa. Ghana, Senegal and Uganda urged the Security Council to encompass all reverberating conflicts, however small, within its surveillance. Senegal could not survive the overflow of Liberian refugees and conflict across its borders, they said.

Concerns like this have implications for the future composition and functions of the Security Council.

There are other more mundane reasons for caution in taking on UN peace commitments. The whole process needs to become more defined and efficient. In its recent comprehensive resolution on peacekeeping, the Assembly urged that henceforth the Security Council, when launching a peacekeeping operation, make clear what it wants to achieve (objectives) and how its action will advance the political process. There should also be much closer coordination with planning and delivery of humanitarian assistance. A time frame should be set. Experiences should be kept under review. The Assembly said the sensible things about adequate resources – financial, military, civilian – and the importance of norms for performance, especially military, and training to that end. Specific arrangements in the Secretariat for direction, management and support were mandated, including the ever-vigilant Situation Centre. While there was no support for a standing UN peace force, governments were urged to have standby forces at the ready, and current moves towards closer contact between the UN and national forces were encouraged. Several governments offered training facilities for peace operations. Canada offered to host technical consultations on the management of peacekeeping in 1994. It remains to be seen how the USA will follow through with substance and how the UN Secretariat can take hold.

Pressure on the Security Council could be relieved to the extent that regional organizations are able to deal with local conflicts. The current General Assembly resolution encourages the sharing of responsibility by regions and asks the Secretary-General to help regional institutions to develop the necessary competence. Performance by regional organizations so far has not been brilliant. After all, they are creatures of the same States as the UN, and function in the same political and resource climate. Europe – the European Community, CSCE, and even NATO – has been unable to take on the former Yugoslavia. For Haiti, the OAS had to turn to the Security Council. In Africa, the OAU summit in June 1993 decided to become active in conflict resolution and has begun to acquire mediating skills. The OAU, the Arab League and the Islamic Conference joined the UN in mediating among the Somali warlords. Their participation was politically important, although no miracles were wrought. ASEAN is a useful arrangement for consultation, but without the Asian giants, India and China. In the shambles of the USSR, successor states are groping for regional security. Kazakhstan and Uzbekhistan suggested that Russia might serve as a peacekeeping arm of the Security Council in that region, and Kazakhstan reported that it had hosted two meetings of experts from 25 Asian countries addressed to building confidence for collective security in the region.

Going one step further, Kazakhstan, with Canada as co-sponsor, made a formal proposal that a Special Session be convened in 1995 for a comprehensive review of UN peacemaking. The Assembly will consider this proposal in 1994.

The risk to UN personnel, military and civilian, and especially humanitarian, has greatly increased since the Security Council has gone into countries where fighting continues. UN casualties are mounting and there was unanimous agreement in the Assembly that much better arrangements to safeguard international staff must be made. Just how this can be done, in places like Somalia and the former Yugoslavia, where local militia and brigands wander about, is hard to see. This Assembly created a special Committee, with Canada's Philippe Kirsch in the chair, to draft a convention to put the full weight of the UN into security for UN staff.

Disarmament

War in pre-industrial times was hardly a gentle art, as a glance at Goya's *Desastres de la Guerra* makes us know; but the orgiastic scale of impersonal horror achieved in modern war attests to the lethal power of scientists and technicians. The enormous arsenals of killing machines built up during the

Cold War are largely intact; and with world military expenditures still standing at well over $500 billion in 1993, disarmament has a long way to go. So does this world's commitment to stopping warfare, as governments balk at sustaining the $3 billion needed for UN peacekeeping last year. At the same time, economic growth is stalled in most regions and resources for basic human services are hard to come by. The linkage of enormous expenditures on armaments to insecurity, warfare, poverty and the environment should be evident. Yet international negotiations about disarmament continue day-to-day in the hands of specialists who may let technical arms issues obscure the larger vision. There are formidable technical problems in this pursuit of disarmament – *e.g.*, verification – but where there is a political will, there is a technical way. This could be seen at the 1993 Assembly, when a favourable wind was blowing from the banks of the Potomac. If President Bill Clinton, speaking at the UN, put a damper on peacekeeping, at the same time he gave a mighty shove to the big one, nuclear disarmament.

The green light shone when, prior to his UN appearance, President Clinton announced his decision to maintain the US moratorium on nuclear testing. This decision was by no means assured. US citizens of all stripes had been urging Clinton to extend the moratorium. There was a mighty sigh of relief when the decision was announced. It is once again evident that the US government is no monolith, and decisions like this come only after a fierce power struggle within that huge and sprawling citadel. With all declared nuclear powers, China excepted, joining in suspension of tests, the General Assembly (confirming the First Committee) was able at last, after many contentious years, to adopt by consensus a resolution in favour of a complete test ban. China came near to upsetting this apple cart when it conducted an underground test on 5 October 1993. The Chinese tried to put the best face on it, saying they will stop testing whenever a comprehensive test ban treaty is concluded: they only have a few bombs for defence, and they advocate the eventual elimination for all nuclear weapons, they say.

Meantime, in a parallel action, the *Geneva Conference on Disarmament* (the CD) at last got its orders to begin, in January 1994, to negotiate a treaty to ban all testing (a comprehensive test ban, CTBT).

The 37–government CD, standing outside the UN, is the mechanism for hammering out multilateral arms control treaties. Last year, after a decade's gestation, the CD brought forth the remarkable *Chemical Weapons Convention* (CWC), banishing stocks and production, and mandating unprecedented intrusive inspections. By September 1993, 148 States had signed the CWC; it will enter into force, with its own staff to oversee implementation, in 1995, if at least 65 States have ratified it. In 1992, the full membership of the UN, at the General Assembly, gave enthusiastic support to the CWC.

Retirement of the nuclear nightmare seems a bit premature: the big powers still have over 20,000 nuclear weapons, and while the "dead man's hand" (the automatic nuclear response to an attack that has severed the internal nuclear command system) has at last been removed, only now are the weapons being redirected away from Cold War targets. But unless some crazy dictator takes over in one of the nuclear states, a steady withdrawal from the brink seems assured. A permanent end to testing would mean an end to developing even worse nuclear devices (like little bombs you could carry around in your brief case). An end to testing is an essential step towards ending production altogether.

Even if the big nuclear powers have stopped scaring each other to death, there remains the real danger that any number of countries might make a few bombs. What about bomb-toting terrorists? The *Treaty on Non-Proliferation of Nuclear Weapons* (NPT), since coming into force in 1970, has been the only institutionalized bulwark against nuclear spread. Three of the declared nuclear powers, USA, UK and USSR, signed early, while China and France signed only last year. South Africa came out of the closet in 1993, destroyed its bombs and joined the NPT. Israel says it will come clean when it is formally recognized by its neighbours. India holds out on the grounds that the NPT, in its different treatment of haves and have-nots, legitimizes the nuclear monopoly. To counter this criticism, NPT lays on the nuclear powers the commitment to end nuclear development and reduce nuclear weaponry in a big way. Since the NPT is due for review and extension in 1995, it would be a splendid prologue to have the CTBT in place by then. Let us not forget that President Mitterand's writ runs out in June 1995. At the recent UN Assembly, the conservative French Foreign Minister, out of step with Mitterand, made atavistic noises about the primacy of national independence, and may want to take his country back down the lonesome road. The Clinton administration at present holds that CTBT negotiations cannot be concluded until some time in 1996 at best. Herein may lie a serious problem. It is tempting to think that a quick decision to create a CTBT would be through a simple amendment to the existing Partial Test Ban Treaty, but strong USA opposition blocks that road. Most encouraging, however, is that Washington is unequivocally committed to achieving a ban and to multilateral negotiations.

Then there is – or was – the *World Court Project*, an international NGO drive, strongly supported in Canada, to get a General Assembly resolution asking the International Court of Justice to rule – to give an advisory opinion – on the legality of the use of atomic weapons. Indonesia, on behalf of the Non-Aligned Movement, tabled a resolution that would have asked for an opinion not only on the use, but also on the threat to use nuclear weapons. Under pressure, the resolution was withdrawn. Canada was of the view that to press this resolution would have been a tactical error: it would have raised hackles to no useful end, since the big breakthrough had already been achieved. The counter argument is that a World Court opinion, almost certainly that using the bomb is illegal, would accelerate the CTBT negotiations and reinforce the NPT. In any case, the World Health Organization, in May 1993 (by a vote of 73 for, 40 against, 10 abstaining), asked the Hague for an advisory opinion on the following question: "In view of the health and environmental effects, would the use of nuclear weapons by a State in war or other armed conflict be a breach of its obligations under international law including the WHO Constitution?" The International Court accepted the WHO petition last September, and invited interested parties to submit statements by June 1994. *On va voir.*

Directly related to all this is the General Assembly resolution just now calling for a treaty to ban weapons-grade fissionable materials. Consensus on this was possible because the USA, led by Clinton, switched from opposition to strong support. Introducing the resolution to the Assembly's First Committee, Canada's Ambassador Peggy Mason recalled that Canada had been advocating this move every year for 15 years. It was part of a "strategy for suffocation" advocated by Prime Minister Trudeau at the *First UN Special Session on Disarmament* in 1978. The other part was the CTBT. Both were now within reach.

Verification is critical for arms control, especially for the big destroyers; and here too Canada has been a leader. This Assembly approved Canada's proposal that the 1990 UN study on verification be updated with the intent of improving international surveillance.

The UN General Assembly (First Committee) also had occasion to look at the international arms trade as partially exposed in the first year of reporting (1992) to the *UN Register of Conventional Arms.* Attempts to get this kind of information into the public domain go back to the League of Nations. No doubt the Gulf War was an important factor in moving major arms exporting nations to take this step towards institutionalizing UN concern. The *Register* got off to a good start, with 80 countries reporting exports and imports. Nearly all exports were covered. Among big customers not responding were Saudi Arabia and Taiwan, the latter not a member of the UN. Other no-shows included Kuwait, Indonesia, Iran, North Korea, Pakistan, Syria, Thailand and Ukraine. The *Register* is limited to seven major weapons categories: battle tanks, armoured combat vehicles, large calibre artillery systems, combat aircraft, attack helicopters, warships, missiles and missile launchers. A great many weapons are outside this system (such as bombs, small arms, ammunition, mortars, ground-to-air missiles, back-up equipment, and dual-use technologies). National production and stocks are not yet included but will likely be added within a year or two. The growing black market in arms, of course, will not show its face in official reports. Hard times and the demise of the USSR have reduced official trade in conventional arms by 50% in the last five years, but it still runs at around $20 billion annually. The UN Register shows the USA far in the lead, followed by Germany, Russia, France, UK and China. We are reminded that the Security Council's Perm-5 account for 85% of the arms trade.

What use is the *Arms Register*? Could it feed a little sanity about huge sales, as in the Middle East? Maybe, but that hasn't happened yet. Public disclosure could build confidence, or the reverse. Only in Europe, through its *Treaty on Conventional Armed Forces* (CFE), is there any regulation of conventional military machines. But with an *Arms Register*, eventually all-inclusive, can the political (read: psychological) will for constraint and regulation forever be denied?

This question can be put to grim test with land-mines. Upwards of 100 million live land-mines now desecrate fields and roadways throughout the world, most of them in developing countries. Civilians, many of them children, are being maimed by the thousand by these cheap, hidden and long-lived devices. Mines have given Cambodia the highest incidence of amputees in the world. Thirty-six countries make and export land-mines. As the UN has learned in peacekeeping in many countries, mine clearance is an extremely slow and primitive process. The exclusion of mines from the *Arms Register* is symptomatic of pervasive ignorance, indifference and neglect of this scandalous evil. On the books is the 1980 *UN Convention on Inhumane Weapons* (*Convention on Prohibitions or Restrictions on the Use of Certain Conventional Weapons which may be deemed to be Excessively Injurious or to have Indiscriminative Effects*), ratified by only 37 countries; and *Protocol II* to that *Convention*, referring only to inter-State Conflicts, prohibits the common practice of scattering mines indiscriminately: minefields should be marked and mapped, mines should be metal-detectable, and every precaution should be taken to protect civilians. This *Convention* has been ignored.

The General Assembly has asked the Secretary-General to convene a conference to revise and strengthen *Protocol II*. Meantime, the USA (which has not ratified the *Inhumane Weapons Convention*) has placed a moratorium on exporting land-mines, and the UN General Assembly in 1993 has also passed a resolution urging all countries to suspend mine exports. This will do nothing to defuse the lethal seeds already in the ground.

Also awaiting enlightenment is the tsunami impact of war and its industries on the environment. The hawks of the world suppressed any serious attention to this at the *UN Conference on the Environment and Development* (UNCED) in Rio de Janeiro in 1992. There have been plenty of studies about it, the latest at this session being the Secretary-General's *Report on Protection of the Environment in Times of Armed Conflict.* This deals with what happens during combat (*e.g.,* the blowing up of oil wells in the Gulf War). It presents the conclusion of experts consulted by the International Committee of the Red Cross (ICRC): existing humanitarian law is adequate for environmental protection, it just needs to be enforced. It says that the provisions in existing law should get into military doctrine, using the prototype military manuals prepared by the ICRC. This will require informed pressure on national military commands. This is important so far as it goes. It is not likely to have much effect in the flux of internal "civil" wars. And it leaves aside the environmental impact of the arms industry: the waste of scientific, technical and physical resources, the pollution of land, sea and air.

Enlarging the Security Council

Last year (1992) the General Assembly decided that all UN members should be invited to submit written proposals on future membership in the Security Council. The seventy-five replies served as a background for a discussion of this tricky question in 1993. The *Charter* gives the Security Council decisive authority on all matters affecting peace and security, leaving to the Assembly a largely advisory role. The Security Council has to report to the General Assembly (the latest report, covering the twelve months ending 15 June 1993, is a 519-page chronological compilation of its official records); and the budget for peacekeeping operations launched by the Security Council must be approved by the Assembly. So far peacekeeping budgets have always been approved.

While the Perm-5 (allies in World War II) are firmly entrenched by the *Charter*, criteria for the other ten members laid down in the *Charter* are:

- "the contribution of members of the United Nations to the maintenance of peace and security and to the other purposes of the Organization";
- "and also...equitable geographical distribution".

The veto power of each member of the Perm-5 is also built into the *Charter.*

Everyone agrees that Security Council membership should somehow be enlarged so as to correspond better to the present-day world. The time has not come for a revision of the *Charter*, so for now the Perm-5 remain. What reforms can be built around that core? This year's preliminary debate yielded many proposals, both as to membership and procedure. Chief among them were the following:

Purpose of reforms:
- To ensure: legitimacy, moral authority, trust and faith, credibility, impartiality, responsiveness, democracy;
- To maintain and reinforce: cohesion (unity), efficiency, manageability, decisiveness.

Criteria for membership: equitable geographical representation (large and small), population, size of economy, support for peacekeeping, funding UN regular budget, participation in UN political and economic activities, strategic location, diplomatic skill.

Procedures:
- Veto – abolish it now, or phase it out, or qualify it;
- Proceedings should be open and transparent, regular, structured;
- Relative to General Assembly – Security Council to be accountable, stronger GA guidance;
- Relative to Peacekeeping Contributors (75 nations) – keep them in the picture with information and consultation.

With this smorgasbord of advice, the General Assembly set up an open-ended Working Group to develop recommendations both on membership and procedures in the future Security Council. These recommendations are to be considered by the Assembly in 1994, and perhaps a decision can be reached by 1995.

War Crimes Tribunal

This special Tribunal was created by the Security Council to handle war crimes committed during the current fighting in the former Yugoslavia. It has now been constituted, with an international panel of eleven eminent jurists, including Canada's Jules Deschenes. The Tribunal will have an outstanding Prosecutor in Justice Richard Goldstone, former chair of South Africa's Commission on Public Violence. Canada has already made an important contribution in gathering evidence. Let us hope that the Tribunal can function with credibility and dignity. But I ask myself how complicit are we who stand by and watch mass murder go unchecked.

International Criminal Court

Preparations for constituting a permanent International Criminal Court, to complement the existing International Court of Justice, have gone ahead much faster than expected a year ago. The International Law Commission completed draft Statutes for the Criminal Court in time for their review by the Assembly (Sixth Committee) in 1993. States have been asked to comment on this draft in time for revised Statutes to be prepared in 1994. There is broad support for creating such a Court. It may come into being before the end of this *Decade of International Law.* If the international community puts teeth into law enforcement, a Court like this could give pause to warmongers and abusers of rights.

Human Rights

You might think that, after Vienna (the *World Conference on Human Rights,* June 1993), the debate and the debaters about people's rights would be exhausted. Not quite, the Assembly discovered. The *Vienna Declaration and Plan of Action* is a strange and wondrous pastiche, ringing the changes from high principles to topical issues like dumping toxic waste. Nothing and nobody is left out. Reading the *Declaration* will dispel any suspicion that a mastermind is at work manipulating a global conspiracy. While the text is prolix and diffuse, it does make you feel that human rights is a live issue, that pro or con, people care, that rights touch on every aspect of our lives, and that a mighty struggle is underway on all fronts. A major achievement of Vienna was the formal affirmation by all current members of the UN that human rights are universal: rights as defined in the *Charter,* the *Universal Declaration of Human Rights,* the *International Covenant on Civil and Political Rights* and the *International Covenant on Economic, Social and Cultural Rights.* The two Covenants are crucial, the first focusing on the individual, while the second deals with emancipation from poverty and its ramifications. In our world, where ubiquitous brutal repression is in foul contrast to high principle, few governments should be comfortable about UN rights surveillance. In Vienna, and again in the General Assembly, the debate among governments therefore came to a head on this very issue: should the UN have a High Commissioner for Human Rights, as it does for Refugees (UNHCR), to give strong leadership and maximum exposure to rights and wrongs? Unable to reach agreement on this, the Vienna Conference referred it to the General Assembly.

Performing automatic reflexes, the Assembly stumbled into a truncated replay of Vienna: don't impose alien values, cultures differ deeply, yes, but basic rights are congenital, universal, *etc.* As it turned out, the ground work had been done in Vienna, many of the "Non-aligned" supported a High Commissioner, the opponents backed down, and the new Under-Secretary post was approved by consensus. This very senior official will oversee the Human Rights Centre and all the UN rights enforcement apparatus. The Assembly also supported the Vienna recommendation that more money and staff be put into rights "enforcement" without promising to put up the funds.

How slow and reluctant has been the acknowledgment of wide-spread and polymorphous violence against women. Canada led in advancing *via* Vienna a draft *Declaration on Violence Against Women* which *inter alia* includes the first international definition of this violence. The General Assembly endorsed the *Declaration* by consensus. Other resolutions approved included one that condemned rape and abuse of women in the former Yugoslavia; and another, regarding human rights among big movements of refugees, asked the Secretary-General to report on what he is doing to anticipate such movements, to safeguard their rights and to provide humanitarian assistance. Canada sponsored the latter resolution.

Countries where rights violations had special attention this year were Cambodia, Haiti, Iran, Iraq, Myanmar (Burma), Somalia, Sudan and former Yugoslavia. Canada's annual *tour d'horizon* touched on all the major scandals including the above, while not omitting Europe, Peru, El Salvador, Guatemala, Syria, Angola, Zaire, Rwanda, Liberia, Nigeria, China, Kashmir, Pakistan, Sri Lanka and little East Timor. Angry protestations and denials show that political leaders are very sensitive to international exposure.

Humanitarian Assistance

International "emergency relief" was transformed into "humanitarian assistance" when, in November 1991, the General Assembly created the high-level post of an Under-Secretary for Humanitarian Assistance, responsible for overseeing UN system-wide aid to natural and man-made disasters. The functions envisaged for this new office were political leadership (*e.g.*, negotiating access during war) and coordination of operations and fund-raising. The office was not to be operational in countries. As the tiny new UN Department of Humanitarian Affairs resulting from this decision has struggled to find its way, the demand for humanitarian assistance has exploded to a level in 1993 of nearly $2 billion flowing through bilateral and UN channels. Much of this increase stems from man-made disasters, armed conflicts at home inside UN States; and these, euphemistically called "complex emergencies", present the most difficult political, conceptual and operational problems. Other baffling problems are coming to the fore. These are seen in UN pioneering forays into restoring order and rebuilding society in Mozambique, Somalia and, one hopes, in Haiti, not to mention Liberia, Afghanistan, Angola and eventually the former Yugoslavia. The most perplexing challenge is how to give humanitarian assistance – meaning the restoration of civil society, of social infrastructures, not just first-aid to war's victims – its proper place in peacekeeping operations launched by the Security Council. The military culture that has been central in peacekeeping has little understanding or tolerance of the slow and uncertain process of civil society, nor does it suffer the same cost-benefit resource constraints. The hit-and-run approach in Somalia, where the military took over the show, at a cost ten times the UN investment in humanitarian aid, is an expensive lesson in blundering enthusiasm. So the humanitarian approach must permeate peacekeeping. But how to maintain impartiality, how to avoid the use of humanitarian aid for partisan military and political ends? Where civil war is primarily directed against the civilian populations, how can humanitarian aid be seen as neutral? And where UN military contingents are used to protect humanitarian operations, how to keep a clear distinction in the field between military and humanitarian roles?

There are two more politically sensitive issues confronting humanitarian operations. One is the impact of sanctions on the civilian population, as in Iraq and Haiti. Despite the attempts to exclude some kinds of medical and nutritional supplies, civilians (especially the most vulnerable such as children) have been badly hit. Will humanitarian aid be treated as a breach of Security Council sanctions? The other issue is land-mines, already touched on in the Disarmament section of this report. Mines are a vicious enemy that prevents the safe return of displaced populations to home and livelihood, and thus prolongs humanitarian operations.

Yet another basic policy issue arises from the North-South dialogue: why so much attention and aid to these spectacular emergencies, asks the Group of 77 (through Colombia, its spokesman at this Assembly), when we have our silent emergency in dire poverty? To this, the UN doctrine, built into the mandate of the Department of Humanitarian Affairs, is that emergency aid should be planned and executed in such a way as to mesh with long-term reconstruction and development.

In the legislative and structural life of the United Nations, a fertile ground for growth is the joint General Assembly–Security Council concern for humanitarian operations. In its current review of peacekeeping, discussed earlier in this paper, the Assembly has insisted that Humanitarian Affairs be closely involved in planning and implementation of field operations; and coming from the humanitarian side, it has confirmed the 1993 ECOSOC conclusion that, in the field, "the Emergency Relief Coordinator should participate fully in the overall United Nations planning...in order to serve as the humanitarian advocate in insuring that the humanitarian dimension, particularly the principles of humanity, neutrality and impartiality of relief assistance are taken fully into account." The Assembly also had serious things to say about training for peacekeeping personnel. So the legislative groundwork is being laid to bring military and humanitarian aspects together. Will this facilitate or will it exacerbate?

All the above is a complicated prologue to saying that last year ECOSOC made a fairly comprehensive review of UN humanitarian assistance; and that subsequently the General Assembly confirmed and elaborated on ECOSOC's conclusions. On policy issues, the Assembly, besides affirming the advocacy role of the Humanitarian Relief Coordinator, touched on problems of access (in war), mine clearance and protection of humanitarian personnel. Nothing was said about sanctions. Both in ECOSOC and the Assembly, however, the main preoccupation was with better coordination of the several UN organs involved in relief operations, management, quicker response and adequate funding. The Assembly asked the Secretary-General to beef up the staffing of the little Humanitarian Department.

Under-Secretary Jan Eliasson has decided to leave his post as Head of Humanitarian Affairs at the end of January 1994. As Sweden's Ambassador to the United Nations, he was a key player in sensitizing the international community to its humanitarian responsibilities. He was the UN mediator who brought Iraq and Iran to the end of their war. His efforts culminated in the 1991 decision that gave the UN its humanitarian mandate. Returning to Sweden, he will be at the University of Uppsala. He tells me that he wants to devote himself to attacking the sources of conflict, and that he will of course be on call to assist the UN.

The Processional of Development

So here we go again into the labyrinth of the development debate at the United Nations. What makes the world go 'round? Is it love, guns or money? Love is having a hard time of it these days with the AIDS pandemic and soaring population. Love will have its day, in a manner of speaking, when the *International Conference on Population and Development* convenes in Cairo in September 1994. As for guns and money, is it guns that make money, or is it money that makes guns? The collapse of the USSR is just the latest confirmation that, in the long pull, the economy comes first. But what makes the world's economic engine work? State Capitalism (so-called Communism), as practised in the USSR, was not able to support that empire. But that negative lesson has left the "international community", that congeries of formal and informal arrangements, with neither a sure understanding of the present-day economy nor efficient tools to stimulate and guide it. Rio de Janeiro enshrined "sustainability" as a stern necessity, but we are slow to change our lavish ways. As of today, the world has adequate primary resources and expansive new means of production – biotechnology, genetic manipulation, automation, the robotics revolution – but we are lacking the political wisdom and skills to meet basic human needs in a fair way, even in many industrialized nations. Unemployment coexists with enormous unmet social needs. And on the scale of economic development there are now many gradations as more and more countries climb up the ladder, especially in Asia and Latin America. As already mentioned, while the Non-Aligned Movement (the South) still speaks with one voice on some development issues – like terms of trade, access to markets and technology – yet there are various national groupings around particular shared interests as manifested, for example, in regional trade associations. The South Commission and the Group of 15 nations have taken a more technical and professional approach to the North–South dialogue. While the fact of one billion people still living in absolute poverty cannot be ignored, rigid polarization between "developed" and "developing" is giving way to a more pragmatic style. With the spewing of capital and capacity into the South and the universal appetite for markets, we are indeed all caught up in a global economy.

Where has the United Nations come into all this? In its preamble, the *Charter* says that one of the UN's aims is, "to promote social progress and better standards of life in larger freedom"; and in *Article I* this statement is elaborated to read, "to achieve international cooperation in solving international problems of an economic, social, cultural or humanitarian character." But the establishment of the Bretton Woods organizations (the World Bank and the IMF) and GATT, outside Mother UN, effectively emasculated the General Assembly as a player in the international economy. This has been the source of chronic frustration as the Assembly has adopted principles, made declarations and formulated strategies, which in practice have had little impact on development. Indeed, not even Bretton Woods has a handle on the vast economic activity generated by the stateless transnationals.

But two happenings are beginning to change this situation. One is UNCED, a distinctly UN affair, which raised the crisis of environment-plus-sustainable-development to the highest political level, and got solid treaty work in process on major facets of that complex. The Inter-governmental Commission on Sustainable Development is charged with seeing that governments follow through on the UNCED programme, *Agenda 21*. And the UN has a piece of the action through the joint UNDP–UNEP–World Bank–Global Environment Facility (GEF).

The other happening is still happening: the probability, indeed the certainty, that Germany and Japan will become members of the Security Council. This means that economic strength, not just military capacity, is recognized as basic to peace and security.

An Agenda for Development

It was against this background that the General Assembly in 1993 addressed the need for an *Agenda for Development*. Remember that this idea was an immediate reaction of the South to *An Agenda for Peace*. A focus on development should be seen not just as parallel or complementary to concern for peace, but rather as putting peace and security, along with everything else, into their proper context. "Development" has come to comprise all meliorative principles and processes: human well-being (people-centred), poverty alleviation, equity, participation (democracy), sustainability, environment conservation and protection.

In the fantasia of the Assembly hall, there was repeated rhetorical resounding of these themes. Development so conceived would create the optimum conditions for peace. This year's active and constructive debate, with 48 nations speaking, indicates that development will be a leading concern of the Assembly in the years ahead. The configuration of speakers was interesting, including Colombia for the Group of 77, Belgium for the European Community's twelve, Finland for the Nordics, Algeria, Brazil, China, France, India, Indonesia, Italy, Japan, Korea, Malaysia, Pakistan and the UK. Why so little African participation? The World Bank and the IMF also spoke.

The yearning of the South to gain substantial influence among economic powers was expressed by Colombia, speaking for the Group of 77: "The United Nations is the only global organization which has a clear mandate in all the relevant areas of development. It is the only one with a capacity to articulate, within an integrated vision, the various economic, environmental, social and political issues." But the tendency to attribute all economic problems to a hostile international environment was modified, along lines taken by the South Commission, with more emphasis on what countries must do for themselves.

The economic powers-that-be must be comfortable with the Caesarean quadrisection proposed to the Assembly by Camdessus of the IMF. His four pillars are: GATT for promoting trade, World Bank (IBRD) for financing projects, IMF for macro-economic stabilization, UN for human, social and environmental development. While this approximates the present state of affairs, its formal acceptance would imply UN abdication of any role in the big game. And M. Camdessus, with his Big Bank Pillars, seems to feel that social and environmental issues are subsidiary, if not marginal. Ideally, the UN should play a leading conceptual and political role, without actually running the Big Banks.

All of this is by way of preliminary scratching in the farmyard. The Secretary-General is now working up what should be a major report for a major debate in the next Assembly. Many will be consulted in preparation for this report as was done for *An Agenda for Peace*.

Coordinating UN Development Operations

Meantime, in 1993 the General Assembly continued its sorting out of development functions within the UN. For policy making, the current Assembly resolution tries to clarify the three levels of responsibility along the following lines:

- the General Assembly, to make overall policy;
- ECOSOC, to review major development issues, to translate overall policy into objectives, priorities and policies for the system as a whole, and to coordinate and evaluate the work of several UN funds;

- Executive Boards of the Funds (UNDP, UNFPA, UNICEF) to provide inter-governmental support to and supervision of the activities of each Fund, in accordance with the overall policy guidance of the Assembly and the Council.

The laudable intent is to make these three UN Funds (the UNDP is called a Programme, but it is the same thing) all point in the same direction, in so far as their programmes interact and relate to overarching objectives. There is the danger that concern over tidy "management" may obscure judgement about substance. Are these Executive Boards to be reduced to the role of auditors and bookkeepers? Coordination and coherence sound good and, if done intelligently, get better results. But the need for specific technical guidance will not disappear when policy-making is raised to a higher level. Is the Assembly endowing ECOSOC with the technical skills and experience now residing in the subsidiary Executive Boards? If not, these Boards will continue to provide technical guidance. Is this the tacit understanding? Anyhow, giving greater authority to ECOSOC will not in itself make ECOSOC politically powerful. Other considerations apart, a council of 54 governments is an awkward machine for agreeing on anything. The Commission on Sustainable Development suffers from this same membership. A strong Development Council, balancing the Security Council, is not yet in sight.

Funding the UN: What's New?

Start by comparing 1992 and 1993:

Unpaid Assessed Contributions at 30 September
(in millions of US dollars)

	1992	1993
Regular budget	826	784
Peacekeeping operations	644	1,502
Total	1,470	2,286

The increase in Peacekeeping operations means that Peacekeeping assessments made during the 12 months since 30 September 1992 are about three times the regular assessments, since the $1.5 billion figure for 1992 includes $708 million authorized only in September 1993.

As of 31 December 1993, the situation has improved a lot:

Unpaid Assessed Contributions at 31 December 1993
(in millions of US dollars)

Regular budget	488
Peacekeeping operations	1,013
Total	1,501

For the moment, the UN does not have a cash-flow problem. Yet with a chronic shortage amounting to around one-third of assessments, keeping the UN afloat is a juggling stunt, as funds are switched about from one pocket to another.

As of 31 December 1993, the big delinquents are:

Unpaid Contributions
(in millions of US dollars)

	Regular	Peacekeeping	Total
Russia	43	484	527
USA	260	193	453
Ukraine	29	74	103
South Africa	53	33	86
Spain	0	39	39
Belarus	6	20	26
Japan	0	25	25
Brazil	12	8	20

Unpaid contributions below $20 million are not listed here. Russia, USA and Ukraine account for two-thirds of outstanding assessments. Ukraine and Belarus are having special dispensation. Most of South Africa's dues are for its years of sanctioned isolation.

Although the Ford Foundation's Volker-Ogata report on financing the UN was circulated as an official document, none of its recommendations was adopted. Keep your eye on government assessments was the tune. "Pay on time", said the Secretary-General. "We'll do better", said Bill Clinton, and indeed the USA has made big strides. But unless the USA restores the UN appropriation for one whole year that Reagan dropped in US fiscal year 1982 (1 October - 30 September), it will always be very late in its payments, since the United Nations budgets for the calendar year. Canada is still among the handful of States that pay on time, in 1994 being the first. As for penalties for delinquents, the only one given any serious consideration was charging interest on arrears, which is not likely to fly in Washington, Tokyo or Moscow.

Complaints

- the new UN regular budget was months late;
- many contributors of Peacekeeping Forces have not been paid;
- you keep asking the UN to do more but you freeze our budget;
- how can we strengthen Human Rights, Humanitarian Assistance, *etc.?*

And so funding and budgeting lead on into the tangle of administration.

The Secretariat– Management

The founders of the UN envisaged an elite international civil service to facilitate intercourse among States and to do their bidding. It is hard enough to create and maintain an efficient and responsible public service for any one country. How can you satisfy many masters who may be squabbling among themselves? UN staff regulations were designed to protect the international service from political influence. As the UN drifted along in the Cold-War doldrums, this ideal was tarnished and a good many people got into the Secretariat through government pressures rather than merit. Their presence further dispirited the core loyal staff, already the scape-goats for international intransigence; and once in, it was hard to get the political floaters out. UN regulations protect the just and the unjust alike, alas and alack. This problem is common to many national bureaucracies, sometimes being the paralytic norm. But the UN should outshine the best.

And then, to the usual arteriosclerosis of aging bureaucracies were added top-level functionaries and functions mandated year after year by *ad hoc* decisions of the General Assembly, to the point that, on arrival, Mr. Boutros Boutros-Ghali had more than 30 Under-Secretaries reporting directly to him. He cut this back to eleven; but now, with a High Commissioner for Human Rights, the number will rise to twelve. At this senior level, the rationale for three departments of economic and social affairs and two departments of political affairs is not clear. The 38th Floor is something of an enigma. Teamwork and direction at the top are also coloured by the Secretary-General's aloof and imperious style. He has brains and vision for his unique responsibilities. Let us hope that, with time and support, he can mellow. We wish him well.

Beneath him, serious problems of administration and management remain. These show up in ambiguities and lacunae in the current budget. The grouping of inspection and auditing functions into a single office, as arranged by the Secretary-General, may tighten accountability, but it won't solve internal management problems. Turf wars must end, and dead wood be put away. A clear head and tough hand are needed, not primarily to expose naughty people, but to make it possible for good people to work well.

Non-Governments

The negative designation of citizens' organizations at the UN, as NGOs, *i.e.*, *Non*-Governmental Organizations, bespeaks the ambivalence of government officials about popular participation in affairs of State, especially on the international stage. The *Charter* starts out with a rhetorical flourish, "We the Peoples...", but after that it's all about governments. Yet in our time NGOs have begun to play a serious role in international affairs, most evident in social and economic issues – the environment, human rights, women, minorities, population – and in aspects of disarmament, *e.g.*, the nuclear tests ban, land-mines. Opening up to further NGO participation is under consideration at ECOSOC. NGOs are not likely to get a seat at the Security Council, but international NGO enthusiasm and ideas about UN reform will surely refresh official corridors. The distinguished Commission on Global Governance in Geneva will surely be heard.

In the spectrum of issues before the UN, I mention just a few where more NGO attention could help. These are:
• international regulations (laws) concerning the environmental; impact of the arms industry and of armed conflict;
• control of the conventional arms trade;
• land-mines: clearance, ban on exports and production.

This is not to detract from the important work of NGOs on many other issues. Like governments, NGOs need to get their act together and bring in their partners from the developing countries. This means travel money. There is the political hazard that NGOs from the industrialized North may take on the cast of neo-colonial intruders.

Another Future?

If history means the repetitive cycle of wars and other disasters, we can rejoice in the announcement that it has ended. At the UN, hopes, fears, threats, compassion, intransigence and goodwill are the order of the day. What future can we build on that? From time to time, we raise our sights and try to see the big picture. This I tried to do when thinking about priorities for Canada's foreign policy. It seemed to me that some sort of strategy – the word is overworked but it still has its validity – would help in making day-to-day decisions. A big strategy would address the big issues, the big problems that must be confronted, mitigated, resolved if there is to be a new kind of future. Here I repeat my outline of the big ones:

(1) *Poverty* – the core evil of our times, from which flow many systemic problems. The great divide between North and South is manifested most clearly in the one billion people living in "absolute poverty" (annual per capita income of below $370 according to the World Bank);

(2) *Population* – increasing at the rate of one billion in this decade, around 90% in the South;

(3) *Environment* – the reckless depletion of the world's resources (mainly by the North), the pollution and the destruction of environmental protection;

(4) *Anarchy* – the lack of an accepted international legal system and an adequate enforcement mechanism (international police); the continuing resort to force (international and civil wars) as a way to settle disputes;

(5) *Tyranny* – the prevalence of arbitrary and brutal political systems, where violations of human rights are customary instruments of government;

(6) *Xenophobia* – or mass paranoia, the widespread source of irrational behaviour.

These are interlocking issues, facets of an organic whole, so that touching on one in the long run affects them all. As we are today, at least we can turn our minds to this whole complex and work towards a useful strategy for steering our ship of fools. Right now we don't have the map and we are wasting our fuel. At the UN, superseding the vague *International Development Strategy*, adopted by the General Assembly in 1990, the elements for a relevant and workable strategy may be taking shape in *An Agenda for Peace*, the UNCED *Agenda 21* and the forthcoming *Agenda for Development*. Within such a framework, piece-meal actions could converge. Even though the UN at present will have only a small operational role in "development", it could become humanity's cartographer. This would be worth a Fiftieth Anniversary celebration in 1995. Many a time in my UN life I have felt that we are just nibbling around the edges. But then, better to nibble away down here than to nibble on pie in the sky.

CHAPTER 3

United Nations Reform: A Systems Approach

Dietrich Fischer

The end of the Cold War, which had long paralyzed the United Nations, offers the opportunity to strengthen it, so that it can better fulfil the roles originally foreseen for the UN and assume some new ones. To reach agreement on reforms to be taken is not easy. It has usually taken a major catastrophe to shake up the international community sufficiently to attempt to create a new world order. After World War I, the League of Nations was formed, and after World War II the United Nations. Both have played a useful role, but not completely fulfilled the hopes of their founders. We had better not wait for World War III before seeking to make the UN more effective.

Several international commissions have recently made proposals for improvements in the international system. The two Brandt Commission Reports (*Independent Commission on International Development Issues*, 1980 and 1983), and more recently the *Report of the South Commission* (1990), chaired by Julius Nyerere, have emphasized the need to reduce inequalities between rich and poor countries, a source of tension. The Palme Commission (*Independent Commission on Disarmament and Security Issues*, 1982) coined the concept of "common security" and pointed out that true security can be achieved only through cooperation. The Brundtland Commission (*World Commission on Environment and Development*, 1987) has stressed the need for "sustainable development," which preserves a livable environment for future generations.

This paper seeks to contribute to the debate on how the United Nations family of organizations may be strengthened on its approaching 50th anniversary to improve human security in a broad sense, reducing all forms of threats to human life and well-being. It focuses on inter-related threats to peace, economic development, a clean environment and human rights. It is based on a report to the United Nations Institute for Disarmament Research on Nonmilitary Aspects of Security (Fischer 1993), which also discusses some strategies at the regional, national, local and individual levels. Only problems that cannot be solved at any lower level should be assigned to the United Nations (according to the principle of subsidiarity), but a growing number of tasks fall into that category. Many of the necessary institutions and programmes already exist today; some need to be strengthened, others are currently under discussion and still others are new.

This paper explores how systems theory – the science of how living systems survive under adverse conditions and adapt to changing environments – can provide some insights into how to improve the international order. Living systems use numerous automatic feedback mechanisms that constantly compare their current state with a desirable goal state and set in motion corrective mechanisms if a deviation is detected. An example is the human immune system, which detects and eliminates disease germs before they can multiply and spread. An example of such a feedback control system and regulatory mechanism in society is the legal system. Laws define norms of behaviour, courts determine violations of the law and the police enforce the laws.

A regulatory feedback system has three main components: (1) a goal; (2) ways to measure deviations from the goal; and (3) corrective mechanisms to reduce deviations from the goal.

Such a system can fail in six possible ways: (1) there may be no agreement on the goal (a matter of conflict resolution); (2) even if the goal is clear, deviations may not be detected (a matter of observation and measurement); (3) even if deviations are noticed, those who could correct them may have no incentive to do so, because others are affected (a matter of externalities, and also ethics, whether we care about each other); (4) even if those who cause a problem will ultimately suffer from it, the consequences may not be immediate and they may fail to foresee them (a matter of planning for the future); (5) people may have accurate information on time but fail to correct a problem due to prejudices or other sources of irrational behaviour (a matter of psychology and culture); and (6) people may be fully aware of a problem and wish to correct it, but not know how or lack the necessary resources (a matter of resources, science, technology and education). The approach briefly outlined here may be called "adaptation theory," because it emphasizes adaptation to changing external conditions for survival.

As an example, consider how these six principles would apply to seeking an end to the war in Bosnia and Herzegovina. To restore peace, there must first be agreement on a political settlement. For this purpose, it is necessary to press the Serbs to stop their aggression.

Second, we need better intelligence. There have been numerous cease-fire agreements, but they all broke down, with each side accusing the other of having started to shoot first, that they acted only in self-defence. There need to be independent observers, who can pinpoint those responsible for violating an agreement so as to put pressure on them to stop it.

Third, the adversaries must have an incentive to stop fighting. As long as aggression is rewarded with territorial gains, there is little to prevent it. It must be clear in the eyes of an aggressor that the costs of aggression far outweigh any benefits.

Fourth, it would have been much better to take action before war broke out instead of reacting to it. For example, in the Fall of 1991, a few months after the war between Croatia and Serbia broke out, a peace conference was called in The Hague to bring the parties together to seek a peaceful settlement. If the conference had been held a year earlier, before fighting began but when tensions were already very clear, it might still have been possible to prevent a war by finding a mutually acceptable solution. Once blood begins to flow, it is much harder to do that. It was wise to station some troops in Macedonia as a deterrent to prevent the war from spreading there. More should be done now to find a just solution to the problem of Kosovo, before it is engulfed in war.

If fighting cannot be prevented in advance, efforts to stop it must be made more quickly. If at the time when Serbian gunners began to shell Dubrovnik and terrorize the civilian population over a year ago there had been a quick international response to silence those guns, maybe other cities, including Sarajevo, might have been spared the same fate. Now that this has been allowed to go on unpunished for over a year, it is much harder to stop.

Fifth, one of the difficult problems is how to overcome the old hatred between Serbs, Croats and Muslims. Jean Monnet found a way to overcome the tension and hostility between Germany and France by bringing them together in the Coal and Steel Union, which has since developed into the European Community that has made another war between Germany and France almost unthinkable. Although Serbia and Croatia were united in the former Yugoslavia, that arrangement was imposed on them at Versailles. If Germany and France had been forced to join the European Community, rather than doing so voluntarily, that might have exacerbated tensions rather than reducing them.

Sixth, the UN needs greater resources for its peacekeeping missions.

Existing UN agencies already address many of these six common sources of problems. Table 3.1 (slightly modified from Tinbergen and Fischer 1987, 148) lists existing global institutions within the United Nations family, classified by four areas: peace, development, environment and human rights. Table 3.2 indicates how these institutions help ameliorate problems of lack of agreement on goals, lack of feedback, distorted feedback, delayed feedback, rejected feedback and lack of remedies, in each area. It also lists a number of institutions that have been discussed but not yet implemented, and some new organizations or initiatives that could fill existing gaps. The following sections focus on potential new agencies.

Clearly, improvements in one area help reduce problems in other areas, *e.g.*, improvements in human rights or economic justice reduce tensions that might lead to war. For this reason, a comprehensive strategy is needed. Efforts to solve one problem in isolation often fail. Security is also enhanced through redundancy, so that if one approach fails, there are others to back it up.

1. Peace

1.1 *Agreement on Goals*
The task of reaching agreement about global policies falls primarily on the UN General Assembly. Most national parliaments consist of two chambers, one representing geographical entities and one representing people directly. This suggests the creation of a second chamber at the UN, often called People's Assembly (Barnaby 1991; Segall and Lerner 1992). It could have, for example, one popularly elected representative for every ten million inhabitants of a country or a fraction thereof. Decisions approved by both chambers would have greater weight and legitimacy. A People's Assembly would also give a voice to people who benefit or suffer from global decisions and would tap a vast new reservoir of ideas for solutions to world problems. It would help make the United Nations more democratic and more accountable to the public. [See Chapter 5.]

1.2 *Detecting Deviations*
Several institutions have been created to verify arms control agreements, including the International Atomic Energy Agency (IAEA) to verify the *Nuclear Nonproliferation Treaty.* They should be strengthened. The IAEA can now only inspect plants that members agree to place under its supervision. If a border guard could inspect the car of a suspected drug smuggler only in places where the smuggler agreed, such an "inspection" would be totally meaningless. The IAEA should be given the authority and the necessary means to inspect any suspected facility, among members and non-members, without advance warning, otherwise rogue governments or terrorists may acquire nuclear weapons. Those who abide by the treaty have nothing to hide.

Verification of arms control treaties could be improved through an International Satellite Monitoring Agency (ISMA), first proposed by France in 1978. ISMA could also reveal preparations for aggression. It is easier to prevent aggression before it is carried out than to reverse it afterwards. Further, it could give advance warnings of droughts or plant diseases to help guard against food shortages, and help monitor the global environment.

1.3 *Incentives*

If violations of agreements are detected, measures are needed to enforce them. UN peacekeepers can help observe cease-fires if invited by both sides. This is useful, but more is needed. As UN Secretary-General Boutros Boutros-Ghali (1992) has recommended, there should also be *Peace-enforcement Units* that can be deployed at the request of one side alone inside its territory, without depending on agreement from the other side. If the police could stop a criminal from attacking a victim only if the criminal agreed it would be powerless.

1.4 *Foresight*

Rather than reacting to outbreaks of war, it would be preferable to anticipate potential conflicts and prevent or resolve them long before they lead to war (Fischer 1991). The same principle applies to other threats to security. Carl Sagan (1983) pointed out that some of the greatest dangers facing us – the greenhouse effect, the destruction of the ozone layer, and nuclear winter – have all been discovered by accident and wondered how many other potential dangers may still be unknown. Mikhail Gorbachev (1987) proposed the creation of a council consisting of about one hundred eminent former political leaders, scientists and writers from around the world, who could study long range global problems and explore possible solutions, free from the pressure to react daily to the latest crisis. Such a council, which might be called a World Security Commission, would cost far less than maintaining millions of troops, yet could contribute considerably more to global security.

1.5 *Overcoming Prejudice*

Long-living, constantly recreated prejudices and hatreds between different ethnic, linguistic or religious groups are a source of war. In an effort to help break down such prejudices, UNESCO publishes history books written by international teams, who avoid stereotyped enemy images and the glorification of victory in war. Even more people could be reached, on a daily basis, if there was a UN Radio and Television Network broadcasting

Table 3.1
Some UN Institutions, Classified by Primary Area of Concern

<u>Peace</u>

IAEA	International Atomic Energy Agency	Vienna
ICJ	International Court of Justice (World Court)	The Hague
UNGA	United Nations General Assembly	New York
UNHQ	United Nations Headquarters (Secretariat)	New York
UNIDIR	United Nations Institute for Disarmament Research	Geneva
UNSC	United Nations Security Council	New York

<u>Economic and social development</u>

ECOSOC	Economic and Social Council	New York
FAO	Food and Agriculture Organization	Rome
GATT	General Agreement on Tariffs and Trade	Geneva
IBRD	International Bank for Reconstruction and Development (World Bank)	Washington
IBS	International Bank of Settlements	Basel
ICAO	International Civil Aviation Organization	Montreal
IDA	International Development Association	Washington
IFAD	International Fund for Agricultural Development	Rome
IFC	International Finance Corporation	Washington
ILO	International Labour Organization	Geneva
IMF	International Monetary Fund	Washington
IMO	International Maritime Organization	London
INSTRAW	International Research and Training Institute for the Advancement of Women	S. Domingo
ITU	International Telecommunications Union	Geneva
UNCHS	United Nations Centre for Human Settlements (Habitat)	Nairobi
UNCTAD	United Nations Conference on Trade and Development	Geneva
UNCTC	United Nations Centre for Transnational Corporations	New York
UNDP	United Nations Development Programme	New York
UNDRO	Office of the United Nations Disaster Relief Coordinator	Geneva
UNESCO	United Nations Educational, Scientific and Cultural Organization	Paris
UNHCR	United Nations High Commissioner for Refugees	New York
UNICEF	United Nations Children Fund	New York
UNIDO	United Nations Industrial Development Organization	Vienna
UNITAR	United Nations Institute for Training and Research	New York
UNRISD	United Nations Research Institute for Social Development	Geneva
UNU	United Nations University	Tokyo
UNV	United Nations Volunteers	New York
UPU	Universal Postal Union	Bern
WHO	World Health Organization	Geneva
WIDER	World Institute for Development Economics Research	Helsinki
WIPO	World Intellectual Property Organization	Geneva
WMO	World Meteorological Organization	Geneva

<u>Environment</u>

UNEP	United Nations Environment Programme	Nairobi
UNFPA	United Nations Fund for Population Activities	New York

<u>Human rights</u>

UNCHR	United Nations Commission on Human Rights	Geneva

Table 3.2
Some Existing (and *Potential – Italicized*) International Organizations and Initiatives to Address Global Problems

	Peace	Economic development	Environment	Human rights
(1) Agreement on goals	UNGA; UNSC; *People's Assembly**	GATT; ICAO; ILO; IMO; ITU; UNCTAD; UPU; Law of the Sea; *UN Space Agency**	UNCED; Earth Charter	Universal Declaration of Human Rights; UN Conference on Minorities
(2) Detecting deviations	UN Observers; IAEA; *International Satellite Monitoring Agency (ISMA)**	UN Statistical Office; UN Centre on Transnational Corporations; WIPO *Global Anti-corruption Campaign*	UNEP (GEMS— Global Environmental Monitoring System)	Commission on Human Rights; *International Democratic Elections Agency (IDEA)*
(3) Moral and material incentives	World Court; economic sanctions; *Peace-enforcement Units**	International Bank of Settlements; *global anti-trust laws, with enforcement*	*Pollution taxes*, global pension plan**	*International Criminal Court**
(4) Foresight	*World Security Commission**	WIDER; Committee for Development Planning	Sustainability Commission	UN High Commissioner for Human Rights*
(5) Reducing prejudices	UNESCO (History Book Project *etc.*); *Global Youth Exchange*; Global radio, TV and press*		*Global Environmental Education Campaign*	
(6) Creating and disseminating knowledge and resources	UNIDIR; International Peace Academy; *Global Peace Service**	FAO; IBRD; IDA; IFAD; IFC; IMF; INSTRAW; UNCHS; UNCTAD; UNDP; UNDRO; UNHCR; UNICEF; UNIDO; UNITAR; UNRISD; WMO; UNU; UNV; WHO; *World Treasury*; NATURE***	UNFPA; debt-for-nature swaps; Global Environmental Facility; *network of global parks*	*Centre for Legal Education and Research (CLEAR)*

* *previously proposed by others*
** *Network of Applied Technical Universities and Research Establishments*

around the world (supplementing but not replacing national broadcasts), which could present a wide variety of viewpoints and promote international understanding. Before the 1993 elections in Cambodia, the UN sponsored a daily radio broadcast of one hour in which the various parties were allowed to present their platforms without censorship. It proved so popular that all transistor radios in that country were sold out. In the former Yugoslavia, on the other hand, President Milosevic had monopoly control over state radio and television and won the December 1992 elections by flooding the country with his propaganda of hate, while the peace candidate Milan Panic had almost no opportunity to get his message across. The West's failure to respond to Panic's urgent pleas for broadcasting equipment was a tragic blunder that may cost many lives in years to come.

An even deeper understanding of different viewpoints and cultures than through radio and television programmes can be gained from living for an extended period in a different country. There exist a number of youth exchange programmes, but usually between countries that already have close ties, and with inadequate funding. Ideally, all young people should be able to spend at least a year in a different country, working with local people and learning their language, through a Global Youth Exchange Programme. Friendships concluded during youth can last a lifetime and help overcome enemy images.

1.6 *Knowledge and Resources*

Even if a country's leaders wish to keep peace, they do not always have the necessary means or skills. UNIDIR (1990) explains principles of nonoffensive defence that can help countries maintain their security without threatening their neighbours (Fischer 1984; Galtung 1984). To help resolve international conflicts even before they lead to war, the UN Secretary-General has often acted as mediator, but he is overburdened. The International Peace Academy (IPA) can help mediate disputes, train future mediators from around the world, and help develop institutions less prone to conflict. Ury *et al.* (1988) have pointed out that the best mediators make themselves unnecessary by enabling people to resolve future conflicts themselves, as the best doctors teach people how to stay healthy. Currently, the IPA has only 30 staff members and is not able to deal with all the potential conflicts in the world. But given that one individual, Terje Larsen, was able to bring Israel and the PLO together to negotiate a peace agreement, while thousands of UN troops in Bosnia are unable to stop the fighting after war has broken out, it would make sense to put greater resources into preventing wars than reacting to them after they erupt.

Robert Muller (1991) proposed a Global Peace Service, in which young people from around the world could work together to alleviate poverty, restore a healthy environment, educate children and care for the ill. Such joint efforts generate good will and can help avert future wars.

2. Economic Development

2.1 *Agreement on Goals*
A whole series of organizations foster international agreement on such issues as trade, transportation, communication, labour laws and the use of global commons. It has become urgent to create a UN Space Agency (Tinbergen 1991a) to regulate the growing use of outer space and prevent future wars over space resources. Greater efforts are also required to reduce the enormous income gap between rich and poor countries. Tinbergen (1991b) points out that, if the developed countries fail to agree to this out of altruism, they should at least do so out of self-interest, to avoid being inundated by streams of future economic refugees.

2.2 *Detecting Deviations*
A variety of statistical offices within the UN system gather information about the state of the world economy, a precondition for informed planning. Another initiative that could help economic development would be a Global Anti-corruption Campaign. Corruption is one of the main obstacles to development. As long as it is easier to gain wealth by controlling the police or the army than by producing goods in demand, the most ambitious people will tend to plot military coups or engage in organized crime rather than investing in flourishing enterprises. The UN Human Rights Commission and Amnesty International have been able to reduce human rights violations by publicly exposing them. A voluntary organization, Transparency International, has been founded this year with the goal of fighting corruption by exposing it.

2.3 *Incentives*
To encourage fair competition at the global level, it would be useful to have enforceable global anti-trust laws that limit the accumulation of monopoly power in the hands of a few transnational corporations.

2.4 *Foresight*
Rather than dealing with the debt crisis in hindsight, it would be easier to explore what forces in the world economy are responsible for the tendency

to concentrate wealth, and what forces automatically tend to reduce income differentials. It should then be possible to alleviate future crises by strengthening the mechanisms that promote greater equality and restraining trends that exacerbate global inequality.

2.5 *Overcoming Prejudice*
Learning more about other people's lifestyles and customs sometimes allows us to recognize wasteful habits and overcome them. International comparisons of diet and health can reveal healthier diets.

2.6 *Knowledge and Resources*
Jan Tinbergen (in Tinbergen and Fischer 1987) noted that some international organization corresponds to almost every government department at the national level, for example, the Food and Agriculture Organization to a ministry of agriculture, the International Labour Organization to a ministry of labour, the World Health Organization to a ministry of health, *etc.* Most national economies have three major financial institutions: a reserve bank, an investment bank and a treasury. The International Monetary Fund corresponds to a reserve bank, although its functions should be extended. The World Bank corresponds to an investment bank. Corresponding to a treasury, there is nothing comparable at the global level. Yet without a treasury, which collects revenue to finance all its operations, any government would collapse. Tinbergen therefore proposes the creation of a World Treasury, which could finance the operation of the UN and its affiliated organizations on a secure basis.

Agreement on world income taxes is not likely soon, but an initial source of revenue could be fees for the exploration of mineral resources on the deep seabed outside any country's national jurisdiction. This would also help avoid future wars over those resources. When oil was first discovered in Texas, some rival oil companies bombarded each other's drilling towers to get at the oil first. Yet they soon realized that they could not make a profit that way. Today they appreciate that the US government grants exclusive drilling rights to the highest bidder for a tract of land. They pay something, but in return they have the assurance that they can drill in peace, without fear that someone else would take away the oil they discover. Similar mechanisms at the global level would not only raise substantial revenue, but also provide a valuable service to the companies wishing to exploit those reserves. Other potential sources of revenue for a World Treasury include a fee for geo-stationary satellites, an auction of the international radio-spectrum and a tax on currency exchanges proposed by

Tobin (1974). Disarmament and economic conversion could also free substantial resources (Sivard 1993). To mention just one example, UNICEF (1990) has estimated that for $1.50 per child, the children in all developing countries could be inoculated against the most common preventable diseases, from which nearly 3 million children under five die each year. This would cost about $150 million per year – less than one tenth the cost of a single stealth bomber.

Perhaps the most under-utilized resource for development is technical knowledge. Unlike physical or financial resources, which must be given up by someone to be given to someone else, useful knowledge, once discovered, can be duplicated without limit, at almost no additional costs. Voltaire said that freedom is used up when it is not used. This is also true about human knowledge. If the least polluting and least resource-, energy- and labour-intensive production methods known anywhere on earth were available everywhere, everyone could be much better off. The weapons research laboratories left over from the Cold War could now join with academic institutions into a global Network of Applied Technical Universities and Research Establishments *(NATURE)* to cooperate towards the solution of global problems, instead of planning mutual destruction. They could do research on non-polluting manufacturing processes, safe and renewable energy sources, disease-resistant and high-yield food crops, new and less expensive cures for diseases, to name only a few, and share their discoveries world-wide.

3. Environment

3.1 *Agreement on Goals*
The 1992 *United Nations Conference on Environment and Development* (UNCED) in Rio de Janeiro has helped increase awareness of dangers to the global environment and the need to embark on sustainable development strategies. Some preliminary agreements have been concluded, but many more are needed. Agreement is easiest to reach if all participants derive some benefits, in "win-win" solutions (Fisher and Ury 1981), instead of some gaining at the expense of others. Saving the global environment is in the strong interest of all.

3.2 *Detecting Deviations*
The implementation of agreements must be monitored to detect and correct violations. UNEP has a small Global Environmental Monitoring System (GEMS), but it is grossly understaffed and should be strengthened.

3.3 *Incentives*

Effective ways to enforce pollution standards and to encourage the conservation of scarce resources are taxes on pollution and the use of natural resources (Baumol and Oates 1975; Orr 1991). Most of these taxes will be raised at the national level, at least initially, but if some (*e.g.*, a carbon tax to reduce global warming) were collected at the global level, they could help fund a World Treasury.

Today's tax systems, which tax hard work and creative initiatives to meet human needs, are counterproductive. Those activities should be encouraged, not penalized. It would be better to tax harmful activities, such as pollution, resource depletion and wasteful consumption. Such taxes would, paradoxically, allow a reduction of overall tax levels, because they would also help reduce the problems governments face, such as environmental cleanup. To see this, imagine that gasoline was distributed for free. Would we pay less for gasoline? On the contrary, we would pay much more, because many people would waste it, and in the end the taxpayers would have to foot the bill anyway. Since today we generally treat a clean environment as if it were free, it should surprise nobody that we pay dearly, if not with money, then with our health.

Environmental taxes would also greatly simplify tax collection. Instead of pursuing each individual and depending largely on people's voluntary declaration of their tax liability, it would suffice to station permanent inspectors at a few factories, mines and harbours where pollution or resource depletion originate. The price system would then automatically propagate these taxes throughout the economy, and simultaneously encourage the use of environmentally more benign products.

The rapid growth of the human population is severely burdening the earth's environment, in addition to wasteful consumption. To stabilize the human population, Arthur Westing (1988) proposed a global pension plan – to be financed by all nations through a progressive tax – to reduce parents' dependence on their children to care for them during old-age, a principal reason for large families.

3.4 *Foresight*

A Sustainability Commission, established at the Rio de Janeiro conference, can project long term future trends regarding development and the environment and recommend strategies to avert impending dangers. Past US policy was to do nothing about global warming until its effects are certain. But once the sea levels rise, we cannot suddenly freeze huge quantities of ocean water and deposit them back on Antarctica. Reacting to crises is like driving a car with closed eyes, waiting to hit an obstacle before trying to change direction, instead of anticipating and avoiding dangers. It is even worse. Many dangers we face, like global warming, ozone depletion, or nuclear war, are irreversible once they are upon us. Waiting to react to them is comparable to driving blindly towards the edge of an abyss, from which there is no return.

3.5 Overcoming Prejudice

To help overcome bad environmental habits, a global public debate is needed. When Louis Pasteur first saw microbes under a microscope and discovered how we infect ourselves with typhus or cholera unless we are careful, education about personal hygiene became commonplace throughout the world, starting in early infancy. Now that we have discovered that we can get cancer and other diseases unless we protect the environment, a similar global environmental education campaign has become necessary.

3.6 Knowledge and Resources

Even if people wish to protect the environment, they may not have the necessary technical knowledge or means to do so. "Debt-for-nature swaps" help preserve rain forests and other natural treasures as a common heritage of humanity. A network of global parks, financially supported by all countries according to their ability to pay, could supplement today's national parks and help developing countries preserve their natural habitats. The Global Environmental Facility created in Rio de Janeiro should fund *Agenda 21*, a comprehensive strategy for sustainable development for the 21st century. However, it is not adequately funded. Of the estimated $125 billion per year needed, only $3.7 billion was pledged. [See Chapter 16.] Yet even full funding would represent only a small fraction of the nearly $1 trillion annual world military spending.

4. Human Rights

4.1 Agreement on Goals

The *Universal Declaration of Human Rights* of 1948, which most countries have ratified, is a clear and comprehensive statement of goals in this area. The 1994 *UN Conference on Minorities* should define the rights of minorities more clearly. The problem is inadequate implementation of these principles.

4.2 Detecting Deviations

The United Nations Commission on Human Rights monitors human rights around the world and condemns gross violations. A strong guarantee of human rights is democracy. It enables people to replace an oppressive government. Many UN agencies provide economic and technical advice, but often the problems lie deeper. An International Democratic Elections Agency (IDEA) could support democracy around the world by monitoring elections and ensuring that all parties have fair access to the media during the preceding campaigns. It is easy to reject accusations of vote fraud from an opposition party as politically motivated and unreliable. It is harder to dismiss observations by a respected international commission, which can therefore increase the credibility of voting results and their acceptance by all parties. To remove any stigma attached to having elections observed by outsiders, countries that take pride in a long tradition of democracy should be the first to invite international observers to their own elections. If that becomes a routine, any government that refused to admit observers would then raise suspicion about what it may try to hide.

An expansion of democracy would not only improve human rights, but also reduce wars. Immanuel Kant predicted that governments elected by the people who would have to fight and die in case of war would not go to war. He was wrong; even democracies have participated in many wars. But there has never been any war between two democracies (Shuman 1991; Russett 1993). It is plausible that if there had been an open debate and a vote in Iraq about the wisdom and legitimacy of invading Kuwait, instead of one man making that decision in secret, reason would have prevailed. Therefore, with the spread of democracy, wars may greatly diminish, if not disappear.

4.3 Incentives

To guarantee human rights, individuals or minorities must be able, if necessary, to seek justice from an International Criminal Tribunal with adequate enforcement powers (Kotliar 1991) [see Chapter 20]. It is an illusion to assume that the highest court within a country will always grant people justice, especially if they are oppressed by their own government and the government controls the courts. The World Court is now only authorized to hear cases between governments and has no enforcement powers.

Would an International Criminal Tribunal violate national sovereignty? Under ancient Roman law, the head of a household, the *pater familias*, had absolute authority over his family. He could sell his children into slavery or beat them to death and the state had no right to intervene in this "internal affair." Today we consider that notion absurd. Similarly, when governments massacre their own people, it is time to abolish the obsolete notion of absolute state sovereignty.

4.4 *Foresight*

Rather than waiting until gross violations of human rights occur and then reacting to them, it is preferable to survey constantly the human rights situation throughout the world and to help prevent violations before they occur. A private team from Princeton was able to get the Rumanian government to allow its Hungarian minority to use its own language in return for a promise not to seek secession, possibly preventing another disaster such as that in the former Yugoslavia (*New York Times*, 20 July 1993 A6). The new office of the UN High Commissioner for Human Rights, which was established by the General Assembly following the recommendation of the Human Rights Conference in Vienna in June 1993, can help improve human rights throughout the world, with relatively modest efforts if applied early.

4.5 *Overcoming Prejudice*

To help overcome racial, religious and ethnic prejudices, laws are important, but can only play a supplementary role. More important is education towards greater tolerance, which should begin during early childhood. Modern communication via satellite, which enables children in classrooms around the world to talk face to face and work on joint projects, may in time help overcome old prejudices.

4.6 *Knowledge and Resources*

Countries seeking to improve their justice systems could learn from the experience of others, without having to repeat the same mistakes. A global Centre for Legal Education and Research (CLEAR) could study the constitutions and legal systems of countries around the world, explore what works well under what conditions, and what does not and why. These findings could be disseminated globally. The world's leading legal scholars could discuss the advantages and problems of various legal approaches and teach their insights to each succeeding generation.

One particular concept that such a centre could investigate is the idea of legal systems based on rewards for exceptional contributions to the public good, rather than only on punishment for doing harm. There is a precedent. Someone who discovers a cure for a disease or contributes significantly to world peace may win a Nobel Prize. But this is rather comparable to selecting "the criminal of the year" from around the world for exemplary punishment, while letting every other lawbreaker get away free. We would hardly consider this an adequate legal system. Today's penal law could be complemented with a form of "remunerative law" which recognizes and rewards those who selflessly work for peace, justice, development and the protection of nature. People respond better to encouragement and rewards than to criticism and punishment ("Why Job Criticism Fails: Psychology's New Findings," *New York Times,* 26 July 1988 C1). Yet law still relies exclusively on punishment. A shift from punishment to rewards to implement legal norms might be comparable to the shift from slavery, where the motivation for work was the fear of punishment, to wage labour, where the main motivation for work is the expectation of a reward.

Concluding Remarks

The growing global interdependence has given rise to some problems that individual states can no longer solve alone. Only through worldwide cooperation can we prevent climate shifts, stem the international drug trade, or prevent nuclear terrorism. Simultaneously, improvements in transportation and communication have made global cooperation easier.

Many governments are still reluctant to join a global authority to deal with global problems out of fear that they would lose part of their national sovereignty. But that fear is mistaken. No country today, for example, has sovereign control over the ozone layer. By joining a global authority that can allocate and enforce emission quotas, we do not give up control over our destiny. On the contrary, we gain added control that we do not now possess and could never achieve at the national level (Mische and Mische 1977).

The first advanced civilizations emerged about 6,000 years ago in the Nile and Euphrates valleys, when farmers faced problems that they could not solve alone. To prevent recurrent floods and droughts, it was necessary to build dams to control the flow of those rivers, requiring the organized cooperation of thousands of individuals. This gave rise to the first states, the development of written language, the codification of laws, and a flourishing of science and the arts. Today we face some problems that not even a superpower can solve by itself. Hopefully, this will lead to greater worldwide cooperation before it is too late.

Modern science and technology have given humanity unprecedented powers. We can use them to make our world more livable, or to destroy it. The choice is ours.

References

Barnaby, Frank ed. 1991 *Building a More Democratic United Nations* (Frank Cass: Portland OR).

Baumol, William J., and Wallace E. Oates 1975 *The Theory of Environmental Policy* (Prentice Hall: Englewood Cliffs NJ).

Boutros-Ghali, Boutros 1992 *An Agenda for Peace: Report of the United Nations Secretary General to the United Nations Security Council* (United Nations: New York).

Dumas, Lloyd J. 1986 *The Overburdened Economy* (University of California Press: Berkeley).

Fischer, Dietrich 1984 *Preventing War in the Nuclear Age* (Rowman & Allanheld: Totowa NJ).

Fischer, Dietrich 1991 "An Active Peace Policy" in Shuman, Michael, and Julia Sweig eds. *Conditions of Peace: an Inquiry* (The Exploratory Project on the Conditions of Peace: Washington DC).

Fischer, Dietrich 1993 *Nonmilitary Aspects of Security: A Systems Approach* (Dartmouth Publishing Co.: Brookfield, VT; Ashgate Publishers: Aldershot, UK).

Fisher, Roger, and William Ury 1981 *Getting to Yes: Negotiating Agreement Without Giving In* (Houghton Mifflin: Boston).

Galtung, Johan 1984 *There Are Alternatives! Four Roads to Peace and Security* (Spokesman: Nottingham UK).

Gorbachev, Mikhail 1987 *Perestroika: New Thinking for Our Country and the World* (Harper & Row: New York).

Independent Commission on Disarmament and Security Issues (chaired by Olof Palme) 1982 *Common Security: A Blueprint for Survival* (Simon & Schuster: New York).

Independent Commission on International Development Issues (chaired by Willy Brandt) 1980 *North-South: A Programme for Survival* (Pan Books: London).

Independent Commission on International Development Issues 1983 *Common Crisis, North-South: Cooperation for World Recovery* (Pan Books: London).

Kotliar, Vladimir S. 1991 "The Question of Establishing an International Criminal Court as Recently Considered within the Framework of the United Nations" (Nuclear Age Peace Foundation: Santa Barbara CA).

Leontief, Wassily, and Faye Duchin 1983 *Military Spending: Facts and Figures, Worldwide Implications and Future Outlook* (Oxford University Press).

Mische, Patricia and Gerald 1977 *Toward a Human World Order* (Paulist Press: New York).

Muller, Robert 1991 *The Birth of a Global Civilization* (World Happiness and Cooperation: Anacortes WA).

Russett, Bruce 1993 *Grasping the Democratic Peace: Principles for a Post-Cold War World* (Princeton University Press).

Sagan, Carl "Nuclear War and Climatic Catastrophe" *Foreign Affairs* 62 (2) 1983, 257-292.

Segall, Jeffrey J., and Harry H. Lerner eds. 1992 *CAMDUN-2: The United Nations and a New World Order for Peace and Justice: Report of the Second International Conference on a More Democratic United Nations (Vienna, 1991)* (CAMDUN Project: London and New York).

Shuman, Michael "A Separate Peace Movement: The Role of Participation" in Shuman, Michael, and Julia Sweig eds. 1991 *Conditions of Peace: an Inquiry* (The Exploratory Project on the Conditions of Peace: Washington DC).

Sivard, Ruth Leger 1993 *World Military and Social Expenditures* (World Priorities: Leesburg VA).

South Commission (chaired by Julius Nyerere) 1990 *The Challenge to the South: The Report of the South Commission* (Oxford University Press).

Stockholm Initiative 1991 *Common Responsibility in the 1990s: The Stockholm Initiative on Global Security and Governance* (Office of the Prime Minister: Stockholm).

Tinbergen, Jan, and Dietrich Fischer 1987 *Warfare and Welfare: Integrating Security Policy into Socio-Economic Policy* (Wheatsheaf: Brighton).

Tinbergen, Jan 1991a *Supranational Decision-Making: A More Effective United Nations* Booklet 29 Waging Peace Series (Nuclear Age Peace Foundation: Santa Barbara CA).

Tinbergen, Jan 1991b *World Security and Equity* (Gower: Brookfield VT).

Tobin, James 1974 *The New Economics One Decade Older* (Princeton University Press).

UNICEF 1990 *The State of the World's Children 1990* (Oxford University Press).

UNIDIR 1990 *Nonoffensive Defense: A Global Perspective* (Taylor and Francis: New York).

Ury, William L., Jeanne M. Brett, and Stephen B. Goldberg 1988 *Getting Disputes Resolved: Designing Systems to Cut the Costs of Conflict* (Jossey-Bass: San Francisco).

Westing, Arthur H. ed. 1988 *Cultural Norms, War and the Environment* (Published by Oxford University Press for the Stockholm International

Peace Research Institute and the United Nations Environment Programme).

World Commission on Environment and Development (chaired by Gro Harlem Brundtland) 1987 *Our Common Future* (Oxford University Press).

CHAPTER 4

Third-Generation World Organizations

Hanna Newcombe

After World War I, the League of Nations was organized; after World War II, the United Nations was created. Mercifully we may avoid World War III. But with the great changes at the end of the Cold War, the kind of changes usually associated in history with a great war (William R. Thompson, 1983), we stand in great need of a more advanced working world organization. We might call this the third generation or the Third Wave (cf. Alvin Toffler, 1980, in a different context). It will also correspond to the end of our century and our millennium, and the dawning of the next one, hopefully less bloody.

The ideal, I would still maintain, even after many disappointments with the performance of governments, is a world federal government. Since we were well taught, however, by such writers as E.F. Schumacher (1973) and many others following him that, "Small is Beautiful," we should be careful not to put the entire stress on centralization. The guide to the future must be the old principle of subsidiarity. This principle states that problems should be solved at the lowest level possible at which there are no significant external effects. There is considerable vagueness in the definition of "significant," since in any system, including the world social system, everything is connected to everything else. Nevertheless, rough judgements can be made, and in social practice they are made routinely. For example, upstream pollution in a river affects downstream communities significantly, and therefore the whole river valley population should be involved in decision-making on such matters; but the rest of the world need not be involved, although strictly speaking the river pollution ends up in the ocean from which it does affect everyone – but, we arbitrarily say, not significantly.

Using the principle of subsidiarity, we might suggest a multi-level world system, in which about six levels of government would span the range from person to planet. It could move up in powers of 100: 100 persons form a neighbourhood government, 100 neighbourhoods (10^4, ten thousand persons) form a town government, 100 towns (10^6, a million persons) form a metro region or province, 100 metro regions (10^8, a hundred million persons) form a state, 100 states (10^{10}, ten billion persons – projecting world population a bit into the future) form the world. Note that the state (we don't say "nation-state" because most present states are in fact multi-national) is only one level among several, not particularly emphasized, and not the most salient level of identification as it is at present.

All this may be a later stage, however, perhaps the fourth generation world organization. Our present problem is how to upgrade our second-generation world organization, namely the United Nations. It may take two or more developmental stages.

As a first step, we can specify what we do not want, although it is in danger of happening. Two undesirable characteristics of a New World Order (the George Bush type) became apparent during the 1991 Gulf War: (1) collective security manipulated through the UN Security Council; (2) hegemony of the remaining superpower, *i.e.*, *Pax Americana* – a unipolar international system replacing the former bipolar system.

Collective security was the old ideal behind both the League of Nations and the United Nations, the first two generations, though never fully realized. The idea was that, if a state committed an aggression against another state, all the other states would be obligated to come to the aid of the victim of aggression. It was a criminal–law model of international law: when a murder is committed, in the criminal trial the whole state is against the accused, not just the representative of the victim seeking compensation as in a civil suit. Or, to employ another descriptive metaphor, it was like a military alliance (NATO–type) with no pre-designated external enemy.

There were four problems with this.

(1) There may be non-compliance with this rigid rule, because of the high cost required of all the states in the world system. This is what killed the League of Nations, when it did not apply the principle in the case of Italian aggression against Ethiopia and Japan's aggression against China. Partial application of the principle by the United Nations in the Korean War was probably illegal, because the permanent members of the Security Council were not unanimous (the USSR was absent, which was arbitrarily declared not to constitute a veto), as well as a bit of a fiction in practice, since the main protagonist against North Korean aggression was the USA, with only minimal participation of a few others.

(2) It is not always possible to pinpoint the aggressor. As we review the approximately 200 wars that have occurred under the UN regime

(*i.e..*, since 1945), most of them began as civil wars which later entailed foreign intervention, while some were escalated mutual provocations, where the exact moment of aggression could be differently defined, depending on one's point of view. This was the case with some of the Arab-Israeli wars. It was more constructive and more to the point to deal with these wars, though not always very effectively, by means of UN peacekeeping than by applying the rules of collective security.

UN peacekeeping does not try to assign blame, or ask, "Who started it?"; it asks the more appropriate question, "How do we end it?." It does this by being impartial towards both warring parties. It assumes a no-fault war, just as there can be a no-fault divorce or a no-fault car accident. The drawback of this new method of dealing with war, invented by our second-generation world organization during its operation, is that it merely enforces an armistice without settling the underlying problem, so that the peacekeeping force can be pinned down sitting on the powder keg almost indefinitely, as in Cyprus. Another problem has emerged now in the former Yugoslavia, when true peacekeeping cannot even begin until there is an armistice: there is no interposition capability at all, since the UN force is too weak to intervene between the belligerents.

(3) Collective security is based on state-centred thinking: states are aggressors, victims, defenders, judges, executioners. This is in accordance with traditional international law, which recognizes only states as judicial "persons." But aggressive acts are in fact ordered by national leaders, or at least a small ruling elite group, not the whole nation. And yet the war of all states against one, which the initial aggression unleashes under the collective security system, punishes innocent persons within the aggressor states, who never took any part in the decision-making that led to the aggression. This is certainly true in modern war, which routinely violates the principle of not harming civilians, a principle that became inoperative long before the nuclear age, with the advent of air power and the technical possibility of attacking cities from the air.

Even conscripts in the army are not the primary guilty persons in aggressive acts ordered by their rulers. True, they are supposed to be obligated by the *Nuremberg Principles* to disobey orders that are illegal under international law, but surely in real-life practice disobedience is usually almost impossible. We should not require of others to do that which we would most likely not have the courage to do ourselves under similar circumstances: I would add this rule to Kant's rules of moral conduct.

In the recent Gulf War, for example, the civilians of Baghdad, especially the babies, did not commit any aggression against Kuwait; they never even had a chance to vote for or against Saddam Hussein, since he took power in a military coup. Yet they were killed in large numbers in the US bombing raids. It is surely no excuse to say that this was "collateral damage."

(4) Above all, the collective security system is not the way to end war. It is a way to enlarge the war that an aggressor began. It tries to fight fire with fire. It hopes to deter potential aggressors from carrying out their criminal designs, and thus assume a preventive role. But this expectation confronts the whole well-known spectrum of problems with deterrence: it assumes rational cost-benefit calculations by national leaders, who may not be totally rational to begin with, and who may be pushed even further from rationality by the pressures of a crisis or economic frustration (*e.g.*, Kuwait siphoning off Iraq's oil from underground deposits). In general, since the means tend to determine the end, it does not seem reasonable to fight a war to end a war.

It has been said that, in the Gulf War, the UN Security Council was finally able to function as the founders had intended when the *Charter* was written. There are three separate points to be made in this regard:

(1) *Charter* provisions were in fact not followed. The Security Council never evaluated the effectiveness of the economic sanctions against Iraq before permitting (note: not ordering) the use of military force. The war against Iraq was not conducted under UN command, nor was it organized by the UN. Military operations were even more openly under US command and direction than in the Korean War, although the forces of other Coalition partners were nominally involved.

(2) The vote in the Security Council was bought or coerced by the USA. The disintegrating USSR was in no shape to resist, since it needed economic aid from the West, and China and some of the non-permanent members were also promised economic benefits. To its credit, China abstained, and some of the non-permanent members opposed the resolution.

(3) Even if there had been no illegalities, irregularities and briberies, this application of collective security principles was unfortunate. The war,

while killing some 150,000 people, did not even remove Saddam Hussein, the primary guilty party, from power. In this particular example, the whole collective security principle has been thrown into disrepute. If the *UN Charter* has indeed been operating according to the founders' original designs, we may have to admit that their designs were seriously flawed.

The second-generation world organization must be transformed into a third-generation system that does not contain this flaw. This is as it should be: we learn as we go, from our mistakes as well as from our successes. Supporting the United Nations (as I do in the absence of a better system) does not mean approving of everything it does, just as I often speak against the government of my own country, while remaining a loyal citizen.

Let us now turn to the second salient point of the New World Order according to George Bush, namely *Pax Americana* (this was, of course, never stated as such, but it is implicit in his words and actions).

World hegemony by one world power is not the way to go, no matter which world power it is or what are its merits and demerits. I say this to defend myself from any charge of anti-Americanism. The real reason why we should reject this model is that hegemonic power can be shown in recent history to have remained stable for only about 100 years at a time, at the end of which time a great war usually occurs with a challenger power, after which a new hegemonic power takes over – not necessarily the challenger (both previous ruler and challenger may be too exhausted by the war).

This "long cycle" has been documented for the last 500 years (William R. Thompson, 1983). The successive hegemons have been Portugal, the Netherlands, Britain twice, and the USA since 1946, a pattern repeating for five cycles already, ever since (or a little before) the nation-state system was established in Europe. Spain was the challenger once, France twice, Germany once, and the USSR once, without any of them ever gaining ascendancy. While this cycle is interesting for political historians and theorists, it is also a warning to us for the future: empire is stable for a while, but not for too long, and eventually it ends in a very large and bloody war.

All the previous great wars happened before the dawning of the nuclear age, though that age dawned ominously at the very end of the last one, World War II; but at the end of the next hegemonic cycle, predicted for about 2050, the result could be catastrophic. The lesson of history is clear: the 100-year cycle must be broken by introducing a radically new pattern into world politics. I assume that we have enough "free will" against "historical forces" to be able to change patterns deliberately, since I am not a determinist. To break this cycle would introduce the real New World Order.

Instead of *Pax Americana*, we should aim at a *Pax Democratica*. It would be a multilaterally structured world system without a ruling hegemon, under the regime of a universal world organization, a revamped United Nations – what we have called the Third Generation System. *Democratica* in this sense means both democratically structured as between nations, and composed of states which are democratically structured internally.

The vindication and general public acceptance of democracy as a superior and generally acceptable political system was the real result of the ending of the Cold War between the social systems, not the vindication of Capitalism over Communism as an economic system, nor a triumph of the USA over the USSR as a world power (this would lead straight to *Pax Americana*). It was also definitely not the end of history in the Hegelian sense (in spite of Fukuyama's 1989 argument), for Hegel was wrong – history in the sense of ideological struggle and the contention of ideas will continue as long as humanity endures, however long or short that turns out to be. The end of history will come only with the end of humanity.

Another excellent reason for championing *Pax Democratica* is the empirical finding of peace research that democratic countries (properly defined in terms of particular and rather stringent indicators) never fight wars with each other, although they fight plenty of wars with non-democratic countries. Whatever the theoretical explanation for this finding might be, and de Tocqueville had some ideas on this, it makes the conversion of as many states as possible to democratic regimes highly desirable from the standpoint of obtaining world peace, as well as, of course, from the well-accepted standpoint of implementing human rights and political and social justice.

So much for certain general principles of the features that we want to see realized in the future better world order, and the features that we should try to avoid. Now we need to translate these principles into specific recommendations for reforming the United Nations, in order to promote it to the full-fledged Third–Generation model. We do not need to change the name, as happened between the League of Nations and the United Nations Organization (the First and Second Generation), which was actually unfortunate. Continuity in the evolution of social structures is a great virtue, and the creation of a more appropriate structure need not and should not require the demise of the UN, or even a name-change that would suggest it.

The reforms of the UN to be discussed fall into several categories:

(1) replace the presumed collective security system;
(2) improve conflict resolution mechanisms and crisis prediction and prevention capabilities of the United Nations;
(3) form a UN Disarmament Verification Agency to supervise and monitor the implementation of present and future disarmament treaties;
(4) create an International Criminal Court to try individual violators of international law;
(5) reform the structure and procedures of the UN Security Council;
(6) introduce weighted voting in the UN General Assembly;
(7) create a Second (People's) Assembly at the UN [see Chapter 5]; and
(8) revamp the UN economic development institutions to reflect the concerns of sustainability.

To replace the presumed collective security system and up-grade the peacekeeping system, we need to affirm and practice the principles of common, not collective, security, as defined in the *Palme Report* of 1982. This involves recognition of the principle that, "we are all in the same boat," and that, in order to improve our own security, we must also improve the security of our opponents. This system was designed for the world of the Cold War, with two opposing alliances facing each other, but it remains applicable to a multipolar world if we conceptually replace "both in the same boat" by "all in the same boat"; it is, of course, also bilaterally applicable to various local and regional conflicts, *e.g.*, that between India and Pakistan.

What this involves is focussing on attempts to prevent war, rather than applying measures after a war has started, as both collective security and UN peacekeeping do. As Dietrich Fischer has postulated (1992), war prevention (an "active peace policy" – pro-active, not reactive) involves three stages: (1) a habit of international cooperation in times of peace (especially on superordinate projects which benefit all and require the cooperation of all, such as action to forestall global warming); (2) conflict resolution when disputes arise; and (3) non-offensive defence if armed conflict becomes an immediate threat or even a fact. I would amend this only to the extent that we should never let situations proceed even to the third stage.

Both international cooperation, which has been shown to deconstruct enemy images as well as having direct benefits derived from fulfilling the goals of the cooperation (Muzafer Sherif, 1961) and conflict resolution can take place under the *aegis* of the United Nations, or at least be encouraged by it.

To accomplish this, however, UN capabilities in these areas need to be upgraded. Agencies of international cooperation in the environmental field should blossom in the wake of the UNCED conference in Rio de Janeiro – but this is not a prediction, unfortunately, only a prescription of what should happen. Cooperation on fostering the proper kind of Third World development and the abolition of dire poverty everywhere is also imperative, as well as cooperation on the implementation of human rights in general. We do not necessarily need new UN agencies in these fields, though we might in some cases; but at least better possibilities of implementation of UN policies. Cooperation on solving problems of refugees, of world hunger, of alternative energy supplies, are all related to this, and to each other. Functional cooperation (as this approach has been called) is not only essential for solving the "world problematique," but would at the same time help unify humanity as we work together shoulder-to-shoulder on solving practical problems.

On conflict resolution too, the UN must do much better. It has from time to time supplied mediators in dispute situations and the Secretary-Generals at various times have practised what has been called "preventive diplomacy." But this has been, and still is, *ad hoc*. There needs to be in place a firm system of a sequence of conflict resolution measures that countries in dispute have to go through (somewhat like the obligatory sequence institutionalized in labour disputes): negotiation, mediation, arbitration, adjudication or the use of referenda – all under UN direction and administration. Something like this has been proposed, I believe, by the UN Committee on Reviewing the Charter.

Another measure is needed by the UN to face up fully to the requirements of common security: a reliable fact-finding and crisis-prediction and monitoring capability of its own. A small beginning has been made in creating the Office of Research and Collection of Information (ORCI). Again, this needs to be greatly upgraded in order to function reliably and effectively in all foreseeable circumstances. Only when the UN has full knowledge of local situations and of threats to international peace and security will it be able to take appropriate measures of war prevention.

To institute and properly supervise the multilateral disarmament treaties already concluded or soon to come (surely they must, in the newly improved world situation), the UN will need a Verification Agency to service these treaties. The argument has been made by Douglas Scott (1990) and by Walter Dorn (1990), that a single verification agency would perform better and more efficiently than a series of separate verification agencies, one for each multilateral treaty.

Another part of common security, as opposed to collective security, is to make national leaders personally responsible for aggressive acts against neighbouring countries; and for that matter, also for gross human rights violations against their own citizens, acts such as genocide, death squads activity, state terrorism, disappearances and torture. We can leave aside for the moment such "minor" human rights violations as press censorship or religious discrimination – serious enough, to be sure, but not in the same class as the first group.

To make national leaders personally responsible for criminal acts against outsiders and insiders is a very difficult matter, but it is necessary to face the need for it squarely, or we shall be stuck forever on the horns of the dilemma of either waging war against their whole nation or letting the evils continue.

To deal with this requirement, the United Nations must organize an International Criminal Court, which has been proposed and is under consideration. The 1993 General Assembly has approved the Draft Statute for such a court drawn up by the International Law Commission. The Draft Statute has certain shortcomings, but it is a beginning. If all goes well, the International Criminal Court will become a reality in 1995. [See Chapter 20.]

The closest the world has come to dealing with international criminal cases were the war crimes trials, in Europe and in the Far East, conducted in Nuremberg and Tokyo at the end of World War II. The crimes for which leaders were condemned there, and sometimes executed when found guilty, were of three types: (1) crimes against peace – initiating war unlawfully, or violating *Ius ad Bellum*, which comes close to what we have termed "aggression" in our discussion of collective security; (2) war crimes – committing atrocities or acts of unnecessary cruelty against soldiers, civilians, prisoners of war, or neutrals during war, *i.e.*, violating the rules of *Ius in Bello*, the Geneva Conventions, *etc.*; and (3) crimes against humanity – genocide of one's own citizens, as in the Nazi holocaust of Jews, Gypsies, and East Europeans.

At the time when these trials were conducted, they were condemned by some as representing "retroactive justice," *i.e.*, trying people for committing crimes which were not defined as crimes at the time they were committed. This objection was overruled by stating that these crimes were so heinous that they offended against the common conscience of humankind, *i.e.*, they were offences under international common law, though not against any codified law.

A more important objection was that the new laws were not applied impartially, since only the losers of the war were judged, not the victors, although it was commonly known that both sides had committed atrocities: on the Allied side, one need only mention the bombing of Hamburg, Dresden, Hiroshima, and Nagasaki. Of course, the Germans bombed Rotterdam and Coventry – but they had to stand trial for this, while Allied leaders were not held similarly responsible for their acts. Admittedly, this did establish a bad precedent.

Since 1945-46, when these trials were held, a whole body of international criminal law has been formulated and codified by the UN's International Law Commission, and also by *Declarations* and *Conventions* or *Convenants* adopted by the UN General Assembly, *e.g.*, the *Convention Against Genocide* and the extensive *Covenants on Human Rights* based on the 1948 *Universal Declaration of Human Rights*. In other words, we do have at least the beginnings of international criminal law, but we still have no court to judge international criminal law violations. Law enforcement is seriously lagging behind law codification.

The nations who are now proposing or supporting the creation of an International Criminal Court at the UN sometimes think of it mainly as a court that would try international terrorists and drug traffickers. These international crimes are serious enough, but surely more international crimes must be added to the list of those that the new court will deal with. We must insist that offenders should also include military aggressors, violators of disarmament treaties (in both the above cases this means the top leaders of nations guilty of these crimes), the three types of Nuremberg crimes described above, and gross international polluters, *e.g.*, those guilty of oil spills at sea, whether they are individuals or corporations. The present *Draft Statute* unfortunately does not cover all these crimes. It does include international aggression, but specifies that the UN Security Council would first have to declare that aggression has occurred. Since this would be subject to the veto, no Permanent Member of the Security Council is ever likely to be found guilty of aggression.

An entirely different class of reforms of the U, that concern decision-making structures is also needed. It is not right that the main guardians of international peace and security, the five permanent members of the UN Security Council, happen to be the five main nuclear weapons powers and the five top exporters of conventional arms. It reminds one of putting the foxes in charge of guarding the chicken coop. The Security Council must be reorganized. One way to do this would be to have large regional organizations, covering whole continents or subcontinental regions, represented rather than nations. Present proposals are to add Germany, Japan, and perhaps India, Brazil, and Nigeria to the Security Council, probably without the veto. However, I consider the regionalization of the Security Council preferable. At least, the European Community should take the place of Britain, France and Germany (if it is added), so as to keep the Security Council from becoming too large and keeping down the relative European presence.

Various modifications of the veto, short of its total abolition, have been proposed. These include the following ways, or combinations thereof: (1) restricting the veto to only some of the enlarged number of permanent members, perhaps only two, the USA and Russia; (2) requiring two or more negative votes by veto-possessing member to defeat a resolution, not just one as at present; (3) imposing a quota of only so many vetoes per year permitted to any veto-possessing member; (4) requiring a qualified majority (*e.g.*, three-quarters of the Security Council) to overcome the veto: in a Security Council enlarged to 20 members, 5 members could in this example block the passage of a resolution, and these might be the present Big Five, if they were unanimous; (5) using a bicameral arrangement with the General Assembly: *e.g.*, a four-fifths majority in the General Assembly could override a Security Council veto; and (6) limiting the application of the veto to certain classes of issues, *e.g.*, excluding membership applications (these have not been a problem lately, but used to be in the early years and could become so again) and conflict resolution.

Let us illustrate the above principles of Security Council reform with an example. Let us assume that we have a Security Council composed of eight permanent members (USA, Russia, China, EC, Japan, India and Brazil and Nigeria) with only two (USA and Russia) having the veto, plus seven non-permanent members, elected as they are now by the General Assembly, thus providing equitable regional distribution. Let us also specify that a resolution will be considered defeated if: (1) both USA and Russia cast negative votes; or (2) or five members (permanent or non-permanent) cast negative votes. Thus, if only the USA votes against and not Russia, it would have to find four other allies to help it block a resolution, which it might be able to do by persuading EC, Japan, and two non-permanents (one of whom customarily comes from pro-Western nations).

Security Council reform is under active consideration now at the UN. The 1993 General Assembly appointed a Working Group to work on this problem and to report back in the Autumn of 1994. Let us hope that they come forward with an imaginative and workable proposal.

The Security Council is becoming a very important body in global decision-making, and that is why a reform of its structure and procedures was discussed first. However, the General Assembly remains the only body in which all UN members are represented, and thus is either an embryo World Parliament or a town meeting of the Global Village for the discussion of issues – depending on whether one is a maximalist or a minimalist. We must therefore also consider how the rules for its decision-making should be modified.

At present, the UN General Assembly adopts important (non-procedural) resolutions by a two-thirds majority, with each nation having one vote regardless of size. It can also adopt resolutions without voting, by the President's ruling, although any member can request and obtain a roll-call vote procedure.

The one nation–one vote rule is, of course, a reflection of the "sovereign equality of nations," a principle of international law also enshrined in the *UN Charter*. However, this principle seems deficient in two respects: (1) it is unfair from a democratic point of view, representation by population being a basic principle of democracy; in the General Assembly system, a citizen of a large nation has relatively less power than a citizen of a small nation; and (2) it is unrealistic from a point of view of power, with the small South Pacific island of Vanuatu having the same decision-making power as the USA, the world superpower. In the world outside the UN, the USA has treated Vanuatu rather roughly, but that is another story.

The obvious voting reform in the General Assembly is weighted voting, some nations having more votes than others. I have studied this rather extensively, as summarized in Newcombe (1983). Twenty-five different weighted voting formulas were compared, including votes proportional to population, or to the square root or cube root of population, or to UN assessment (budget contributions), or to GNP, or to linear combinations of two of these factors (always including population as one of them). These were compared with eight different criteria: flexibility, less skewness, political balance, future representation by population, additivity, simplicity, accessibility of data, and incentives. It would take us too far afield to define these in detail here, but the reader can get the flavour of these comparisons from the names of the criteria.

A very important one among the criteria is political balance, which was judged by approximate equality between the main bloc alignments (East *vs.* West and North *vs.* South), so that no bloc would be permanently outvoted. The alignments, however, have changed drastically since 1989.

In any case, in the 1983 publication, the best formulas on all eight criteria were the two-factor formulas, population plus a wealth factor (UN contribution, GNP, energy consumption, or health and education expenditure), in equal proportions. From the standpoint of incentives, the health and education expenditure indicator would be preferred, while lawyers might like the UN contribution indicator, economists the GNP one, and physical scientists (though not environmentalists) the energy consumption one. In actual fact, all these two-factor formulas give almost the same numerical results in terms of vote numbers, since all the wealth indicators are strongly inter-correlated.

Finally, to democratize the United Nations further, we should consider adding a House of Peoples or a People's Assembly to the present "House of Nations" (the General Assembly). This could be done without formal *Charter* revision, if the General Assembly were to use its powers, conferred on it in *Article 22* of the present *Charter*, to create an auxiliary body. As such, the People's Assembly (sometimes called a Second Assembly) would have only advisory functions, but these could later be expanded to formal decision-making. After all, even the resolutions of the present General Assembly are not binding (unlike those of the Security Council), but are only recommendations; though they have customarily been considered part of international law if adopted unanimously.

Proposals for a Second UN Assembly have been studied extensively at three *Conferences on A More Democratic United Nations* (CAMDUN), one held in New York in 1990, the second one in Vienna in 1991, and the third one in New York. The first CAMDUN conference published its proceedings in a 1991 book edited by Frank Barnaby, former head of the Stockholm International Peace Research Institute (SIPRI), which lists a multitude of different proposals by participants. My own summary in that book lists ten major and six minor schemes. Space does not permit here discussion of more than two of these.

One is based on NGOs (Non-Governmental Organizations), the other on parliamentarians from national legislatures. One might argue that a People's Assembly based on parliamentarians is more representative democratically, since parliamentarians are directly elected in their own countries, at least in those that are democracies internally. However, a People's Assembly based on NGOs would represent, though in a somewhat haphazard self-selected manner, the informed or politically involved sector of each nation's public opinion, skipping the apathetic or uninformed population sector. The ultimate ideal, of course, is direct elections, but the above two are suggestions for intermediate states.

A UN Parliamentary Assembly (UNPA) is described in Chapter 5 (see also Heinrich and Newcombe, 1991). Briefly, national parliaments would appoint the required number of delegates to the UNPA from among their own members, by whatever method they choose, but preferably including some from opposition parties, not only the governing party. This proposal is based on the EC model, where a European Parliament was first introduced in this way as an advisory appointed body, but has now evolved into an elected parliament with some real powers. It is hoped that this process might be duplicated at the global level.

Our example of a UN Second Assembly based on NGOs comes from actual experience with the Swedish People's Parliament in the early 1980s, followed by an even wider experiment in the Nordic People's Parliament. The Swedish Peace Council and Swedish UN Association organized the Swedish People's Parliament on Disarmament. Participants were NGOs of all sorts, not only peace groups: labour unions, churches, women's groups, professional groups, etc. The process was quite elaborate and took a year or more. First the NGOs were asked to submit resolutions or "bills" for the People's Parliament; these were then circulated to all the NGOs which met at their annual meetings to decide what their position would be on each resolution, and to choose their delegates to the Parliament; finally, the Parliament met, debated the resolutions, and voted on them. The ones adopted were then publicized and passed on to the Swedish government. The whole exercise was a very successful model of democratic decision-making.

In subsequent years, this was repeated and then widened to include all the Scandinavian countries in a Nordic People's Parliament. Some sessions were on various topics, not necessarily disarmament; one was on South African apartheid. These meetings have now stopped, because it was too much work for the organizers and took time away from other activities.

However, Gunnar Ekkegard (see references) from Sweden, who was involved in several of the People's Parliaments, has devised a scheme by which this process could be globalized: (1) organize People's Parliaments on the Swedish/Nordic model in all world regions; (2) pass the adopted resolutions to the next higher (perhaps continental) level for similar processing; and (3) pass those successful in this second stage to a World People's Parliament, which would be an adjunct to the United Nations (the officially recognized Second Assembly), where the final decision-making would take place, the results to be passed on to the UN General Assembly.

Altogether, this is an admirable model, using the principles of subsidiarity with democracy and federalism at all levels right up to the global; but it would require great amounts of energy, which the NGOs, already overworked and underfunded, might not be able to mount. Another difficulty might be that most NGOs operate in the industrialized countries, and there might not be enough active NGOs in the Third World to participate to the same extent. What will probably happen in the real world is a gradual upgrading of direct participation of the NGOs in existing UN processes, partly with ECOSOC and the Specialized Agencies. There are already groupings of NGOs affiliated with the Economic and Social Council (ECOSOC), called Consultants A, B, and C; other NGOs affiliated with the UN Office of Public Information, groups of disarmament NGOs both in New York and Geneva, the Peace Messenger Organizations who received UN awards for peace-related work, CONGO (Congress of Non-Governmental Organizations) which meets periodically, and parallel conferences (People's Foras) at big governmental UN Conferences, such as the recent UNCED in Rio de Janeiro. In fact, UNCED was preceded by four intensive sessions of the preparatory committee (pre-negotiating sessions hammering out the text of various documents), to which the NGOs were invited and in which they actively participated. At the three *UN Special Sessions on Disarmament* (1978, 1982 and 1988) and at the *UN Conference on the Link Between Disarmament and Development* (1986), many NGOs were able to address the General Assembly and distribute their documents to governmental delegates. At UNCED in Rio de Janeiro, NGO activities were greatly intensified and cooperation between them implementing environmental decisions continues.

Finally, something must be said on reorganizing the UN's economic system of economic agencies. It has often been suggested (*e.g.*, in the *Bertrand Report* of 1985) that streamlining and elimination of areas of overlap would greatly improve the efficiency of that system. This is true, but I have something else in mind. Surely after UNCED we must introduce the concept of long-range sustainability into all our development planning in a much more systematic way, if the *Brundtland Report's* (1987) phrase "sustainable development" is to have any practical meaning at all.

This is not primarily a matter of rearranging the various agencies, or even of adding new agencies or upgrading the powers of the old ones. It is a much more fundamental matter, the need to rethink economics from the ground up, in order to link it firmly with ecology. The new "eco-eco" system must internalize the maxim that, "the economy and the ecology are married till death do us part." We can no longer regard natural resources as an infinite reservoir, or the streams, oceans and dumps as bottomless sinks for our wastes. We are bumping our heads against inexorable limits. We cannot dismiss undesirable side-effects of our activities as mere "externalities," a term that reminds me of the phrase "collateral damage" that military writers use when they mean killing civilians. We must pay for new projects, especially contemplated mega-projects, not only in the human-created currency of money, but in nature's currency of entropy and free energy, as suggested by Georgescu Roegen in 1971. Economists had better learn about thermodynamics real fast. If that means double bookkeeping in our cost-benefit analyses, so be it.

Even the Native People's way of thinking seven generations ahead, while much superior to the span of the four or five years of most nations' election cycles, is not good enough, for we humans aspire to lasting for longer than that if possible. It certainly is not possible at the present rate of attrition of stocks. This kind of thinking must totally permeate the plans of all the UN development and money-lending agencies, as well as the thinking of national leaders in both industrialized and developing countries. In economic thinking, it is a far more fundamental revolution than merely switching from socialism to capitalism.

In conclusion, this outline of steps in building a truly new world order has only scratched the surface. It could and should be both widened by discussing additional reforms, and deepened by providing more details on each. Until this is done by comprehensive studies in which many dedicated and capable researchers should take part, may this paper serve as a suggestive introduction to this enterprise.

References

Barnaby, Frank ed. 1991 *Building a More Democratic United Nations* (Frank Cass: London).

Bertrand, Maurice 1985 *Some Reflections on Reform of the United Nations* (Joint Inspection Unit, United Nations, Geneva, JIU/REP/85).

Dorn, Walter "UN Should Verify Treaties" *Bulletin of the Atomic Scientists* 46 July/August 1990 12-13.

Ekkegard, Gunnar, c/o Swedish World Federalists, P.O. Box 224, S-10122 Stockholm, Sweden.

Fischer, Dietrich "Components of an Active Peace Policy" in Newcombe, Hanna ed. 1992 *Hopes and Fears: the Human Future* (Science for Peace Series, Samuel Stevens: Toronto) 47-66.

Fukuyama, Y. Francis "Have We Reached the End of History?" RAND Paper 7532, February 1989.

Heinrich, Dieter 1992 *UN Parliamentary Assembly* (World Federalist Movement: New York).

Newcombe, Hanna 1983 *Design for a Better World* (University Press of America: Lanham MD).

Newcombe, Hanna "Proposals for a People's Assembly at the United Nations" in Barnaby, Frank ed. 1991 *Building a More Democratic United Nations* (Frank Cass: London).

Palme, Olaf, and Independent Commission on Disarmament and Security 1982 *Common Security: A Blueprint for Survival* (Simon & Schuster: New York).

Roegen, Georgescu 1971 *Entropy Law and Economic Process* (Harvard University Press).

Schumacher, E.F. 1973 *Small Is Beautiful: Economics as If People Mattered* (Harper & Row).

Scott, Douglas, and Markland Policy Group 1990 *Disarmament's Missing Dimension* (Science for Peace Series: Samuel Stevens: Toronto).

Sherif, Muzafer *et al.* 1961 *Intergroup Conflict and Cooperation: The Robbers' Cave Experiment* (University of Oklahoma Press: Norman, OK).

Thompson, William R. "Uneven Economic Growth, Systemic Challenges and Global Wars" *International Studies Quarterly* 1983 341-355.

Toffler, Alvin 1980 *The Third Wave* (Morrow: New York).

World Commission on Environment and Development (chaired by Gro Harlem Brundtland) 1987 *Our Common Future* (Oxford University Press).

CHAPTER 5

A United Nations Parliamentary Assembly

Dieter Heinrich

Our increasing global interdependence brings with it a growing need to develop a new global politics based on the ideals of community. Increasingly, political decisions and actions need to be taken from a global perspective in the global interest. The UN may be the locus of such a political community, but only if it proves capable of being reformed.

The *UN Charter* begins with the words, "We the Peoples of the United Nations ..." In practice, the UN is a meeting place not of the peoples but of the governments – and only the executive branch of governments at that. One of the first reforms might best be to establish the citizen dimension at the UN, and give the UN, finally, to the world's people. This would help ensure that any expansion in the UN's authority will be accompanied by an increase in democratic accountability. An equally important consideration is that introducing a citizen dimension to the UN may be essential to driving the reform process itself.

The whole realm of global politics has heretofore been considered the domain of governments, who purport to act as the exclusive agents of their citizens. The estrangement of citizens from this realm has consequences for global political culture. It results in a systematic under-development among citizens of a sense of global responsibility, which is an essential foundation stone of genuine global political community. Not only does the present system fail to illicit the greatest degree of citizen initiative, it also increases the likelihood that at critical moments an unprepared, inward-looking citizenry will not support measures that their governments might be prepared to take in the global interest, whether it be providing troops to the UN, opening borders to freer trade, or increasing foreign aid.

Excluding citizens from the UN also entails the consequence of retarding any process of UN reform. If all official input to the UN, including all proposals for change, can come only through the inherently conservative structures of the foreign affairs bureaucracies of the nation-states, then change will not only come slowly, but it will be change that favours the institutional interests of those bureaucracies over the real needs of the world. The first tendency of any bureaucracy is self-preservation, including the jobs of its members. This tendency in foreign ministries will mitigate against an expansion of the UN's role, regardless of the objective merits of proposals for doing so. This is one reason governments cannot be relied upon to undertake the reform of the UN with real commitment.

Citizens have a human right to be represented as directly as possible in political decision-making as it affects their lives. This is a fundamental of democracy. The extension now of this principle to the global level is both a moral imperative and a matter of sound governance. Democracy is not only right – it works. It has proven, on balance, the most reliable model for the management of public affairs. This being so, there is *a priori* reason to suppose that the application of democratic principles of citizen representation and direct accountability will also produce the most satisfactory management of global affairs. This suggests that opening the United Nations to the involvement, imagination and energy of the world citizenry – not only the select who speak for the institutions of national government – would ultimately make the UN more effective. If effectiveness is the issue, given the scale of our global problems, we can hardly afford to pass over such a basic approach to improving our capacities to govern ourselves.

The single most appropriate and important institution for enabling citizens to be represented at the UN, as in any political community, is a parliament. The European Parliament of the European Union provides an important example of how a supranational parliament can develop. The experience there suggests that the first stage of a UN parliament could be a consultative Parliamentary Assembly made up of representatives chosen by the national parliaments. This would enable a UN parliamentary chamber to be created easily and inexpensively in a way which nevertheless creates a valid democratic link between the UN and the world's citizens through their representatives in the national legislatures.

A Parliamentary Assembly could be established relatively easily without *UN Charter* reform. The General Assembly could create it under *Article 22* of the *Charter* as a consultative body. In creating such an assembly, it would help greatly if states would explicitly declare it to be part of a longer term process of building a global political community. This again draws on the lesson of Europe, where the end goal of a closer union was stated at the outset. This created a context of legitimacy and an overarching rationality for the whole developmental process that followed, and which resulted in the European Parliament becoming a directly elected body. A UN Parliamentary Assembly should be founded, in other words, with a sense of destiny. In this case, the assembly becomes justified not only for what it is, but for what it is becoming. Once established, a Parliamentary Assembly could lead the process of its own evolution by proposing appropriate ways for governments to increase its function and responsibilities on the way to transforming it eventually into a directly elected parliament.

A Parliamentary Assembly would, however, be useful on its merits from the very beginning, even with only a consultative role in its initial stages. It would be a vital new link between the UN and national parliaments and could increase awareness and support for all aspects of UN activities. It would be a new source of proposals and a new source of initiative within the international system for the solution of global problems, especially problems related to the reform and strengthening of the UN where a global perspective is especially critical.

Most importantly, a UN Parliamentary Assembly would become a symbol of a new kind of world order for the future. In place of today's state-centric ideology, which makes a virtue of national selfishness and exclusivity, a Parliamentary Assembly would stand for the idea of the world as an emerging democratic community of citizens who share common vital interests and values. The world depends on such a new earth- and citizen-centred perception, because it provides the essential moral basis for any real political cooperation on the critical problems of our age. A Parliamentary Assembly would help recondition some of the deep assumptions about the world which underlie all political decision-making.

From the very beginning, it would be a very different kind of "voice" within global politics. The General Assembly is composed of representatives of governments who ultimately represent institutional interests within the nation-state system. A Parliamentary Assembly would be made up of individuals whose mandate it would be to speak for the citizen interest. Parliamentarians are free to take positions of conscience in debate with their colleagues. We would have for the first time a body composed of officials who would be free of governmental instruction, free from the constraints of *raison d'état,* free to take a global perspective – free, among other things, to call upon the governments in the General Assembly to take action in the way they think citizens would want them to.

In establishing a UN Parliamentary Assembly (UNPA), a number of issues would need to be addressed, none of them insurmountable:

Representation: The founding of the Parliamentary Assembly of the CSCE in 1990 shows how easily a chamber for "we the peoples" could be established by drawing on existing parliaments of Member States for representation. In the case of the parliamentary assemblies of the CSCE and the early European Coal and Steel Community, the representatives were first of all sitting members of national parliaments. This approach enhances the stature of the resulting body, but comes with a cost: busy parliamentarians have limited time to meet. The UNPA might rather consider an important modification to our precedents by having national parliaments send non-parliamentarian delegates. These might be former parliamentarians, or distinguished citizens-at-large. In this way, a full-time global body could be created. Some combination of the two approaches might also be considered. On another point, travel costs and salaries of UN parliamentarians should be paid by the budget of the Parliamentary Assembly itself, not the national governments. This will help assure the independence of UNPA politicians and a greater equality of participation.

Selection of representatives: One unique feature of UNPA is that it could include representation from minority parties within national parliaments, and so reflect more truly the complexion of the citizenry. There may need to be measures, however, to deter a majority party of a parliament from arbitrarily choosing only its own. One approach might be to require that national parliaments elect representatives by secret ballot. In the case of one-party states, election of representatives in this way could reduce the likelihood of interference from the executive. It might also be considered so subversive a practice by non-democratic regimes that they refuse to participate, helping us with the next point.

Representation from non-democratic countries: It would be possible, no doubt, to have non-democratic countries excluded from participation in the UNPA through ingenious criteria only democracies could satisfy. But a case can be made for admitting parliamentarians of all countries. A parliamentary assembly with only consultative status is not yet a parliament, after all, and so the inclusion of even a large number of dubious members may be of little practical consequence in the short term. Parliamentarians, unlike diplomats, could be directly challenged to defend their views or change them. Collegial persuasion might have an educational effect on non-democratic representatives, and so hasten the spread of new ideas to non-democratic countries. The fear of this might keep some dictatorships from participating, thus solving the problem in another way.

Powers: The UNPA, as a consultative body, would have no formal powers initially. Its resolutions, however, would have a moral influence on governments the way today's General Assembly resolutions have. A more ambitious proposal would be to empower the UNPA to be able to request debate in the General Assembly on at least some of its resolutions as though they had been introduced by a member state.

Size and composition: The question of how many representatives each country should have can be addressed in various ways. The ideal would be representation by population, but this would be impractical in the beginning, especially if it meant giving a 20 per cent share of the assembly to the world's largest non-democracy. Alternatively members could be apportioned on a sliding scale with ever larger increments of population needed for each additional representative from a state. The smallest countries might have one, the largest 10 to 20.

Financial issues: A more effective UN would ultimately save governments money. The cost of the UNPA should be regarded as an investment in wiser global decision-making that could help solve many global problems before they become expensive nightmares.

CHAPTER 6

Reforming the United Nations Administration

Robert I. McLaren

Since 1980, it has not been difficult to find articles and reports recommending changes and reforms in the administration of the United Nations. For example, the decade could be said to have begun with John Renninger's policy study for UNITAR.[1] The middle of the decade saw an increased pace for reform proposals with Maurice Bertrand,[2] the Group of 18,[3] and the American United Nations Association[4] each making significant recommendations. The end of the decade saw two more significant sets of proposals – those of Urquhart and Childers[5] and the Nordic UN Project.[6] Indeed, the difficulty has been in keeping track of all of the different proposals from all of the different potential sources. The above is surely no more than a listing of those studies that have received the most attention.

Reform proposals for the United Nations can normally be categorized into one of five types:

(1) making the UN more relevant – this usually is a request to downgrade the Western orientation and hegemony of the UN and upgrade the organization's relevance for the Third World, thus calling for holistic change, whereas each of the remaining four types of proposals are incremental;[7]

(2) coordinating the UN system – this usually means to make the specialized agencies adhere to the wishes of the United Nations Organization, a desire which has been previously dismissed by this writer,[8] who finds an appropriate metaphor for this perennial multi-organizational problem in a perceptive chapter by Anthony Jay:[9] "The struggle between the king and the barons is the great recurrent theme in the domestic politics of medieval England. Sometimes the barons are up and the king is down (Stephen, John, Edward II); sometimes it is the king who is on top and the barons who are repressed or quiescent (Henry I, Henry II, Edward I). There was a time when I found it puzzling that England should have bouts of tearing itself to pieces in domestic strife, even when there were great

dangers threatening (or great opportunities beckoning) from outside her borders. After all, they were all part of the same kingdom, weren't they? Surely they could see the advantages of all pitching in together?";

(3) reducing the complexity of the UN Organization – this usually refers to the plethora of funds and programmes, some of which mandates vie with those of the UN's own departments;

(4) improving the management of the UN Secretariat – including human resource practices as well as structural considerations; and

(5) altering the manner in which the UN is financed.

The focus of this chapter will be on (3) and (4), since these are the areas that seem to be most acceptable for reform in the UN these days.

As for the other three areas, it can be asserted that the UN's member governments hold the key to any reforms in these areas and the "sovereignty gap" (which will be further explained below) is at present unbridgeable for these three potential reform areas – *i.e.*, the problems in these three areas are straightforward and do not need the advice of outside consultants to indicate the compromises and trade-offs. When the member governments are willing to pay what needs to be paid, and/or are intent on making the king and the barons cooperate,[10] and/or wish to sit down and create a brand-new UN, these problems will be resolved; until then, they will not be.

Far more difficult than locating attention-getting studies is to find within the sets of proposals some criteria by which to judge the merits of the recommendations. Statements to the effect that the present United Nations is a mess are often assumed to be sufficient justification for making any and all recommendations. Empirical analyses of the UN's failings are rare; belief statements about the supposed failings prevail. For example, the *Nordic Report* ends its overview of *Challenges for the 1990s* with the simple statement: "We feel that the UN is not always equipped to deal with these matters effectively. This is why it is high time to address the issues of reform of the United Nations."[11] The writers of the *Nordic Report* may well be correct in their assessment, but one would like more concrete evidence of the problems.

A follow-up set of two studies by Urquhart and Childers[12] does indicate an array of objectives for assessing their plan to rationalize the UN Secretariat. These objectives are:[13]

• facilitating the Secretary-General's discharge of a now formidable range of responsibilities;

- better distribution and delegation of responsibility for assisting the Secretary-General and simplifying the chain of command;
- freeing the Secretary-General for leadership functions and for particular tasks that can only be performed by the Secretary-General;
- ensuring improved multi-disciplinary approaches to challenges that require input from two or more departments, through a more coherent scheme of organization and better coordination;
- providing for continuity, flexibility and substantive response within the Secretariat to significant trends, as well as swift response to increasingly frequent emergencies;
- facilitating and making more efficient the complex and often simultaneous field operations which are more and more requested of the United Nations;
- better use of human resources, and stimulation of the staff through more consistent demand on their skills and their commitment;
- achieving more efficient working practices, more expeditious follow-up, and routine evaluation to support all of the above objectives.

In addition, the authors note that any reorganization involving the staffing of the UN Secretariat must satisfy *Article 101.3* of the *UN Charter* – to wit, "the highest standards of efficiency, competence and integrity" must be integrated with "recruiting the staff on as wide a geographical basis as possible."[14]

However, other than the Organization Chart to demonstrate how complex is the present UN Organization, the authors provide the reader with little explanation as to why the above objectives are the required tools for solving the UN's problems. There is no doubt that these objectives can constitute proper administrative practices, but that is not enough – it must be shown why these are the proper practices for whatever problems it is deemed exist. Administrative practices are tools, not principles. A hammer is neither better nor worse than a saw as a tool; its comparative advantage as a tool depends upon the problem to be solved. A proper administrative practice, whether it is the delegation of authority or a more efficient way to operate, is still only a tool, not an end in itself.[15] More than objectives, one needs principles in order to gauge the merits of proposals. The key questions involve *what* and *why* things are being done, not *how* they should be done.

One of the reports does establish an important principle against which to assess reform proposals. It is derived from the report's observation that key to any reform of the United Nations is the attitude of the member governments. If the member governments are not in favour of any reform proposal, it little matters how splendid are the particular merits of that proposal, for it will not be implemented. Basic to any reform of the United Nations has to be the desire by each and all of the member governments to accede to and support it. The *UNA–USA Report* refers to this as, "bridging the sovereignty gap,"[16] and explains the principle as follows:[17] "Too often prescriptions for an expanded role for international institutions are volunteered to national policymakers in a language that has little meaning. It is a language of generalities about 'interdependence' or 'mutual gains' that are passionately averred and specifics about means and modalities that are weakly conceived and unconvincingly presented. Clearly, the mere facts of interdependence and the growth of national limits, while axiomatic among most governments, will not themselves induce governments to choose a multilateral tool over the alternatives. Unfortunately, advocates of internationalism, after invoking 'interdependence' as a kind of abstract imperative to cooperate, frequently fail to show how such cooperation would translate into a method of issue management that is more attractive than unilateral alternatives. Nor can the rationale for the existence as well as the refurbishing of international organizations be established by abstract assertions of collective self-interest or mutual gains. Gains are often mutual but rarely equal. In fact, the nature of most international problems is such that the risks, costs and sacrifices involved in managing them are rarely distributed evenly.

The case for international institutions can be compelling, but only if articulated in the language of national self-interest and combined with incontestable common goals. An easy way to understand their role in an era of sovereign states is to consider that, while the term 'sovereignty' means absolute power within a limited geographical sphere, it is only in the legal and political sense that state power is absolute. In every other way that matters – military security, the economy, the environment, public health, and social conditions – authority may be unlimited, but effective power is not. In the late 1980s that gap between abstract sovereignty and the means to exercise it has grown particularly large, even for the so-called 'superpowers.' If participation in international institutions is seen as helping to close this 'sovereignty gap,' then a greater investment in them will seem justified; if it is seen as widening the sovereignty gap, then it will not.

The task for international institutions and for those who would expand their use in the 1990s and beyond is, therefore, to strengthen their appeal to national governments as a means to bridge the sovereignty gap without encroaching upon sovereignty's still very vital core ..."

Five years have passed since this explanation of a sovereignty gap was made; since then, the legal concept of sovereignty has come under greater attack due to crises in Iraq, the former Yugoslavia, Somalia, *et. al.* Still, the perspective contained within the explanation seems valid as a procedural criterion for assessing the merits of reform proposals. The UN is still a creation of its member governments.

However, a second criterion, a substantive one, is also required. Administrative reform cannot exist in a vacuum; it must be oriented to some purpose. It must not only be acceptable to member governments, but must also be seen to accomplish something purposeful.

But there is a vacuum at this point. Without an agreement as to what the UN should be doing, there can be no meaningful recommendation as to how it should be organized. The set of objectives provided by Erskine and Childers[5,12] is merely a set of sound practices; their additional statement, that Equitable Geographical Distribution of the staff must be observed, is an additional procedural principle, not a substantive one. What is it that we want the UN to accomplish?

The set of reform proposals listed at the beginning of this chapter provide us with a grape-shot of answers to this question. Renninger discussed four options for reforming ECOSOC; Bertrand stated that the "lack of coordination and definition of priorities is due to the extraordinary complexity of the structure";[18] the G–18 Report focused on rationalizing and simplifying inter-governmental structures;[3] the *UNA–USA Report* recommended the establishment of more bodies to strengthen what the UN can oversee;[4] the first study of Urquhart and Childers[5] proposed to improve UN leadership with recommendations dealing with the Secretary-General and the selection process for this person, with the specialized agencies, with UN Funds and Programmes, and with the senior echelon; and the *Nordic Report* made several recommendations to improve and strengthen various parts of the UN system in order to foster economic and social development.[6] While there is some overlap from one of these studies to another, in general it can be stated that the only thing they have in common is their piecemeal incrementalism – each study sees a different hole in the dike. If the UN is so porous, one has to wonder how anything is accomplished there? If nothing is being accomplished, why is there not more impetus for a holistic reform?

Once again, we are drawn back to a search for the problem that needs to be solved. What is it?

A complex organization is not necessarily bad; a simple organization is not necessarily good. A lack of coordination is not necessarily bad; coordination is not necessarily good. If the problem in the UN Secretariat is so obvious, why does one study (the G–18) recommend a reduction of staff and bodies while another (the UNA–USA) recommends the opposite?

Another example can be given. In their second set of reform proposals, Urquhart and Childers have recommended that the UN Secretariat be reorganized from its present situation of 30–plus distinct departments or offices, all reporting to the Secretary-General, into one where the Secretary-General will be assisted by an Executive Office, while each of the 30–plus entities will be combined into one of four units: (1) Political, Security and Peace Affairs; (2) Economic, Social, Development and Environment Affairs; (3) Humanitarian and Human Rights Affairs; and (4) Administration, Management and Conference Services.[19]

This is a very logical proposal and would provide the outsider with greater ease in understanding the organization of the Secretariat. However, it should be noted that, like all organizational designs, it is totally artificial – that is, a construct of the logical mind, not necessarily of any reality. One can argue just as validly, as Secretary-General Boutros Boutros-Ghali has, that:[20] "… peace and security, and economic and social development are integrated. To be successful, peacemaking and peacekeeping must be integrated with comprehensive efforts to identify and support structures which will consolidate peace and advance a sense of confidence and well-being among people. In addition to the traditional military tasks in such situations are new responsibilities, such as monitoring elections, advancing human rights, attending to refugee needs, protecting minorities, reforming or strengthening governmental institutions and promoting political participation. For the long term, peacebuilding will entail cooperative projects which link two or more countries in mutually beneficial undertakings – for example, in agricultural development, shared water resources, transportation networks and educational exchange."

Furthermore, will this Urquhart and Childers proposal actually improve the work of the Secretary-General? That is the real criterion for determining its merits. Is it important that outsiders understand the organization of the Secretariat, or is it important that the Secretary-General have the best mechanism for obtaining his given objectives, no matter how complex and uncoordinated this mechanism appears to outsiders? What is the problem with having 30-odd departments reporting to the Secretary-General? Where is the evidence that their work is not being done, that their mandates are not being obtained?

In his first attempt at reorganizing the UN Secretariat in February 1992,[21] Secretary-General Boutros Boutros-Ghali subscribed partly to the recommendation of Urquhart and Childers. Twelve offices and departments were "discontinued as separate entities"; however, the four new positions of Deputy Secretary-General that were recommended to head the four major parts of the Secretariat in the Urquhart and Childers proposal[5] were not created and so neither were the offices and departments collected into four sections. Instead, "... eight undersecretaries-general will report to him directly, down from about 30 top officials under the old system. But the plan disregards the representatives' suggestion that the five permanent Security Council members – the United States, Britain, France, Russia and China – agree not to claim any top posts for a few years."[22]

Thus, although the Secretary-General agrees that some simplification of structure would be beneficial to him, the area of recruitment to positions is different. Here, it would appear that the sovereignty gap has not yet been bridged. The five permanent powers do not yet see it as being in their interest to give up their "right" to certain positions, even though Urquhart and Childers called for this,[23] and even though the General Assembly called for this as far back as 1980.[24]

Perhaps a contrary perspective needs to be taken on UN reform. Instead of focusing so often on "sins of commission" (without explaining what "commission" has occurred), perhaps the emphasis would be to allow the present operations to continue and focus instead on "sins of omission." In this regard, the second report by Urquhart and Childers is worth noting again.[12]

The second half of *Towards a More Effective United Nations* is a set of recommendations dealing with, "Strengthening International Response to Humanitarian Emergencies."[25] Like the *Nordic Report*[6] and that of the USA-UNA,[4] the focus here is on enabling the UN to respond better to what is considered to be its mandate. This approach has considerable merit in accepting the *status quo* for what is currently being done, and then scanning the environment for the present *lacunae*.

However, once again, niggling questions arise: Do these recommendations arise from the UN's mandate or the authors' perception of such a mandate? Will there be a sovereignty gap that needs to be bridged, and if so, how will it be bridged? What is the actual problem? And how will this increase in activities help to alleviate the supposed problems of complexity and lack of coordination that were cited in the other studies?

Reform proposals to fill in the gaps of the present UN fare no better than those to repair present damage – they both must first create a vision of what the member governments should want the UN to be and do. Without a detailed specification of that agreed-upon scenario, the reform proposals will simply continue to mount in a pile of documents.

In the absence of a holistic reform of the UN, it must be concluded that only incremental changes to the Secretariat's present operational procedures are possible. But incrementalism is only piecemeal, "muddling through," unless some kind of vision exists in people's minds. If there were such a vision, it would have to be founded on holistic principles – and now we have a Catch-22 situation.

Organizational design cannot and should not be an end in itself; it is at best a means for implementing agreed-upon purposes. All organizational structures have simultaneous advantages and disadvantages, assets and liabilities, solutions and defects. No organizational structure can achieve everything; at best, it can achieve some things at the cost of others. An organizational design proposal, therefore, whether *de novo* or a reform, must be oriented towards a particular purpose. And it is the responsibility of the organizational designer, at the same time, to indicate then what problems will simultaneously be created by that particular design, what *lacunae* will exist, what defects will soon be obvious. This "how" stage of the process, however, only comes after the "what" and "why" stage has been completed.

Notes

1 Renninger, John P. 1981 *ECOSOC: Options for Reform* (Policy & Efficacy Studies 4, UNITAR: New York).

2 Bertrand, Maurice 1985 *Some Reflections on Reform of the United Nations* (JIU/REP/85/9: Geneva).

3 *Report of the Group of High-Level Intergovernmental Experts to Review the Efficiency of the Administrative and Financial Functioning of the United Nations* (A/41/49: New York, 1986) commonly referred to as the *G-18 Report*.

4 UNA-USA 1987 *A Successor Vision: The United Nations of Tomorrow* (United Nations Management & Decision-Making Project: New York).

5 Urquhart, Brian, and Erskine Childers 1990 *A World in Need of Leadership: Tomorrow's United Nations* (Dag Hammarskjold Foundation: Uppsala, Sweden).

6 Nordic UN Project 1991 *The United Nations in Development: Reform Issues in the Economic and Social Fields* (Almqvist & Wiksell International: Stockholm).

7 This is especially the perspective of Andy Knight in his submission to the ICFUN Working Group, "The Managed Change Process in the United Nations." Although Knight's paper will not be discussed in detail

here, it enshrouds our whole paper because of the following perspective taken from the Abstract of his paper: "Because it has a predominantly Western-oriented, technocratic and incrementalist bias, this approach to change is suspect to the charge that it places the Western states and technocrats within the system at a distinct advantage. As a result, it is increasingly challenged by an emerging counter-hegemonic position which places the focus of organizational change on delivery systems, equitableness, fairness and justice. What is required, according to the challengers, is a major transformation or overhaul of the UN system; not piecemeal 'reforms' that effectively result in forestalling needed change. [The Knight] study explores this dialectical conformation, using specific case studies, and demonstrates that a process of acquiescence and compromise form both the hegemonic and counter-hegemonic groups operating within the organization is most often the result. Concomitantly, UN reform results fall considerably short of what is required to meet the challenge of relevance."

8   McLaren, Robert I. "The UN System and Its Quixotic Quest for Coordination" *International Organization* 34 Winter 1980 139-48.

9   Jay, Anthony 1967 *Management and Machiavelli* (Holt, Rinehart & Winston: New York) 35.

10 McLaren, Robert I. "Coordination of the United Nations System" *International Review of Administrative Sciences* 53 1987 383-94.

11 See note 6, 15.

12 Urquhart, Brian, and Erskine Childers 1992 *Towards a More Effective United Nations* (Dag Hammarskjold Foundation: Uppsala, Sweden).

13 See note 12, 14.

14 See note 12.

15 McLaren, Robert I. 1982 *Organizational Dilemmas* (Wiley: Chichester, UK).

16 See note 4, 55.

17 See note 4, 55-57.

18 Bertrand, Maurice, in Taylor, Paul, and A.J.R. Groom eds. 1988 *International Institutions at Work* (Pinter: London) 195.

19 See note 12, 12-20.

20 UN/Press Release SG/SM/4777, ECOSOC/5364, 6 July 1992.

21 UN/Press Release SG/A/479, 7 February 1992.

22 *New York Times* 9 February 1992.

23 See note 12, 14-15.

24 As cited in note 12, fn. 6.

25 See note 12, 41-85.

PART III

PEACE AND SECURITY

Commentary on Part III

Henry Wiseman

The world has changed. Everyone knows it. Everyone senses it. And we all hope that the UN too will change; that it will evolve in authority, structure and competence to the better management of international peace and security. So much for the obvious. Here we have six short and succinct papers beginning with a clear and historical presentation by Geoffrey Pearson that delve directly into the practices, pitfalls and promises for the new generation of peacekeeping, a generational shift from the seemingly simple to the confusingly complex. These are not simple tributes to the past nor are they utopian proposals for reform. They delve with penetrating insight into the fundamental issues that must be addressed if meaningful UN reform is to take place.

Here we learn of the multitudinous functions of contemporary peacekeeping, which span the full range from the monitoring of cease-fires to the restoration of failed states; such as maintaining dishonoured cease-fires, the provision of law and order, delivering of humanitarian aid, the conduct of elections and the assumption of governmental authority – in brief, from peacekeeping to peacebuilding, from bloody conflict to constructive stability.

With eighteen new operations since 1988, what have we learned about intervention?

What are the criteria for UN intervention. Walter Dorn in a few pages provides a graphic picture of the stages of conflict escalation and the possible points of entry for preventive diplomacy, early warning, crisis management, conflict resolution and finally enforcement operations. Therein arises the question about the use of force, when appropriate, when not? "With all necessary measures" is too broad an authorization, contends Venkata Raman. Should all this be left to the determination of the permanent members? If so, argues John Polanyi, "Force ... should be used according to prescribed guidelines, as a last resort and to the least extent. But these conditions having been met, it should be used as it would also be used domestically to halt violent crime." Nevertheless, Raman reminds us that the primary UN function is not to perfect its enforcement muscle, but to explore its usefulness as an agent for change and peace. Furthermore, should the UN create arrangements for a "permanent" military force, as recommended by the Secretary-General in *An Agenda for Peace*, Arnold Simoni lays out some of the problems related to the possible structure, command and control, and the guidelines for implementation.

Yet a further difficulty arises, as we are warned by Newton Bowles, that in the case of Somalia past colonialism bears much of the blame for later conflict. And while the UN intervened in an impartial manner for the delivery of humanitarian aid, hybrid arrangements with the United States resulted in the partisan use of force and the subsequent distortion and failure of the operation.

It is to the credit of the authors that they do not shy away from the troublesome questions such as the reconciliation of the principle of national self determination with that of territorial integrity, as in Bosnia. Have we reached a stage where nationalist behaviour far exceeds the norms of international law?

The world is undergoing radical transformation. But the rise in the frequency and intensity of conflict, the disintegration of states and the general erosion of state sovereignty are not, unfortunately, compensated by a commensurate development of the authority and competence of the UN. There are many wild cards afloat in the international system, some benevolent, others not. Non-Governmental Organizations have become significant actors in the international system, particularly in respect to the delivery of humanitarian assistance and the management of conflict. The media have also become part of the early warning system. How can they best be coordinated in the complex UN peacekeeping and peacebuilding operations? These are but a few of the significant issues raised in this section on peace and security.

The great value in asking different authors to deal with the several aspects of "peace and security" is that among them most of the key issues will be raised from a variety of perspectives. And in this regard these authors have eminently succeeded. But they have done more than that. Each has gone beyond analysis and presented a number of essential, important and practical recommendations. Finally, I am drawn back to Geoffrey Pearson's reminder, quoting the Prime Minister, that "the UN's central vocation in the defence and promotion of peace and security is Canada's vocation as well." Whatever the reforms proposed for the UN as it celebrates its 50th Anniversary, in preparation for the enormous responsibilities it will face in the 21st century, our task is to ensure that Canada plays a vital part in its transformation.

CHAPTER 7

Peacekeeping and Canadian Policy

Geoffrey Pearson

Introduction

As the end of the century approaches, there is new hope that the United Nations will begin to do what its founders hoped it would do in 1945 – keep the peace. Such hopes had evaporated by 1948 as the Cold War and the prospect of atomic destruction froze the policies of the superpowers into an icy standoff. For almost forty years the UN appeared to be an adjunct of Cold War politics, conscripted in 1950 to fight on the Western Side in Korea, but otherwise permitted to intervene only when the interests of the two great antagonists ran roughly parallel, as in the containment of conflict in the Middle East and in Cyprus. The absence of the communist government of China from UN councils until 1971 prevented any UN mediation in East Asia, especially in respect of war in Indochina. Soviet intervention in Afghanistan in 1979, and civil war in Central America during the 1980s, proceeded without significant UN response. Yet, since 1988, eighteen new peacekeeping operations have been authorized by the Security Council, some of which have greatly expanded the traditional UN functions of observation and warning. The challenge now is to give these precedents institutional form and political legitimacy. To this task, Canada can make a unique contribution if her political leaders can muster the resources and the public support to do so.

The Canadian Record

In 1947 the Secretary of State for External Affairs defined as a principle of Canadian foreign policy: "security for this country lies in the development of a firm structure of international organization." This remains the case. In 1993 the Prime Minister told the General Assembly: "the UN's central vocation – the defence and promotion of peace and security – is Canada's vocation as well." Frustrated by the failure of the UN to conclude agreements with its members for the provision of armed forces as the *Charter* stipulated, Canada nevertheless earmarked a brigade for UN duty in

Korea, and when this device proved to be impractical for other UN missions, was ready to respond with various forms of military assistance from the creation of the first UN peacekeeping force (UNEF) in 1956 to the present day. 100,000 Canadian soldiers have served in peacekeeping missions since 1956. As a middle power with professional armed forces, capacity to pay the costs, a reputation for impartiality, and diplomatic influence, this readiness to contribute to peacekeeping was matched by an equal readiness in New York to look to Canada for advice and help. In 1993 Canada was the fourth largest contributor of peacekeeping personnel, ranging between four and ten percent of the total. Recent Canadian experience in the former Yugoslavia and in Somalia has brought home to Canadians, however, the risks and costs of UN intervention in conflict-ridden countries, providing a strong motive to press for measures that improve UN effectiveness and strengthen its authority.

The Nature of Peacekeeping

To keep the peace implies that peace (in the sense of the absence of war or armed conflict) already exists, either because the disputants have agreed to cease fire or have reached a settlement of their differences. They may not live in harmony, but they agree not to pursue their disputes by violence. In fact, there have been few examples of peaceful settlements between states since 1945, except in cases of de-colonization. Most peacekeeping operations have helped only to maintain an uneasy *modus vivendi*; Cyprus, Kashmir, and Israel's relations with Syria and Jordan offer conspicuous examples. In such cases the presence of the UN has required the consent of the Parties, the purpose has been to observe and report, and the use of force is excluded except in self-defence.

In the last two or three years, peacekeeping mandates have been extended to encompass the monitoring of elections, *e.g.*, in Namibia and Nicaragua, and of human rights, *e.g.*, in El Salvador, as well as the delivery of humanitarian relief, *e.g.*, in Somalia and Rwanda. The latter function in particular has been based on a strengthened interpretation of peacekeeping mandates under *Chapter VII* of the *Charter*, which allows the use of "all necessary means," including the use of force, for the accomplishment of the mission. The use of force has varied, depending on the circumstances, but has fallen short of the requirement to defeat cross-border aggression, as was the case in Korea in 1950 and in Kuwait in 1990.

One may therefore distinguish three types of UN action to respond to threats to peace and to acts of aggression – actions to keep the peace agreed to by Parties, enforcement actions against one or more of the Parties designed to facilitate relief or restore order, and enforcement actions required to repel aggression. The term "peacemaking" is sometimes used to describe actions involving the use of force, but it is more properly applicable to diplomatic activities aimed at achieving the political settlement of disputes after fighting has ceased [see Chapter 8].

Peacekeeping in all three senses is a transitional activity between the law of the jungle and the law of humanity ("over all nations is humanity," in the words of Prime Minister Mackenzie King at the San Francisco Conference in 1945). The fact is that the application of international law to the use of force remains at an early stage. A law of nations implies agreement on the definition of nations and of the rights and duties of governments and citizens. But no such agreement exists, and in a world of continuing gross disparities between rich and poor, citizens cannot hope to have equal access to any judicial process. When, in addition, the rights of both individuals and minorities are not subject to international enforcement, the use of other means to claim such rights is understandable. In these conditions, peacekeeping can only be a method of helping to establish a minimum of civil order and social welfare. Keepers of the peace cannot be justices of the peace until the rules of global society are more securely in place than at present.

Collective Security

These rules, it was hoped in 1945, would be based on the provisions of the *UN Charter*. Chief among them would be a prohibition of "the threat or use of force against the territorial integrity or political independence of any state." The means of enforcing the rule was to be entrusted to a concert of those great powers which had emerged victorious from the war. Neither the principle nor its means of implementation survived the two major phenomena of the post-war world – the growth of East-West hostility, exacerbated by fear of atomic destruction, and de-colonization. The first paralyzed the activity of the Security Council, and the second undermined the principle of territorial integrity, leading instead to the development of a second principle enshrined in the *Charter*; equal rights and self-determination of peoples. Action by the Council to repel aggression in Korea in 1950 was only made possible by the absence of a Soviet veto and by the ability of the USA to muster the military force and the political influence to dictate subsequent events, including the co-operation of the General Assembly to act in the place of the Council if the veto should make this necessary. But a second lesson of Korea was that there were severe limits to use of force by the UN, whatever the circumstances, given the possibility that the Cold War could lead to a war fought with atomic weapons.

The concept of "collective measures" (the term "collective security" is not used in the *Charter*), implying the use of force, therefore developed into ways of taking collective action to police cease-fires and to encourage political settlements rather than to suppress aggression. It found its first large-scale expression in the UN Emergency Force (UNEF) deployed in Sinai in 1956. It was a way of containing conflict rather than meeting it head-on, although in 1960-64 the UN force in the Congo was obliged on several occasions to resort to a limited use of force in order to carry out its mandate, the first example of operations that were to become more frequent after the end of the Cold War. But for the most part in the peacekeeping era from 1956 to the late 1980s, the UN had to depend on the consent of the Parties involved in disputes to the mandate of its forces as defined by the Council. It suited both sides in the Cold War as well as the Non-Aligned that UN flags should only be present in areas, such as the Middle East, from which their own forces were absent. But Soviet suspicion of an organization that remained largely under the influence, if not the control, of its Western members until well into the 1970s helped to ensure that peacekeeping remained an *ad hoc* activity, improvised on each occasion in haste and confusion, and kept under close watch by a Security Council that had no collective will to build, as well as to keep, the peace. It was a poor substitute for the grand design of the *Charter*, enjoying little public support in most of the world, but it did allow the UN to learn from experience and to prepare discreetly for the future.

New Directions

The end of the Cold War has accelerated a major trend in the politics of the 20th century, a trend on which the peacemakers of 1918 conferred legitimacy and which the *UN Charter* of 1945 confirmed – the self-determination of peoples. The Soviet Union paid lip service to this ideal in theory, while effectively suppressing its realization in practice, and Soviet power, countered by US policies of containment, acted to repress national sentiments in most of Eastern Europe. The struggle for independence in parts of Africa, Southeast Asia and elsewhere was converted into a contest for power, and democratic movements languished. Once this contest began to dissipate and the last of the great European empires – the Soviet Union – had collapsed, the march towards a world of self-governing peoples resumed, less restricted by foreign dictate and puppet regimes, and following the examples of others, such as India, which had escaped the strictures of Cold War rivalry. In addition to the emergence of this underlying trend, however, new factors complicated the task of peacemaking: the absence, instead of the imposition, of political authority in some states, the flight from poverty and disaster, and what has been called a clash of civilizations based on culture and religion that is demonstrated *in extremis* by a new form of genocide. Together, these phenomena portend anarchy rather than aggression as the major threat to peace, and they point to the delivery of humanitarian relief and the reconstruction of civil institutions as the principal objectives of UN peacekeeping.

It is the UN, indeed, that will have to maintain and develop its new found purposes if global turmoil is to be limited to something short of global conflict. Other means of keeping peace are available, whether by national fiat or regional cooperation, but they may work too well or too little. Regional organizations may lack the capacity or the will to police recalcitrant members or, as in the former Yugoslavia, to use sufficient force in the face of determined resistance to outside pressure. No doubt such will exists in Washington, Moscow and Beijing, and in other capitals, if and when vital interests are perceived to be in jeopardy, but the unilateral use of force by strong states is surely not the model one would wish to see followed at the end of this century of war by mass destruction. The nuclear stalemate of the past forty years is by no means guaranteed to continue if the number of guarantors increases much beyond its present level of five declared nuclear powers.

Formidable obstacles, however, confront the UN as it struggles to work out *An Agenda for Peace*. The *Charter* injunction against intervention in the domestic affairs of Member States still carries a powerful resonance, despite the recent determination by the Security Council that the situation in Somalia justified such intervention [see Chapter 9]. Is Somalia a special case? If not, where else might similar criteria justify the use of UN force? No consensus exists about the answers to such questions, nor is one likely to emerge soon as governments around the world grapple with challenges from minorities and individual citizens to their right to govern. Consequently the reputation of the UN is bound to suffer from the accusation of double standards, whatever the merits of the decision on Somalia.

Publics are further confused by the notion of obligation. If UN forces are to be engaged more often in civil wars, where the concept of the enemy is ambiguous and controversial, whose soldiers should be called upon to run the risks of keeping the peace? American and Russian reluctance to send ground troops to Bosnia illustrates the dilemma, and the casualties suffered by UN forces in Somalia underline it. Moreover, even if Member States are obliged to accept the decisions of the Security Council, are they obliged to contribute to the costs, much less to supply the troops? The costs for 1993 may be close to $4 billion, despite the fact that arrears from past operations continue to mount and that the two worst offenders are the USA and Russia. In these circumstances, the ideal of collective security and therefore collective responsibility will be hard to realize any time soon.

Nevertheless, real progress has been made. Encouraged by the spirit of cooperation in the Security Council (only one veto since May 1990), seventy or more Member States have supplied military, police or civilian personnel to UN operations, including, for the first time, Germany and Japan. The experience thus gained is already beginning to transform traditional roles for armed forces by demonstrating their utility for the delivery of humanitarian relief and the protection of refugees, despite inevitable incidents of the misuse of force or, on the contrary, an inability or unwillingness to use the military strength implied by the concept of collective security. Political settlements have been reached in Namibia, El Salvador, Haiti and Cambodia, and there is hope for success in Mozambique and in Somalia. Conflict continues in Angola and Afghanistan, but at least outside intervention in both countries has largely ended. In other cases – Israel and her Northern neighbours, Cyprus and Western Sahara, for example – UN forces or observers continue to supervise a fragile peace, and in the former Yugoslavia UN intervention, however hesitant and confused, has served to bring relief to many who otherwise would have long since perished and to give hope for a negotiated settlement that would otherwise have been savagely imposed.

What Is to Be Done?

One may compare the international scene of the years between 1950 and 1990 to a landscape shrouded in mist. The contours of human development were difficult to discern beneath the fog of Cold War rivalry and the menace of mass destruction. Once the fog was swept away by the breeze of revolution in Moscow, epitomized by Gorbachev's emphasis on "universal human values," the realities of global politics were soon revealed. Fears of world domination by one or other great powers or systems of belief gave way to concerns about more complex symptoms of strain – the rise of nationalist passions and the assertion of minority and individual rights on the one hand, and the global dangers of resource depletion and social breakdown on the other. Armed with old, but now exploitable grievances, and freed from the restraints of alliance and the threat of military intervention, it is not surprising that political forces have emerged in old and new states alike that encourage the temptation to resort to violence. Yet the organization of lawful procedures for the international control of violence remains at a primitive stage, stunted by the failure to develop legitimacy in the Cold War years. Not since 1945 has the community of nations, now almost four times more numerous, faced a greater challenge to re-build the structure of peace through law.

Both short- and long-term goals are at stake. In the short term the UN has to feel its way, one step at a time, learning painfully from experience. The Secretary-General provided a road map, *An Agenda for Peace*, in June, 1992, a map that Member States are still examining with a mixture of hope and anxiety – hope that the UN might show the way to a more peaceful world order, but anxiety about how the rules of the road are to be decided. Some steps are generally agreed: a more complete inventory of standby forces and equipment to be called upon in emergencies, the better organization of headquarters staff and thus of the control of operations, more regular consultation with contributors, and the standardization of training and equipment. Such improvements would apply to peacekeeping operations as traditionally understood, implying the consent of the Parties to the dispute, impartiality between them, and the use of force only in self-defence. There is no agreement, however, on the rules of enforcement action, nor on the circumstances which would call for the use of force, despite the precedent of the Gulf War, and in part because of the way in which force was authorized and used against Iraq. As a result, operations authorized under *Chapter VII* of the *Charter* that implied the use of economic or military sanctions have been subject to *ad hoc* decision-making and divided counsels in New York and in the capitals of the main contributors. Controversy over the use of limited force in Somalia and disagreement about the proper response to coercion in the former Yugoslavia are cases in point. In Cambodia, on the other hand, the issue could be safely by-passed once the Parties agreed to allow elections to proceed and (apparently) to accept the results. In the long term, a doctrine to govern enforcement actions will have to be formally or tacitly accepted by the members of the Security Council. A UN case law will gradually accumulate that may make this possible, including some consensus on what constitutes a threat to peace and how the members should share the costs, both military and financial, of dealing with it. Any consensus will be dependent on the willingness of Member States to accept the legitimacy of Security Council decisions, and this in turn will almost certainly require reform of its membership and powers. Any redistribution of permanent seats on the Security Council will be a difficult feat of diplomatic bargaining, but the longer it is delayed, the more the authority of the Council will suffer, and the longer it will take to consider seriously more ambitious goals, such as formation of a UN volunteer force ready for instant action when required. In the meantime, governments that agree to earmark military units for UN duty are bound to attach reservations about the use of force. The measure of UN success in keeping the peace will depend in each case on the degree of consensus achieved by Security Council members and the major troop contributors to take "all necessary means" to this end.

Canadian Priorities

The major obstacles to such consensus appear to be two: the reluctance of some states to make the sacrifices and to run the risks involved in operations not under their direct control, and in places they may regard as peripheral to their vital interests; and the contrary suspicion, held in particular by some Islamic states and by China, that the Security Council is too easily persuaded by Western interpretations of "threats to peace." The absence of a strong Western response to aggression against Bosnia-Herzegovina is symptomatic of fears of the first kind; and the occasional use of force by the UN in Somalia arouses the kind of anxieties provoked by the second reaction to UN decisions. Canadian forces have served under UN command in both places, and Canadian officers seconded to the UN Secretariat are familiar with problems in New York. Canadian advice could help persuade Washington, and perhaps Moscow, that the strengthening of UN command and control of operations, under the overall authority of the Security Council, is preferable to unilateral action, even if the latter is taken under UN cover. This will be more difficult to do if the number of permanent members of the Security Council is increased to reflect the actual distribution of power in the world; but both objectives will have to be sought if the UN is to enjoy the confidence of its members and to fulfill the purposes of its *Charter*.

Canadian experience and influence would also suggest that Canada is well qualified to act as a centre for the training of personnel, both military and civilian, earmarked for the UN duty. As noted above, the use of force by units under UN command, even though authorized by the Security Council, is a highly sensitive and controversial subject. Unit commanders, as well as their troops, would benefit from advance training on the kinds of circumstances that might lead to such use, especially as the Secretary-General has recommended that Member States begin to recruit "peace enforcement units" to consist of volunteers. They would also benefit from better knowledge of the work of UN and other agencies engaged in humanitarian relief and economic development, activities which sometimes appear to be at cross-purposes with military action. A second area of training, therefore, is to learn how to coordinate the peacekeeping and peacebuilding aspects of UN operations.

Closely related to peacekeeping are efforts to limit the supply of arms to contending parties. A middle power, not significantly dependent on arms production as a factor of employment or export earnings, Canada could urge a larger role for the UN in monitoring the production and supply of sophisticated weapons. The UN arms register is a modest first step. It needs to be strengthened and then complemented by measures to discourage local arms races and to penalize the export of certain categories of weapons. Perhaps a new UN agency, on the model of the IAEA, with broad powers of inspection and required to report to the Security Council should be created.

In February 1993, the External Affairs Committee of the House of Commons recommended that a fundamental objective of foreign policy in the years ahead should be, "the building of a UN-centred system of international security and development." The question that remains to be answered is whether, at a time of political uncertainty, Canada's leaders can pursue this objective with the will and the imagination it deserves.

CHAPTER 8

From Peacekeeping to Peace Making

John C. Polanyi

If on that foundation we do not build something more permanent and stronger we will once again have ignored realities ... and betrayed our trust.

Lester B. Pearson, on peacekeeping,
Nobel Peace Prize acceptance speech, Oslo, 1957

For Canadians, and not only for Canadians, the story of United Nations peacekeeping begins with Lester B. Pearson. For a scientist it could well begin with the explosion of the first nuclear weapon, in 1945. As a Canadian and a scientist, I start with both.

In 1945, the year in which the *Charter* of the UN was formulated, Pearson (in a speech in Quebec) spoke of the need to subject "the annihilating forces of science to ... social control," and of the central role that the United Nations must play in bringing this about. As advisor to the first Canadian delegation to the UN, at the San Francisco Conference that year, he was bold enough to argue, on behalf of Canada, against the notion of a great power veto. He felt strongly that the rule of law, vested in this new body, must be made to supplant the rule of force symbolized by "great power" status.

Of course, he failed in the idealistic aim of denying the great powers their veto. But his courage in pursuing his principles contributed to the success of the *Uniting for Peace Resolution* of the UN five years later, in 1950. This *Resolution*, to which he gave his strong support as, by then, Canada's Secretary of State for External Affairs, allows the General Assembly of the UN to be convened at 48 hours notice following the use of the veto, in order to pass judgement on the question. The *Resolution*, which remains in force today, reduces the power of the veto.

But what, one is entitled to ask, can the General Assembly, empowered by this *Resolution*, do in the face of great power intransigence? The answer is that, by marshalling world opinion, it can do a great deal. The moral authority of the UN is its most precious asset.

Pearson understood, that in order to sustain this authority, the UN must both speak for justice, and act for it. Act first of all through diplomacy, but then, if need be, through diplomacy backed by force. The use of force by the UN is a contentious issue. I introduce it at the outset, since we should be aware that it had a place in Pearson's agenda.

In Pearson's view, which many share, whatever force was judged to be needed by the international authority, it must first be made evident that it was needed, and then be made evident that only such force as needed had been used. These rules are, of course, the same as those that would be observed by a police force engaged in upholding domestic law. It is one important way in which the police are distinguishable from the criminals. The other way, I need hardly add, is that they act within a framework of law.

These considerations served as Pearson's guide in regard to the Korean crisis of 1950. The Korean conflict was the seminal moment for UN peace-enforcement – though it fell short of being UN peace-enforcement.

On June 25, 1950, North Korea launched an attack on the South. The UN Security Council, in the fortunate absence of the USSR, denounced this "unprovoked aggression," and called for prompt withdrawal and cease-fire. Within two days President Truman, in consultation with the Security Council but on his own initiative, announced that he was sending air and naval forces to Korea.

Prime Minister St. Laurent (following the advice of Lester Pearson) committed Canada to participate on condition that this be a "collective police action under the control and authority of the UN." Sadly, the action was not under the control, and no more than formally, under the authority of the UN. But the intention on the part of Canada was clear.

Canada supported the UN's involvement in the Korean crisis of 1950. The UN, our government believed, was justified in meeting the force of aggression with a countervailing force, so long as the objective was restricted to repelling attack and thereby creating the conditions for a cease-fire. The US action taken in conjunction with the UN offered, as Pearson remarked at the time, "a promise of hope for the future … this time the collective conscience of the democratic world has expressed itself in action and not merely words."

Only three years after the ending of the Korean War, in July of 1956, the world was taken by surprise once more by a major outbreak of hostilities, this time precipitated by Nasser's seizure of the Suez Canal on behalf of Egypt. Shortly after this, two great powers, Britain and France, together with Israel, attacked Egypt. The UN Security Council could not take action in the face of the British and French veto. But under the "Uniting for Peace" provision the General Assembly was able to proceed, within days, to call upon the aggressors to desist.

We have, of course, seen a string of similarly feeble UN *Resolutions* up to and including recent times. Pearson sought for a way in which the *Resolution* could be strengthened by tangible evidence of the UN's resolve. The instrument that he proposed was, as he put it, an action "half way between the passing of *Resolutions* and the fighting of a war." A United Nations Emergency Force (UNEF) would be deployed in the contested area in order to supervise a cease-fire while further negotiations proceeded. Realizing the need for quick action (another vital lesson for our times) he used his negotiating skills to ensure that only two days later the General Assembly adopted this proposal. In the face of public pressure, the four governments involved in fighting agreed to the necessary cease-fire and permitted this UN Peacekeeping Force to be deployed.

Pearson referred to the UNEF with due modesty the following year (1957) in his Nobel Peace Prize acceptance speech. "I do not exaggerate the significance of what has been done," he said. "There is no peace in the area. There is not unanimity at the United Nations about the functions and future of this force. But it may prevent a brush fire from becoming an all-consuming blaze ... We made at least a beginning then. [However,] if on that foundation we do not build something more permanent and stronger we will once again have ignored realities, rejected opportunities and betrayed our trust."

Pearson was under no illusion that the UN had suddenly leapt to maturity. The world has, unfortunately, found it difficult to take the succeeding steps. This is in part because the most powerful nations were, until recently, locked in the frozen embrace of the Cold War. But it is also in part because the danger of the global predicament has only gradually penetrated the consciousness of a sufficient fraction of humankind.

Yet we should take heart from the fact that the education of the world's population is proceeding. The proposition that war between nations armed with nuclear weapons is too dangerous to contemplate, is widely accepted. The fact that preparation for war is impoverishing those who can little afford it, and that the resort to war is adding to the global burden of misery, including homelessness and statelessness, is becoming evident to anyone with access to a television set.

And to the danger of nuclear explosion, which provided the impetus for Pearson's long search for peace, there is being added an awareness of the consequences of the explosions in population and poverty. For many wealthy nations, Canada among them, these constitute by far the greatest external threat – the threat of a just claim being made upon the world's resources by its poor. This is not a threat against which we would want to mount a military defence, nor could we hope to succeed in doing so.

The pent-up impetus for change, deriving from these historic forces, was evidenced by the sudden increase in demands being made upon the United Nations in the few years since the end of the Cold War. Not only were the demands numerous (eighteen new operations since 1988, exceeding the number in the previous 42 years), but the nature of the demands was far broader, extending to humanitarian assistance, maintenance of law and order, supervision of elections, protection of minorities, and the assumption of a wide range of governmental functions. The UN has heard a global cry for help from the threatened, the hungry and the disenfranchised.

This new centrality of the UN shows how much the world has changed. Now the UN too must change, if it is to fulfill its mandate.

That mandate is made clear in the first paragraph of *Article I* of the UN *Charter*. The primary purpose of the UN is, "To maintain international peace ... and to that end to take effective collective measures." This, it is explained, has as its purpose the building of a world in which international disputes are settled peacefully, on the basis of justice and law. If that detracts from the traditional prerogatives of states, it is implied, so be it.

Reading the *UN Charter* one realizes that the New World Order, rather than having been invented after the Cold War, was postponed by 45 years because of it. Over that time the need for a New Order has grown more pressing due to the global increase in armaments, in population, tribal conflict and environmental strain. The desire for it has never been greater.

What are the avenues open to us for addressing the hunger for peace with justice? A document prepared by the Secretary-General of the UN for the Security Council in the summer of 1992 addressed this question. *An Agenda for Peace*, as it is called, distinguished four broad categories of UN activities on behalf of peace: Preventive Diplomacy, Peacemaking, Peacekeeping and Peacebuilding.

Preventive Diplomacy attempts to bring hostile parties to agreement before conflict leads to war. This as yet poorly developed field includes conflict identification as well as a warning function. Currently the UN Secretariat has 40 staff in the area of Preventive Diplomacy and Peacemaking, as against almost 80,000 peacekeepers in the field. But peacekeepers arrive late, and at a heavy cost. We need to invest much more in Preventive Diplomacy and Peacemaking. The operation of one element, the warning function under the heading of Preventive Diplomacy as it operates presently, can perhaps be judged from the fact that the UN Secretariat, one is told, had to send out for maps showing the Falkland Islands when the Falklands invasion occurred.

Peacemaking makes use of many of the same diplomatic skills as the Preventive Diplomacy that I have just been discussing, but does so after a dispute has become an armed conflict. The aim, then, is to reduce the intensity of the conflict through negotiation, as a step on the path to a cease-fire.

Peacekeeping, as we have already seen, involves deployment of armed UN personnel to help defuse a conflict. It differs from Peacemaking in one crucial way: the Peacekeepers arrive when a cease-fire has been agreed to, with the purpose of seeing that it is honoured.

Peacebuilding, the final category of operation, involves the building of all sorts of "structures" (such as social services, a judiciary and responsive government) that strengthen peace and order. Peacebuilding can occur before or after a conflict, but is certain to be badly needed in the aftermath of war.

These pedantic categories for UN action are, as you can imagine, both overlapping and incomplete. One thinks of the modest UN force that today separates the Kosovo area of Serbia from the former Yugoslav Republic of Macedonia. This UN force is something new. Since armed personnel are involved, it is not Preventive Diplomacy. For the same reason, and also since there has been no conflict, it cannot be Peacemaking. Since there has been no shooting and therefore no cease-fire, it cannot be Peacekeeping. By elimination, it must therefore be Peacebuilding. Whatever it is, this "trip-wire" is sensible and farsighted – provided that there exists something for it to trip.

It is evident that there are a broad range of actions – referred to as "Peacemaking" in the title of this paper – before, during and following conflict, which the UN, provided with the proper mix of military and civilian personnel, can undertake. None should be neglected.

If one of these categories is to be made flexible so as to cover a spectrum of actions, it should be Peacekeeping, which has already gone into the language. Two Nobel Peace Prizes have acknowledged that. The institution became tangible one might say on the day in 1956 when, in order to distinguish UN Peacekeeping troops in Suez from a large number of others, an unused pile of helmet-liners were painted blue and distributed to the troops to wear. Little by little the blue helmet is taking its place as a respected symbol of courage and service. This is not to deny that the blue helmets will at times be suspect, or even disgraced. But the symbol must be strong enough to withstand that, and is becoming so.

In recent times, we have come to group under the heading of *Peacekeeping*, activities that go beyond the monitoring of a cease-fire to the enforcing of one. We are gradually coming to terms with the fact that our Peacekeepers cannot be held hostage to the first malcontent, as would be the case if they were withdrawn if one of the warring parties decided to violate a cease-fire or attack the UN troops. The right to self-defence on the part of the blue-helmets should be real. Additionally, the obligation to enforce a cease-fire, rather than merely monitor it, should sometimes be placed upon the peacekeepers.

The case for such *Peace-enforcement* will be strong in instances where the UN believes a cease-fire has a chance, and where the international community has the resolve to follow through till the action is made effective. Both Bosnia and Rwanda provided opportunities for a great deal more action than was taken, but, tragically, the resolve was lacking.

There are people of good conscience who argue against the use of force by the UN on the grounds that peace cannot come from the barrel of a gun. I respect that viewpoint, but am not persuaded by it. Force, it cannot be too much stressed, should be used according to prescribed guide-lines, as a last resort, and to the least extent. But these conditions having been met, it should be used as it would also be used domestically to halt violent crime.

The argument that force inevitably begets force gives too little weight to the difference between legality and illegality, between right and wrong. If a criminal is apprehended in the act of committing a crime, as has been so horribly the case in Bosnia, Rwanda and elsewhere, there is an obligation, when exhortation fails, to take action. Our slowness to act has not been one of principle, but lack of it.

There are, of course, many deserving UN causes (and non-UN causes) on behalf of peace, but Bosnia has for over three years been central: in part, I grant, because of television. But that is a legitimate factor. It is a worse crime to ignore what you know than what you do not, and more damaging to fail in what you have begun than in what you have neglected.

Additionally there are realities that do not depend on television: in Bosnia the Christian world meets the Muslim. It is a fateful meeting. We need a civilized peace in Bosnia for all our futures. If we succeed in this we do so not only for Bosnia, but also for the UN on which so much depends. If we fail, the political opportunists and thugs around the world will take note and make their plans to fill the vacuum that our failure has created.

What broad implications does all this have for Canada? Participation in UN Peacekeeping, starting with the Suez crisis of 1956 and extending to virtually every UN Peacekeeping operation since that time, has helped to define this country, a country not over-burdened with definability.

The UNEF of 1956 served as a springboard from which Canada moved up the ladder of global influence. That is a credit to Mr. Pearson, but still more to the tradition that he helped to establish. It was in that tradition that Mr. Trudeau, as Prime Minister of Canada, addressed the UN General Assembly in 1978 and once again in 1982, on each occasion making specific proposals for slowing the arms race in weapons of mass destruction. The following year, 1983, Mr. Trudeau set out on a global crusade for peace. The intention was to jolt the feuding nations out of their mood of helplessness in the face of their own paranoia.

The apotheosis of their deranged state of mind came later in 1983 when President Reagan on behalf of the USA asked the USSR to agree to spend hundreds of billions of dollars on a defence system that the two superpowers would erect against one another's nuclear missiles – the alternative being to agree not to fire them. But the latter path presupposed the existence of free will. UN Peacekeeping is based on the more hopeful view that human conduct is to some extent under human control.

One of the most dazzling testimonials to the notion that even under the most adverse circumstances we remain the masters of our fate, was surely the collapse of numerous Communist dictatorships just a few years ago. These terrible regimes fell to no foreign invader, nor to internal *force majeure*, but were the victims of popular disgust. In human affairs, it would appear that what people sufficiently wish to change, they can. The message of these events was read in this light at points as widely separated as South Africa and China.

In the same spirit of change, the UN was subsequently called upon to bring peace and stability to a dozen places around the world where people were suffering, among them Angola, Kuwait, El Salvador, Cambodia, the former Yugoslavia, Somalia and Mozambique, and now Rwanda. Canada was involved in every case, at some significant financial cost to the country and risk in Canadian lives. As much as any nation on earth we have embraced the new definition of security as constituting a common goal and responsibility.

Not only do we regard this as a civilized attitude, we recognize, as I have suggested, that the greatest external threat to our country derives from the consequences of conflicts abroad. To name only one aspect, there is a limit to the rate of immigration that a nation can accommodate, and still be that nation. World-wide, the number of political refugees will soon exceed 50 million. The number of economic and environmental refugees already runs into the hundreds of millions. And yet, given the choice, almost all of these people would prefer to live their lives in the places they know best, if only that were possible.

The record of success in UN operations, though marred by failures, is sufficiently good that demands for UN assistance continue to escalate. In the future, quite obviously, we need to improve the functioning of the UN in regard to Peacekeeping. Canada can contribute to this. We shall also have to start to be selective in our participation. Canada cannot be everywhere.

Peacekeeping, if people but realized it, is an incredible bargain compared with war-making. To put costs into perspective, it should be noted that Canada's major involvement in peacekeeping in the various parts of the former Yugoslavia has (according to our Department of National Defence, as reported in the Globe and Mail, 11 March 1994) cost $170 million p.a. This amounts to 1.5% of our defence budget. In contrast to the parts of our defence expenditure that fulfill the traditional purposes of guarding the nation against foreign attack, this is a 1.5% that can be justified to the hilt.

It is true that at present our Peacekeeping forces, with at times up to 4,500 military personnel on duty around the world, extend our 78,000 person armed forces to the limit. However, it should not strain credulity to suppose that a force of this total size can, with reassessment of priorities and reassignment of duties, be made to yield fifty percent more peacekeepers. That is what is proposed within the compass of item (1) of the following brief list of proposals – four in all:

(1) It is proposed that Canada contribute in the region of two to three thousand peacekeepers to a UN stand-by force. Such a commitment would add to, not replace, our present contribution of roughly four thousand peacekeepers on world-wide duty.

(2) The provision of standby troops would be a pioneering action. It is most likely to be imitated by other nations, and adopted by ours, if it is accompanied by a move to create a more effective Peacekeeping command system within the United Nations. With our long experience of Peacekeeping as well as our technical competence in DND and External (Foreign) Affairs, we should be able to make a substantial contribution to this, and should undertake to do so.

(3) This item takes cognizance of the special importance of the new concept of Peacebuilding in the critical period just following the cessation

of hostilities. Unless we assist in reconstructing the fabric of society, through the provision of humanitarian relief workers, electoral officers, police, educators, and so on, the gains made through Peacekeeping can very easily be lost. Let us insist therefore that in any Peacekeeping operation in which we participate there shall in future be (with or without our active participation) an integrated Peacebuilding effort.

(4) The fourth and final item of this short list aimed at increasing the effectiveness of Canada's contribution to UN Peacekeeping, involves the provision of improved training. This could be achieved through the establishment of a Canadian Peacekeeping and Peacebuilding Training Centre. Training would include languages, negotiating skills, and acquaintance with the setting of possible future operations.

So much for instrumentalities. But instrumentalities are only part of the story. Unless Peacekeeping is more than an instrument, it will fail. The professional impartiality of the Peacekeeper must exist within a framework of values. The *UN Charter*, for example, is not a value-free document, but a statement of shared beliefs.

Mr. Pearson liked to insist that all that we do on the world stage must be in response to the question: "What kind of world do we want?" His own guide to the world he wanted is to be found in a favourite homily: "Human sovereignty transcends national sovereignty." Human rights must take precedence.

If individual rights are indeed to be protected from the collectivity, within a nation or a world, this will only be achieved – paradoxical as it may seem – through collective action. We should recall Edward Jenner who, in 1798, discovered that a small dose of virus protects you forever from a lethal dose.

We in this country, on many days in the year, rejoice in our diversity. But, as some among us have been insisting, in the absence of willingness to share, diversity will inevitably lead to fragmentation. We can see this happening at many points in the world, Canada among them.

The slippery slope begins with an entirely proper recognition of cultural identity, then proceeds more dangerously to political division along cultural lines, culminating all too often in territorial division. In this perverse algebra, human sovereignty, instead of transcending national sovereignty, multiplies it.

At what point in this tragic progression do we abandon the pre-eminence of the individual for the pre-eminence of the collectivity, the state?

Surely at the point that we decide to seek equity through erecting boundaries – through excluding others. The pursuit of equity through the exclusion of others leads to the pursuit of greater equity through more rigorous exclusion until, with hideous justice, it excludes those who set the process in motion.

There is, in truth, no grouping exclusive enough to guarantee justice, not even the family, as Cain and Abel found out some time ago. Instead, justice must be defended in the widest possible arena. That should be the aim of the people of this diverse grouping called Canada, as it should also be the aim of the widest grouping of all, the United Nations.

Of course, the future of Canada matters less than the future of the United Nations. Curiously, nothing can better serve the future of Canada than to realize this truth. Since 1945 a succession of Canadian governments have committed our country – all of it – deeply to the UN. Their motives were global. Had they, however, wished to do a service to the Canada that was emerging, a country in which ethnicity is distributed over a hundred different cultural-linguistic heritages, they could have done no better than to strengthen our commitment to the United Nations.

References

Axworthy, T.S., and P.E. Trudeau 1992 *Towards a Just Society* (Penguin Books).

Centre for International Studies 1994 *Canada 21; Canada and Common Security in the Twenty-First Century* (University of Toronto). The author was a participant in the *Canada 21* study; the four proposals for Canadian initiatives are based upon that study.

Evans, Gareth 1993 *Cooperating for Peace* (Allen and Unwin).

Pearson, Geoffrey A.H. 1993 *Seize the Day* (Carleton University Press).

CHAPTER 9

Somalia: Learning the Hard Way

Newton Bowles

The UN Security Council broke new ground when it decided on 3 December 1992 to use force to make humanitarian aid available in Somalia. In so doing, the Council said it was alarmed by reported violations of international humanitarian law; and also said that this humanitarian tragedy was a threat to international peace and security. Early in his tenure as Secretary-General, Dr. Boutros Boutros-Ghali had criticized the Western powers for their preoccupation with the Balkans, while ignoring starvation in Somalia. His criticism might have had little effect but for the enormous influence of the mass media.

In 1992, all through the year, the TV windows of the world opened up on scenes of starving children amidst a plague of armed banditry in Somalia's sandy wastes. You could see the generous outpouring of humanitarian aid from the West being carried off by bands of brigands roving uncontrolled in heavily armed "technicals." International and private agencies were frustrated, with more and more aid workers in danger of their lives. What a relief it was on 9 December to switch on the TV and see the orderly landing of 20,000 US troops, under the UN banner, dedicated to a new kind of war, getting food to children. In the weeks that followed, TV audiences were soothed by images of rolling relief convoys and children snatched from the verge of death. Village elders were arrayed in support of the benign invasion. The humanitarian war had been won.

Or had it? Nine months later, on the streets of Mogadishu, bloody scenes of battle flashed across TV screens, with the multinational UN force trying to capture General Aidid, the Somali clan leader in control of South Mogadishu. General Aidid had been the main holdout against disarming. In June, as the UN went about its disarmament mission, twenty-four Pakistani soldiers were killed. To take the lead in capturing Aidid, the USA sent in a contingent of Rangers. But Aidid was not only elusive; he was formidably armed and a skilled warrior. Nigerian and US soldiers were killed or captured. Women and children died in the cross fire. Humiliated, US political bandleaders found convenient scapegoats: the United Nations and their own President. Bill Clinton's wings were clipped: US forces must leave Somalia before April 1994 and henceforth it was unlikely that any

US boys would serve under UN command. What went wrong?

First of all, there is television. It was television that propelled the massive US and UN intervention in Somalia. But the generous impulse to help suffers from the short attention span in the TV fantasy world. TV demands a happy ending now. Fix it and move on. Next show? When the next show parades "our boys" shot down and captured, the TV mood swings all the way to wounded pride, anger and withdrawal. TV is a fickle instrument for sustained and difficult engagement.

Second to television is machismo. It is hard to make the John Wayne formula work in real life. The debacle in South Mogadishu, as seen on TV, in fact was triggered by the US special forces, acting independently of the UN command, even though the second-in-command of the UN operation at the time was an American general. Consequently, a brash raid by air on Aidid's directorate was launched without sufficient back-up on the ground. Hence the tragic fiasco of helpless US troops in the streets of Mogadishu when helicopters were shot down.

Third was the miscalculation by all parties of Aidid's strength. The time to bring Aidid into line was December, when the overwhelming military intervention could hardly have been ignored. The moment passed and Aidid held his ground.

Such are the explanations of the unhappy denouement of this drama as seen in television's foreshortened lens. But what do we see in the wide lens of history and the evolving United Nations? The capacity of the UN to mitigate conflict is being tested all across the globe. What is it that gives Somalia its special poignancy?

Let us indulge in a little history. European imperial rapacity came late to Somalia. In the nineteenth century, the British took Somaliland, *i.e.,* Northern Somalia, as an adjunct to the port of Aden, while the French took the port of Djibouti. In the early years of the twentieth century, the Italians consolidated their hold on the South. After World War II, in 1950, the UN General Assembly gave the Italians a ten year Trusteeship over Southern Somalia to prepare for its independence. The British went along in Somaliland, so that North and South were joined in the new state of Somalia in July 1960. France let go in 1977 when the tiny Republic of Djibouti was born.

Unlike most African states spawned by the colonial powers, Somalia was homogeneous in ethnicity, language and religion (devoutly Islamic). There are perhaps 5 million Somalis all told, of whom a few hundred thousand live in Ethiopia (the Ogaden) and in Northern Kenya. Apart from a few agricultural communities in the South and the commercial ports, Somalis were nomads living a precarious life as cyclical droughts threatened their fragile existence. Their survival system centred on fierce loyalty to family and clan. Cultural identity was split vertically by clan. Disputes over access to water were usually settled by negotiation between clan elders. Under colonial rule, a sense of national identity and national political organizations began to emerge. Rudimentary elements of civil administration, a legal system, police and a modern economy were introduced in different forms by the Italians and British. Embryonic health, veterinary and education services were begun. But in 1950 the fledgling United Nations was more interested in accelerating political independence than in endowing Somalia with the capacity for governance.

Somalia was precipitated into independence with the outlines of a democratic state, but with no experience of national politics. The first elected government got caught in the spoils of power and in 1969 was thrown out by modernizing young military. The USA supported the new government. Their idealism was soon subverted by General Syad Barre, who masked his ruthless dictatorship under the facade of Scientific Socialism. The USA pulled out and Russia moved in with massive military aid. But in 1978, when Syad Barre lent his support to the powerful Somali uprising in Ethiopia, the Russians, with their Cuban allies, organized the Ethiopian attack that defeated the Somalis. Syad Barre threw the Russians out. Defeat by Ethiopia undermined Syad Barre, and in his last desperate days, rival clans formed separate armed forces. Hargeisa, the main base of opposition, was destroyed. After the fall of Syad Barre in January 1991, the country lapsed into anarchy. All this took place in Somalia's first thirty years.

This simplistic sketch shows that Somalia's internal difficulties have been greatly exacerbated by intrusion from the outside, first by the colonial powers, and then by the cold warriors who left behind an enormous arsenal. The United Nations brought Somalia to nominal independence, but was unable to serve as protector or mentor. Statehood and modern arms were thrust upon the nomadic clans called Somalia.

The clock of history cannot be turned back: somehow the Somalis must find their way to live together. But the great powers, through the United Nations, have a special obligation to the Somalis.

What has the UN done about Somalia? There have been two reactions: the first political, the second humanitarian. The political reaction is to promote a political resolution to civil war. The humanitarian reaction is to feed and protect the people.

The UN intervention in Somalia started in 1992 as a peacemaking operation. The objective was to defuse clan conflict and to promote a political settlement. At first, things seemed to go well. In February 1992, the two warring factions in Mogadishu agreed to a cease-fire. In March, Ali Mahdi and Aidid agreed to the deployment of UN observers to monitor the cease-fire. In April 1992, the Security Council created the UN peace-keeping operation in Somalia, and at the same time asked the Secretary-General to get on with preparations for a national conference on reconciliation. The Arab League, the Islamic Conference and the OAU were associated with the UN in the ensuring consultations that continued throughout the year. A reconciliation conference was held in Addis Ababa in March 1993, at which all 15 Somali clans agreed to disarm, to settle their differences peacefully and to establish a representative national government within two years.

But even while the political negotiations were taking place, anarchic violence was preventing food from reaching the starving. This led to the American-led deployment of enough force to get relief supplies flowing. By mid-summer, after the US troops had left, UN forces totalled over 20,000 from 27 countries, plus around 1,200 US Rangers outside the UN command. An ominous sign, however, was that, against the UN 1993 humanitarian requirements of $163 million, only $16 million had been forthcoming. Overall, the UN is spending ten times as much on military as on humanitarian operations in Somalia.

Nevertheless, in most of the country, a good start was made in implementing the Addis Ababa agreement. By mid-summer a good harvest was in the fields, livestock exports had resumed, the return of over one million uprooted Somalis had begun, and health and education systems were beginning to function again. By December, 52 District and 8 Regional Councils were in place.

From June onward, following the killing of 24 Pakistani soldiers, international attention was focused on Mogadishu, the Headquarters of UN Representative, Admiral Howe, and of the UN and US military command. TV and newspaper reporters were also concentrated in Mogadishu. All eyes were trained on the hunt for General Aidid, another TV drama. It appears that the UN itself fell into Aidid's trap, becoming obsessed with a military solution to a political problem. The outcome of this episode is well known. Following military stalemate, a non-military solution is now being sought. In December 1993, the UN convened another conference in Addis Ababa, this one devoted to Somali humanitarian aid and reconstruction. Twelve of the 15 Somali clans were there; Aidid stayed out. The UN and the donor governments announced that, in effect, they were tired of inter-factional bickering and that, unless Somalis put their own house in order, external aid would dry up. Meantime, for practical as well as political reasons, external aid would be directed to those areas in Somalia where political reconciliation has made for security and stability. In an eloquent and impassioned plea for indigenous reconciliation, the UN Under-Secretary for Humanitarian Affairs, Jan Eliasso, observed: "Without peace and security, there can be no rehabilitation, no recovery, and no development." At this conference, the twelve clan leaders reaffirmed the commitments made in March.

Right after the *UN Humanitarian Conference*, the President of Ethiopia, on behalf of the OAU, engaged the same clan leaders in political consultations and Aidid was induced to come, but no progress towards a political settlement was achieved. The UN military presence is being turned over to India, Pakistan and Uganda, as all European and US forces are being withdrawn. There is evidence, as of January 1994, that the fragile security in much of the country is deteriorating. What are the prospects for Somalia and what does this mean for the UN?

In Somalia, the script for the next show is now being written. Instead of a grateful people embracing the benign UN, there persist strains among clan-based forces jockeying for power, the banditry of restless unemployed youth, and an incipient resentment of the UN military presence. Without social healing and political construction, the UN forces will lapse into the status of an army of occupation. Recent UN military action in Mogadishu has fed the fires of xenophobia; and has reminded us that the military presence, while necessary for immediate security, is not the prime instrument for nation building. How to proceed?

A people with fierce family and clan loyalties, displaced and battered in violent internecine fighting, lacking a strong tradition of national cohesion or national identity – this is Somalia. Enter the UN as pacifier and giver of good things: authority or friend? To the complex of internal hostilities is added suspicion of the outsider. How to create a sufficient degree of confidence and trust in the UN as disinterested mediator? The best hope lies in the humanitarian role of the UN, not just emergency first-aid, but engagement in solid long-term rehabilitation and construction. Social and political stability create the optimum conditions for humanitarian aid. Non-Governmental Organizations and UN organs like UNICEF have been in Somalia for many years; they know the country well and they are accepted and trusted. The UN can make better use of this credit of trust to facilitate political conciliation. The UN needs the partnership of humanitarian agencies in its function as nation-builder. Somalia will see the humanitarian face at many critical points along the road to peace.

What can the international community learn from UN experience in Somalia? There are many lessons of different orders: lessons of history, lessons about how domestic crises reverberate internationally, lessons about the inseparability of humanitarian and political issues, lessons about steadfast commitment and lessons about tactics. Here are some lessons to think about:

(1) The first lesson is that the cold warriors carry a continuing responsibility for bloody conflicts in many fragile states. This is not to say that violence began with the Cold War. But conflicts were exploited and killing capacity was vastly increased by Washington and Moscow.

(2) Second, procrastination does not simplify or solve problems like Somalia. UN intervention in 1991 would have had a much greater chance of success and might have forestalled immense human suffering.

(3) Third, it is conventional arms that are killing people. The international arms trade continues uncontrolled, with the USA and Germany in the lead.

(4) Failed states create instability and cannot be ignored. Look at the refugees if nothing else. Refugees are the main export of Afghanistan, Liberia and Somalia, not only to their neighbours, but also spilling over to the West.

(5) Humanitarian aid will go down the drain unless there is concomitant social and political healing and reconstruction.

(6) Military force cannot by itself bring about social and political healing. Prolonged and patient negotiations will always be necessary. For failed states the UN must develop a comprehensive nation-building strategy and capacity, using military force only as the last resort. In effect a new form of Trusteeship is needed.

(7) Humanitarian aid that includes social and economic reconstruction can be a strong inducement to cease fire and make peace.

(8) In a complex situation like Somalia, where active hostilities are confined or localized – in this case, Mogadishu, and maybe the Southern border later on – a workable UN strategy may be to seal off the volcanic area while keeping peace elsewhere.

(9) It follows that a step-by-step approach may be the best pathway towards an eventual comprehensive national settlement.

(10) UN success depends on unconditional and sustained commitment and unconditional acceptance of UN leadership. Dropping out when

the going gets rough not only wrecks current operations, but also undermines confidence in the UN in general.

(11) Ultimately, the UN must have its own international force. This is the only way to ensure that governments do not run away when their own troops face death in the service of the United Nations. Who will pay for a standing UN Force, you ask. Who pays for failure? Can the UN afford another Somalia?

The massive US/UN intervention in Somalia has precipitated the UN into uncharted territory. How can a benign international entity, backed by military force, facilitate the mending of a broken society where even the forms of national governance no longer exist? There is plenty of imperial or colonial experience of imposing government, but there is no analogue to UN undertakings like this. This engagement calls for the highest level of statesmanship, of diplomatic, mediating and professional/technical skills. The UN must look beyond skirmishes and arsenals in the foreground, to the background of Somali society and tradition. The most and the least that the UN can do is to facilitate a process in which Somalis themselves achieve some sort of civil society. Only when Somalis can go about their lives in conditions of peace and predictability will the UN have done its job.

CHAPTER 10

Keeping Watch for Peace: Fact-Finding by the United Nations Secretary-General

A. Walter Dorn

Introduction

In the post-Cold War world, the United Nations has found itself with new missions, expanded roles and growing responsibilities.[1] The trend is expected to continue over coming years because, in an interdependent world with many unresolved problems and new challenges, a world no longer dominated by a mammoth superpower struggle that severely curtailed international efforts at peacemaking, the UN offers a unique source of authority, talent and experience. Admittedly, the UN has shortcomings and many limitations, but nevertheless it remains the foremost avenue in the minds of many for advancement towards a world based on respect for international law and order.

A focal point in UN activities to keep the peace is the Office of the Secretary-General. For nearly a half century, the UN Secretaries-General have built up, through experience, precedence and a flexible interpretation of the *UN Charter*, responsibilities that include preventive diplomacy, early warning, crisis management, peacekeeping and conflict resolution. The Security Council, which has primary responsibility for maintaining peace and security, and the General Assembly, which may discuss and make recommendations on these matters, often entrust the Secretary-General with the detailed planning and implementation of the international operations envisioned in their resolutions.

The range of tasks carried out by the Secretary-General and his Secretariat staff in the field of peace and security is truly awe-inspiring.[2] In

---

A condensed version of this chapter was presented at the *Monitoring and Fact-Finding Session of the Third International Workshop on Verification of Arms Reduction*, Geneva, 23-25 August 1993, hosted by the Geneva International Peace Research Institute.

the past five years, the Secretary-General has: verified the withdrawal of Soviet forces from Afghanistan and Cuban forces from Angola; supervised the cease-fire in the Iran-Iraq war; overseen Namibian transition to a independent, democratic nation, climaxing 70 years of international involvement; assisted in the implementation of the Central America peace plan (including the disarmament and demobilization of the Contras); provided for the protection of UN efforts for Kurdish and other refugees in Iraq; verified Iraq's declarations about its weapons of mass destruction and is overseeing their elimination; supervised elections or referenda in Nicaragua, Haiti and the Western Sahara (pending); won the release of hostages in the Middle East, monitored human rights nation-wide in El Salvador; tried to ease the Civil War in former Yugoslavia; kept the peace in Cyprus while promoting a lasting settlement; guarded supply routes in Somalia; and administered Cambodia during its transition period before supervising successful but suspenseful elections.

Table 10.1 at the end of the paper describes instances, from the foundation of the UN up to the end of 1991, when the Secretary-General has alerted the Security Council to a potential threat to international peace and security. In any operation carried out by the Secretary-General, a reliable and independent capability to gather information is essential. Currently he has a variety of information-gathering means, but on the whole the financial and technological resources at his disposal are incongruous with the demands that these complex operations entail.

The Scope of Fact-Finding

In many cases, information gathered by the UN Secretary-General relates directly to the security and vital interests of nations, as well as to international peace and security. Thus the information can sometimes be very sensitive and must often be kept secret. The Secretary-General often requires what would, by some definitions, be called intelligence.

The term intelligence is avoided in UN discussions because, as one authoritative handbook for UN peacekeepers noted, it "implies undercover activities and the use of covert means for obtaining information about the parties in a dispute."[3] No UN body or Member State has authorized the Secretary-General to gather information using clandestine or illegal means. While information obtained in such a manner might, at various times, be offered by a Member State, the Secretary-General must avoid giving even the impression of deliberate concealment of the methods used in his own information-gathering operations. Transparency in UN methods will always be necessary to maintain confidence and trust in the organization. At the same time a good system to maintain the confidentiality of information is also required.

Instead of "intelligence gathering," the term used in UN circles is "fact-finding," which can be taken as equivalent to information gathering, enquiry, inquiry or investigation.[4] In the *Declaration on UN Fact-Finding*,[5] endorsed by the General Assembly on 9 December 1991, fact-finding is defined as: "any activity designed to obtain detailed knowledge of the relevant facts of any dispute or situation which the competent United Nations organs need in order to exercise their functions." This broad definition gives wide scope to the fact-finding activities of UN bodies, the main limitation arising from the word "facts." Webster's Dictionary defines a fact as a "piece of information presented as having objective reality." A fact can be information about both physical and non-physical entities. This could include, for example, the location of a tank, the government policy or instruction that justifies the deployment of the tank in that position, and the intentions of the leaders in making those policies. Since it is harder to claim "objective reality" about intentions, the Secretary-General often has a limited range of possible fact-finding areas. He must not risk the prestige of his office by making unsubstantiated statements or basing his actions upon rumours or conjecture. Facts need to be supported by evidence. In the practical world of international diplomacy, a fact is a statement that cannot be easily contested.

Facts presented by the Secretary-General have on occasion been disputed, but he is widely regarded as an objective source of information. A criticism more often made about the holders of the office is that they are too cautious in stating the facts, desiring not to offend or alienate any Member State, and careful not to present conclusions that cannot be easily substantiated. Sometimes it is necessary to read between the lines of the conclusions of a UN report to determine where blame lies. The current Secretary-General, however, appears to be less inhibited in this respect and he does, on occasion, make bold and challenging statements to the Security Council and other international bodies.

Ironically, the UN often performs some of its most valuable services when the world knows least about what it is doing. At the early stages, simmering disputes are often not public knowledge and are not covered by the media. At these times, actions by the Secretary-General are often kept secret. If his mission is successful, then there is little or no news; in the event of failed efforts leading to conflict, the events take front page. It is often in situations where disputes have not been the subject of public attention that the Secretary-General's inquiries and actions can be most effective.

Figure 10.1 presents a conceptual view of the fact-finding process, in which information is first collected, then sifted through and analyzed, on a continuous or case-by-case basis, before the facts are established. If there are conflicting claims, as is often the case, then an effort may be made to investigate more thoroughly. In many cases, witnesses must be interviewed, and third parties consulted before a coherent picture is formed. During the process, information must constantly be evaluated to determine if it is relevant to the Secretary-General's mandate. Some information obtained in the course of fact-finding may turn out to be irrelevant, superfluous or even none of the Secretary-General's business. This must be minimized or avoided where possible. The Secretary-General may use fact-finding to assist him in carrying out any variety of functions, as listed in Figure 10.1. The legal and political sources of his authority for fact-finding are also listed.

The 1991 Declaration on UN Fact-Finding

The 1991 *Declaration on UN Fact-Finding* adopted by the General Assembly provides the Secretary-General with an enhanced and explicit mandate for fact-finding that goes beyond the conduct of *ad hoc* missions requested by a state or a UN body for a specific purpose: it encourages him to carry out continuous monitoring for the larger UN goal of maintaining peace. In *Section IV*, the *Declaration* states: "The Secretary-General should monitor the state of international peace and security regularly and systematically in order to provide early warning of disputes or situations which might threaten international peace and security." The *Declaration*, adopted unanimously, represents a milestone in the development of UN fact-finding, especially as it relates to the Secretary-General. After decades of heated debate over the extent of the Secretary-General's authority, including steadfast opposition from the Soviet Union to fact-finding free from the Security Council veto, the Secretary-General has now been given an explicit and wide-ranging mandate to monitor situations as he sees fit.

The *Declaration* stops short of giving the Secretary-General the right to pass legal judgments or assigning blame after establishing the facts. Nevertheless, he will need to analyze gathered information *vis-à-vis* his many responsibilities and to decide on a course of action – some options are listed in Figure 10.1. Under specific resolutions and agreements, the Secretary-General may be given additional authority to interpret an agreement, as well as to establish the facts, in order to verify compliance or even to lay the blame on one state or another.[6] In *Article 99* of the UN *Charter*, he is explicitly authorized to "bring to the attention of the Security Council any matter which in his opinion may threaten international peace and security." The *Article* has seldom been explicitly invoked in the Security Council – relevant cases are described in Table 10.1 – but the Secretaries-General have reasoned that *Article 99* carries with it the power to carry out wide-ranging inquiries and good offices functions, a power that is enhanced by the explicit wording in the *Declaration*.

Uses of Information

Fact-finding may be used before, during and after a conflict. Figure 10.2 presents a conceptual view of the roles of the Secretary-General (or any other entity) in the maintenance of international peace and security. The seven roles, listed in Figure 10.1 and illustrated in Figure 10.2, are based on a chronological view of a generalized conflict.

Ideally, the Secretary-General should be able to detect and defuse a dispute before it ignites into armed combat or escalates to higher levels of intensity. This activity of the Secretary-General, called *preventive diplomacy*, requires early knowledge of developing disputes and the cooperation and good will from involved parties, as well as tacit or formal support from members of the Security Council [see Chapter 8]. In order to minimize the chances that a conflict will erupt, the Secretary-General may request permission from the Security Council to establish a *preventive deployment* of UN peacekeeping forces. One such force was deployed in Macedonia in 1992, in a successful effort to prevent the expansion of conflict in Bosnia and Herzegovina to other volatile regions of the former Yugoslavia. In cases where the Secretary-General feels the necessity of alerting more powerful bodies, he may issue an *early warning* of impending danger to a greater authority such as the Security Council, the General Assembly or certain Member States. Because early knowledge of a conflict has not been readily available in the past, good examples of preventive diplomacy and early warning are hard to come by. Preventive diplomacy was used in resolving the UK-Iranian dispute over Bahrain (1970) and early warning was used to some extent in both the Congo (1960) and the Vietnam War. The Secretary-General's confirmation of aggression in Korea on 25 June 1950, coming a half-day after North Korea launched its attack, is an example of "late" warning, but one which still proved useful in encouraging a prompt and united response from the Security Council. As with Korea, the Secretary-General usually becomes aware of fires once they have been lit for all to see.

In cases of *conflict/crisis management,* he may offer his good offices for conciliation, mediation or facilitation. Often he will send identical letters to the heads of state of the warring parties calling for restraint, as U Thant did during the Cuban Missile Crisis (1962). He may put forward specific proposals for the parties to consider. Important plans were presented by the Secretary-General in the cases of the Status of West Irian (1962-63), the Cuban Missile Crisis (1962), the Congo crisis (1962), the Vietnam War (1965) and the Falkland Islands dispute (1982), among many others. To increase his effectiveness, he often appoints a personal or special representative to gather information in the area, to make contacts with officials and to help him prepare his proposals. When the parties are ready to consider a cease-fire, the Secretary-General may suggest one of the most useful tools to keep armed clashes at bay: peacekeeping. Peacekeeping operations may be set up under Security Council authorization for observation and supervision or to act as a buffer between parties. In both cases the operations serve as confidence-building measures, and can provide a steady stream of information to the Secretary-General as well as allowing diplomats the time to settle the dispute peacefully.

Cessation of fighting is usually not enough to bring enduring peace. The Secretary-General has a duty to resolve the conflict at a deeper level so that fighting does not reoccur. This is *conflict/crisis resolution,* or "peacemaking" as it is sometimes called [see Chapter 8]. It is sometimes a long, painstaking process requiring "patient diplomacy." Examples of recent successes include the independence of Namibia (1989-90), which had been a concern of the United Nations and its predecessor the League of Nations for 70 years, and Central America, where the Secretaries-General have long been active in the transformation of the region. In both regions, the Secretary-General stationed large teams of UN observers to enhance stability during the peacemaking process.

The Security Council has the authority, under *Chapter VII* of the *UN Charter,* to demand and enforce compliance with its decisions. The two main instances of such *enforcement* action were in Korea (1950-53) and Iraq (1990-). The Secretary-General had only a minor role in UN operations during the Korean War, but in the aftermath of the Gulf War he was given significant responsibilities, which included the development of plans for UNSCOM, a Special Commission to inspect and supervise the destruction of Iraq's weapons of mass destruction. UNSCOM collected information using a variety of means, including American U-2 photo reconnaissance aircraft, and also received intelligence reports from nations. After UNSCOM had developed an effective information gathering and analysis system, UNSCOM information was eagerly sought after by these same nations.

Peacebuilding activities are designed to assist states to develop and maintain the infrastructure which is necessary for peace. They include economic and technical aid, assistance through development, education and health programmes [see Chapter 8].

In a given conflict the Secretary-General may proceed from one role to another. The Congo crisis provides a good example. In January 1960 Secretary-General Dag Hammarskjold made a tour of Africa, "characteristically meeting trouble halfway by going out to look at the problems of its emergent states."[7] During his visit to the Belgian Congo and other African nations, he observed the complete inadequacy of preparations for independence. Being anxious about what might happen, and eager to help ease the transition, he dispatched Ralph Bunche, a top Secretariat official, to the Congo. At the Independence Day celebrations on 1 July 1960, Bunche read out the Secretary-General's message, which promised that "the United Nations stands ready, when called upon, to afford the Government of the Congo the fullest measure of [development] assistance." Bunche stayed on to discuss such assistance. Thus Hammarskjold was attempting to play a preventive role. However, chaos broke out within days, with mutinies in garrisons throughout the country and with a secession led by the President of the Katanga province. Belgium dispatched paratroops, against the will of the Congolese leaders, to protect Belgians and other Europeans. The Congolese government cabled the Secretary-General for military assistance. Hammarskjold called for a meeting of the Security Council, where he described the situation and suggested that UN forces be sent, which they were. Thus Hammarskjold, explicitly invoking *Article 99*, played a warning role by bringing the matter to the attention of the Security Council. As the forces were being dispatched, focus shifted to crisis management and "peacemaking." Tragically, Hammarskjold lost his life in a mysterious air crash while travelling in the region to negotiate an end to the crisis. A year later, Acting-Secretary-General U Thant proposed his *Plan of National Reconciliation*, which, after many ups and downs, formed the basis of the final settlement. UN forces were withdrawn from the Congo in 1964, after the Secretary-General observed that law and order had been largely restored.

The Secretary-General's *An Agenda for Peace*

In his 1992 report, *An Agenda for Peace*, Secretary-General Boutros Boutros-Ghali reaffirmed that conflict prevention must be "based on timely and accurate knowledge of the facts" and "an understanding of developments and global trends." He called for increased resort to fact-finding and requested Member States to provide information and promised, "to supplement his own contacts by regularly sending senior officials on missions of consultations in capitals." A group of states, incorporating Australia, Canada, New Zealand and the Nordic countries, made a submission to the Secretary-General in which they pointed out that, "Member States have a duty to inform the United Nations of potential threats to the peace." They further called upon the United Nations," to rationalize and enhance its capacity to collect, analyze and disseminate information" on such threats. The time has now come to move from a recognition of these needs and benefits to institutional implementation of a fact-finding unit within the Secretariat with sufficient resources to gather and analyze wide-ranging information in a timely manner.

Eventually, the Secretary-General should be given broad authority (by the Security Council or by states in an international treaty) to conduct inspections in connection with certain types of disputes in the territories of nations without giving the states the right of refusal. The possibility of an Open Skies regime, using aerial and satellite reconnaissance, under the UN can also be considered for the long term.

Conclusion

Fact-finding can help preventive diplomacy and conflict resolution in a number of ways. First, the mere announcement of a fact-finding mission can ease tensions and lessen false propaganda. Second, the impartial determination of the facts can clarify contentious issues and aid parties to reach agreement. Third, by accepting the conclusions and interpretations of the UN Secretary-General, a nation can save face when it might otherwise not feel capable of accepting the facts, however valid they may be, as presented by an antagonist. Finally, facts reported or publicized by the Secretary-General can allow UN bodies or individual Member States to apply pressure on a delinquent state. The main problem with UN fact-finding is that once the facts are established, there is an expectation and a responsibility for the UN to act, and Member States are not always ready to undertake bold initiatives.

Besides the domain of peace and security, there are other important areas where the Secretary-General has significant fact-finding responsibilities, and where an increase in his fact-finding capability would be beneficial. Many of the points made in this paper can be applied to his activities in the social, economic, humanitarian, human rights and environmental fields.

In anticipating and resolving disputes in the international community, the office of the Secretary-General must have the financial, technical and human resources to gather, process and distribute information on a broad basis. While the track record is impressive, the Secretary-General could do much more if he/she had an autonomous, effective, wide-ranging and timely system for information gathering and analysis. For instance, the possession of advanced observation technologies and resources (including regular satellite imagery of "hot spots")[8] would enhance the quality and quantity of information. A modern data gathering and analysis system within the Secretariat would increase the Secretary-General's capacity for peacekeeping and peacemaking, and allow him to fulfill his new role of regular and systematic monitoring of the state of the world, thereby helping to identify and hopefully resolve threats to international peace and security as they arise.[9]

Notes

1   The number of new UN peacekeeping missions in the field has, for instance, more than doubled in the past five years, and the size and scope of certain missions (like UNTAC in Cambodia) is unprecedented. New roles assumed by the United Nations include supervision of elections in sovereign states and broader, integrated peacekeeping operations. The responsibility of the Security Council for maintaining international peace and security has been given new impetus (as well as presenting new dangers). And in 1991, the Secretary-General was explicitly given new responsibilities in the *Declaration on UN Fact-Finding.*

2   The Secretary-General is now directly involved in virtually every major dispute brought before the United Nations. In the first ten years, he was an important player in only one out of every four disputes. This observation is based on a survey of the disputes listed in Allsebrook, Mary. 1986. *Prototypes of Peacemaking, The First Forty Years of the United Nations* (Longman: Harlow, Essex, UK).

3   International Peace Academy 1984 *Peacekeepers Handbook* (Pergamon Press: New York).

4   The *Charter of the United Nations* uses the term "enquiry" (*Article 33*) while the *Covenant of the League of Nations* uses the term "inquiry" (*Articles 12* and *17*). These synonymous terms suggest that facts are examined, not simply gathered, in order to arrive at conclusions or recommendations. Fact-finding, as used in this paper, is slightly broader: it involves the development of conclusions and recommendations as well as the reporting of results. Fact-finding may incorporate observation and inspection and it is an essential part of supervision and verification.

5   The full title is *Declaration on Fact-Finding by the United Nations in the Field of the Maintenance of International Peace and Security*. The *Declaration* was endorsed in General Assembly resolution 46/59, which was adopted without a vote (*i.e.*, by consensus).

6   This kind of legal discretion is not often given to the Secretary-General in the area of treaties, since the interpretation of treaties is seen as largely the prerogative of sovereign states and the International Court of Justice. However, he is frequently called upon to monitor compliance with resolutions of the Security Council and the General Assembly.

7   *Economist* 2 January 1960 "Mr. Hammarskjold, We Presume."

8   See Dorn, Walter 1987 "Peacekeeping Satellites: The Case for International Surveillance and Verification" *Peace Research Reviews* 10 No. 5/6 (Peace Research Institute – Dundas, Canada.).

9   Since this paper was written, the UN has established a Situation Centre in the Department of Peace-Keeping Operations. The SITCEN functions primarily as a focal point for communications with the UN's peace-keeping missions, but it is gradually developing an information-gathering and analysis capability to use other sources. This is a promising start.

Figure 10.1
From Fact to Act: A Conceptual View of the Procedures and Uses of
Fact-Finding by the UN Secretary-General

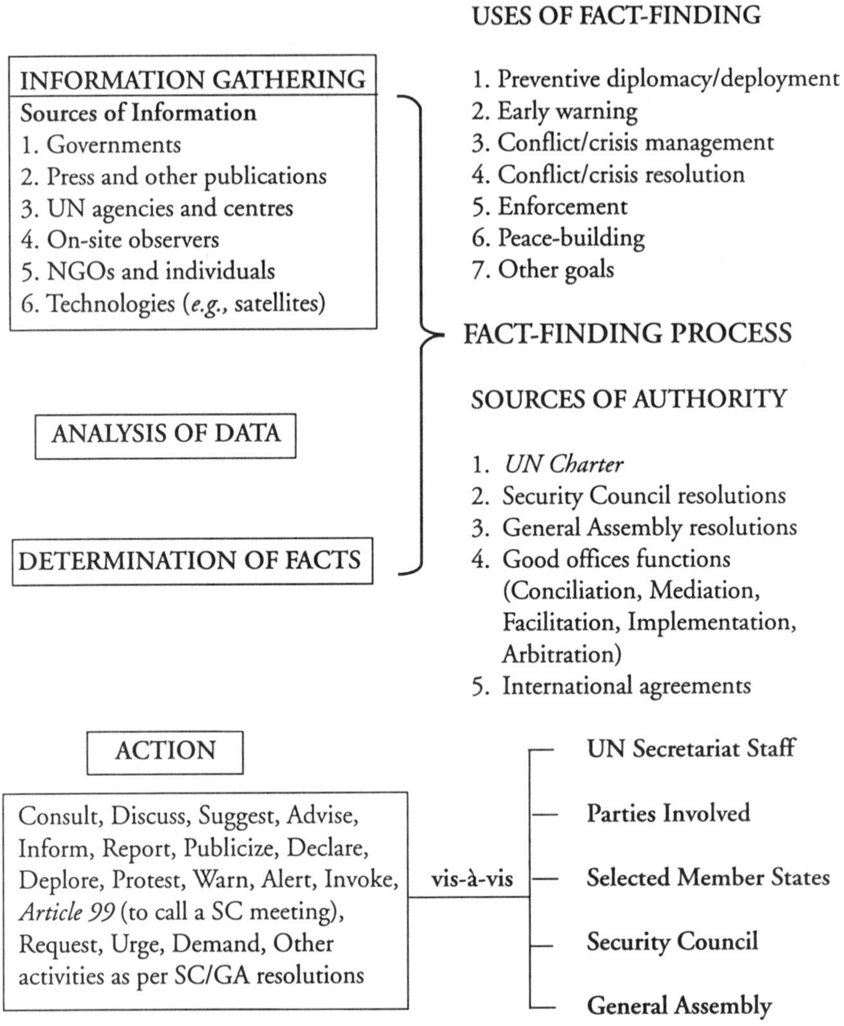

USES OF FACT-FINDING

| INFORMATION GATHERING |
| Sources of Information |

1. Preventive diplomacy/deployment
2. Early warning
3. Conflict/crisis management
4. Conflict/crisis resolution
5. Enforcement
6. Peace-building
7. Other goals

Sources of Information
1. Governments
2. Press and other publications
3. UN agencies and centres
4. On-site observers
5. NGOs and individuals
6. Technologies (*e.g.,* satellites)

FACT-FINDING PROCESS

ANALYSIS OF DATA

SOURCES OF AUTHORITY

1. *UN Charter*
2. Security Council resolutions
3. General Assembly resolutions
4. Good offices functions
   (Conciliation, Mediation,
   Facilitation, Implementation,
   Arbitration)
5. International agreements

DETERMINATION OF FACTS

ACTION

Consult, Discuss, Suggest, Advise,
Inform, Report, Publicize, Declare,
Deplore, Protest, Warn, Alert, Invoke,
Article 99 (to call a SC meeting),
Request, Urge, Demand, Other
activities as per SC/GA resolutions

vis-à-vis

— UN Secretariat Staff

— Parties Involved

— Selected Member States

— Security Council

— General Assembly

Figure 10.2
A Schematic View of the Secretary-General's Roles in the Field of Peace
and Security, as They Relate to the Stages and Intensity
(with Sample Profile) of Conflict

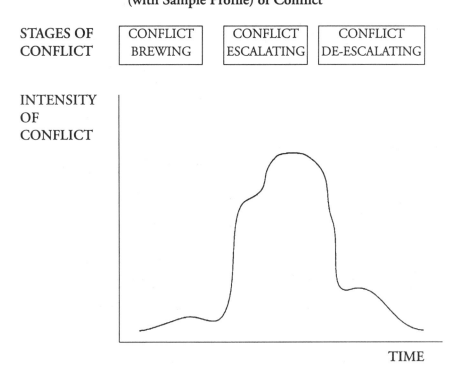

| STAGES OF CONFLICT | CONFLICT BREWING | CONFLICT ESCALATING | CONFLICT DE-ESCALATING |

INTENSITY OF CONFLICT

TIME

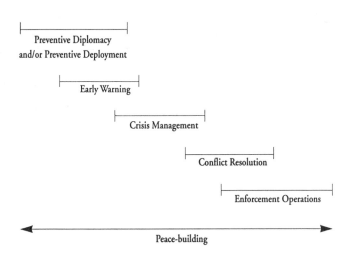

SECRETARY-GENERAL'S ACTIVITIES

Preventive Diplomacy and/or Preventive Deployment

Early Warning

Crisis Management

Conflict Resolution

Enforcement Operations

Peace-building

Table 10.1
The Secretary-General Alerts the Security Council

This table describes the instances, from the foundation of the United Nations up to the end of 1991 when the Secretary-General (SG) has brought to the attention of the Security Council (SC) matters that in his opinion may pose a threat to international peace and security. Thus, the Secretary-General exercised the substance of the responsibilities conferred upon him by *Article 99* of the *UN Charter*. *Article 99* states: "The Secretary-General may bring to the attention of the Security Council any matter which in his opinion may threaten international peace and security." In preparing this table the following criterion, broader than those conventionally used to classify an invocation of *Article 99*, were used: (1) the Secretary-General must be the first to address the issue formally in the Council *or* be the first to call for a meeting (but not necessarily both) and (2) he/she must announce the existence of a threat to the peace. The criteria for a formal, explicit invocation of *Article 99* are narrower, and this has occurred only three times, arising from the crises in the Congo (1960), Iran (1979) and Lebanon (1989).

Secretary-General	*Meeting Date/Situation*	*Description*
Trygve Lie (1946-53)	25 Jun 1950: North Korea attacks South Korea. USA notifies SG of attack. SG obtains independent confirmation and details of attack from the UN Commission on Korea.	At an emergency SC meeting, requested by the US (and boycotted by the former Soviet Union), SG speaks first, stating that "military actions have been undertaken by North Korean forces" which were a "direct violation" of General Assembly resolution 293 (IV) and of the *UN Charter*. He said that the situation was "a threat to international peace ... I con sider it the clear duty of the SC to take steps necessary to re-establish peace in that area." SC passes resolutions con deming attack as breach of the peace. On 27 June, SC calls upon UN Members to furnish assistance to repel the attack. [Lie, pp. 323-33]
Dag Hammarskjöld (1953-61)	7 Sep 1959: Laos alleges Vietnamese aggression and requests SG to send an	SG asks SC President to "convene urgently" a SC meeting, which President does under his own authority. USA desires to introduce a draft resolution to establish a fact-finding body as a proce dural matter, and thus avoid Soviet veto. At meeting, SG states he is not invoking *Article 99*, which would cause matter to

be considered substantial, but is only reporting to SC on agenda item introduced by SC President. He states that he has insufficient knowledge to make judgement as to the facts. US draft resolution is carried, over Soviet objections, and fact-finding Committee is established. Committee reports indicate that Lao allegations are over stated. No UN force is sent. [UNYB 1959, pp. 62-65]

13 Jul 1960: Congolese government cables SG with a request for UN military assistance against Belgian paratroops. These had been dispatched to protect Belgian interests (including inhabitants) in the former colony. The country is in chaos.

SG requests urgent meeting of the SC for that evening on "a matter which, in my opinion, may threaten international peace and security." At meeting, he recommends a UN force be sent to Congo, so that Belgian forces could be withdrawn and to prevent other countries (esp. former Soviet Union) from sending troops. SC authorizes him to send the UN force. ONUC, which at its peak numbers about 20,000 troops, is established to help keep law and order. [Cordier & Foote, vol. V, pp. 16-27; UN Docs. S/4381, S/PV.873]

22 Jul 1961: Fighting intensifies around Bizerta, Tunisia, between French forces (which occupy the city) and Tunisian soldiers and civilians. Tunisia had blockaded the French naval base at Bizerta.

At the second SC meeting dealing with the Bizerta question, SG speaks to SC: "News reaching us from Tunisia indicates that the serious and threatening development which the Council took up for consideration yesterday continues, with risks of irreparable damage to international peace and security." In view of the "obligations of the Secretary-General acting under *Article 99*", he appeals to SC to make an immediate call for cease-fire and return of all armed forces to original positions. SC adopts a resolution with these provisions by vote of 10-0, with France refusing to participate. [Cordier & Foote, vol. V, pp. 526-530]

U Thant
(1962-71)

29 Apr 1963: The Imam of Yemen is deposed in a *coup d'état* by republicans. The UAR recognizes new regime, while Saudi Arabia supports the Imam. Fighting breaks out. UAR sends troops.

SG informs SC of his initiatives to ensure against "any development in the situation which might threaten the peace in the area." Explains that the three parties have agreed to the stationing of a UN observer mission (UNYOM) and will pay for it. UNYOM is established to observe disengagement and withdrawal of foreign forces, including supervision of a demilitarized zone. At 11 June 1963 meeting Thant warns that "disengagement may be jeopardized if the United Nations observation personnel are not on the spot." SC passes resolution approving observation force, which conducts operations until 4 Sep 1964. [Cordier & Foote, vol. VI, pp. 328-30]

20 Jul 1971: Awami League declares the independence of East Pakistan in March 1971. Pakistani President Yahya Khan requests army to suppress independence activities, resulting in bloodshed. U Thant maintains almost daily contact with India and Pakistan but refrains from calling SC meeting because both sides consider the conflict an internal matter.

SG distributes a confidential memorandum to SC members, "warning them that the conflict could all too easily expand, erupting the entire subcontinent in fratricidal strife, and that the UN must now attempt to mitigate the tragedy." The memorandum was made public in August. SG describes it as "an implied invocation of *Article 99*." Yet SC does not meet in emergency session until the Indo-Pakistan War begins on 3 December, four months after SG's warning. SC is unable to decide on action. SG confines himself to the humanitarian aspects of the problem, including the organization of international aid for refugees in India. [U Thant, p. 423]

Kurt Waldheim
(1972-81)

16 Jul 1974: Cyprus crisis is ignited when Greek Cypriot National Guard stages a *coup d'état* on 15 July against President Makarios, who flees from the Island.

SG requests SC President to convene an emergency meeting, in view of the seriousness of the matter in relation to international peace and security and in view of the UN involvement in Cyprus. The permanent representative of Cyprus also requests meeting. SC endorses continued UN peacekeeping efforts and authorizes SG to attempt to mediate the dispute. However, it was only on 20 July, the day of the Turkish intervention that the Security Council passed a resolution calling for a cease-fire. [UNYB 1974, p. 262]

30 Mar 1976 & 16 Mar 1978: Syria deploys troops in Lebanon in Spring 1976 in an effort to end civil war. In March 1978 Israel retaliates against PLO bus attack by invading southern Lebanon.

In both cases, SG brings to the attention of the Security Council the gravity of the situation in Lebanon, transmits the communicatons that he has received, and offers his good offices. [UN Chronicle, Apr 1976 and Apr 1978]

4 Dec 1979: US Embassy in Tehran is invaded by revolutionary students on 4 Nov 1979, with support of Iran's new government. On 9 Nov, after consultations, SC President calls for the release of the hostages.

SG writes to SC President on 25 Nov 1979 drawing attention to the continuing crisis and requesting SC meeting, saying that it was his opinion that the crisis posed a threat to international peace and security. SC meets formally on 27 Nov. SG speaks first, calling upon the USA and Iran to exercise maximum restraint. In resolution of 4 Dec SC calls for release of hostages, restoration of diplomatic immunities and authorizes SG to "take all appropriate measures" to implement the resolution. On 31 Dec 1979 he travels to Tehran. The Iranian government paints his visit as a fact-finding mission to examine cruelties of the Shah's regime. SGs four-point proposal is rejected and he returns empty handed. [UNYB 1979, pp. 307-312; S/13646]

26 Sep 1980: From mid-May to mid-Sep SG receives accusations fromboth Iran & Iraq, indicating a deteriorating situation. Iraq invades Iran on 22 Sep, beginning the Iran-Iraq war. SG appeals to both parties on 22 & 23 Sep for restraint and a negotiated settlement.

SG states in letter to SC President (25 Sep), that fighting had intensified and that the situation undoubtedly threatened international peace & security. SG suggests SC consultations. Mexico and Norway request formal meeting of SC. At meeting on 26 Sep, SG summarizes developments leading to the meeting. SC adopts resolution 479 (1980) calling for a cease-fire and urging parties to accept mediation or conciliation. [S/14196; UNYB 1980, pp. 312-314]

| Javier Pérez de Cuéllar (1982-91) | 15 Aug 1989: Fighting in Lebanon escalates, especially in and around Beirut. There is danger of even further involvement of outside parties. | In a letter to the SC President, the SG notes that violence in and around Beirut "had escalated to a level unprecedented in fourteen years of conflict." He states his belief that an effective cease-fire is imperative: "in my opinion, the present crisis poses a serious threat to international peace and security. Accordingly, in the exercise of my responsibility under the *Charter* of the United Nations, I ask that the Security Council be convened urgently ..." [S/20789] Meeting is held ... |

References for Table 10.1
Cordier, Andrew W., and Wilder Foote, eds. 1969-1974. *Public Papers of the Secretaries-General of the United Nations*, vols. I-IV (Columbia University Press: New York).
Lie, Trygve. 1954. *In the Cause of Peace: Seven Years with the United Nations* (MacMillan: New York).
U Thant. 1978. *View from the United Nations* (Doubleday & Co. Garden City: New York).
Repertory of Practice of the United Nations Organs, vols. I-VI, with supplementscovering period 1946-1978 (United Nations: New York), 1956- .
UNYB (United Nations Year Book) (United Nations: New York), 1946.

CHAPTER 11

A United Nations Peace Force

Arnold Simoni

If the United Nations is to fulfil its mission as set forth in the *Preamble* and *Chapter I* of its *Charter*, it will have to be thoroughly reformed. Its first priority should be the formation of an effective and viable Peace Force. Without such a force at its disposal, the UN cannot assure the conditions essential to make and maintain peace. Solutions have to be found for overcoming the difficulties identified below, if the UN is to fulfil its peacekeeping mission:

(1) **Sovereignty:** The creation of a Peace Force as an effective arm of the UN will necessarily entail some degree of infringement of national sovereignty. This, it may be argued, is already the case with decisions taken by the Security Council in the name of the UN Security Council. These decisions are, however, often the outcome of pressure wielded by a bloc or by individual nations. Thus, it is not the United Nations itself that infringes upon the sovereignty of nations, but rather those nations that exert political pressure on the Security Council. In these cases it is questionable whether such decisions have contributed to the establishment of lasting peace, while at other times the UN failed altogether to take action when the situation called for a collective response.

(2) **A Reformed International Court of Justice:** To establish the rights and limitations of the UN Peace Force, a code of international law will be required, and the parties responsible for implementing them will also have to be clearly defined. This code furthermore will determine the framework under which the UN Peace Force could and should intervene. Such a reformed International Court will have to be neutral. To be effective, it will also have to be swift in arriving at its rulings and be equally swift in implementing its decisions.

(3) **Military Peace Force and Its Responsibilities:** An essential element for establishing a UN Peace Force will be the establishment of a model demonstrating how a military department at the UN might

work. Such a department would be responsible for the recruitment, arming, training and stationing of the Peace Force. The military section would also make decisions concerning the cost-effective deployment of the Peace Force. This would be especially important at times when a number of simultaneous conflicts might present a situation beyond the total capacity of its forces.

(4) **Personnel:** The Peace Force should comprise volunteers. They will have to renounce their nationality for the period of their service, which might be about two years. The Peace Force might be modelled in some respects after the French Foreign Legion.

(5) **Funding:** Funding for the military forces, including armament and operational costs, will have to be obtained through taxes, which should be imposed on all nations in proportion to their wealth. These contributions will, to a degree, represent a partial transfer of expenditures that are now allocated to national defence budgets; the existence of an effective UN Peace Force would enable nations to reduce their own military forces, and with it their defence budgets. A possible source of armament would be the arms rendered surplus by national military forces. Nations making such contributions would receive appropriate credit for them. The military department of the United Nations will determine the need and the value of such contributions.

(6) **Checks and Balances:** To prevent the misuse of UN forces, checks and balances will have to be clearly defined and imposed. The increase in military power required to make the Peace Force effective will also make it dangerous if misdirected.

(7) **Other Ramifications:** The creation of an effective and credible peacemaking and peacekeeping force will also entail some changes in the Security Council and the General Assembly, as well as the Permanent Secretariat of the United Nations.

(8) **The Need for Political and Economic Stability:** Studies have demonstrated that authoritarian regimes, human rights abuses and poverty are contributing factors to political destabilization, upheavals and conflicts. These factors need to be considered to forestall conflicts and wars.

These are the major problem areas inherent in the creation of a workable and credible United Nations Peace Force. Because the changes required are so profound, it might be argued that one will have to wait for action until cataclysmic crisis conditions occur that undermine the *status quo*. However, long before the conclusion of World War II, nations were willing to think of new ways for avoiding future wars, namely the United Nations Organization. When it was formally instituted in 1946, however, the urgency and importance of forming a viable United Nations Organization was inadequately considered. After two years of intense negotiations, the "Realpolitiks" overcame the "Idealists." The latter were persuaded that, with the formation of such a body, humankind could in the future control conflicts and maintain peace. The *Preamble* and *Chapter I* of the *UN Charter* does in fact declare that the purpose of the organization is the avoidance of war and maintenance of peace. The *Charter* has, however, not provided the means to achieve such an ambitious goal.

With the radically changing world conditions and the proliferation of weapons of mass destruction, it has become essential that we return to the basic problem: how can the UN become viable in the context of real politics? We certainly cannot wait until breakdown and war occur before making the necessary changes, especially since it is not even clear what kind of changes are necessary to make the UN workable. It is crucial to analyze and study the problems now. One hopes and expects that positive and acceptable methods of resolving the difficulties can be found. A comprehensive study and research project to investigate the problem areas might contribute to the prevention of future collapse of the international order and help right now to reduce conflict and avoid war.

The United Nations, backed by a strong and viable Peace Force, would be able to solve current and future security problems. The failure to address these problems, however, would condemn the UN to the same fate as that of the League of Nations in the 1930s. If we believe that the necessary changes are unattainable, then we should "reform" the UN by eliminating the *Preamble* and *Chapter I* of its *Charter*, thereby limiting its work to issues like human rights, health, cultural cooperation, concern about the environment, and similar matters. This would end the illusion that the United Nations, as presently constituted, can contribute to the establishment and maintenance of lasting peace around the globe.

CHAPTER 12

Law, Politics and United Nations Enforcement of Peace

K. Venkata Raman

In 1945 the world community established the United Nations with the explicit purpose of undertaking a collective responsibility for international peace and security. This collective responsibility was enshrined in *Chapter VII* of the *Charter of the United Nations* and became pragmatically the only choice open, given the political situation created by the advent of nuclear weapons. No nation is secure unless the whole world is secure. This fundamental common interest obliges states not to resort to use of force except in self defence, and to take collective decisions to punish violators of *Charter* principles. Such activities must be conducted in accordance with a rule of law acceptable to all nations. Further, it was understood that the system created by the *Charter* must be used in an inclusive, non-discriminatory manner. There was great suspicion that selectively chosen precepts of convenience or narrowly perceived national self interest, if allowed to influence the common front against tyranny and aggression, would damage the authority of the UN itself. The traditional right of states to resort to use of force is specifically limited to the narrow context of individual or collective self defence, as indicated in *Article 51* of the *Charter*, and the principal responsibility for determining the lawfulness of such actions is assigned to the UN itself.

During the four decades of Cold War, superpower rivalry prevented this collective system from becoming operational, and the attendant process therefore remained dormant. That did not alter the juridical character of the system, nor its underlying legal principles. Indeed, it is a measure of the *jus cogens* quality of the norm against aggression that the *Charter* requires even non-members to comply with its mandate. The recent political changes in Eastern Europe and the former Soviet Union created unwarranted optimism that the operational matrix of the UN collective security system might be used in its present form to serve its intended purpose. The success of the UN-endorsed coalition action in the Gulf War no doubt has raised hopes that the UN process might now become effective to play its intended role. While this favourable turn in the global security process is to be applauded, the basic objectives of the *Charter*, and the principles of international law governing the rights and obligations of sovereign states remain unchanged.

Concerns about the rule of law remind us of some basic tenets which have great influence on any impartial third party process. These require that decisions affecting peace and security be made by the UN system in accordance with established procedures, and not in a selective, secretive or opportunistic manner. Deference to such basic principles as the sovereign equality, independence and territorial integrity of Member States may limit the situations appropriate for collective action, especially when it is initiated under the auspices of the UN. The objective of all external interventions must normally be directed towards peaceful resolution of disputes, with sensitive human rights issues handled fairly and in a consistent and non-intrusive manner. Have any of these objectives changed now?

It is necessary to ask this question because the decision-making process of the Security Council is not inclusive as it is at present constituted; the major powers still call the shots and only one or two of them possess the wherewithal to enforce UN decisions. This political reality is not the only one likely to stifle the ability of the UN to make objective and democratic decisions. The UN system has become vulnerable to misuse through unilateral interpretations of its decisions by the dominant powers in the Security Council. This factor poses a far greater danger than an inactive UN to its institutional integrity, and thus to its authority, as an impartial third party institution. Why is this prospect so alarming to the future integrity of the organization? What is so wrong in allowing it to play on a purely *ad hoc* basis the global policing and corrective or sanctioning functions? This paper is intended to canvass the reasons why notions of the rule of law are of fundamental importance to UN decision process. While it does not pretend to offer any definitive solutions, its purpose is to alert the reader to the dangers present if these considerations are not addressed in some manner.

The UN is not just a voluntary organization of sovereign states. Neither admission to, nor withdrawal, from the UN is really any longer at the discretion of any state. The UN has become, in the expectations of "the Peoples of the United Nations", in whose name its *Charter* was proclaimed, a lot more than a ritual assembly of Heads of State and Foreign Ministers convened every September. There now exists an impressive array of international non-governmental and private organizations and pressure groups, whose views influence UN deliberations and significantly affect its decisions.

Both the constitutive policies sustaining a global authority structure, and the consensually structured operational arrangements through which these policies must be maintained, demand respect. The recent trend to invite UN involvement in some internal conflict situations appears, however, to be of a character not anticipated by the founders of the UN system. Lately most disputes inviting international attention have included largely ethnic, religious and nationalistic conflicts arising within the internal political arena of individual states. The *ad hoc* nature of the "enforcement" measures mounted for them, sometimes with little consideration of available alternatives, appears to worsen the relations between the fighting factions, thus compromising the above stated objectives of the UN.

It must be remembered that the UN is not an independent political actor, because its decisions, including those made under *Chapter VII*, are essentially the result of major power agreement and decision. Even then they are limited to specific outcomes in such situations, and cannot usually create policies of broad general scope. In any case, they cannot reflect any strong consensus of the UN system as a whole, even when agreement among the key power-brokers to enforce peace is found to exist. The new opportunity to engage the UN in decision making affecting the internal dynamics of states, unless carefully circumscribed, is likely to exacerbate rather than resolve the tensions within unstable political communities. When decisions to involve the UN in such situations are made, the authorization for individual members to use "all necessary measures" to restore order, if not simultaneously accompanied by vigorous activities on the diplomatic and political fronts, is likely to be counterproductive in practice. The inability of the UN system to establish and supervise effectively a common "command and control structure", with final authority exercised by the UN to ensure the implementation of its enforcement decisions, as envisaged by *Chapter VII* of the *Charter*, has unavoidably resulted in misuse of power by the *de facto* forces in charge of the operations. There appears in recent practice some intentional fudging of the assigned third party roles by the Security Council, when authorizing specific functions, as to whether they are labelled peace observation, peacekeeping, peacemaking or enforcement: this results in some confusion of the scope of the *Charter* obligations of Member States.

In the absence of agreed UN policies to influence the specific outcomes in a conflict, general international law and the *Charter* principles must be deemed to govern the legitimacy of UN action. What is proscribed for individual states in their inter-state relations is likewise prohibited when the relevant actions emanate from the authority of the Security

Council or from the Secretary-General of the UN. While general international law governs the responsibility of states for their conduct, and they may even be brought to account for their actions before other fora, such as the International Court of Justice, the Security Council's decisions under *Chapter VII* of the *Charter* are not liable to such a review. [See Chapter 19.] Nevertheless, in the final analysis, the authority of UN actions and the lawfulness of its decision-making process in particular situations cannot but be affected by these considerations.

The *Report* of the Secretary-General of the UN entitled *An Agenda for Peace* provided a valuable summary of the prospects for an active UN role in the cause of peace. An active Security Council role in resolving internal conflicts is called for. However, if in pursuit of UN goals an authorization to "enforce" peace is handed over to a small group who have shown some interest in providing the necessary muscle, there must be proper checks and balances to ensure that its members will be allowed to use only the means necessary to achieve the desired outcome. The "Charter System" is a term that embraces not just the enforcement provisions of *Chapter VII* of the *Charter*, but refers also to other contingent obligations of Member States, and permits in *Article 51* use of force in self-defence, either individually or in concert. That contingency, although present in *Chapter VII*, is, however, outside the "enforcement system" of the UN itself. This vital difference cannot be obfuscated by invoking the legitimizing shield of the Security Council, no matter how compelling a justification is present in individual situations for the use of armed force. The latter falls outside the norm of collective responsibility of the UN, and therefore does not entail Member States' obligations under *Articles 25* and *103* of the *Charter* read together. In other words, a blanket authorization cannot serve to justify indefinitely all use of such force, which must be authorized in each instance by the Security Council. During the past four decades, when the Security Council has often been paralyzed, the traditional collective self-defence system under customary international law has permitted resort to use of force.

The post-Cold War scenario has not only altered the dynamics of UN decision-making, but has opened floodgates to claims of self-determination, thus rekindling long-suppressed desires of minority groups within multicultural communities for recognition as autonomous and separate independent nations. The fundamental *Charter* principles of "territorial integrity" and "self determination" appear to coexist uneasily, and indeed may at first glance appear to contradict each other, but they are not antithetical legal notions. They are complementary norms of the international legal system. In almost all legal systems, fundamental legal principles occur in pairs of complementary opposites. Striking an acceptable balance in any particular situation depends upon of its context and cannot remain absolute. In the case of UN action, it will be impossible to escape inconsistencies in practice among the various situations considered by the Security Council, with a positive response in some conflict situations and inaction in others. The post-Cold War world may appear tempting for the UN to initiate collective action by the use of force, but it is unlikely to be disciplined by the forces of the Security Council alone, as it is presently constituted, or by any coalition of like-minded countries, in the absence of some legitimate authorization embodying a collective consensus endorsed by the majority of Member States of the UN. There is undoubtedly a clear need to contain violence even when it does not pose a serious threat to international peace and security. But it is a very different thing to say that the Security Council of the UN, as it is presently constituted, is the proper instrument for that purpose.

The uncertainty of the political situation in pluralistic societies, mentioned above, is aggravated further by the unsatisfactory nature of the mandates emanating from the Security Council to achieve peace through the use of force. The reasons for this are obvious: the voluntary character of the operations; open-ended authorizations to Member States to "utilize all necessary means" for achieving broadly defined and sometimes loosely stated outcomes; and the absence of any central command and control structure to police the day-to-day functioning of such operations. In some instances these deficiencies have made the UN enforcement mechanism both improper under the *Charter* law and counterproductive in real practical terms.

The tensions between "domestic autonomy" of sovereign states on the one hand and the upsurge of "micro-nationalism" on the other, evident especially in many recent situations of conflict, seem a lot more complex than the academic literature or international practice is prepared to acknowledge. They all pose essentially two inter-related problems that demand fundamentally different approaches for their effective management. The first is clearly the human rights dimension which, thanks to the modern technology of instant global communication, can no longer be hidden by any nation, or claimed as its private matter. Yet, unless the human rights situation within a country reaches the scale and proportion of a serious threat to international peace and security, not much can be done by the UN system as it is presently constituted. It can neither offer any useful assistance nor play a positive role in resolving the underlying conflicts. That does not imply that the international community should abandon its collective security interest, or not attempt to contain the effects of the conflict to minimize the loss of life and suffering.

The second feature of the micro-nationalism conflict relates to the particular outcomes that the parties involved are willing to accept. The international community may have a direct interest in the end result, although thus far such a concern has rarely been manifested. The issue here can be framed thus: What are the outer limits of a claim for self-determination that the UN system is willing to support, even if necessary by the use of force? According to traditional international law, the fact that a significant threat, or even a massive violation, of some fundamental human rights is occurring in a country fighting ethnic, linguistic or religious minorities claiming self determination is in itself no blanket invitation for UN "intervention" in that country's domestic affairs. Besides concerns of national integrity, any adventurist intervention is likely to fuel further unrest, and give rise to more irredentist claims. Secretary-General Boutros Boutros-Ghali has warned that the result might be an increase in UN membership by a factor of two or three. That is, of course, not a valid argument for the world community to ignore human suffering. A more liberal, human rights-driven perspective, on the other hand, advocates the use of "humanitarian intervention" in an extreme case, thus internationalizing the process of secession, perhaps against the wishes of the majority of the population.

This dilemma cannot be resolved by positing the relevant issues in such extreme terms. The notion that "humanitarian relief operations" can be distinguished and therefore managed separately from the traditional instances of "humanitarian intervention" will be difficult to maintain indefinitely. *An Agenda for Peace* appears to suggest that the changed post-Cold War context is now conducive for an active UN role in internal conflicts. The international community's primary interest in the use of force in such situations does not arise unless massive human rights violations exist, leading to serious threats to international peace and security. Involvement in internal affairs to minimize serious breaches of peace, or to provide active peacemaking aimed at seeking a solution to such internal problems, would require extensive peacebuilding efforts, calling for very different kinds of resources and diplomatic skills. These are unlikely to be made available to the UN by Member States unless it is in their immediate national interest.

Considerations such as these suggest that the proposed reforms of the UN system must include not only the study of procedural issues, such as internal reorganization of administration and restructuring the Security

Council, but also, more importantly, a reconsideration of the fundamental legal principles of the *Charter*, and of general international law, in relation to the peacemaking tasks in specific conflict situations. Consider for instance the Middle East peace process, and imagine the worth of any settlement negotiations which downplay, if not ignore, the fundamental norm that belligerent occupation or a population transfer confers no sovereign right to the territory. The issue of "illegal settlements" may be papered over for temporary political gain, but can be ignored only at peril. Or for that matter, consider the issue of "self determination" and the establishment of a new Kurdistan in the Turkey-Iraq border region. An opportunity opened up in the fallout of the Gulf War to establish "safe havens" by the use of force. Yet it seems manifestly discriminatory to differentiate between the two Kurdish minorities in Iraq and Turkey, who are both clamouring for the same outcome. Examination of the internal political situations causing "local disorders" in Angola, Mozambique, Sudan, Somalia, Haiti and in many of the newly established nations from the former Soviet Union all present difficult social, political and ethnic problems that make the choices of the relevant legal norms difficult, if not arbitrary. Not all of them can be resolved by demonstrating "military muscle", as has been suggested. The political process of nation building in many of these cases is very fragile and international law must extend its protection to all relevant legal claims in such situations.

In addition to substantive legal considerations of the kind mentioned above, UN reform should be mindful also of procedures used for providing its peacekeeping/peacemaking assistance. Some of these considerations may be briefly summarized:

(1) Where serious political unrest among distinct minority groups clamouring for self-determination presents itself as a source of violence, it is imperative for the UN system as a whole – not just the new *entente cordiale* of the Permanent Members of the Security Council – to engage in active peacemaking. The tragic experiences of recent UN peacekeeping/peacemaking in such conflict situations as Somalia, Haiti and in the former Yugoslavian state of Bosnia, to name only a few, suggest the need to show prudence when personnel from Permanent Members of the Council are posted to enforce Security Council's decisions.

(2) Peacekeeping assistance, which is always the result of mutual consent of all the parties involved, should be made available along with the necessary peacemaking assistance. However, the one role cannot be

allowed to slide into the other through coercion or threats of use of military force.

(3) The composition and structure of peacekeeping forces, even when these are engaged in distributing only humanitarian relief assistance, should reflect sensitivity to ethnic, religious and political concerns in the region. The high visibility of the Permanent Members, given the political baggage they convey, may not always be conducive to the realization of the goals set by the UN.

(4) Enforcement of Security Council decisions through the use or threat of military force may be unavoidable in some situations, but is no substitute for effective peacemaking. In both the Gulf War and recently in Bosnia use of such a force, endorsed by the UN, helped to achieve the short term goals. In other situations where general consensus within the UN system (not just in the Security Council) is not clear or is at best vague, the Secretary-General has a duty to consult with a wider segment of key nations in the General Assembly. The dynamics of war-making through a general, omnibus Security Council endorsement, is not always the answer. Formalism aside, the absence of veto does not now signify full agreement even of the Permanent Members.

(5) It is imperative that institutions implementing such far-reaching decisions affecting political independence and territorial integrity of states be open, accessible and inclusive, and that their processes be as transparent as possible, and the Secretary-General should ensure that the mandates are properly and fairly exercised in practice.

(6) The Secretary-General must ensure that the authority and prestige of the UN system should not be used in a manner compromising the fundamental principles of the *Charter* and general international law. It is part of his independent role, under *Article 99* of the *Charter*, to ensure that efforts are made to promote greater resort to the International Court of Justice for advice where controversial decisions steam-rollered through the Security Council in panic or haste appear to compromise such legal principles, even though a serious threat to international peace and security may demand a quick decision.

(7) Consensual peacekeeping can, under appropriate circumstances, lead to peacebuilding and even provide an opportunity for active peacemaking. Yet during the past four decades of Cold War, the UN has rarely been allowed, or even seemed able, to play such a positive role. Recall the resolution of disputes such as the Indus waters between India and Pakistan, the Bahrain situation between Iran and the

United Kingdom, or the Trieste dispute between Italy and former Yugoslavia – to name only a few – which demonstrate the strength of an active third party role in peacemaking. The UN's primary function is not to perfect its enforcement muscle, but to explore its usefulness as an agent for change and peace. *An Agenda for Peace* offers few insights into how non-governmental and private agencies, institutions and individuals may be enlisted towards this end. The potential role and the authority of the organization in these areas is unexplored and therefore requires fresh thinking and innovative action.

PART IV

HUMAN RIGHTS

Commentary on Part IV
Craig Scott

A common theme unites the two chapters in Part IV: human rights, the UN, and the politics of inclusion – that is, the need rigorously and systematically to make questions of representation and participation central to the collective project of giving effective content to the concept of human rights within the institutional order of the United Nations. In turn, each paper can be read as cohering with a broader tendency within late 20th century social movements, at least in North America, to struggle to give content to the ideal of the *universal* moral worth of every person through a critical focus on the need to inject the *particularity* of experience of and perspectives on the world into the processes (social, political, legal and economic) and institutions that have the power to influence or dictate the allocation of entitlements and responsibilities in the name of various conceptions of justice. Within this frame of reference, the universality of human rights as a substantive commitment involves a procedural corollary, namely that the elaboration and implementation of the substantive content of human rights requires an ethic of universal inclusion of persons or their representatives in the institutional processes that give concrete shape to what human rights mean. The democratic premise is that more inclusive process will generate (more) just substantive outcomes. The result of this approach is that a critique of human rights concepts, doctrine or machinery fuses with a critique that focuses on the question of which actors and sectors of society control the process of making human rights a reality. Who is in and who is out? Whose self-image and partial interests become hegemonic in the name of a universal ideal? These are the forms of inquiry that characterise much of fin de siècle critical discourse and community-based political and social movements. In the Western world, such discourse has come to be variously labelled, in pejorative terms by some and in empowered terms by others, as the "politics of difference", the "politics of recognition", the "politics of identity" and the "politics of voice". For present purposes, I shall refer to the politics of inclusion.

Yet, it is important to note that neither of the following papers privileges procedural inclusiveness over substantive commitment; rather, the latter conditions the former. If we know that the world (including the world of the UN) is organised in such a way that certain perspectives are privileged, the call for inclusion appeals to the ideal of universality that is being compromised as the basis for an imperative need to introduce a kind of counter-privileging energy into the system. In this sense, we can justify a notion of the priority of perspectives as structured by an over-all substantive commitment to the elimination of suffering, of intolerance, of cruelty. Those who we have every reason to believe disproportionately endure suffering, bear the brunt of intolerance and are subjected to cruelty are the ones whose voices not only should be heard in an act of levelling the playing field but also should be given priority on the basis that they know of what they speak.

Laurie Wiseberg, as the director of Human Rights Internet, was an active and tireless participant in the event that she critically describes in her paper, the *World Conference on Human Rights* held in Vienna in the summer of 1993. She discusses a number of different relationships defined in terms of inclusion/exclusion, including the fascinating debate over whether Australia should be identified as a part of the Western (and Other) regional group or part of the Asia Group. She also alludes to, while not discussing in detail, the fundamental inside/outside dynamic that characterized the entire Vienna Conference. According to this dynamic, Non-Governmental Organisations (NGOs) convened in one part of the UN complex (downstairs) and state delegations in a separate part (upstairs). This prompts Wiseberg's wonderfully evocative metaphorical sub-title of "Upstairs and Downstairs: Everything a UN World Conference Ought Not to Be". This architectural insider/outsider split level arrangement was subsequently replicated in the way in which the final *Vienna Declaration and Programme of Action* was drafted, namely in closed session open only to states (and representatives of various UN bodies) and barred to NGO representatives.

The most extensive and significant discussion by Wiseberg of the politics of inclusion pertains to the way in which such a politics played itself out within the organisation of the *NGO Forum* at which marginalized NGOs (mainly from Southern grassroots organisations) "wanted and demanded more than token participation" and succeeded in prompting a kind of people's revolution "which forced the Joint Planning Committee [the organising body for the NGO Forum] to resign and led to the election of a new and more representative NGO Liaison Committee...". As Wiseberg puts it, the leaders of many established NGOs who currently take up so much of the space in giving content to human rights from the non-state sphere "believe[d] they kn[e]w best because they regularly walk the UN corridors". Wiseberg's critique of the capacity of the human rights movement itself to reproduce patterns of exclusion and subordination that are mirrored in relations between states (North/South) and in transnational societal relations generally (rich/poor) is a sobre reminder that 'human rights', as with all abstract concepts that seek to project a progressive message (equality, freedom, justice, dignity, community), are not self-defining. They are intimately bound up in the social production of knowledge from which claims of truth are generated. In this regard, Wiseberg's paper goes far in dispelling a complacent belief that the simple inclusion of more NGO participation and representation within the UN institutional order is, unproblematically, a good thing. Instead, we must be aware that indiscriminate inclusion in many instances serves only to reinforce privileged perspectives about what count as human rights and as human rights violations.

Shirley Farlinger's paper nicely complements that of Laurie Wiseberg in her emphasis on the exclusion of women in all facets of the international order. As she puts it, "when women look at this new era they find themselves largely invisible in decision-making bodies, both global and local". Her paper opens with the reminder that "women" have been implicitly excluded from the "human" in the real world of human rights. The lack of representation and participation of women at every stage and in every facet of activities relevant to human rights has made possible a stultification of the potential of the concept of human rights to help forge a more just world. It is male experience that has predominated in creating "the" human rights perspective(s) on the world.

One strength of Farlinger's paper is that she identifies the absence of women as a phenomenon occurring at every level: within the United Nations bureaucracy; within the apparatus of states; and, consistent with the Wiseberg paper, within organisations of civil society (which overlaps to some degree with the NGO movement). She spends some time illustrating both how gender deficits might be creatively eliminated and how such attention to fairer representation might be expected to stimulate new solutions to old problems (such as civil war) and to allow us to perceive 'new' problems that need prioritized attention (such as violence against women). Much of her paper has a utopian flavour to it, but therein lies its power. Is it really out of the question to take seriously Farlinger's suggestions that we consider a gender partnership model according to which "the Secretary-General's responsibilities [would be] ... split in two and a woman ... chosen in addition to a man" or to consider the similar suggestion of Johan Galtung, to whom Farlinger refers, that half of the members of UN peace-keeping missions be women?

A second strength of Farlinger's essay is her attention to the structural, largely economic, realities that are constitutive of the power relations that have always defined and continue to define human relations. A focus on achieving justice through attention to representation and participation in all decision-making contexts is necessary but cannot be taken as sufficient. In the same way that Wiseberg's essay gives prominence to the appalling lack of financial resources allocated to human rights matters within the United Nations, Farlinger notes that "[even] if all the top positions at the UN were occupied by caring, concerned women (and not all are caring or concerned), this would be an improvement ... [b]ut it would not be enough to stem the tide of global degradation, if the present structures remain." It is in this context that Farlinger refers to "the Other Government" of international capital, a term coined by James Laxer.

Wiseberg focuses on the Vienna *World Conference on Human Rights*. Farlinger also places considerable emphasis on the potential of United Nations world conferences (apart from Vienna on human rights [1993], there is Rio de Janeiro on environment and development [1992], Cairo on population and development [1994], Copenhagen on social development [1995] and Beijing on women [1995]) to provide moments of opportunity for making advances, if only small ones, towards greater justice. Each holds out some hope for a meaningful alliance between the human rights NGO realm and the institutions of the United Nations. Farlinger, however, is more optimistic than Wiseberg. In her discussion of what transpired at Vienna, Farlinger is inclined to see a link between "more than 2700 delegates from 1500 NGOs from around the world [coming] and critiq[ing] the draft document" and "women's rights ...now being integrated into all human rights work" (at least according to the recommendations contained in the *Vienna Conference's Plan of Action*); Farlinger goes on to conclude her essay by saying that she "believe[s] that a reformed United Nations and an energized, gender equal society can transform society and restore the Earth." Unfortunately, the utopian force of this statement is unlikely to be matched in the empirical unfolding of events, at least in the near future. As an on-site observer of the Vienna conference (an academic member of the delegation of Canada), I can attest to the fact that the network of women's NGOs was singularly effective (as compared to other NGOs) in normatively barraging the Vienna interstate process, despite the organisational barriers described above. However, as a wider collectivity, the NGOs at Vienna displayed what Wiseberg correctly refers to as a "lack of coordination and strategic thinking" with respect to how the NGO process of deliberation was to interact with the interstate negotiations over the Vienna draft text. The rifts that appeared in Vienna amongst the NGOs extended to a collective stalemate and indecision over the most appropriate approach to take to that interaction. On the one hand, the NGOs could have organised around creating their own alternative declaration and plan of action in the manner of the alternative treaties that were produced by the NGOs in attendance at the Rio *Conference on Environment and Development*. On the other hand, they could have rigorously based their work on the draft interstate text and sought to influence the negotiations on that text as much as possible. Cogent justifications can be advanced for either strategy. However, in the end, a lack of consensus resulted in neither of these strategies being pursued with any vigour; the *NGO Forum* fell between two stools. When the September 1995 Beijing conference takes place, it will be interesting to see whether a fruitful and effective NGO-UN interaction will occur or whether the problems of Vienna will reproduce themselves to one degree or another.

CHAPTER 13

The Vienna World Conference on Human Rights

Laurie S. Wiseberg

Human rights is one of the central pillars of the United Nations system, both a goal in its own right and a crucial instrument for achieving the other UN goals of international peace and security. This is clearly set out in *Article 1* of the *UN Charter*, which lists among the UN's purposes, "To develop friendly relations among nations based on respect for the principle of equal rights and self-determination of peoples" and, "To achieve international cooperation ... in promoting and encouraging respect for human rights and for fundamental freedoms for all, without distinction as to race, sex, language, or religion." It is restated in *Article 55*, under the heading of *International Economic and Social Cooperation*, which calls on the UN to promote, "universal respect for, and observance of, human rights and fundamental freedoms for all without distinction as to race, sex, language or religion."[1]

Despite this, less than one percent of the United Nations budget is devoted to human rights, and over the course of nearly 50 years of UN history, there have been only two world conferences devoted to human rights: the first, in Teheran, 22 April–13 May 1968, which produced the *Declaration of Teheran*; the second, in Vienna last year, 14-24 June 1993, which gave us the *Vienna Declaration and Programme of Action*.

A Conference That Almost Wasn't

During the three year lead-up to the *Vienna Conference*, the signs were not auspicious. The proposal to hold the Conference, which was adopted by the General Assembly in Resolution 45/155 on 18 December 1990, had originated with Jan Martenson, a Swede, who in June 1987 assumed the post of Director General of the UN Office at Geneva and Head of the *Centre for Human Rights*. However, on 1 March 1992, Martenson was swept out of office by the incoming Secretary-General Boutros Boutros-Ghali in his first phase of "restructuring and streamlining the UN." This was just a few weeks prior to the *Second Preparatory Committee (PrepCom) Meeting*, and Antoine Blanca, the Frenchman who replaced Martenson, seemed to have little real interest in the *World Conference*. In any event, Blanca lasted only a year, resigning by announcing he was returning to diplomatic service. He was replaced in early 1993 by Ibrahima Fall of Senegal, who assumed leadership of the *UN Centre for Human Rights* and became Secretary-General of the *World Conference*.[2]

In addition to the changing helmsman, there was the problem of the changing port-of-call. Originally, the *Conference* was to have been held in Berlin and hosted by the German government. But the Germans rescinded their offer in early 1992 and a new site had to be found. Venice was considered and rejected because there was too little lead time to ensure adequate hotel space. Vienna was finally selected at the *Second PrepCom Meeting* in April 1992, which was about all that meeting agreed upon. There was, for example, no agreement on agenda, on the question of the participation of Non-Governmental Organizations (NGOs), or on participation in the regional preparatory meetings. When the *Third PrepCom*, in September 1992, again failed to agree on the agenda, there was serious talk of possibly postponing the *World Conference*. In the end, the General Assembly salvaged the meeting by adopting an agenda at the eleventh hour.[3]

Problems continued on almost every front right up to and through the *Fourth* (and final) *PrepCom Meeting* in April 1993. The Asian regional meeting was postponed twice because a *coterie* of Asian countries – China, Indonesia and Syria among them – which would have preferred the *Conference* initiative to collapse, were adamant that Australia was part of the WEOG (Western and Other Group countries) and was therefore not eligible to participate in the Asian meeting. Australia, equally adamant that it was Asian, eventually gave in. There was the UN's dilemma of how to put together a list of NGO invitees that went beyond NGOs with Consultative Status.[4] While the hard-line "violative" states wanted to restrict NGO participation, a further obstacle to NGO access emerged when WEOG opted not to have a regional meeting. Since the formula that determined which NGOs could register in Vienna depended upon participation in a regional meeting, there was a fear that Western-based NGOs would be left out in the cold.

And then there were the substantive concerns. In the year leading up to the *Conference*, many – NGOs and governments alike – spoke in terms of damage control rather than possible positive achievements. There was a very real fear that the principle of the universality of human rights would be undermined by those states (largely, but not exclusively, Asian) that were arguing for the need to recognize cultural and religious specificities.

There was a related fear that violative states, unhappy about coming under the scrutiny of the United Nations' human rights machinery, might use the occasion to try and dismantle the human rights infrastructure that had been so laboriously crafted over the past 25 years. While everyone acknowledged the shortcomings of that infrastructure – especially the lack of coordination between and among the UN Commission on Human Rights, its Sub-Commission on Prevention of Discrimination and Protection of Minorities, their Working Groups and Special (thematic and geographic) Rapporteurs, and the treaty-supervisory bodies – those who wanted to strengthen the protective capacity of UN human rights bodies feared possible subterfuge. And there was the disturbing fact that governments were going into a *World Conference* with a 50-page draft document in which almost every paragraph was "square-bracketed," *i.e.*, where there was no agreement on the language.

Finally, there were a myriad of concerns surrounding the organization of the *NGO Forum*, scheduled to take place just prior to the *World Conference* (10-12 June); about the lack of resources to get NGOs to Vienna;[5] and about the lack of coordination and strategic thinking on the part of NGOs.[6]

A Document Emerges Well Past Midnight

Given this inauspicious beginning, what emerged from Vienna is quite remarkable. Representatives of 171 States took part in the *Conference*, as did observers from 95 international and national organizations and 841 Non-Governmental Organizations. Although it was well-past midnight on 23 June when the *Vienna Declaration* and *Programme of Action* were finally adopted, a document was produced that went considerably beyond damage limitation. Specifically:

- The principles of the universality and indivisibility of human rights were clearly, if not quite unequivocally, reaffirmed.
- A major advance was made with respect to women's rights: "The human rights of women and of the girl-child are an inalienable, integral and indivisible part of universal human rights," states the *Vienna Declaration*. "The equal status and human rights of women should be integrated into the mainstream of UN system-wide activity ... The World *Conference* (WC) stresses the importance of working towards the elimination of violence against women in public and private life, the elimination of sexual harassment, exploitation and trafficking in

women, the elimination of gender bias in the administration of justice and the eradication of any conflicts which may arise between the rights of women and the harmful effects of certain traditional or customary practices, cultural prejudices and religious extremism." The WC also encouraged the UN Commission on Human Rights to consider the appointment of a special rapporteur on violence against women at its next session (which it approved in March 1994).

- The WC reaffirmed the important role of NGOs active in human rights and/or development in the promotion and protection of human rights at the national, regional and international levels.

- It also confirmed the role of autonomous national institutions in rights protection and promotion.

- The WC endorsed the proclamation of a decade of the world's indigenous people, though the indigenous lost the fight to keep the "s" on people, which would have affirmed their right to self-determination.

- The WC contains recommendations on the human rights of vulnerable groups, including migrant workers, persons with disabilities and refugees.

- The WC reiterated "the principle of 'First Call for Children' and underlines the importance of major national and international efforts … for promoting respect for the rights of the child to survival, protection, development and participation."

- The *Declaration* contained a separate paragraph on genocide and ethnic cleansing, and recognized the important role of human rights components in specific arrangements concerning peacekeeping operations of the UN, recommending that the Secretary-General take into account the reporting, experience and capabilities of the Centre for Human Rights and human rights mechanisms.

- Finally, and most importantly, the WC called on the General Assembly to begin "as a matter of priority, consideration of the question of the establishment of a High Commissioner for Human Rights for the promotion and protection of all human rights."

We will return in a moment to this last recommendation, potentially one of the most important of the achievements of Vienna. But one should first note a few of the major disappointments. For example, there was dismay that the *Final Declaration* seemed to give states the right to decide which NGOs are "genuine" and which are not. There was dismay that freedom of expression was made conditional on national law. At the level of protective mechanisms – the violations in the former Yugoslavia and Angola notwithstanding – there was no sense of urgency expressed about the need to establish an international criminal court. Most notably, there was no real commitment by states to give the United Nations the resources that are essential if there is to be effective monitoring and implementation of UN standards, beyond requesting the General Assembly to take immediate steps to increase substantially the resources for the human rights programme from within the existing and future budgets of the UN.

Upstairs and Downstairs, Everything a UN World Conference Ought Not to Be

In assessing the *World Conference*, however, the sharpest criticisms were directed at the process rather than the results. Amnesty International's Secretary-General, Pierre Sané, rendered his verdict early, describing the first week of the government conference as "a week of shame." "The people who have the torturers and the killers on their payroll are here in Vienna mouthing phrases about human rights," said Sané, "and there is no evidence that these diplomats have given a single order to stop on-going torture, disappearances, political arrests or killings."

Clarence Dias, director of the International Centre for Law in Development, argued that "the *UN World Conference* ended up epitomizing everything that a *UN World Conference* ought not to be." "Most NGOs from the South and the North alike," he said, "were dismayed that a number of abusive governments used the conference to attack the universality of human rights. NGOs were especially concerned that the Conference Secretariat displayed a disturbing willingness to succumb to the wishes of certain governments with abusive human rights records." In particular, he pointed to the fact that "a few abusive governments sought to impose the procedural chaos of the UN conference onto the NGOs. Planned NGO activities and events were proscribed, participants excluded and attempts were made to curb what NGOs discussed within their own Forum. This was unprecedented and deplorable."[7]

The process did, indeed, leave a great deal to be desired, not only upstairs, where the governmental meeting took place, but also downstairs, where the *NGO Forum* and parallel activities were organized. There were over 2,000 NGO delegates in Vienna – the largest and most diverse human rights NGO gathering ever. They came to represent not only the international NGOs (the INGOs in Consultative Status with the UN), but also regional, national and local NGOs. For many, especially those from the South, it was their first encounter. And an encounter it was, not only with UN protocol, procedures and jargon, but also with delegates from the Western-based INGOs who Southerners perceived to be orchestrating the NGO proceedings.

Those who travelled thousands of miles to get to Vienna wanted and demanded more than token participation. They wanted their own voice and vote. They were angry about the way in which the Joint Planning Committee (JPC), created to steer the *NGO Forum,* caved in to UN demands – that the programme be sanitized to omit references to country situations, that the Dalai Lama be denied access to the *NGO Forum* – and they were angry that the JPC was insensitive enough to invite former US President Jimmy Carter to give a keynote address at the closing session of the *NGO Forum.*

But these were the catalysts, not the cause. At the root of the anger was a clear frustration that those on the front lines of the human rights struggle, those at the grassroots, were once again marginalized by the NGO leadership from Geneva and New York who believe they know best because they regularly walk the UN corridors. Hence the rebellion which forced the Joint Planning Committee to resign and led to the election of a new and more representative NGO Liaison Committee (NLC) to guide the NGOs through the official *UN Conference* and "Beyond Vienna."

A Year after Vienna

On 13 December 1993, five months after the close of the *World Conference,* the General Assembly adopted by consensus a resolution[8] recommending the creation of the Office of High Commissioner for Human Rights (HCHR). This was the culmination of a short, but intense process of lobbying that started in Vienna, continued in the Third Committee of the General Assembly, and ended in the Special Working Group established to set out the mandate of a High Commissioner.

That resolution determined that the HCHR would be "the United Nations official with principal responsibility for United Nations human rights activities under the direction and authority of the Secretary-General." He/she would be appointed for a term of four years (with the possibility of one renewal); be of the rank of Under-Secretary-General; and report annually to the Commission on Human Rights and, through the Economic and Social Council (ECOSOC), to the General Assembly. The individual was to be "a person of high moral standing and personal integrity" and "possess expertise, including in the field of human rights, and the general knowledge and understanding of diverse cultures necessary for impartial, objective, non-selective and effective performance of the duties of the High Commissioner."

The resolution defined the responsibilities of the HCHR to include, *inter alia*: "Promoting and protecting the effective enjoyment by all of civil, cultural, economic, political and social rights" (*Art. 4(a)*); "Promoting and protecting the realization of the right to development and enhancing support from relevant bodies of the United Nations system for this purpose" (*Art. 4(c)*); "Providing, through the Centre for Human Rights and other appropriate institutions, advisory services and technical and financial assistance, at the request of the State concerned and, where appropriate, the regional human rights organizations, with a view to supporting actions and programmes in the field of human rights" (*Art. 4(d)*); "Playing an active role in removing the current obstacles and in meeting the challenges to the full realization of all human rights and in preventing the continuation of human rights violations throughout the world" (*Art. 4(f)*); engaging in a dialogue with all Governments in the implementation of his/her mandate with a view to securing respect for all human rights" (*Art. 4(g)*); "Coordination of human rights promotion and protection activities throughout the United Nations system" (*Art. 4(i)*); "Rationalization, adaptation, strengthening and streamlining of the United Nations machinery in the field of human rights with a view to improving its efficiency and effectiveness" (*Art. 4(j)*) and "Overall supervision of the Centre for Human Rights" (*Art. 4(k)*).

Jan Bauer, analyzing the mandate of the HCHR, draws attention to two key provisions which had appeared in earlier drafts of the text but which were omitted from the final resolution: 1) The first of these would have specifically authorized the High Commissioner "to initiate measures, contact governments and take other appropriate action to prevent serious violations of human rights, or to respond to them wherever they occur, including with the consent of governments, through the dispatch of fact-finding missions." The significance of this provision is that it assumed a proactive rather than reactive role for the High Commissioner. It also assumed a role in the prevention of violations rather than limiting the High Commissioner to responding once human rights violations have occurred and been brought to the international community's attention; 2) The second reference that was dropped would have specifically entrusted to the High Commissioner the task of "co-ordination as appropriate, of the human rights dimensions of other United Nations activities, including *inter alia* the areas of peacekeeping, electoral assistance and development activities, in conformity with the recommendations of appropriate organs." Had this provision stood it would have ensured that the High

Commissioner was authorized to confer and to develop cooperative approaches to human rights violations with UN agencies such as the High Commissioner for Refugees and the UN Peacekeeping Forces, both of which almost inevitably must respond to crises in which the violation of human rights is a fundamental feature.[9]

These limitations notwithstanding, the mandate of the High Commissioner is broad and open-ended enough to permit the Under-Secretary-General to play a key role in prevention, protection and coordination, if the political will and commitment to do so is there. The big question for NGOs and governments alike is whether José Ayala Lasso, the Ecuadorian diplomat who was appointed in December as the first HCHR, will be forceful, determined and creative enough to do so.

Whether Ayala Lasso is successful or not will also depend in large part on his ability to convince the Secretary-General and the UN General Assembly to provide him with the resources necessary to implement the *Vienna Programme of Action* and to be proactive. It will, for example, be impossible for him to undertake fact-finding missions, to send envoys to trouble spots, to develop an effective early-warning system, to develop a much needed computerized documentation and information system for the UN Centre, or to coordinate the myriad of UN agencies and bodies involved in human rights work (especially when it is defined to include the right to development), unless he has the staff and the money to do so. The UN Centre for Human Rights is stretched well beyond its resources. This should surprise no one, given the enormous expansion in human rights mechanisms – special rapporteurs, working groups, treaty-bodies – while the monies have largely stagnated below the one percent mark of the no-growth UN budget.

Finally, Ayala Lasso's effectiveness will, in part, depend upon his ability to forge a strong alliance with governments that respect human rights, on the one hand, and human rights NGOs, on the other. The former would give him the political clout and political profile he will need, while the latter would give him the necessary information and expertise.

The role of human rights NGOs in the post-Vienna scenario is, at present, also somewhat problematic. In June, an Open-Ended Working Group of ECOSOC will begin reviewing the entire question of NGO access to the UN, with particular attention to the question of Consultative Status and participation in world conferences.[10] Despite the NGO revolution in Vienna, and despite the decision of the NGO Liaison Committee "Beyond Vienna" (now renamed the NGO Interim Liaison Committee) to extend its mandate until February 1995, it is not yet clear whether grassroots pressure on the UN human rights system will continue to be effectively exerted. It is unclear, for example, how many Southern-based NGOs will attend the Open-Ended Working Group reviewing NGO status, even though critical decisions affecting their future participation will be made there in the coming year. It is equally unclear how many of the 2,000 NGOs that participated in the *Vienna World Conference* will continue to invest energy and resources in an effort to impact directly in the international (as opposed to local, national or regional) arena.

However, what is indisputable is that the *Vienna World Conference* has to be assessed not as a one-off event but as part of an on-going process to strengthen the preventive, the protective and the promotional capacity of the United Nations human rights system. It may, therefore, be necessary to reserve judgment on whether the *Conference* was a success or failure – whether it merited the enormous time and energies that human rights NGOs poured into it – until we see the extent to which the *Vienna Declaration and Plan of Action* makes a difference to the status of human rights in the real world. For, in the final analysis, the bottom line for human rights advocates must always be: it was worth it if it saved lives, stopped torture, tipped the scales towards justice, made people more tolerant, protected the vulnerable, improved the quality of life, or empowered the powerless. And it is precisely in such terms that we must eventually evaluate the new office of the High Commissioner for Human Rights.

Notes

1 This point was made in a talk by Ross Hynes, Deputy Director and Departmental Coordinator for Human Rights, on the High Commissioner for Human Rights, sponsored by the United Nations Association of Canada, Ottawa, 13 April 1994.

2 In the new UN restructuring, the post of Director-General of the UN's Geneva Office was severed from that of the Head of the UN Centre for Human Rights.

3 The agenda was adopted by the UN Third Committee on 2 December 1992.

4 In the end, the UN Centre for Human Rights turned to Human Rights Internet and other NGOs for assistance in compiling the invitation list.

5 Some of the funding came through so late that it did not reach NGOs – especially the African-based organizations – in time for them to use the tickets to go to Vienna.

6 For general background on the problems leading up to the *Vienna World Conference*, see articles in *Human Rights Tribune* (a quarterly publication of Human Rights Internet, Ottawa) 1 (1-4) and 2 (1) Winter 1992 through June 1993; 2 (1) was a special pre-Conference issue.

7 Dias, Clarence "Five not Twenty-five should be our post-Vienna motto" *Human Rights Tribune* 2 No. 2 November 1993 31-32.

8 A/C.3/48/L.85.

9 Bauer, Jan "Cooperation between Specialized Agencies of the United Nations for the Enhanced and Effective Promotion and Protection of Human Rights," a draft paper prepared for the *Human Rights Working Group of the United Nations Reform Satellite Committee, Canadian Network on United Nations Reform* 21 March 1994 5-6.

10 For a more detailed treatment of this issue, see Wiseberg, Laurie, and Pauline Comeau "NGO Self-Examination is the Missing Link in ECOSOC Review" *New World* (Newsletter of the Canadian Network on United Nations Reform) No. 2 April 1994 4-5.

CHAPTER 14

Human Rights and Gender Equity

Shirley Farlinger

"Women's rights are human rights" is a motto that should never have been necessary. Are women not humans?

The question should be put, "Are women being treated in inhuman ways?" The answer is a resounding, "Yes!" Whether one is looking at political power, salaries, employment, health care, literacy, land ownership or just plain respect, women are not accorded the same rights as men.

Does the United Nations have a responsibility to bring health and happiness to all people? Does this clash with the original mandate of the UN to end all wars?

The *United Nations Charter*, which is the constitution of the UN, came into being on 24 October 1945, when the UN had 51 Member States. It now has 184. It is an organization charged with peacekeeping responsibilities, with the development of friendly relations among nations, including international cooperation on economic, social, cultural and humanitarian matters, and with the promotion of human rights and fundamental freedoms for all human beings without discrimination (*UN Charter*, *Articles 4* and *55*). The *Covenant of the League of Nations* of 1920 contained no general provisions dealing with human rights, so progress in this area has been made. However, other *Charter* provisions have discouraged the UN from intervening in the domestic affairs of the members even in the face of gross violations of human rights. This is changing.

The main organs of the UN are the General Assembly, the Security Council, the International Court of Justice, the Economic and Social Council (ECOSOC) and the Secretariat, which has the Secretary-General and staff. In the General Assembly, any matter within the scope of the *Charter* may be discussed. Most of the Assembly resolutions are non-binding, yet they do have an effect on global thinking and the formation of customary international law. The *Universal Declaration of Human Rights* was adopted by the General Assembly in the form of a resolution in 1948, and has acquired a legal character.

The Security Council, made up of the five nuclear nations with the heavy-handed veto and 10 other states elected on a rotating basis, has binding power. It may use sanctions against countries and has approved military interventions. The presence of both the USA and the former USSR on the Security Council led to many stalemates in decision making. Hopefully a new era is dawning.

Yet when women look at this new era they find themselves largely invisible in decision making bodies, both global and local. But they are very visible among the marginalized; they are the majority of the victims of war, of the malnourished, of the illiterate, of the refugees and of the handicapped.

Marilyn French writes,[1] "While men strut and fret their hour upon the stage, shout in bars and sports arenas, thump their chests or show their profiles in the legislatures, and explode incredible weapons in an endless contest for status, an obsessive quest for symbolic 'proof' of their superiority, women quietly keep the world going. Women know that men will not do this; that either they do the job or it will not be done. They grow or buy, they carry and prepare food for the essential, inevitable, necessarily female-prepared dinner; they give birth to the children, feed them and bathe them, hold them and teach them, and hope they will survive."

It is not just in the best interests of women but also of men and children that women's ideas for reforming structures and changing global institutions be heard and taken seriously.

Muhammad Yunus, Director of the Grameen Bank, a unique institution that grants small loans in Bangladesh to local businesses, has found that money going through women in the household brought more benefits than money entering the household through men. The immediate beneficiaries are the children and then improved living conditions. Men have different priorities that do not give the family the top position.

It is with this background that I discuss some approaches to UN reform at the time of its 50th Anniversary. There will be many UN experts intent on altering the Security Council, the General Assembly and other UN bodies. I will not repeat their ideas, but will concentrate on changes for and by women that I believe are essential to men's health and happiness as well.

Globally the percentage of women is 49. Yet in Canada, where women have better health care, the percentage is 52. In a world population of 5.6 billion this means that millions of women are missing; girl babies have died; women have been killed, and female fetuses have been aborted. These are signs that, in many countries, women are not valued.

The UN has been working on the question of gender equity for decades. In 1946, the 45-member Commission on the Status of Women was designed to collect data on women's rights in political, social and educational fields, and make recommendations. The same year the United Nations International Emergency Children's Fund (UNICEF) was set up that links children's welfare with that of women. In 1969, The United Nations Population Fund was initiated and now issues guidelines for involving women in population and development activities. The *First UN Decade for Women* began in 1975 and resulted in the creation by the Economic and Social Council (ECOSOC) of the International Research and Training Institute for the Advancement of Women (INSTRAW). It coordinates training and research for women from its headquarters in Santo Domingo in the Dominican Republic, but is financed only by voluntary contributions. States that have ratified the 1979 *Convention on the Elimination of All Forms of Discrimination Against Women* (CEDAW) select the 23 experts who monitor the implementation of that Convention. But monitoring is not the same thing as ensuring. Finally, in 1985, the Division for the Advancement of Women was set up with the task of monitoring and implementing the Nairobi *Forward-Looking Strategies for the Advancement of Women*. Other UN bodies, such as the United Nations Development Programme and the International Fund for Agriculture Development, and even the World Bank, have added a women's division. On paper it all looks impressive, but some signatories to the conventions have added so many reservations against them that they have little power. Other countries simply ignore what they have signed.

Eleanor Roosevelt, wife of US president Franklin Roosevelt, served as Chair of the UN Commission on Human Rights from 1946 to 1951 and as the delegate of the USA to the UN. The *Universal Declaration of Human Rights* was adopted on 10 December 1948, largely as the result of her vision and personal diplomacy. Eleanor Roosevelt was one of the first civilian witnesses to speak with Holocaust survivors, to tour concentration camps and to consider the needs of the future. This experience no doubt influenced her life. She was alarmed at anti-black racism in the USA, and personally carried her commitment to liberty, individual freedom, equal rights, civil rights and human dignity into tiny villages and hamlets, as well as into the citadels of government authority.[2] She remains a role model of the independent, influential woman. Her dreams of freedom, equity and dignity, unfortunately, are still dreams for most of the world. There has not been, since her time, anyone of influence promoting the UN within the USA Instead there has been a steady disparagement of the organization in the USA from such well-funded groups as The Heritage Foundation.

So a first recommendation is to improve the status of the UN in all countries and to help women learn about the UN instruments that are already available to assist them. This will depend partly on raising the literacy rate of women. Women will need preferential treatment until as many as possible are literate. This will assist women to take part in "civil society" or Non-Governmental Organizations (NGOs), which are gaining influence at the UN.

The poor standard of living and lack of power of most women are reflected in the condition of children. On 30 September 1990, James Grant, executive director of UNICEF opened the *World Summit for Children.* On the same day, as on every day of the year, it was estimated that 20,000 children died from preventable diseases, 100,000 became malnourished, 115,000 dropped out of primary school and untold millions faced another day of exploitation and abuse.[3] Grant brought together the largest group of the heads of nations, 71 in number, that had ever been assembled, and showed them in a video the good news and bad news of the condition of children around the world. He tried to alert the world's leaders to conditions of the next generation of global citizens. Soon after the *Summit* the *Convention of the Rights of the Child* became international law. Unfortunately, conditions for women and children have still not improved overall. But the *Children's Summit* did place the condition of women, their literacy and health, as a priority in improving the health of children. The *Convention* needs to be tracked in each country to ensure that the signatories are following up with legislation and action.

Since then many UN summits have been held. The *Earth Summit* in Brazil, in June 1992 brought the heads of more nations together, and subsequently three treaties were signed on biodiversity, climate change and reforestation. The UN has since been trying to incorporate the environment into the mandate of its organizations. Such international instruments as *The Law of the Sea* have finally been ratified by enough nations to become international law. The *Montreal Protocol* on saving the ozone layer is reducing the use of ozone-depleting chemicals.

But the exciting story of the *Earth Summit* was the presence of hundreds of NGOs, who wrote their own treaties and were not afraid to point to the connection between excessive military expenditures and lack of resources for the environment [see Chapter 15]. Women, 1,500 of them from around the world, held their own preparatory meeting in Miami and produced their own *Women's Action Agenda 21.* It is fair to say that men dominated the official summit and women made up the majority of the NGOs. The *Earth Charter* was written by the NGOs and is being promoted as principles of action for individuals, organizations, corporations and states at the local, national and international levels. One of the principles states: "Women constitute half of the Earth's human population. They are a powerful source for change. They contribute more than half the effort to human welfare. Men and women agree that women's status in decision making and social processes must equitably reflect their contribution. We must shift from a society dominated by men to one that more accurately reflects the valued contributions of men and women to human and ecological welfare."

The 50th Anniversary of the UN is the time the UN will be asked to adopt the *Earth Charter* and commit to a second *Global Forum* in 1999. The UN already had a United Nations Environment Programme but this has now been expanded and a special fund has been set up. The 53-member UN Commission on Sustainable Development met in May 1994 to oversee implementation of the commitments made in Rio de Janiero, especially *Agenda 21*, the blueprint for sustainable development. Yet military spending continues to eat up the world's resources and there has been little official recognition of the connection between disarmament and development or disarmament and environmental restoration.

There has, however, been a recognition that women should be part of all decision making bodies. This received its first impetus in 1975 when the *UN Decade for Women* began. At the end of the first decade, at a UN conference in Nairobi in 1985, a document called *The Forward Looking Strategies for the Advancement of Women to the Year 2000* was adopted by consensus. It spelled out in nearly 400 paragraphs, which listed both recommendations and blocks to progress, exactly how women should be part of all decisions. It is one of the little known triumphs for the advancement of women and will be taken up again at the *Fourth UN Conference on Women* in Beijing in September 1995. The Secretary-General for this conference is the Tanzanian diplomat Gertrude Mongella, who states that women must be treated as equals and their strengths, skills and talents welcomed and used to the full. The change from having women's talents tolerated to their being "welcomed" is like the blossoming of a flower.

In 1991 the UN began publishing *The Human Development Index* (HDI)[4] to measure the overall well-being, military expenditures, gender gaps and education levels for all countries. It might better be called The *Human Deprivation Index* as more and more people sink into poverty. A *Human Freedom Index* has also been added. These indices show that peace, human development and human rights are inseparable. A second recommendation is for the indices to be determined so that the figures for men and women are separated. When this was done for Canada, we moved from number one to number eight on the HDI. These indices also measure disparity: one rich person and one poor person are not two middle income people, except as a meaningless average.

Following on this idea it is also recommended that UN statistics include the value of the unpaid work of women. Marilyn Waring shows that, when women's work is invisible in UN figures, it is less likely to be supported or even understood.[5] And this practice leads to the exclusion of women from the calculations of every country's Gross National Product (GNP), a figure widely used to determine economic strategies.

The next *Summit* was on population in Cairo in September 1994. This will be followed by a *Social Development Summit* in Copenhagen in March 1995, and then the *Women's Summit* in Beijing in September 1995. These large conferences, with the participation of hundreds of NGOs, could be thought of as a reform of the UN. Certainly the drafters of the UN *Charter* did not envision such global consultations. But the good news is that the Secretary-General has recognized that the participation of NGOs is essential to the attainment of UN goals. NGOs are inexpensive and keep the pressure up on their own governments to adhere to the agreements that have been signed. NGOs are made up largely of women. However the summits are valuable only if the rhetoric is translated into genuine advances.

The urge to reform the UN is not new. The organization that suited the victors of World War II and the decolonizing nations is not likely to suit a world of 5.6 billion people recovering from the effects of the Cold War and now embroiled in 79 vicious civil wars. With the problems of poverty and militarization escalating and the environment deteriorating, reform of the UN is imperative. Although nations of the North see the new calls for UN Peacekeepers around the globe as a sign of positive change, many nations of the South see the UN as a male club run by and for the richest members, particularly the nuclear powers.

Was there ever a time or place in history when people lived in peace, and were fed, clothed, housed, healthy and respected? Perhaps the past has something to teach us now. Women historians, theologians and feminists have been unearthing, sometimes literally, evidence of gender equality and partnership between the sexes. In ancient Minoa on the island of Crete, a society existed for over 1,000 years that was both peaceful and prosperous, as described by Riane Eisler.[6] There were both female and male deities, no armies, no weapons and gender-equal participation, even in dangerous sports. This much is evident from the frescoes on the walls of the ancient palaces, in the absence of written evidence.

The Minoans were fortunate to live on an island and to be self-sufficient in food and wine. The society was not perfect but it has now inspired
women and men to set up partnership groups where people learn to relate
to each other without dominating anyone. It is the "dominator model,"
contends Eisler, which keeps the guns of war blazing, the patriarchy in
control, and explains the disparities that exist between rich and poor.
Studies agree that women did enjoy a broad spectrum of rights and freedoms early in history but that these have been diminished or even abol-
ished. Civilization has not brought progress for all.

Goddess worship was common throughout the ancient world before
patriarchal religions began to persecute women and so-called pagans. There
is now a move towards liberation theology, creation theology and gender
balance. The Pope has just announced that girls will be allowed to serve as
altar girls at communion, a small concession to gender equality. A more
female-affirming theologian is Chung Hyun Kyung, who surprised the
World Council of Churches with her brand of Asian theology. She writes:[7]
"In their struggle for survival and liberation in this unjust, women-hating
world, poor Asian women have approached many different religious sources
for sustenance and empowerment. What matters for them is not doctrinal
purity ... What matters to Asian women is survival and the liberation of
themselves and their communities." She describes her spirituality as one
that, "dances with the cosmic rhythm of the universe, not against it."

How would the "partnership model" and liberation of oppressed
women look at the UN? Starting at the top, imagine that the Secretary-
General's responsibilities have been split in two and a woman has been
chosen in addition to a man. This sharing of leadership would send a powerful message to all countries that, from now on, women will take their
places as equal in status and in decision making power. Imagine that this
caught on with the UN ambassadors and half of them were women, or a
man and a woman shared the job. Imagine that this extended to all the
many agencies of the UN.

Tinkering with the present machinery of the UN, altering the membership on the Security Council, *etc.*, will not however bring the needed
sea-changes. There must be agreement on the ethics and the purpose of the
UN. Once it has been decided that the UN exists, first of all, to preserve
Planet Earth, for without that the rest is immaterial, and that the UN
must benefit the poorest people and raise them up to a decent standard of
living, and that this can only be accomplished when there is peace, then
the necessary reforms will be clearer.

One woman at the UN who understands its potential role is Sharon

Capeling-Alakij, the new Director of the Office of Strategic Planning for the United Nations Development Programme. She was born in Canada and spent many years working on development in Africa before heading up the United Nations Fund for Women. This agency, called UNIFEM, was created in 1976 to provide direct support for women's projects and promote the inclusion of women in the decision making processes of major development programmes. Although this agency and other UN bodies have done good work, they are simply too small and underfunded to accomplish their tasks. Her promotion to the UNDP will give her more scope for helping women.

So the third recommendation is to increase the status, size and funding of The Status of Women Commission and its agencies, to improve the monitoring of the countries who have signed the various conventions and urge the other states to sign and ratify them.

There is evidence that the equal participation of women in politics makes a difference to the legislation that is proposed. In Norway, for instance, the Labour Party adopted a rule that neither sex should drop below 40 percent of the political candidates. This proved so popular that it has been adopted by other parties, and the percentage of women in parliament is almost up to the 40 percent mark in Norway and Sweden. At about 40 percent, it has been observed that the type of legislation brought forward changes to reflect women's concerns. Very few parliaments have achieved this and certainly the UN is far from this representation in the General Assembly.

The fourth recommendation is that all bodies of the UN strive for the standard whereby the representation of each of the sexes does not sink below 40 percent. As the members of the General Assembly see how this benefits both males and females they may change their own thinking and improve the representation of women in their national governments.

Sheer numbers will not produce significant changes if the women are all at the non-decision making level. Sadako Ogata of Japan, as the UN High Commissioner for Refugees, has broken the glass ceiling at the UN. This job must be one of the most difficult as the number of refugees increases and resources dry up. Streams of sick, starving and terrified people head for UN feeding stations on the periphery of civil wars. She will have to be given more say in addressing the root causes of these problems.

Joni Seager describes how powerful decision-makers can have a far-reaching effect:[8] "The environmental crisis is not just a crisis of physical ecosystems. The real story of the environmental crisis is a story of power and profit and political wrangling; it is a story of the institutional arrangements and the cultural conventions that create conditions of environmental destruction. Our environmental problems are the progeny of very particular clusters of powerful institutions acting in particular ways ... Large scale environmental degradation is the product of three or four clusters of large institutions that include, prominently, militaries, multinationals and governments (often in collusion.)."

Much the same could be said of global poverty, of civil wars, of soaring population and of the exclusion of women from decision making positions. If all the top positions at the UN were occupied by caring, concerned women (and not all are caring or concerned), this would be an improvement. But it would not be enough to stem the tide of global degradation, if the present structures remain. A new approach to the question of how decisions are made and how money and resources will be allocated in all countries and at the global level has to be the first building block in a reformed UN.

Since improving standards of living and the condition of our global home will cost money, the present monetary drain from poor countries into rich ones, and from the poor within countries to their own rich elites, must be stopped. This will mean the dismantling or complete reordering of priorities in the International Monetary Fund (IMF) and the World Bank. A *New World Economic Order*, long delayed by the developed world, must begin.

The IMF and World Bank are agencies of the UN and they could be cancelled by the UN. It would be quite revealing if the struggle for the right to cancel these world bodies were taken to the International Court of Justice. The World Bank is actually called the International Bank for Reconstruction and Development, which suggests a mandate for reconstruction and development. It is time this mandate to improve conditions around the world by loaning money to needy countries to raise their standard of living was compared with the results. For every one dollar lent to developing countries two are returned in interest and other payments. The IMF "Structural Adjustment Programme" for economic recovery includes reducing government budgets, cutting social services, privatizing industries, devaluing currencies and increasing exports, even exports of food in places of high malnutrition rates. The Third World debt has soared from $751 billion in 1981 to $1,300 billion in 1992. New institutions, or at least a new code of conduct, are needed[9] [see Chapter 18].

The present international banking system is also part of the problem. James Laxer, writer on economics, notes:[10] "Today central bankers are special people because in every major country they run what can quite accurately be called the Other Government ... In an age when the volume of international capital movements dwarfs trade, the central bank has emerged as a state within the state, whose job is to safeguard the interests of lenders everywhere ... The 'money government' and its cheerleaders have a very clear agenda for Canada – cut government spending by slashing spending for social programmes. If you don't, we'll cut your credit rating and charge you even more for the money we're only too happy to lend you." However this form of financial bondage can only end in collapse. The stones have no more blood.

The *UN Code of Conduct for Multinationals*, vetoed by nations such as the USA, must be reintroduced and rewritten to take into account new rules for preserving the environment and to raise standards of living, especially for the poor. It may be necessary to initiate a licence for companies to do business, a licence that would not permit toxic dumping, the use of child labour, the destruction of rain forests, the export of needed food, *etc.* This might also be a good way to limit military trade. My fifth recommendation for UN reform is therefore to establish a new code of conduct for multinationals and a UN licence or seal of approval for them to conduct business.

Commerce cannot be let off the hook when considering the condition of the environment. Two of the major contributors to ozone depletion and global warming are military activities and global trade. The military is a major user of oil for training, testing, war exercises and its thousands of personnel. Shipping goods around the world uses oil for transportation, but it also has other ill effects. It discourages local production, indigenous foods and products and therefore local culture, and, through mass production, agribusiness and increased use of technology, it tends to decrease the total number of jobs.

By taxing global trade with a UN tax, and this is my sixth recommendation, the United Nations itself, the environment and grassroots organizations would all benefit. The UN simply cannot continue to go beret-in-hand to beg for money for each budget item. A tax on global trade and/or a percentage of foreign currency exchange, now almost $1 trillion ($1,000,000,000,000) per day, with only one of every seventy dollars that are traded actually paying for goods and services,[11] would put the UN on a more secure footing and eliminate the over-strong influence of some powers on what is to be funded. As more countries become impoverished, there is more defaulting on UN dues. Even the USA is $260 million in arrears for the regular budget and $193 million behind for peacekeeping. It is estimated that the Gulf War cost the coalition and Japan $60 billion.

Poor countries are liable to acquiesce to the demands of richer countries in exchange for monetary support. This was clearly demonstrated in the formation of the coalition to fight the Gulf War.

Within countries too, it is difficult for people on the edge of survival to turn down a job, no matter how poorly paid, dangerous, anti-social or degrading. Women supporting children are especially vulnerable. And men often enter military service because it provides food, clothing and support for the whole family. Of course plantation owners and multinational corporations welcome the large pools of employment-desperate people created by poverty and landlessness.

The attitude of Reagan, Thatcher and Mulroney towards the poor was described by economist John Kenneth Galbraith. He said that these leaders agreed that the rich do not have enough money; the poor have too much; and more money should be transferred from the poor to the rich. This also transfers more money from women to men.

In many ways the global village is becoming a Victorian workhouse with a few Victorian mansions. Child labour is on the rise, labour union members are decreasing as a percentage of workers, water and air pollution are increasing and safety standards in the workplace are declining. Conditions were improved in various countries, such as Canada, by the introduction of child labour laws, health and safety standards, free medical care, a minimum wage, and the right to strike, protest and form unions. These are all in danger of being lost in the *North American Free Trade Agreement* (NAFTA). Human rights were not in the agreement, but nevertheless are severely curtailed by it.

The UN must become the catalyst for introducing those kind of reforms at the global level. The present situation of global competition, where factories and capital move to the area of lowest wages and least protection for workers, must be altered. Band-aid solutions of famine relief and refugee support are necessary, but will not change the basic conditions. When each country can feed its own and take care of its people instead of creating refugees, the costs to the UN and all aid agencies will be reduced. When people have sufficient income to purchase goods, business activity will increase. Why is this so hard to understand?

If the UN is seen primarily as a keeper of the peace, then UN reform must address this mandate as well. I began with a discussion of human rights as women's rights, alleviation of poverty and environmental protection because I believe that a more prosperous, just, healthy and gender-equal world will reduce many of the tensions that lead to war. But there are still a host of changes that could be made to reduce conflict.

One of the most difficult situations is in Sarajevo, the site of the beginning of World War 1. What might women have done to avoid war in the former Yugoslavia and what implications does this have for the UN? Whether under Austro-Hungarian rule from 1102 AD, or Ottoman rule from 1459 AD, or Nazi rule during World War II, the territory of the former Yugoslavia has been a cauldron of military aggression. Along with the violence of war has gone the patriarchal rule of three religions, Eastern Orthodox, Roman Catholic and Muslim. All three exclude women from positions of authority and decision making and a feminist theology has never penetrated the country. Under Communism, women gained the advantages of family planning, professional careers, and daycare, but had the triple burden of work, homemaking and child care. There was little activity by NGOs. Women's groups and peace NGOs are now working across religious and ethnic lines to assist refugees and further the peace processes. The UN could give more assistance to these efforts and provide good offices for non-partisan groups to begin peace negotiations. The work of male outsiders such as the Vance/Owen/Staltenburg team has not brought peace.

We are very fortunate that nuclear weapons have not, as yet, entered the picture. But there are unlimited numbers of conventional weapons being brought in or taken from the many stockpiles left from the Tito regime. The weapons must be relinquished to a UN unit, as was done in Nicaragua after the end of the Contra War and in Mozambique. Arms sales to the area must be stopped.

The UN Peacekeepers should withdraw from the areas of combat and only return when there is a ceasefire. And when they return they should come in larger numbers, in the words of peace researcher, Dr. Johan Galtung, "a blue carpet of peacekeepers." Only peacekeepers trained in conflict resolution should be sent. The tragic cases of rape and murder make this an imperative. Galtung recommends half of the members be women. I would concur with that idea if women were part of the decision making about when and where to deploy the personnel. Certainly no soldier trained in traditional aggressive warfare, or one who is likely to rape or mistreat people, should be part of this (or any other) assignment. Recommendations for the UN would therefore be to implement appropriate training for UN Peacekeepers and have the means of organizing that force quickly.

Training in conflict resolution is already going on in places such as the European Peace University in Austria, but it should be expanded to all citizens and taught in schools. Anti-racism material will also be needed. Some of the problems in Somalia seem to stem from the racist attitudes of individual soldiers.

Teachers in many countries are pioneering the use of peace tactics in classrooms. Trained children approach the quarrelers and state, "I am a peacemaker, would you like some help?" Family counsellors and labour union negotiators also use conflict resolution strategies.

In the former Yugoslavia, the UN has relied on NATO and this has led to selective bombing. This tactic is liable to add to the problems. Since the region is in such turmoil, and there will be many valid reasons for revenge, it is important that a neutral body, respected by all sides, begin work on bringing the parties together. Galtung estimates that the peace process will take four or five years. The peaceful division of the former Yugoslavia will be much more difficult than, for example, Czechoslovakia, because so many countries and parts of countries have a stake in the outcome.

There is a very special role for citizens, particularly women, to play. In the churches there should be more ecumenical activity, especially involving Muslims, and more protests by clergy against the use of violence to solve problems. Both the Koran and the Bible are filled with exhortations to love one another and bring peace.

Within families a gender balance has to be established, so that women's ideas for ending the war are given a chance to be tried out and accepted. Women's groups around the world must continue to act in solidarity with their sisters in the former Yugoslavia, whether they be Muslim, Christian or any other religion. Children must be raised so that they can all live in harmony with each other because, sooner or later, the international workers, the UN and the negotiators will be gone.

Women must gather the stories of love and cooperation that exist even in the midst of war, and tell them to the people and to the media. Local peace meetings must continue in every possible corner. Strategies for dealing with the awful trauma of neighbour killing neighbour and friend betraying friend must be found to bring healing to all the former citizens of the former Yugoslavia.

The UN could assist with this kind of education and activity. Conflict resolution and second track diplomacy are not visions of the future but are current. The Blue Beret peacekeeping intervention must be followed by teams skilled in resolving conflicts, and these teams need to be trained now. The UN could have such teams ready for service at any time. The UN Protection Force (UNPROFOR) has encountered enormous problems, but has been successful in reducing casualties and containing the war in some areas. The people of Yugoslavia have had unrealistic expectations of what UNPROFOR could do. The mandate of the forces should be made clear.

The direction of the UN in peace strategy should not be in the hands of the Security Council. Canada's former ambassador to the UN, Stephen Lewis, described the situation before the Gulf War:[12] "In my view, the United Nations served as an imprimateur of legitimacy for a policy that the United States wanted to follow and either persuaded or coerced everybody else to support. The Security Council thus played fast and loose with the provisions of the *UN Charter*. For instance, sanctions were invoked under *Article 41*, but there was never any assessment of whether those sanctions were working or might work sufficiently before the decision was made to resort to force under *Article 42*. Moreover, no use was made of the Military Staff Committee, which under *Article 47* is supposed to direct any armed forces at the Security Council's disposal ... I think it's heartbreaking that the United Nations should be conscripted into the role of providing cover for US foreign policy." The Security Council must be drastically changed or removed.

Economic sanctions have not proven to be a good measure: the hardest hit are the most vulnerable and usually the most innocent. There are however about 200 examples throughout history of the use of civil disobedience to stop aggression. The whole field of defensive defence and civilian non-cooperation with the enemy is expanding. Women are inventing new strategies. For instance, the tree-huggers in India are saving the forests, and the indigenous women of the Philippines stopped the engineers of the World Bank's proposed dam by baring their breasts and screaming. Are these serious tactics? Anything that works is worthy of consideration. The killing fields are no longer acceptable.

Cynthia Enloe describes the relation between women's rights and international politics:[13] "Conventional international politics commentators have put power at the centre of their analyses – often to the exclusion of culture and ideas – but they have underestimated the amount and varieties of power at work. It has taken power to deprive women of land titles and leave them little choice but to sexually service soldiers and banana workers. It has taken power to keep women out of their countries' diplomatic corps and out of the upper reaches of the World Bank. It has taken power to keep questions of inequity between local men and women off the agendas of many nationalist movements in industrialized as well as agrarian societies ... Male officials who make foreign policy might prefer to think of themselves as dealing with high finance or military strategy, but in reality they have self-consciously designed immigration, labour, civil service, propaganda and military bases policies so as to control women. They have acted as though their government's place in world affairs has hinged on how women behaved ... International politics has relied not only on the manipulation of femininity's meanings but on the manipulation of masculinity. Ideas about 'adventure', 'civilization', 'progress', 'risk', 'trust', and 'security' are all legitimized by certain kinds of masculine values and behaviour, which makes them so potent in relations between governments."

We have used the all-encompassing term "civil war" to describe some of the present conflicts. In Yemen it is the North against the South, but it is also President Ali Abdullah Saleh against Vice-President Ali Salem Beidh. In the former Yugoslavia, Tudjman and Milosevic are fanning the fires of nationalism. There is a fatalistic acceptance of military conflict, violence and force as the arbiters of right. The Croatian Defence Minister said,[14] "We have been waiting for this moment for eight centuries." To what extent is this male domination of the levers of power the real basis for the problems? Perhaps these are not civil wars so much as struggles for territory and control, born of male ego-driven bravado.

The saddest example of this machismo is the systematic rape of hundreds of women in the detention camps. By repeated rape the women became pregnant in an exercise of ethnic domination called ethnic cleansing. Women around the world united to protest and send aid.

The *World Conference on Human Rights in Vienna*, in June 1993, provided a forum for women to demand that the UN recognize women's human rights and that rape be declared a war crime under international law. Thousands of signatures were collected from around the world to a petition that denounced domestic violence, rape, sexual harassment, traffic in women, female infanticide and all forms of gender violence, as violations of human rights. An International Criminal Court to hear cases from individuals was proposed. And this conference saw women of all races and cultures affirm their solidarity on human rights as women's rights. Men can no longer claim that women's rights differ from one culture or religion to another.

There is still no mechanism for enforcing compliance with human rights other than global public opinion. The US State Department issues an annual report on the human rights practices of most other countries but refuses to submit reports on its own practices. In fact, the USA has yet to ratify the *Human Rights Covenants* and most other international human rights treaties.

Two recommendations from the Vienna conference have been instituted: there is now a High Commissioner for Human Rights and a UN Special Rapporteur on Violence Against Women. Now it will be possible for anyone to take a case to the High Commissioner without having to go through their own government, a dangerous procedure in some countries.

Canada is a recognized leader in human rights and has been re-elected for a third term to the UN Commission on Human Rights. In 1993 Canada became the first country in the world to recognize domestic violence and other forms of persecution targetting women as a basis for refugee claims, by developing guidelines on women refugee claimants fearing gender-related persecution.

The work of the NGOs in Vienna was impressive. More than 2700 delegates from 1500 NGOs from around the world came and critiqued the draft document.[15] For the first time ECOSOC and non-ECOSOC organizations were invited to the government plenary meetings to present briefs and speak. Women's rights are now being integrated into all human rights work. The Conference called for the universal ratification of CEDAW, with no reservations, by the year 2000.

Marion Mathieson, one of the Canadian NGO representatives said, "Humanity is the loser if the international community does not begin with greater ability to tackle the major human rights deficits of war, poverty, "domestic" violence, discrimination and oppression. Much of the longer term benefit of such conferences comes as a result of having been able to establish contact and network with like-minded people pursuing similar aims in other countries. Human rights principles were offered in this way in a thousand different encounters some of which will have sown the seeds of many future human rights activities. Let us hope for better results, not for the sake of those who attended, but for the vast majority of the world's population who will never dream of setting foot in such places."

NGOs have called for the abolition of war through disarmament and demilitarization as preconditions for peace and security. Both aggressive nationalism and extreme poverty affect human rights adversely. Does the UN have to wait until leaders discover how a civilized, just and peaceful global society could benefit everyone? Or should the UN lead the way? I believe that a reformed United Nations and an energized, gender-equal civil society can transform society and restore the Earth.

Notes

1   French, Marilyn 1992 *The War Against Women* (Ballantine Books: USA; Random House of Canada: Toronto).

2   Cook, Blanche Wiesen 1992 *Eleanor Roosevelt* Vol. 1 (Penguin Books: Canada).

3   *The World Summit for Children* 1994 produced for UNICEF by P&LA, Benson: Oxfordshire, UK.

4   United Nations Development Programme *Human Development Report 1991* (Oxford University Press).

5   Waring, Marilyn 1988 *If Women Counted* (Harper & Row: San Francisco).

6   Eisler, Riane 1988 *The Chalice and the Blade* (Harper Collins).

7   Chung, Hyun Kyung 1992 *Struggle to Be the Sun Again: Introducing Asian Women's Theology* (Orbis Books: Maryknoll, NY).

8   Seager, Joni 1993 *Earth Follies* (Routledge: New York).

9   *The New Internationalist* 257 July 1994.

10   Laxer, James *The Toronto Star* .

11   Dillon, John *Canadian Forum* June 1994.

12   Lewis, Stephen "The United Nations After the Gulf War, A Promise Betrayed" *World Policy Journal* Summer 1991.

13   Enloe, Cynthia 1989 *Bananas, Beaches and Bases: Making Feminist Sense of International Politics* (Pandora Press: London).

14   *Yugoslavia War* 1992 edited by Kuzmanic, Tonci, and Arno Truger (Peace Institute, Ljubljana, Slovenia, and Study Centre for Peace and Conflict Resolution: Schlaining, Austria).

15   Human Rights Centre for Research, Education and Public Policy, University College of Cape Breton, Sydney, NS, Canada.

PART V

ENVIRONMENT AND DEVELOPMENT

Commentary on Part V
David Runnalls

In many ways, the *United Nations Conference on Environment and Development* (UNCED) held in Rio de Janeiro in June 1992 was a great triumph for the UN system. The *Conference* attracted an enormous crowd. There were more than 5000 official government delegates, more than 8000 members of the press registered with the Conference Secretariat and a lively *NGO Forum* featured several thousand representatives of what has now become fashionably known as civil society.

If the *Stockholm Conference* of 1972 was to be the environment's coming-out party, then Rio de Janeiro was designed to put it on the map as one of the principal political/economic issues for the remainder of the century and beyond. The *Conference* was called for in the final report of the Brundtland Commission – the World Commission on Environment and Development.

Our Common Future, the Commission's landmark report, demonstrated that the earth's environment and its economy were so closely interlocked that policies in one sphere that ignored the other were bound for failure. Its policy prescription for the human dilemma – sustainable development – demands nothing else than the reorientation of the world's economic systems. We must remember that concerns over sustainable development arose from the growing judgment that a planetary increase in production and consumption to meet the needs of the 10 billion who will be on the earth by the middle of the next century is simply not supportable by the earth's natural systems, given current patterns of resource use and technology. The Brundtland Commission reminded us how close many of the earth's vital systems are to collapse.

Sustainable development therefore requires not only growth of the economy, but a sea change in the quality of growth to make it less raw material- and energy- intensive and, above all, to make it far more equitable in its impact. It requires measures to limit population growth and to respect the rights of future generations. It requires measures to reduce the consumption of raw materials and energy in the North, while allowing space for the South to expand its use of these commodities. It requires measures to reduce drastically pollution in both North and South. These changes are required globally, as part of an interconnected package to maintain and improve the earth's stock of ecological capital, to improve the distribution of income, and to reduce our vulnerability to economic and ecological crises.

It also requires massive infusions of capital for the transition to sustainable development. Sustainable development is subject to many definitions. Some prefer a more "bottom up" community-based road to sustainability. Others prefer the more traditional approach set out in *Agenda 21*, with national governments playing the key role, assisted by the traditional foreign assistance donors. And there are innumerable variations between these two extremes.

There is little disagreement, however, that the road to sustainable development will be expensive. The costs of cleaning up the tremendous social deficits in the developing world in water supply, housing, food supplies and education, and making the transition to more resource- and environmentally- efficient technologies, will be very high indeed. The UNCED Secretariat estimated the annual cost at $562 billion.

The Brundtland Commissioners knew that governments could not be trusted to deal with issues of this magnitude on their own. So they called in their report for a global conference five years later to review progress towards sustainable development.

Maurice Strong, the Canadian who had headed the earlier *Stockholm Conference* (and no mean hand in the UN reform business himself), was selected to head Secretariat for this *Conference*. Rather than hosting the customary two-week intergovernmental exercise, Strong determined to raise the ante. He knew that the usual assortment of Environment Ministers and middle level bureaucrats were not going to be able to cope with the financial and political challenges of sustainable development. He knew that, if sustainable development were to join peace and security and economic progress at the top of the international pantheon, then he would have to involve Heads of State. He knew that only they could release the massive amounts of capital needed to achieve sustainability. In the words of René Lévesque in another circumstance, he took *le beau risque*.

Eventually, more than one hundred Heads of State attended the *Conference*. And they each made a speech. And by and large, they each made a speech which indicated that they realized that sustainable development was not just more environmental protection. And, with some notable exceptions, they signed two new international agreements, on the preservation of biodiversity and on climate change. They agreed on a vast and comprehensive action plan, *Agenda 21*, which aims to change the way governments do everything: from preventing urban pollution to coping with radioactive waste; from preserving forests to preserving the way of life of indigenous peoples. Finally, they agreed to create a new UN institution, the Commission on Sustainable Development, whose mandate was to follow up the Rio de Janeiro decisions at Ministerial level.

Yet UNCED was, at best, a mixed success. In the end it failed to deliver the goods. Northern parliaments are becoming even more parsimonious with aid money. The dismal performance of George Bush took much of the steam out of the climate change and biodiversity conventions, and the developing countries felt let down by the system again. Once again they were being asked to change their development patterns to cope with problems largely caused by the North. And the money and technology to help them to cope with the transition were simply not there.

The papers in Part V illustrate some of the difficulties with UNCED and reveal some glimmers of hope for the future.

Many feel that the Rio de Janeiro process may have changed the international system by involving non-governmental actors in a much different way than the traditional stultifying UN Non-Governmental Organization (NGO). Peter Padbury, the author of V.1, was himself instrumental in the convening of the global *Forum*, and especially in its treaty negotiations. The treaty process involved NGOs trying to sort among themselves how civil society should react to the challenges of sustainability. Rather than sit back and criticize the *Conference* itself, they set about developing solutions of their own. Padbury speculates how the permanent networks among NGOs created at Rio de Janeiro could lead to a new UN system, which spreads ownership of problems and their solution far more widely than now.

As mentioned above, the transition to sustainable development will be expensive. The Brundtland Commission, in a special meeting held just before the *Earth Summit*, speculated that at least $50 billion would need to be on the table to ensure that the global bargain between rich and poor would succeed. The developing countries held preparatory meetings in Beijing and Kuala Lumpur, and proposed that a separate fund (the Green Fund) be created within the United Nations to finance the transition towards sustainable development. The developed countries wanted most of the funding to be from their bilateral coffers. They preferred any multilateral money to be channelled through the Global Environmental Facility (GEF), an experimental vehicle cooked up by the World Bank (with UNDP and UNEP in lesser, supporting roles) to deal with global environmental issues. Although conceding that the GEF would emerge from Rio de Janeiro with the lion's share of the new resources, Strong preferred a

UN solution, arguing for a major role in capacity building for UNDP.

The war over money dominated much of the Rio de Janeiro discussion. The developing countries finally capitulated to the donors and the World Bank on the supremacy of the GEF, but only after extracting a commitment to reform its governance. Robert Matthews documents in Chapter 16, the transition of the pre-Rio de Janeiro GEF to its current status with an interesting hybrid governing structure.

James Busumtwi-Sam in Chapter 18 carries further the discussion of the role of the World Bank and its sister Bretton Woods institution, the IMF. Although cast in a framework somewhat wider than the remit of the *Rio de Janeiro Conference*, his paper identifies the critical issues raised by the Group of 77 at the *Earth Summit*. He calls for major changes in conditionality and in the operational governance of the World Bank. He recommends the kinds of changes in Structural Adjustment programmes to make them more attuned to poverty alleviation and local circumstances that characterized the debate on sustainable social development. Finally, he brings us back to one of the issues that the *Rio de Janeiro Conference* conveniently neglected – the Third World debt burden.

Perhaps the major insight of the *Rio de Janeiro Conference* is the need to integrate environmental considerations into all aspects of economic decision making. For under sustainable development the environment becomes a big ticket economic item – up there with economic growth, employment opportunities and export performance when Finance Ministers sit down to develop their budgets. This makes it difficult to assign responsibility for the issue within the international system. Coordination is a much used and almost always abused word in the UN system. Urs Thomas in Chapter 17 describes the ill-fated attempts at coordination that the UN Environment Programme has attempted to play in the system, and he speculates on the prospects for the child created at Rio to coordinate sustainable development initiatives – the Commission on Sustainable Development.

Finally, he tackles what might be the toughest issue of all. *Trade and the Environment* has emerged as an issue with impressive speed. In 1987 the Brundtland Commission produced its report and the GATT contracting parties began negotiations on the Uruguay Round. At the time, the two events were thought to be unrelated. Now we realize that the new World Trade Organization must find ways to develop trade policies that take the environment into the centre of trade policy.

Despite the temporary failure of the Rio de Janeiro process, sustainable development is an issue that is here to stay. And it poses a host of problems of coordination, finance and the relationship with the Bretton Woods institutions that the United Nations system must face. But it also offers new opportunities for the UN to build its own constituencies directly with non-governmental groups, if it opts to broaden the range of stakeholders both in the identification and the solution of problems.

CHAPTER 15

UNCED and the Globalization of Civil Society

Peter Padbury

What Lessons Can We Learn from UNCED?

Context
The *UN Conference on the Human Environment* held in Stockholm in 1972 put environment on the official agenda. But by the late 1980s it was clear that protection of the life support system of the planet was a secondary concern for most governments at both the national and the international level. In 1987 the Brundtland Commission report, *Our Common Future,* noted a number of highly inter-linked problems and called for a UN conference to address these problems in an integrated fashion. The UN General Assembly agreed (in a contorted way), and established the *UN Conference on Environment and Development* (UNCED) in December 1989. There was a two and a half year preparatory process with thousands of meetings involving tens of thousands of people all over the world. Officially, there were five long and intense *Preparatory Committee* (*PrepCom*) meetings in Geneva and New York and a short heads-of-state *Earth Summit* in Rio de Janeiro in June 1992.

"Conference" is a strange word to use in a UN context. It is not much like a regular conference; it is more like a session of the General Assembly on a special theme. Government diplomats or government appointed experts are the only participants with power to speak when they want. Special rules govern the behaviour of Non-Governmental Organizations (NGOs) with consultative status, UN Agencies and invited others. Over the last few decades there had been a long series of UN conferences on various sectoral themes (energy, women, children, *etc*). UNCED was by far one of the most ambitious. There are many things we can learn that would have implications for UN reform.

What Did the Secretariat Do?
Maurice Strong was chosen as Secretary-General for UNCED. Strong, who was also Secretary-General for the 1972 *Conference* in Stockholm, rec-

ognized that another UN conference by itself was unlikely to solve the problem – he needed allies. His external strategy was to open the doors for innovative relationships with all sectors of civil society. Business, science, youth, indigenous peoples, women's organizations and NGOs responded and organized themselves in different ways to take advantage of the opportunity to influence the global conference. His strategy with the governments was to prepare background papers and initial negotiating text that opened the debate as widely as possible and later in the game to focus on what was feasible. He used the media, visits to heads-of-state and the NGOs to raise expectations and to put as much pressure on the governments as possible. Unfortunately, the world media, which had a key role to play, failed to cover the all-important negotiating process and ignored the big picture at the Summit.

What Did the NGOs Do?
One thousand four hundred NGOs asked for accreditation to the preparatory process. Many of these groups were national, regional or issue networks. Throughout the five *Preparatory Committee (PrepCom) Meetings*, NGOs had access to meeting rooms, got copies of negotiating text, could speak in plenary, lobby everywhere and circulate their own position papers. NGOs had their own meeting rooms to organize and strategize as well, *i.e.*, almost the same access as consultative status NGOs. For many of these groups, this was their first participation in the global policy dialogue.

NGOs started off by being critics. But very soon the diplomats (who knew relatively little about sustainability) started to ask the NGOs for concrete ideas about what to do. A synergistic relationship emerged. NGOs organized daily NGO/government dialogues. NGOs started to identify friendly governments in both North and South. NGO ideas, data and text started to appear in the negotiating text.

NGO networks around the world started to exchange papers and ideas about what to do at the next *PrepCom Meeting*. Most of the major group networks organized series of meetings at the national, regional and international level to make commitments, contribute ideas and develop position papers. Some started to use electronic mail in *ad hoc* issue networks. There were several attempts to organize all of the independent sectors under one umbrella committee.

In their position papers, many NGOs saw a global system in crisis and the need for a new paradigm, if we were to keep economic activity within the environmental carrying capacity of the planet in a way that was equitable, just and sustainable. By the *Third PrepCom Meeting*, two things were becoming clear: Governments were not interested in a paradigm shift, and no one, including NGOs, could describe alternative policies and strategies which would both affect the shift and attract the interest of governments.

By the time of the *Earth Summit* in Rio de Janeiro, the NGOs who might have been critics at the government meeting had dramatically shifted their strategy, but this significant shift was not covered by the media. In Rio de Janeiro, several thousand of the most articulate NGO leaders sat together for two weeks with translations in four languages to draft 39 NGO treaties. The treaties describe mechanisms for NGO cooperation and work plans that NGOs would carry out to build alternatives. While the outcome of the NGO treaty process is not yet clear (negotiations are continuing), the vision that motivates it invites our attention.

NGOs in the treaty process moved from being critics of the system to seeing themselves as co-creators of the future. They saw the need to integrate the local, national and global dialogues on problems, options and strategies. They saw the need to invent and test policies and strategies that would facilitate the transition to sustainability. They saw the incredible potential of civil society to mobilize its own resources, to share, teach and learn, and to empower itself to act. One African participant said that we have been working at the local level for forty years doing good projects; but our good work is frequently undermined by national and global policies that ignore our needs and realities. Many participants were aware that globalization of business and technology was occurring in a vacuum, and there was a need for a parallel globalization of civil society to provide moral and ethical checks, if not an alternative vision. The NGO treaty process is an innovative example (there are others) of elements of local and national civil society attempting to organize themselves to address complex global problems.

One of the most notable features of all of this activity is that civil society was using its own limited resources to help change global policies and programmes. Twenty-five heads-of-state and many diplomats and observers said that NGOs made a very significant contribution. Unfortunately, the UN, as a forum of sovereign governments, was unable to respond in a strategic or constructive fashion to all of this creativity.

What Did Governments Do?
It is important to state that a lot was accomplished at UNCED, particularly in expanding cooperation on environmental issues. UNCED failed however to reach its goal. It failed to agree on the strategies, policies, tools and new institutions that are needed to ensure that the planet's economic

processes do not destroy the ecological system on which they depend.

The background documents prepared by the Secretariat were generally quite good. As negotiations proceeded, the wording become more general and the commitments less precise. Many times during the UNCED process the negotiations did not seem to be connected to problems or actors in the real world. One wondered whether anyone was really reading the documents back in the capitals. The principal strategy of governments seemed to be to ensure that nothing happened that obligated their country to make any changes.

UNCED was a real learning process for several thousand diplomats, national and international civil servants and NGOs who worked together through months of meetings. It was strange to talk with the negotiators in the coffee shop or bar. Many of them wanted the same things. Many of them saw the need for fundamental change, and pushed for it in small ways whenever they could. Several diplomats said the problem was that the people back home had not sat through the same learning process – the capitals were not ready.

The debate on financial resources to pay for *Agenda 21* was illustrative of many of the problems. The South wanted the industrial countries of the North to pledge new and additional resources to carry out the action plan. They argued that all of the aid money they currently received was committed to essential services. The North was in a recession and could not promise new resources. It wanted to get higher synergy out of existing resource flows and to use new economic instruments to generate new resource flows. NGOs proposed two credible solutions: (1) if civil society was more involved it might be willing to pay for some of the changes; and (2) if there is no new money, start with the things that do not cost much money. These suggestions were ignored. A great deal of time was spent on the finance question. Both sides were prepared to put significant chunks of reality up for debate. The finance discussion was a stalemate that was never formally resolved. It had its roots in forty years of unresolved UN debate on questions like debt, trade, militarism, *etc.* The finance stalemate served to highlight the inability of the inter-governmental process to look strategically at all of the relationships as one inter-related system.

In Rio de Janeiro, the governments approved a change process that effectively had two elements. Heads-of-state promised to implement *Agenda 21* and the two conventions. In UN style, implementation would be done in an *ad hoc* fashion and at their convenience. Also, a new UN body, the Commission on Sustainable Development, was established to review progress in implementing *Agenda 21* on an annual basis (and in a significant way by 1997). Its unstated role was to put pressure on governments to act. The implicit assumption is that civil society, nationally and globally, has a key role to play, because governments tend not to embarrass each other. However, no provisions were made to make it easy for civil society to play that role.

Two years after Rio de Janeiro, many low-cost UNCED-initiated activities are still moving through the environmental bureaucracies of the planet. The Commission on Sustainable Development meets for two weeks annually to monitor progress in implementing *Agenda 21* (based largely on voluntary country reports). However, sustainability is not high on any finance or development minister's agenda. Little has fundamentally changed. A couple of hundred people have read *Agenda 21*. For most people on the planet, it is still business as usual.

UNCED was a heroic effort to put sustainability on the global agenda. It had a very promising start. There were good people in all of the key position, good initial negotiating documents and adequate finances for the process. It was as if the UN had assembled a very impressive team numbering in the thousands. But it soon encountered all of the unresolved problems of the UN. It was a 19th century institution trying to solve a 21st century problem.

Implications for UN Reform

UNCED was an amazing process, but, like many UN conferences and permanent fora, it suffered from a number of problems:

(1) *Emphasis was on negotiation, rather than an effective change process.* The negotiating processes of the General Assembly and related committees and commissions are amazing. Unfortunately, there are other phases to effective action than just negotiation; there are thousands of unimplemented UN resolutions that prove the point. Processes for problem identification, generation of alternative visions, prioritizing, strategizing, getting the commitment and support of affected populations, implementing, assessing and learning are definitely not evident in the decision making fora of the UN. Indeed, anyone with a modicum of process skills would be hard pressed to find in the UN any of the processes that are common in a modern government department, corporation or NGO. If we have to rely on the UN, it is going to take a thousand years to solve complex problems like the transition to sustainability, because we need more than a negotiating forum.

(2) *Emphasis was on nation state rather than planetary system.* The UN is principally a forum for sovereign states. Governments cooperate and carry out UN agreements if it is in their interest. When the UN was founded, the nation state and the associated policies and institutions were more or less effective. But now many problems (crime, disease, pollution, poverty, *etc.*) travel freely across international borders. Many of the most difficult economic, social and environmental problems can only be solved when viewed as part of an evolving global system. Many UN decisions, shaped by the self-interest of nation states, are more appropriate to the world of the 1960s.

(3) *Emphasis was on sectoral – rather than system – level change.* UN bureaucracies parallel national bureaucracies in many amazing ways. National health departments relate to each other, but health departments do not talk to energy departments; women's departments are marginal everywhere; economic institutions listen to no one. Each sector has its own plan, its own experts, its own annual meeting, its own UN agency and even its own UN decade. The system is overloaded with sectoral meetings, one after another, in an un-integrated fashion. Unfortunately, many of our most pressing global problems, *e.g.*, poverty or sustainability, do not easily fit in these old boxes. Solutions require an integrated response across departments, across disciplines and across borders. The institutional infrastructure to develop a credible consensus to solve a system-level problem does not exist yet.

(4) *Many of the principal stakeholders are not present or committed to act.* Effective solutions to many system-level problems will require participation and agreement by many different stakeholders at every level across the planet. Businesses, consumers, investors, educators, professionals, workers, managers, parents, peasants and NGOs all have key roles to play in solving problems like the global transition to sustainability. Many of them know that they own part of some global problem that is a barrier to their success. Together, they have all the resources necessary to solve the problems, but few of them see the UN as an appropriate channel. The UN is dominated by overworked, well-intentioned diplomats and departments of foreign affairs. Most UN meetings are seen as irrelevant. The negotiations move so quickly that many government departments (other than foreign affairs) and affected populations have little time to take advantage of the opportunity to use the UN to help them solve their problem. Few people in the world know or care what is happening at the UN. The structure and process-

es of the UN do not encourage creative new kinds of partnerships to solve global problems in an effective and coordinated fashion.

Towards a New Vision of the UN

Let us briefly summarize the political decision making process in the General Assembly and subsidiary bodies of the UN, and then describe how the UN could be reformed to resolve some of the problems mentioned above.

Currently, most countries maintain missions in New York and Geneva. While the size varies considerably, many are quite small. This small group of several hundred overworked diplomats go to an endless round of meetings. They are supported and directed by foreign affairs departments back in the capitals. The foreign affairs departments involve other government departments and experts as issues dictate. The overloaded UN Secretariat consults with governments and others and prepares the initial discussion papers for the meetings. Often these papers are late and do not circulate widely. Other UN agencies, governments and NGOs may also prepare papers. The meetings often have three phases: general statement on the text; negotiating the text; approval of the final text. All decisions are based on consensus. Paradoxically, governments that have no intention of implementing the agreement will water down the text to the lowest common denominator. Regardless of the objective of the meeting (monitoring, norm setting, coordinating, *etc.*), the outcome is left up to each government to implement. Often nothing happens because of limited resources or other priorities.

The UN has served us well in dealing with highly focused problems like peacekeeping and sectoral cooperation. It is most effective at preserving and extending the *status quo*. This system would probably work if we were not facing a system-level transition.

The key to successful UN reform is to know what problems we need to solve. I have argued above that one of the central flaws of the current system is that too few people are trying to solve global problems. No one else knows or cares. A key element of the solution is to broaden the ownership of the global problems we face as well as of the UN processes needed to solve them. Broadening ownership will contribute to a new orientation towards a systems view, a planetary perspective, and effective management of change. UNCED proves that, unless we start building a world wide constituency for change, we are not going to be able to solve the problems that threaten life on this planet.

It would be logical and fashionable to extend a long-term historical trend and call for the democratization of the UN. Over the last 250 years we have seen an expansion of representative democracy that involves elections at the village, province/state and national level in a number countries, and even at the regional level in the European Union. The next step would be to do the same at the international level. The result could be either a parliamentary assembly (national parliaments choose from among their members: see Chapter 5) or a people's assembly (direct election: see Chapter 4) at the UN.

I am doubtful that such strategies would improve the current situation. They would suffer from the same problems of credibility and legitimacy that all governments currently face. The mechanisms for developing global consensus and accountability would be even weaker. The people's assembly would raise the difficult issue of a democratic *vs.* a shareholder model. Are the rich countries going to allow themselves to be outnumbered? In all likelihood a parliamentary assembly would become an extension of the current state system at the UN with similar problems.

I suggest that, in the short term, the solution lies in two emerging and related trends:

* Many organizations are behaving and becoming more like networks than hierarchies. Forces like downsizing, fiscal constraints, and complexity are forcing organizations to develop processes to collaborate. A network is not a structure or an institution. It is a set of roles and processes for information sharing, resource sharing, visioning, consensus-building, strategizing, decision making and learning;
* Empowerment involves all of the key stakeholders working together to create policies, institutions, processes and tools that support communities and organizations to provide the services they need themselves or to act for the benefit of the whole.

These trends have already begun to shape the emerging elements of global civil society. One of the remarkable features of UNCED was the emergence of issue networks and national coalitions of environment, development, labour and women's NGOs that linked local concerns to global problems. They held public fora and prepared position papers as a contribution to a global process. They did not want to give up their autonomy to a central office in New York or Geneva. They wanted to be part of a global network actively working on change. Some of those networks still exist. It is significant that they are building new relationships with each other around the UNCED follow-up, other UN conferences and other initiatives. These networks are different from traditional international NGOs, which tended to have a narrower focus and mandate, limited membership involvement and limited and less proactive involvement in the global policy dialogue.

As more people recognize that important decisions that affect their lives are increasingly made in international rather than national fora, we can anticipate the emergence of more national and regional networks as well as more issue networks. A number of forces support this trend: modern communication technologies such as electronic conferencing, financial constraints that encourage collective action, increasing attention to identifying and coping with root causes. Indeed, processes like the NGO treaty process are developing norms and mechanisms for networks to work together to develop alternatives and influence the global policy dialogue. With increased globalization, we can expect many sectors of society to be more and more engaged in the international dialogue to protect or extend their interests.

Assume for one moment that these trends were allowed to reshape the UN. What would it look like? In the old UN, a handful of people sat in meetings in New York and owned the problems. In the reformed UN, people and organizations around the planet would collaborate in decentralized networks to solve the problems. The UN decision making fora would not be seen as the top of a government pyramid, but rather as nodes in a vast network of collaborating governments and organizations. The UN's unique role would be as caretaker of a series of processes that broadly engage all levels of government and interested elements of global civil society, in an effort to create consensus on integrated strategies, policies and action plans to solve global problems.

Who would participate in these processes? The participants would be organizations and networks, whose members own parts of a global problem and want to find a solution. They would include all levels of governments, businesses, unions, women's groups, associations of farmers, people's organizations, teachers, health workers, NGOs, *etc.* During UNCED, the questions often asked were, "Whom do NGOs represent? How large is your constituency?" Some would argue that governments have been elected (in some countries) and thus are the legitimate spokespersons for the people of their country. Others would argue that peoples organizations and associations have as much legitimacy, especially if they are directly accountable to a constituency and are already working on the problem under discussion. It may be more important that the full range viewpoints be represented to ensure that workable and empowering solutions are developed.

What would they do? Interested organizations, associations, networks and governments would participate in a consensus-building process to build ownership of the problem and commitment to a solution. The process would be more than a consultation. The participants would be actively involved in working with others around the world to develop, test and implement solutions.

What would be the advantage? Broadening the involvement of civil society in UN processes would have several benefits:

(1) it would bring creative and credible solutions to the government fora and help to focus on the highest common denominator among those solutions;
(2) it would challenge self-interested sovereign governments to act on collective and system-level problems;
(3) the involvement of civil society would bring significant new human and financial resources to solve global problems;
(4) it would build understanding, commitment and ultimately political will to solve global problems;
(5) and finally, it is likely that the emerging global civil society would provide a smooth transition towards an effective world parliament.

The speculations above are based on the assumption that in the next fifty years we face a number of system-level problems. These problems will require considerable global effort to solve. For many global problems there are no answers: we need to invent the solutions. We need a set of tools and processes and relationships that identify fruitful strategies and then bring forward those issues that require international cooperation and negotiation to resolve. We need to build the institutional infrastructure *now* to solve those problems, because it will take several decades before it is fully operational. Part of the solution involves broadening the ownership of the problems as well as of the UN processes to solve them. It is proposed that a global civil society is emerging and that it has a key role to play in the process.

Recommendations and Strategy

Below are several concrete suggestions to help realize this vision and make the UN a far more strategic, catalytic and action oriented forum:

(1) Make UN fora and agencies more welcoming of civil societies' contributions.

(2) Encourage and support the globalization of civil society through the development of effective national, regional, global and issue networks. These networks require resources to support information sharing, consensus-building and decision making processes, and most donors are reluctant to fund such processes.

(3) Invent processes to allow a broad cross-section of the people of the planet to participate in prioritizing issues and agenda-setting for UN fora.

(4) Support an open, transparent drafting process. The preparation of negotiating documents should be a much more open process. The Secretariat should distribute widely an outline paper and then successive drafts, inviting analysis, examples and creative solution- oriented input. This would allow government departments and others to use the process in more constructive ways. It would allow major groups who cannot afford to come to these meetings to have a say. It would make it much easier for writers to focus their contribution, and for the Secretariat to incorporate contributions. This is a very simple but important innovation that could significantly increase ownership and participation.

(5) Assess the state of the world: the Secretariat should prepare in one concise document a strategic overview of the state of the planet. This document would summarize and analyze information from government and non-government sources. The overview should offer an assessment of strengths, weaknesses, threats and opportunities that we face in solving global problems. It should recommend priorities, and issues for discussion and negotiation at the UN, as well as for action by others.

(6) Open the process of developing national government positions for key UN meetings to debate and broad public involvement. Consider joint drafting processes in which the government prepares reports in cooperation with civil society (as was done for the Canadian national report for UNCED).

(7) Encourage and support civil society representatives on government delegations to appropriate UN meetings.

(8) Support innovative processes and new kinds of multi-level partnerships to address system-level problems. To solve system-level problems it is necessary to work at the micro- and the policy-levels at the same time.

CHAPTER 16

On Reforming the Global Environment Facility

Robert O. Matthews

The Global Environment Facility (GEF) was formally launched in 1991 as a 3-year pilot programme to assist developing countries in their efforts to protect the global environment in four focal areas: global warming, pollution of international waters, loss of biodiversity and depletion of the ozone layer. The GEF was conceived of by its founders as a funding mechanism to be managed by the World Bank, the United Nations Development Programme (UNDP), and the United Nations Environment Programme (UNEP). Either through contributions to the GEF's "core fund" or through parallel financing arrangements, the donor countries pledged a sum of $1.2 billion over three years to cover the incremental costs involved in developing projects that benefited the global (rather than the local) environment.

From an historical perspective the GEF can be viewed as the culmination of a difficult and lengthy "search for ways to channel increased financial resources into programmes designed to reverse the declining state of the global environment."[1] This search began at the Stockholm *Conference on the Human Environment* in 1972, at the conclusion of which a UNEP Environment Fund was established on a voluntary basis to finance environmentally sound development. In 1987 the Brundtland Commission called for "serious consideration to be given to the development of a special international banking programme or facility linked to the World Bank ... to marshal and support investments for conservation projects."[2] Two years later, in a report commissioned by the UNDP, the World Resources Institute recommended the creation of a Global Environment Trust Fund. Later in the same year, this idea was put forward as a proposal by the French and German governments at a meeting of the World Bank's Development Committee. The World Bank was then instructed to ascertain what additional funding would be needed and the level of support for such a mechanism within the donor community. Out of a series of meetings sponsored by the World Bank, and attended by representatives of the major donor countries and of several developing countries and UNDP and UNEP officials, emerged an "enabling memorandum" calling for the establishment of the GEF. This memorandum was formally approved by the Board of the World Bank on 14 March 1991. In October 1991, the tripartite agreement formally established the GEF, specifying the responsibilities of the three Implementing Agencies (the World Bank, UNDP and UNEP). Thus was born the GEF. It was to be an experimental project, lasting from July 1991 to June 1994.[3]

Calls for Reform

From its very beginning, however, the GEF has been the subject of reformist pressures. This should come as no surprise as it had been put together hurriedly and without widespread consultation. Indeed, the GEF was launched as an experiment with the understanding that the lessons learned from its operations could be used to fashion an innovative approach to environmental issues. Calls for reform came from a variety of sources but mainly from the community of Non-governmental Organizations (NGOs) and from the developing countries of the Third World.

NGOs

Since the first meeting of the Participants' Assembly in May 1991, NGOs and particularly those that had extensive dealings with the World Bank, have sought to influence the direction of the GEF. Through consultations with their own governments and through the bi-annual consultations with the GEF and its participant governments, NGOs have launched a searching critique of the GEF, its mode of operation, and its overall approach to the global environmental crises. And as David Reed of the World Wide Fund for Nature has commented, their efforts have had modest success: "While it is clear that relatively few of the reforms promoted by the NGO community have been implemented ..., we nonetheless believe that our combined efforts have helped shape the debate over the policies, practices, and procedures of the GEF and the implementing agencies."[4]

It would be incorrect to suggest that there is an NGO community that has voiced a single set of clearly defined reforms. In fact, there is no consensus on how to reform the GEF. Only a few NGOs are especially interested in the GEF and within that group each organization has articulated its own interests. Some have called for radical change, while others are prepared to work for modest reforms within the existing framework of the GEF. Notwithstanding these differences, it is quite remarkable that at an

NGO consultation in Cartagena, Colombia, a consensus did emerge around six major points. Above all, the NGOs believe that the GEF lacks "a clear strategy and set of objectives that overarches focal areas and guides project selection."[5] As a consequence the GEF has tended to "become a mechanism to palliate the effects of existing development approaches, rather than a means for opening new development strategies that could internalize global environmental costs."[6] Secondly, this absence of objectives and strategies is observed at the level of each of the four focal areas. Thirdly, the NGOs note the "failure to reconcile national and global environmental interests and responsibilities to guide programme and project design."[7] Fourthly, fundamental differences do exist between developing and industrial countries as to what the GEF goals and strategies should be. Fifthly, the NGOs express their concern that the present Facility does not allow for adequate consultation with them and local communities and precludes their obtaining observer status. Finally, they note the "lack of a systematic learning process."[8] If the GEF is to be an effective organization, it has to develop a permanent and independent body to evaluate continuously its own work. In addition, the NGOs have called for increasing the organizational and functional independence of the GEF from the three implementing agencies, in particular the World Bank. Only in that way can the GEF, as distinct from the implementing agencies, approve or reject projects and programmes.

The South

Somewhat belatedly the developing countries of the South have taken an interest in the GEF and expressed their concern with its mode of operation and direction. This interest and concern grew out of the parallel debates that were taking place in the preparatory meetings leading up to the *United Nations Conference on Environment and Development* (UNCED) in Rio de Janeiro in 1992, as well as the inter-governmental negotiations for a *Framework Convention on Climate Change* and a *Convention on Biological Diversity*. In all these fora the debate was dominated by questions relating to the need for additional environmental funding and an appropriate financial mechanism. By the time of the *Third Preparatory Committee (PrepCom) Meeting*, held in August 1991 in Geneva, the South had fashioned a consensus within its own ranks. In sharp contrast to the industrialized countries that championed the cause of the GEF, the developing countries called for its demise, for the GEF was in their view an institution that had been controlled, from its very establishment, by the North. As the

South Centre, a Third World think tank, argued, the creation of the GEF was nothing but "a pre-emptive institutional and political move by the North and the World Bank" to establish "the facility on their own terms … thereby making it easier to deflect likely demands from the South."[9] In the early stages of these discussions the South favoured the development of a new Green Fund as a mechanism to administer new and additional[10] resources to be allocated for the environment. By the end of the *Fourth PrepCom Meeting* (April 1992) the South agreed to accept the GEF as long as the scope of its activities was broadened and the structure of its governance made more open and democratic.

By early 1992 it had thus become clear that, if the GEF were to continue and to become an umbrella for all future environmental funding, important changes in the way in which it operated would be essential. At a meeting convened in Washington, DC in late April 1992, the participants, recognizing the inevitable, accepted the general framework for reform presented to them by the GEF Administrator. Membership in the GEF was to become universal; the scope of its activities was to be extended to include, within the four focal areas, land degradation issues, principally desertification and deforestation; the World Bank, UNDP and UNEP were to continue to fulfil the roles they then played; a Participants' Assembly made up of all the participating governments would direct the implementation of the GEF; and decisions would normally be made by consensus, but when that proved impossible a system of voting would be devised to "guarantee both a balanced and equitable representation of the interests of developing countries, as well as give due weight to the funding efforts of donor countries."[11]

A similar set of principles, in some instances identical, was incorporated in *Agenda 21*, the action plan designed at UNCED to achieve sustainable development in the 21st century. *Chapter 33* of *Agenda 21* spells out the terms of the compromise reached by North and South. The GEF was acceptable as a funding mechanism as long as it was restructured in such a way as to "encourage universal participation;" "ensure a governance that is transparent and democratic in nature, by guaranteeing a balanced and equitable representation of the interests of developing countries as well as give due weight to the funding efforts of donor countries;" "ensure predictability in the flow of funds by contributions from developed countries;" and distribute these funds "without introducing new forms of conditionality." Almost identical wording is to be found in the *Framework Convention on Climate Change* (*Articles* 11 and 21) and the *Convention on Biological Diversity* (*Articles* 21 and 39).

From Rio de Janeiro to Geneva

While a compromise had been struck at Rio de Janeiro on the basic principles guiding the restructuring of the GEF, there still remained the difficult
task of translating these principles into practice. What, for instance, would
be the governing structure and the actual voting procedures? How would
transparency be assured? The answers to these questions were not obvious,
nor free of conflict. Nor did the compromise address the larger concerns of
the NGOs; as they were to be part of the discussions on restructuring,
their interests could not be ignored. Finally, the donor countries had to
reach agreement on a new level of funding.

To resolve their differences on restructuring and replenishment the
parties to the GEF (their numbers had increased to 73 by March 1994)
held a series of seven *Participant Assembly Meetings*. At the first such
Meeting, held in Abidjan in December 1992, it was decided to open up
membership to all states; the principle of universality was to be honoured.
At the same *Meeting* the participants requested an independent evaluation
of the Pilot Phase of the GEF to be completed by the end of 1993. With
such an evaluation in hand the participants could fashion a new instrument that not only reflected the interests of the developing countries, but
also incorporated the lessons drawn from the earlier experience of the GEF.

Subsequent *Meetings* were held in Rome (March 1993), Beijing (May
1993), Washington, DC (September 1993), Paris (November 1993) and
Cartagena (December 1993). Some progress was made, but underlying differences over governance and levels of funding remained. With the publication of the *Report of the Independent Evaluation of the GEF Pilot Phase* on
23 November 1993, the stage was set for what was expected to be the final
session. The parties assembled in Cartagena in the first week of December
to finalize the restructuring and replenishment of the GEF. The first day of
the *Meeting* was taken up with presentations by the NGOs and the team of
independent evaluators. Both argued in favour of institutional reforms that
would strengthen the role and independence of the GEFs Council and
Secretariat from the three implementing agencies, the UNDP, UNEP and
the World Bank. They also recommended that the process of preparing,
implementing and monitoring projects should be opened to greater participation of NGOs and affected local communities. It is difficult to ignore
the far-reaching conclusions of the *Report of the Independent Evaluation*:
"The GEF is a promising, and presently the only significant, mechanism
for funding programmes relevant to the protection of the global environment. However, the promise of this significant new fund will not be real-

ized unless there are fundamental changes in the GEF strategies, the functions and relationships of its organizational components, and operating procedures."[12]

As the week progressed, the participating governments focused their attention less on reform than on the sharing of powers between the North and South within the GEF's Governing Council. This conflict was reflected in two contentious issues. The first related to how many seats there would be on the Council, how those seats would be distributed between industrialized and developing countries, and the kind of majority required for the making of decisions. The second revolved around the question of who would Chair the Council, the Chief Executive Officer (CEO) of the Secretariat or someone elected from among its members. The developed countries preferred to have 30 seats on the Council, with 14 from the industrialized bloc, 2 from economies in transition, and 14 from the South, and with the CEO serving as Chair of the Council. The Group of 77 insisted on having a clear majority in the Council and on the right of the Council to elect its own Chair. Agreement appeared to be very close when, on the last day, the industrialized countries returned to the table with two options. However, at the very moment that the Group of 77 was reviewing these alternatives, France insisted on returning to the original OECD proposal with the CEO serving as Chair. Linking its policy to France's, Germany withdrew its support for the compromise as well. "Amidst accusations of bad faith, and of failing to live up to the promises of new levels of cooperation made in Rio de Janeiro, the negotiations collapsed."[13]

After intensive consultations among governments, following the collapse of negotiations in Cartagena, talks resumed in Geneva on 14 March 1994. Two days later, on 16 March, agreement was reached on new structures for the GEF and on the level of funding for the next three years. The final outcome was a compromise between the positions adopted by the industrialized and developing countries. The Governing Council is to compose of 32 seats, 16 for Group of 77 countries (6 from Africa, 6 from Asia, and 4 from Latin America), 2 for countries whose economies are in transition, and 14 for the principal donor countries. Decisions in the Council will normally be taken by consensus, but where that is impossible to achieve, an affirmative vote will require a 60% majority of the total number of participants and a 60% majority of the total contributions. Finally, there will be two chairs, the CEO of the Facility and one elected by the Council. As the latter only serves during the sessions of the Council, which meets twice a year, the former is left with the most power;

it is the CEO who "will actually approve funds, check projects and their implementation and run the GEF on a day to day basis."[14]

An Assessment

"The Geneva agreement marks a significant step forward in alleviating the growing pressures on the global environment," claimed Mohamed T. El-Ashry, Chairman of the GEF.[15] A new institution has thus been borne. But has it really? Have the Third World's demands been answered and NGOs concerns been met? Any evaluation undertaken at this time must of necessity be tentative, as the newly reformed GEF will not begin operations until mid-1994, but it should be possible now to situate the new instrument "for the establishment of the restructured global environment facility" within the context of Third World demands and NGO concerns: To what extent does the revised GEF reflect earlier pressures for reform?

The Third World's demands can be captured in three words: size, governance and scope. Clearly expectations following Rio de Janeiro were very high. The industrialized countries had pledged "new and additional resources" to give effect to the decisions of UNCED.[16] When the question of replenishment of the GEF was first raised, the figure most commonly mentioned was 3 billion SDRs (Special Drawing Rights on the IMF). That later fell to 2 billion SDRs and when the final agreement was reached at Geneva, it had sunk further to $2 billion. That does constitute a substantial increase from the $1.2 billion allocated to the Pilot Phase of the GEF, and this includes a greatly increased contribution to the NGO Small Grants Programme. But it falls far short of what the developing countries had expected. Obviously, the Third World was willing to pay the price of fewer resources for the creation of an instrument that was not driven by the donor countries, that resembled the Multilateral Fund established to finance the Montreal Protocol.

And to a certain extent, the GEF does mark an advance on most other international financial institutions. It has three organs, the Assembly, the Council and a Secretariat. The Assembly, which consists of representatives of all the Participant governments, will meet once every three years and has the responsibility of reviewing the general policies and operations of the Facility. It was the Third World's initial desire that the Assembly "be the supreme organ of the GEF and main forum for taking decisions."[17] In the end the Group of 77 had to accept more limited powers for the Assembly. It is in the Council that real power resides, and thus it is not surprising that its composition was the most conflictual issue in the negotiations.

Rather than being simply an "administrative board," as the Group of 77 had wanted, the Council has become the principal deliberative body, reviewing and approving the work programme, directing the utilization of GEF funds, appointing the CEO and overseeing the work of the Secretariat. The Third World does not constitute a clear majority of the Council's membership, but with 50% of its members the developing countries can effectively veto decisions by the Council. So of course can the donor countries, both because they make up more than 40% of the membership and because four donors (France, Germany, Japan and the USA) hold 63% of the vote on the basis of contributions. The key role played by the CEO, who serves as the Chair of the Council and who in all likelihood will be a staff person drawn from the World Bank, does give to the donor countries a decided advantage in managing the new GEF. Although the Secretariat is to "operate in a functionally independent and effective manner," its links with the implementing agencies, especially the World Bank, do give understandable cause for concern to the Third World. In sum, Third World countries have reason to be cautious in their overall assessment of the GEFs new structures. As Razali Ismail, Malaysia's Ambassador to the UN and the first chair of the UN Commission on Sustainable Development, remarked, "I will suspend congratulations till we can see that it (the GEF) is viable. I cannot say that it represents a serious change to the previous relationship between donors and recipients."[18]

The final demand of the Third World, and one that links the demands of the developing countries with those of the NGO community, relates to the scope of the Facility. For both groups the four focal areas offer too narrow a field on which to promote global environmental benefits. They argued that the scope of the GEF should be broadened to include such problems as soil erosion, the lack of potable water, rapid urbanization and its attendant problems of pollution, and even more broadly, poverty and its problems. The South Centre put the problem very succinctly: the "GEF is rooted in a vision of the environmental *problematique* which has arisen from the experience of the industrialized countries and their efforts to deal with pollution as an externality of economic activities. This approach tends to gloss over the causes of environmental problems and does not question the socio-economic structures which give rise to such problems." Instead of its present focus the agenda of the GEF "should reflect needs based on an integrated approach to the problems of the South ... it is essential to start from the global agenda as charted and agreed to at the *Rio de Janeiro Conference.*"[19] Notwithstanding these arguments, the scope of the GEF has remained unchanged.

The concerns of the NGO community were more far-reaching in nature. Their calls for reform were very much in line with the general recommendations of the formal *Independent Evaluation*, which was highly critical of the Pilot Phase of the GEF and urged radical changes before rushing into a new programme. As far as the NGOs were concerned, the real issues were not debated. Negotiations focused almost entirely on the political issues of who would control the new GEF rather than on a discussion of such questions as the strategy and set of objectives that overarch the focal areas, the project cycle and the engagement of NGOs and local communities, and the lack of a systematic learning process. In their view very little has been done to address the recommendations of the independent evaluation; too much has been left for the Council to debate and ultimately act upon. While the new instrument does wax lyrical on the need to consult with NGOs and other groups and to involve them in the GEF project cycle, the NGOs are not convinced that the Participants have created "an open, inclusive, democratic instrument in which all stakeholders find their place."[20] Just as the developing countries have reserved judgment on the GEF, so too have the NGOs.

The Global Environmental Facility has undergone considerable changes since its beginning in 1991. Its funding has almost doubled, and its structures have been substantially altered. The final instrument, however, falls short of Third World demands and fails to address all NGO concerns. While GEF funding has increased, the level of support is far less than what had been expected and is limited to financing the agreed incremental costs of global environmental benefits. As many donor countries have cut back their overall development assistance, the resources committed to the GEF are in all likelihood part of earlier commitments rather than new and additional. Since the focus of the GEF remains limited to the four original areas, areas of principal concern to the industrialized world, many of the environmental issues facing the South are ignored. Finally, the structures of the GEF have been made more democratic by allowing for universal membership, by developing a voting system that gives considerable weight to the poorer countries of the South, and by promising to open the project cycle to the participation of NGOs and local communities. Some of these changes, however, remain promises for the future; decisions on both principle (NGO observer status) and modes of operation (public participation) are left to the new Council to make. A further weakness of the present structure lies in the establishment of the GEF's Chief Executive Officer as both head of the Secretariat and effective Chair of the Council. In linking these two positions in one person the new instrument has created "a clear conflict of interest," one that threatens to blur "the lines of accountability."[21]

Only time will tell whether or not the promise that the *Independent Evaluation* saw in the GEF will be realized. Unfortunately, many of the changes that this team of independent assessors called for have either been ignored or deferred for later consideration by the Council. Under the circumstances, both the South and the NGO Community can be counted on to continue representing forcefully their beliefs and constituencies at future meetings of the Participants.

Notes

1 Reed, David 1991 *The Global Environment Facility: Sharing Responsibility for the Biosphere* (WWF-International) 1 3.
2 World Commission on Environment and Development (chaired by Gro Harlem Brundtland) 1987 *Our Common Future* (Oxford University Press).
3 On the origins of the GEF, see *Report of the Independent Evaluation of the Global Environment Facilit*, 23 November 1993 v-vi. See also note 1, 3-4.
4 Reed, David "GEF Consultation: Discussion Paper" 25 May 1993.
5 Introductory NGO Statement to the Tri-Partite GEF NGO Consultation, Cartagena, Colombia, 5 December 1993 1.
6 See note 1, 29.
7 See note 5, 1.
8 See note 5, 2.
9 South Centre 1993 *Developing Countries and the GEF: For a Strategy of the South* Geneva 1993 5.
10 At the Climate Convention negotiations, the Group of 77 defined the two terms as follows: "Additionality must mean in addition to, or over and above the target set by the United Nations for ODA (Official Development Assistance) flows (0.7% of GNP) ... 'new' means flows of a quantitatively different sort. It is not assistance or aid, but transfers to compensate developing countries for adopting and pursuing costly measures to combat climate change." (See Group of 77, "Statement by the

Group of 77 on Financial Resources and Transfer of Technology in Working Group 1 of the Inter-governmental Negotiating Committee for a Framework Convention on Climate Change" 26 June 1991. Reprinted in *Eco Newsletter* 26 June 1991.)

11 *UNDP Global Environmental Facility: The Pilot Phase and Beyond* Working Paper Series No. 1 May 1992 7. See also Matthews, R.O. "United Nations Reform in the 1990s: North-South Dimensions," *ACUNS Reports and Papers* No. 5 1993 19-21.

12 *Report of the Independent Evaluation of the GEF Pilot Phase* 23 November 1993 xvi, with emphasis added.

13 *Earth Negotiations Bulletin* 5 13 2. Much of the information concerning the Cartagena negotiations is drawn from this source.

14 Chatterjee, Pratap "Environment: New Two Billion Dollar Environment Fund Launched" *Inter Press Service* 16 March 1994.

15 *GEF Press Release* 03/16 25 March 1994. For the text of the new GEF, see *Instrument for the Establishment of the Restructured Global Environment Facility* 31 March 1994.

16 The estimated cost of implementing *Agenda 21* alone was $600 billion, of which $125 billion was to come from the industrialized countries, and thus the $2 billion replenishment for the GEF represents a drop in the bucket.

17 Statement of the Colombian Representative on behalf of the Group of 77 at the *Global Environment Facility Participants' Meeting* in Beijing, China, 26-28 May 1993.

18 Quoted by Chatterjee, Pratap: see note 14.

19 South Centre *Developing Countries and GEF: For a Strategy of the South* 6-7. In a statement to a Tri-Partite GEF NGO consultation in Cartagena, the NGOs commented in a similar fashion when they stated that "the programmes and projects of the Pilot Phase have been largely donor and agency driven."

20 NGO Statement on the GEF Evaluation *GEF Participants' Assembly*, Cartagena, 6 December 1993 3.

21 Walsh, Kenneth *Cartagena Meeting* 22 December 1993.

CHAPTER 17

Environmental Politics, Trade and United Nations Reform

Urs P. Thomas

Introduction

The reform of the UN system is an ongoing process that will hopefully obtain a stimulus from the 50th Anniversary activities. In particular, concern for the environment and sustainable development has already substantially changed inter-governmental cooperation over the past twenty years. Multilateral environmental and development activities and structures have been shaped profoundly by four events over a six year period:

- the General Assembly's support for the 1987 *Brundtland Report* through *Resolution 42/187*;
- the creation of the Global Environment Facility (GEF) by the World Bank, the UN Development Programme (UNDP), and the UN Environment Programme (UNEP) in November 1990;
- the June 1992 *United Nations Conference on Environment and Development* (UNCED) in Rio de Janeiro;
- the December 1993 conclusion of the *GATT, Uruguay Round.*

This article will accordingly place UN reform in the post-Rio de Janeiro and post-Uruguay context. The most important result of UNCED[1] was to make people in the North aware that we share our greenhouse earth with a great many people in the South, and that their collective decisions will increasingly have an impact on our own environment and on our own quality of life. UNCED has forcefully brought home the fact that the North and the South are more and more interdependent. That is why global environmental change "will increase dependence among nations and regions, thereby substantially increasing the political leverage of the South." (MacNeill, Winsemius and Yakushiji, 1991:73).

The connection between providing additional funds to ensure the protection of the environment in development projects, and tying conditions to official development assistance funding is not new. A conflict between "additionality" and "conditionality" was already at the heart of negotiations at the Stockholm *UN Conference on the Human Environment* back in 1972 (Caldwell, 1990:62). The fact that UNCED included development in its basic mandate represents a victory for the South. Developing countries tend to show little interest in discussing environmental issues in isolation. They insist on linking them with economic concerns such as access to Northern markets, better terms of trade, and forgiveness of debts. The developing countries managed, during the third of four preparatory conferences in Geneva in August 1991, to link environmental negotiations explicitly with their developmental concerns. This common Third World position had been strengthened at a ministerial conference of the Group of 77 in Beijing in June 1991 (Matthews, 1993:17). In spite of these antecedents over the last twenty years, the perceived need to link environment and development at UNCED is less obvious than might appear. As late as Summer 1989, for example, some US and German diplomats whom I interviewed in New York, were seeking a "technical" conference on the environment, with no linkage to development issues.

The discussion of UN reform needs to be placed in the context of the present wide and deep recession and the re-emergence of nationalist sentiments. The European Union, for instance, which was actively involved in the UNCED process, is now very reluctant to engage in joint environmental initiatives, not only because of the recession, but also because of a nationalist backlash emerging from the *Maastricht Treaty* (MacKenzie, 1994:12). In view of the present harsh economic and political climate, it is not surprising that the short term financial consequences of UNCED have been meagre, even taking into account the fact that the industrialized countries' pledges to the Third World were very disappointing to start with. Runnalls (1992:3) surmises that, "in 10 years time, the world may remember the *Rio de Janeiro Summit* more for the re-emergence of the Group of 77 as a real force to be reckoned with than as an event which produced the cash to do the job."

The 1980s were particularly disastrous for most developing countries, which are still suffering from a massive South-North transfer of capital. Many of them cannot realistically envisage investing in the environment as long as interest payments on their national debt strangle their policy options. This adds to the urgency of bringing environmental concerns to future North-South negotiations, such as the March 1995 *World Summit for Social Development* in Copenhagen.

For the foreseeable future, multilateral development activities will continue to account for by far the biggest part of UN expenditures, although peacekeeping and peacemaking activities are presently increasing their share. Nevertheless, international environmental affairs now constitute an essential part of the development process. They have undergone profound changes in the past few years, and are now one of the key forces driving the UN reform process.

Coordination of the UN's Environmental Activities

The main coordinating problem at the UN is that the specialized agencies of the UN system, such as FAO or UNESCO, and the World Bank enjoy a very large degree of autonomy. The governments that make up their membership usually send delegations from the pertinent Ministries, *e.g.*, agriculture, education or finance. Since most governments have great difficulty in coordinating their own national environmental policies, it is not surprising that these problems are reflected in the inter-agency relationships at the UN.

The United Nations Environment Programme (UNEP) is a major UN body with an annual budget of approximately $100 million, including voluntary government contributions and trust funds. The Secretariat and over 500 of UNEPs total staff of approximately 700 are located in Nairobi.[2] Its primary tasks can be loosely subsumed by four C's: (1) convincing the diplomatic community of the necessity to protect the global ecosystem; (2) compiling and disseminating scientific information; (3) catalyzing environmental programmes and projects; and (4) coordinating environmental activities throughout the UN. UNEPs mandate is essentially of a facilitating nature, and the actual projects in the field are usually carried out by other organizations in cooperation with UNEP. During its first twenty years, from 1972 to 1992, of which the last 16 were under the leadership of the Executive Director, Mostafa K. Tolba, UNEP has lived up to expectations in the first three tasks, but has failed its coordination mandate (Thomas, 1993).

We shall accordingly focus our discussion here on UNEPs coordinating activities. Perhaps their most critical feature is the organization's Nairobi location. Nearly all the UNEP officials in Nairobi that I have questioned on the impact of UNEPs location there on its coordination activities answered that it is really no problem. In fact, it is even claimed to be an advantage, because offices are cheaper and salaries are lower than in Geneva and New York, while modern telecommunications overcome any inconveniences. On the other hand, nearly everybody questioned on this issue at about thirty UN and government institutions in Europe and North America said that it is a very serious handicap for coordination activities.

The selection of a developing country as the site for a major UN secretariat was overdue, but UNEP is unique. Apart from considerations of international equity, which can be addressed in many different ways, the Nairobi location needs to be analyzed in the light of a variety of UNEP mandates that do not all have the same organizational needs. Dr. Tolba has fortified the UN General Assembly's institutional set-up by concentrating UNEP's decision making and control in Nairobi. From an administrative standpoint, it may well be easier to manage the numerous programmes when decision making is concentrated at a single location. This presumably facilitates efficient financial control and effective streamlining of policy implementation. For most of UNEP's functions a concentration of control in Nairobi may well be considered an asset. One has to wonder, however, how the intersectoral character of environmental projects can be taken into consideration in this kind of an organizational constellation. In fact, at a colloquium on global environmental problems, a participant noted that, "UNEP at first avoided the turf-building which plagues the UN system but has since succumbed to it, becoming sectoral, defensive."[3] The concentration of environmental coordination in a remote location does *de facto* strengthen the perception that environmental activities constitute a specific sector. This notion, however, violates the basic concept underlying the sustainable development philosophy, namely that the environment should be considered a dimension of development and not a separate sector dealing with the restoration of damages.

The question I want to analyze here is whether the concentration of decision making power that is politically and managerially desirable may be detrimental to UNEPs coordinating mandate. It is another question whether it should indeed have such a coordinating mandate. This issue is actually debated in some quarters, for instance at FAO, UNESCO and UNDP. The fact of the matter is that, as things stand and for the foreseeable future, UNEP does have an official policy guidance and coordinating mandate. This was reconfirmed explicitly at UNCED through *Section 38.21* of *Agenda 21*: "The Governing Council should within its mandate continue to play its role with regard to policy guidance and coordination in the field of the environment, taking into account the development perspective."[4]

In view of the independence that the specialized agencies enjoy, thanks to their prerogative of raising operating funds from their member-countries, and to the fact that they govern themselves through their own legislative bodies, coordination in the UN system does not have the same meaning as in most other organizational settings. Coordination traditionally implies, at least in principle, some sort of ruling powers. In public institutions this power is often quite vague and ineffective. Graham Allison, in his classic organizational study (1971:145), considers that public sector institutions in a decentralized arrangement enjoy "baronial discretion."

At the UN, this discretion is particularly pronounced. Coordination can only be done through moral persuasion and voluntary cooperation. A coordinating mandate does not connote a regulatory power, as it usually does in industry or in national governments. It implies instead gathering and dissemination of information, and organizing negotiations about the implementation of mandates. In view of the autonomy of cooperating agencies, the distinction between coordinating and cooperating can become quite blurred. Skilled coordinators will obtain some influence from this function, but all participants understand this to be rather limited. Even if an organization has received its coordination mandate from the General Assembly, it may have little power for the execution of this mandate. If the organization delegates certain tasks to other institutions, they may well ignore or perhaps exceed them, or they may interpret them according to their own interests.

As far as UNEP is concerned, the first problem with its coordination mandate is the fact that Nairobi is really out of the way for people travelling to such UN locations as Paris, Geneva, Vienna or Rome that are all located within about one hour's flight from each other. From these cities, reaching Nairobi takes longer than a flight to New York. It happens frequently that ministers and senior UN and government officials visit several agencies on the same trip for intersectoral and interagency discussions, which is what environmental coordination is all about. But usually they cannot include three additional days for talks in Nairobi, so that UNEP is often left "out of the loop." Telecommunications have long been a problem. They have improved within the UN network, but it still remains to be seen if telecommunications outside the UN system, and especially fax connections, can be maintained at an adequate level.

Nairobi, unlike Geneva and New York, lacks a large number of Permanent Missions staffed with technically well informed staff. Instead, UNEP's direct link with the Embassies and High Commissions consists of the Committee of Permanent Representatives, whose members are generally not specialized in environmental matters and have to deal with many other issues at the same time. Furthermore, again due to the Nairobi location, the members of this committee are in many cases not well connected with their governments' ministries, especially in the case of small countries. In fact, ambassadors of developing countries often represent several countries. These factors have resulted in a committee which, according to several observers, is not very effective as a liaison mechanism between UNEP and its Member States.

Last, but not least, it is doubtful if the Nairobi location really serves developing countries' interests. An official in a bilateral development agency concluded that the Nairobi location serves to marginalize UNEP and therefore makes it more difficult for its secretariat to defend the interests of the South. UNEP is represented in New York only by a very modest liaison office; an even smaller office in Washington, DC was recently closed down. These are grossly understaffed for the double role as a liaison with the UN organizations based in New York, and as a bridgehead in North America. As of 1991, the New York office was staffed with only three professionals. For UNEP to achieve more political weight, a stronger presence in New York and also in Geneva is absolutely essential.

The Nairobi location of the secretariat has nevertheless served UNEP reasonably well for wide range of activities during its first twenty years. It should also be acknowledged that, during his long tenure, Dr. Tolba has managed to compensate the negative effects of his centralizing style with a widely recognized diplomatic *fingerspitzengefühl* (sensitivity and discernment). The substantial increase in UNEP's budget a couple of years ago gives its leadership a considerable freedom to deal with the problem of the isolation of the Nairobi location. UNEP could strike a deal with Kenya and the other African members, whereby Nairobi would end up with an enlarged staff thanks to the larger budget, while at the same time those positions and functions in the area of political, financial, technical and legal coordination, which suffer most from the Nairobi location, could be transferred to New York and Geneva. Indeed, UNEP's present Executive Director, Elizabeth Dowdeswell, seems to be in the process of reorienting the organization in this direction.

New Challenges for UNEPs Coordination Role

In this section I want to demonstrate that, in the emerging inter-organizational competition over an important part of UNEP's traditional domain, a transfer of environmental coordination to the political, financial and technical decision making centres is more urgent than ever. In the wake of UNCED, environmental and development aspects of multilateral cooperation are converging more and more, while substantial and increasing sums are earmarked for environmental projects. This trend opens up new opportunities for UNEP, but at the same time it faces an increasing challenge from developmental organizations such as the World Bank, UNDP, UNESCO and FAO, which are very interested in securing these additional funds for themselves by stressing their environmental credentials to the donor countries.

The World Bank upgraded its environmental activities substantially in 1987 when it added an Environment Department, largely as a result of pressures from US NGOs, which were able to rally political support from the US Congress. In 1992 it established a new vice presidency for environment and sustainable development. The World Bank has increased its lending for "primarily environmental objectives" from $404 million in fiscal year 1990 to $1.6 billion in 1991, and to a record $2 billion in 1993.

The UN Development Programme also is getting more and more involved in environmental management. In an environmental policy document submitted at the 1990 UNDP Governing Council, the *Report of the Administrator* explains that, ... "the reporting on statistics has been reassessed to include more comprehensively environmental projects of a human living and development planning nature that are being promoted via the *UNDP Environmental Management Guidelines.*"

This "reassessment," articulated in somewhat contorted English, includes projects which are "likely environmental, in a socio-cultural sense" in areas like education, women in development, and public administration, as well as projects that are "potentially environmental in a developmental sense," like urban management or clean industry and biotechnology. Clearly, UNDP is making great efforts to strengthen its environmental profile. UNESCO and FAO are also stressing the importance of the environment in their developmental policy-making. UNEP can evidently expect much more competition from its sister institutions than it used to have. In particular, these developments will make its coordinating efforts inherently even more difficult than they were in the past.

This institutional theatre has recently become still more complex by the addition of two new players. The first is the Global Environment Facility (GEF), a joint structure comprising the World Bank, UNDP and UNEP, which will not be discussed here because its present mandate is not directly related to coordination activities. It is focused specifically on projects in the areas of climate change, ozone depletion, biodiversity and international waters. In the long term, however, once it is reconstructed from its recently terminated three-year pilot phase into a more permanent institution, there are good reasons to expect that the GEF will also play an active role in international environmental coordination, especially since at the *Rio de Janeiro Conference* it was given the mandate to finance the climate change and the biodiversity conventions, at least on an interim basis [see Chapter 16].

The second new entrant in this highly dynamic and politicized domain is a high-level Commission on Sustainable Development (CSD) comprised of the representatives of 53 states, whose creation was decided at the Rio de Janeiro Conference. Like UNEP, it reports to ECOSOC. Many analysts (*e.g.*, French, 1992:8) would have preferred a more autonomous stature which would have been achieved if CSD had been made to report directly to the General Assembly.

The mandate of this new Commission consists essentially in "monitoring progress in the implementation of *Agenda 21*," including financial resources, technology transfer, the implementation of the conventions and private-sector activities.[6] A special feature of the CSD is that it will seek input not only from the UN network, but also from other sources, such as "international financial institutions and other relevant inter-governmental organizations, including industry and the business and scientific communities."[7] Of particular significance to UNEP is the fact that this Commission also has the mandate, "to provide a high-level nerve centre that aids in the effort to coordinate the UN's far-flung responses to the environment-and-development challenge posed at Rio de Janeiro." (French, 1992:8). This coordinating effort notably includes not only the World Bank but, for the first time, also the IMF, which so far has managed to isolate itself from the environmental ramifications of its actions and policies. This coordination mandate may go very far. For instance, CSD is required to: "... enhance international cooperation and rationalize the intergovernmental decision making capacity for the integration of environment and development issues."[8]

At the first Substantive Session in June 1993, which attracted the presence of about fifty ministers, CSD decided to set up two working groups on technology transfer and finance, and it scheduled a thematic programme for the next few years. The actual work of CSD, however, began with the 1994 Session. This raises two separate issues. First of all, the coordinating activities of UNEP's Governing Council (GC) and the CSD need to be coordinated, which presumably will not be an easy task. Furthermore, UNCED has resuscitated, through *Article 38.17* of *Agenda 21*,[9] a top-level task force on sustainable development of the Administrative Coordinating Committee (ACC), which consists of the agency and programme heads or their deputies. This task force was first created in 1988 in Oslo at an ACC meeting convened by Mrs. Gro Brundtland, but it never got off the ground because of inter-agency quarrels. This means that the UN now has three bodies that are officially mandated to coordinate environmental and sustainable development issues: UNEP, CSD and ACC's task force. One should mention also a recently created Inter-Agency Environment Coordination Group[10] (ECOSOC), the General Assembly's Second Committee, and internal organs of the UN Secretariat that are also very much involved here, such as the Department of Policy Coordination and Sustainable Development. This seems not to be the most effective setup, and one wonders if anybody does indeed coordinate all these coordinators.

In view of the autonomy of the agencies and their loose coordination in the UN context, there is trade-off between monitoring UN agencies (let alone policing them) and coordinating their activities with sister organizations. No organization is going to be particularly cooperative with a coordinating authority that may at any time blame it for some environmental misdeeds. This suggests that, by burdening CSD with important coordinating functions, its creators have consciously reduced its monitoring role.

The only way to reduce the political trade-offs between monitoring and coordination would be to give these two tasks to two separate organizations. Clearly, the international community is not ready yet for the creation of an effective monitoring body with some teeth. In fact some countries, *e.g.*, the UK, agreed only reluctantly at or after the last *UNCED Preparatory Committee Meeting* to the establishment of CSD. In the light of this resistance to environmental monitoring, the creation of CSD, with all its limitations, represents significant progress. In any case, as Sand (1990:33) has shown in the case of the International Labour Organization, the UN hardly ever uses adversarial procedures to enforce compliance by member countries. He considers annual or bi-annual reporting by the Member States, complemented by expert evaluation and public debate, to be more effective.

One might hope, nevertheless, that the movement favouring the establishment of a more autonomous and effective sustainable development monitoring agency will gain momentum. CSD's monitoring function should be strengthened, while its coordinating tasks should be moderated. CSD should limit its coordinating activities to general policy issues and to backing up a revitalization of UNEP's coordinating mandate. For instance, it might give a higher profile and respectability to its System-Wide Medium-Term Environment Programme, which has been ineffective so far. Coordinating sustainable development at the UN can only be effective if there is a clearly expressed delineation of levels of coordination. The ACC task force should set the basic parameters, CSD should develop general policy guidelines, and UNEP should negotiate detailed arrangements with the agencies, based on the System-Wide Medium-Term Programme.

As far as UNEP is concerned, which has no mandate to monitor sister organizations or governments, CSD represents the first explicit institutional challenge to its traditional monopoly on environmental coordination. MacNeill (1992:34) considers that CSD has a great potential to become the "primary forum for international leadership, North-South dialogue and action on the road from Rio de Janeiro," as long as it "doesn't simply disappear in the huge, amorphous sponge that is the UN system." He calls not only for ministerial-level government participation and a strong secretariat, but also for the inclusion of women's groups, other NGOs, indigenous peoples and the business community. MacNeill warns, however, that several important countries, as well as some UN agencies concerned about losing their autonomy, are trying to diminish the Commission's potential influence by pushing for a weak secretariat integrated into another UN body.

Clearly, these initiatives show a considerable amount of dissatisfaction with the principle of UN-wide coordination from Nairobi. Perhaps the main reason why coordination from Nairobi was largely seen as quite adequate until recently is the fact that environmental issues were simply not considered to be of major political importance. Furthermore, many observers feel that UNEP has never been taken seriously by the specialized agencies, whose decision-makers were presumably quite satisfied to see its secretariat at a safe distance. In Nairobi it is less threatening to their autonomy than if it had a powerful presence in New York or Geneva. Now, however, with the growing awareness of global environmental problems and the fear of millions of environmental refugees, perceptions of the fundamental design of the UN system are beginning to change. It is in this context that the Nairobi venue of UNEP's coordination role has to be reconsidered. If UNEP maintains its coordinating function in Nairobi, the UN system will simply develop other environmental coordination mechanisms closer to the action, especially at the political level in New York, and UNEP will be marginalized in the areas of policy-making and coordination.

While New York is the UN's political centre, Geneva is the hub of technical cooperation, which is particularly important in the case of the environment due to its inherently interdisciplinary nature. Some diplomats interviewed consider that there is a trend in the UN Secretariat's decision-making process to concentrate more and more political and economic control in New York at the expense of the Geneva facilities. This goes hand in hand with a general expansion of UNDPs influence at the expense of the specialized agencies. Instead of automatically using UN Agencies such as FAO or UNESCO to execute UNDP-financed projects, UNDP will increasingly give NGOs and private consultants a chance to compete against them. This of course indicates an increasing concentration of financial and political power in New York, and provides additional backing for the proposal to transfer there the coordinating functions of UNEP.

Most developing countries, and in particular China, are resisting any attempts to transfer UN activities out of Nairobi. From 14-19 June 1991, China hosted in Beijing, a ministerial-level *Conference of Developing Countries on Environment and Development* , which was attended by 41 countries. They issued the *Beijing Declaration* which contains the following paragraph: "We support the strengthening of UNEP and all its programme activity centres in Nairobi, considering the success the Programme has achieved to date from this venue and the need to have it better equipped for carrying out its work." (emphasis added)

Unfortunately for this view, even under the best institutional constellation, UNEP will be more and more challenged to defend the need for its role in environmental coordination. Some observers in the "epistemic community" (Haas, 1992) of international environmental affairs argue that UNEP should essentially have not much more than a scientific and technical environmental support function, whereas for coordination UNDP would be more effective, since it has a budget of $1.3 billion, which would go a long way towards persuading the specialized agencies to accept its coordinating schemes. That would presumably not be acceptable to the World Bank, however, which would mean that the two institutions would share coordination either through GEF or through some other joint structure.

The developing countries would be the losers in any such scenario. UNCED has clearly shown that they vigorously resisted – without success so far – the interim financing of the conventions on biodiversity and climate change through GEF, where they have presently much less influence than the industrial countries. The principal issue of contention is the extent to which environmental conditions imposed on development projects are financed by additional funds, and these financial arrangements tend to be negotiated in New York and Washington, not in Nairobi. The inclination of the industrialized donor countries, on the other hand, is to favour multilateral development banks, which are gaining ground at the expense of the specialized agencies.[12] For all these reasons, it would seem that the efforts of the developing countries to maintain UNEP's coordinating function geographically separate and far remote from the most crucial political and financial negotiations will turn out ultimately to be contrary to their own interests. It is also contrary to the ideal of sustainable development, because UNEP has more of a long-range orientation than both the World Bank and UNDP.

Trade and the Environment

The end of the twentieth century is characterized by an increasing trend towards a technology-driven globalization of the economy. Transnational corporations are managing their operations in a world where national borders are less and less important to them. When products and services are subdivided into components that can be designed, managed, produced and sold in any of a number of countries on different continents, the question of their nationality or the nationality of the transnational corporation whose label they carry, or the national origin of the funds making any given operation possible, becomes secondary or even meaningless. "National champions everywhere are becoming global webs with no particular connection to any single nation." (Reich, 1991: 131).

We shall now consider the impact on the environment of the more liberal trade policies catalyzed by this technology-driven globalization. The relationship between trade and environment received very little attention until recently. In the last three years, research on this topic has mushroomed, and a recent bibliography takes up 26 pages (Charnovitz, 1994:23).

Trade is an essential element of development. The *Earth Summit* dealt with the development process in *Principle 4* of the *Rio de Janeiro Declaration on Environment and Development* as follows: "In order to achieve sustainable development, environmental protection shall constitute an integral part of the development process and cannot be considered in isolation from it."[13]

In order to assess whether this fundamental principle is being respected in the negotiation of agreements concerning the international economy, the *Uruguay Round of* GATT that was concluded recently, culminating in the decision to create a World Trade Organization (WTO), is a revealing test case. The WTO will be an essential but autonomous component of the wider UN system, to which *GATT* did not want to belong. The conclusion of the *Uruguay Round* should therefore be considered as an essential and dynamic element of the ongoing UN reform process. The environment has not been completely forgotten. The preamble endorses the notion of sustainable development, and it should now become easier to bring scientific evidence and advice bearing on the environment into dispute settlement panels (Jones, 1994:22). The fact of the matter is, however, that none of the key issues in the trade-environment relationship, such as full cost pricing to reflect environmental externalities, trade-environment measures, or cross-border environmental liability, have been seriously dealt with in this round of trade talks. Environmental issues have been mostly ignored, perhaps put aside for a future, less comprehensive round of trade talks. In the meantime, nations will be trading with each other according to the new GATT rules, but otherwise it will be business as usual. GATT's acting director of the Trade and Environment Division, Richard Eglin, confirmed (1993: 34) GATT's unwillingness to get involved in global policy-making in this area: "GATT is not equipped to become involved in the tasks of reviewing national environmental priorities, setting environmental standards or developing global policies on the environment, and there is no intention for it to do so."

As a consequence, one cannot escape the conclusion that the dozens of governments which have signed both the Rio *Declaration* and the *WTO Agreement* have not only violated the above-mentioned *Principle 4*, but have put the fledgling WTO from the beginning on a conflict course with the very notion of sustainable development.

I do not wish to imply that institutionalized trade liberalization is fundamentally incompatible with environmental priorities. On the contrary, a rather straightforward argument supporting the WTO may be made on theoretical grounds. The linkage between ecology and economy is the core principle of sustainable development. Global environmental problems such as ozone depletion, climate change, or the protection of the oceans, require global mechanisms to deal with them, which in a crisis situation need to be able to override the antiquated principle of national sovereignty. The crucial point here is that, in order to implement global sustainable development policies, one needs to establish global instruments to manage both the environment and the international economy. This means that we shall need the WTO for sustainable development. This conclusion follows directly from the postulate that the economy and the environment are linked. We now have an essential tool of international management that urgently needs to be adjusted to environmental imperatives. I have in mind a restructuring process after a pilot phase, comparable to the one implemented by the World Bank in 1987, or the GEF at the end of its three year pilot phase.

One of the principal arguments made by the critics of the *Uruguay Round* is that it favours transnational corporations that act according to selfish principles based on the objective of short-term profitability. This results in destructive socio-economic and environmental consequences, especially in developing countries. This criticism is certainly justified in many cases, but that does not mean that small local firms are less destructive. The average such firm may even be worse than the transnational corporations because, unlike small fly-by-night operators, the transnationals have to keep in mind their reputation with institutional shareholders and international markets. It should be noted, however, that transnational corporations do not really need the GATT for their protection and prosperity. They are quite able to look after their interests under any trade regime. Historically they have been successful in adapting to either protectionism or to free trade.

The WTO Agreement is particularly inadequate in the area of trade in natural resources, which cannot be regulated sensibly by the same rules as trade in manufactured goods. De Bremond's (1993:157) argument that free trade imposes a high cost on the environment is pertinent. The "decoupling" of prices for natural resources from environmental considerations that GATT demands, i.e., the prohibition of providing subsidies and other support mechanisms to protect the environment in agriculture, forestry, fishing, or in the mining industry, has wide-ranging negative environmental consequences. Soil-erosion management, crop-rotation techniques, integrated pest-management systems, reforestation efforts or policies aimed at protecting small diversified farms from being merged into huge cattle ranches with serious environmental problems will all be undermined by free trade policies.

An additional threat looms from transgenic biocides made possible by genetic engineering, which will further increase the push towards exploitation of huge and ecologically fragile monocultures. This will further increase the farmers' need for chemical supplies and their dependence on the biological engineering support system (Hindmarsh, 1991:204). The current annual global market for synthetic pesticides is estimated at $20 billion, and it is estimated that, by the year 2000, genetically manipulated plant varieties will amount to $12 billion. The seed, fertilizer and pesticides suppliers and other components of the more and more invasive agribusiness are tightening their control of agriculture both in the North and the South, with ecological consequences that are unknown and indeed unpredictable.

GATT has addressed environmental issues in a 1992 position paper for UNCED,[13] where the secretariat denounces environmental import standards that attempt to influence the behaviour of another country. It furthermore vigorously attacks unilateral initiatives to tackle environmental problems and consistently insists that only a multilateral approach should be used. It is obvious, however, that the negotiation of multilateral agreements tends to be a long and cumbersome process, which may not be appropriate for a fast response to environmental problems. Charnovitz (1992:208) concludes his discussion of unilateralism as follows: "Since nations face different environmental challenges and have different values and temporal preferences, it is natural that countries will want to formulate their own standards for production, consumption, and disposal – which could apply to imported as well as domestically produced goods. A world where countries marched in environmental lockstep would depress standards to the lowest common denominator."

The UN Conference on Trade and Development (UNCTAD), a misnomer because it is not just a conference but a permanent agency mandated to promote the developing countries' trading interests, supports GATT's aversion to unilateral environmental initiatives. It even managed to introduce a clause to that end into *Principle 12* of the *Rio de Janeiro Declaration* (Charnovitz, 1993:154): "Unilateral actions to deal with environmental challenges outside the jurisdiction of the importing country should be avoided." This point is further emphasized by the fact that it is mentioned twice in *Agenda 21* in *Chapters 2:22(i)* and *39.3(d)* (Charnovitz, 1993).

GATT is clearly not sympathetic to the need for catalyzing multilateral environmental agreements through unilateral action. As Charnovitz (1993:157) points out, environmental regimes such as those covering trade in endangered species or driftnet fishing were preceded by unilateral actions, which were not justified by domestic environmental damages, but instead had the objective of changing the behaviour of foreign governments. Instead of trying to block unilateral actions, a "restructured" WTO should use them strategically to catalyze multilateral agreements.

Conclusions

GATT is arguably the most powerful civil institution in the world, even in its pre-Uruguay form. Unlike the Bretton Woods institutions for instance, it is has an important leverage, not only over poor countries, but over rich and powerful ones as well. This cannot be said for UNEP. Nevertheless, signs are emerging to indicate that inter-governmental policy makers should start thinking about environmental crises that will necessitate a global environmental agency with far more power than UNEP. A limited summit meeting in The Hague in 1989 called for the creation of an innovative New International Authority with environmental enforcement powers for dealing with climate change and ozone depletion, which may not necessarily be based on consensus (Starke, 1991:22). Such an authority would represent a potential infringement of the hitherto sacrosanct principle of national sovereignty. Over 20 government heads (including Canada's Prime Minister) signed this declaration, because they considered that the severity of international environmental problems may make the respect of diplomatic traditions impossible. There may be environmental crises where the intervention of a supranational policing authority is required, and for which the present UN system is not prepared.

Last, but not least, an area where UNEP, as well as some of the specialized agencies such as UNESCO, IMF and FAO, need to be substantially strengthened, is their support function for the negotiation of environmental agreements. UNEP especially is intensely involved in many international environmental negotiations in areas such as regional seas, biodiversity, shipments of toxic wastes and the protection of the ozone layer. Young (1993:251) comments on the role of inter-governmental organizations in the negotiation of environmental regimes: "Some observers have suggested that organizations loom larger in some phases of the negotiating process than in others. Specifically, the idea has surfaced that international organizations are more central to the prenegotiation phase and the implementation phase than they are to the actual bargaining phase. There is some merit to this idea."

The two UN institutions primarily discussed here, UNEP and GATT, have until now not cooperated a great deal. They appear not to see much need for intensive exchanges. One of the principal objectives of UN reform should be to create a UN system that will take seriously the idea that environmental concerns are an essential dimension of every phase of the development process from its very inception. I conclude from recent interviews in Geneva that UNEP is indeed interested in initiating a more intensive dialogue with GATT. I am less convinced that at this time there is as much interest for exchange on the other side of the fence. It is to be hoped very much, that an invigorated UN reform process will bring the two institutions closer together.

Notes

1 The specific achievements of UNCED include:
   - *Framework Convention on Climate Change*;
   - *Convention of Biological Diversity*;
   - *Statement of Forest Principles*;
   - *Agenda 21*;
   - *Rio de Janeiro Declaration*;
   - Commission on Sustainable Development;
   - Additional financial support for environmental and sustainable development projects;
   - A decision to hold three UN conferences on population, desertification, and migratory fish stocks.

2 *United Nations Environment Programme 1991: Annual Report of the Executive Director* 1991 (UN Publications: New York) 151.

3 *Environmental Problems: A Global Security Threat. 24th UN of the Next Decade Conference* 1989 (The Stanley Foundation: Muscatine Iowa) 25.

4 *Earth Summit – Agenda 21: The United Nations Programme of Action from Rio de Janeiro* 1992 (UN Publications: New York) 277.

5 UNDP Governing Council, D/1990/27, 1 *Environmental Dimensions of Development, Annex III, UNDPs Expanded Definition of Environmental Projects* (UN Publications: Geneva) 18.

6 "Institutional arrangements to follow-up UNCED" (draft resolution prepared by the issue-coordinator on the basis of A/C2/47/WGI/CRP.10 after informal consultations) 25 November 1992 10 p., provided by the Centre for Development of International Law, Washington DC, 2.

7 *Environmental Policy and Law* 22 (4) August 1992 220.

8 See note 6, 1 and 7.

9 See note 4, 276.

10 "UNEP – 17th Governing Council" *Environmental Policy and Law* 23 (3/4) June 1993 118. This new IAEG may replace the Committee of Designated Officials for Environmental Matters, which was never very successful in alleviating conflict between UN agencies.

11 *Brundtland Bulletin* Issue 13 September 1991 (Centre for Our Common Future: Geneva) SF1.

12 Nordic UN Project 1991 *The United Nations in Development: Reform Issues in the Economic and Social Fields* (Almquist & Wiksell International: Stockholm).

13 See note 4, 9.

14   *Trade and the Environment,* Advance copy dated 7 February 1992 51 p., published by the GATT secretariat (it does not represent the official position of the Contracting Parties).

References

Allison, Graham 1971 *Essence of Decision* (Little Brown: Boston) 338.

Bremond, Ariane C. de "The Hidden Cost of 'Free' Trade: Environmental and Social Consequences of Economic Liberalization in the Enterprise for the Americas Initiative" *Journal of Environment and Development* 2 (1) Winter 1993 151.

Caldwell, Lynton Keith 1990 *International Environmental Policy-Emergence and Dimensions* (Second Edition, Duke University Press).

Charnovitz, Steve "Trade and the Environment: Four Schools of Thought" *Ecodecision* 11 January 1994 23-24.

Charnovitz, Steve "Environmental Trade Measures: Multilateral or Unilateral?" *Environmental Policy and Law* 23 (3/4) June 1993 154-158.

Charnovitz, Steve "GATT and the Environment: Examining the Issues" *International Environmental Affairs* Summer 4 (3, 1992 203-232.

Eglin, Richard "GATT and Environment" *Ecodecision* 8 March 1993 34-36.

French, Hilary F. "Hidden Success at Rio de Janeiro" *World Watch* September 1992 7-8.

French, Hilary F. "From Discord to Accord" *World Watch* May 1992 26-32.

Haas, Peter M. "Introduction: Epistemic Communities and International Policy Coordination" *International Organization* 46 (1) Winter 1992 Special Issue: "Knowledge, Power, and International Policy Coordination" ed. Peter Haas 1-36.

Hindmarsh, Richard "The Flawed 'Sustainable' Promise of Genetic Engineering" *The Ecologist* 21 (5) September 1991 196-205.

Jones, Skip "Environment" *Business America – The Magazine of International Trade* (Special Issue on the Uruguay Round) January 1994 22-23.

MacKenzie, Debora "The Winding Down of the European Environment" *Global Environment Business* 4 (1) January 1994 10-17.

MacNeill, Jim "The 1992 Rio Conference: Setting the Global Compass" *1992 Rio Reviews* (The Centre for Our Common Future: Geneva) 1992 33-35.

MacNeill, Jim, Pieter Winsemius and Taizo Yakushiji 1991 *Beyond Interdependence – the Meshing of the World's Economy and the Earth's Ecology* (Oxford University Press: New York).

Matthews, Robert O. "United Nations Reform in the 1990s: North-South

Dimensions" *ACUNS Reports and Papers* No. 5 1993 15-42.

Reich, Robert R. 1991 *The Work of Nations – Preparing Ourselves for 21st Century Capitalism* (Vintage Books: New York).

Runnalls, David "Summit Recap: No Cash, More G-77" *Earth Summit Times* 14 June 1992 3.

Sand, Peter 1990 *Lessons Learnt in Global Environmental Governance* (World Resources Institute: Washington DC).

Starke, Linda 1990 *Signs of Hope – Working Toward Our Common Future* (Oxford University Press: New York).

Thomas, Urs P. 1993 *The United Nations Environment Programme – An Evaluative Analysis* PhD thesis, Department of Political Science, Université du Québec à Montréal, 425 p.

Young, Oran R. 1993 "Perspectives on International Organizations" in *International Environmental Negotiations,* Sjöstedt, Gunnar ed. (Sage Publications: Newbury Park CA and IIASA: Laxenburg) 244-260.

CHAPTER 18

The Role of the IMF and the World Bank in International Development

James Busumtwi-Sam

We look back on a record of frustration. The rich countries had hoped to resolve the problems of the South – poverty, hunger, high population growth rates, low productivity, economic stagnation, debt, drought, desertification – by channelling aid through international and national institutions which were created almost fifty years ago. The time has come to take a critical look at aid patterns of the past.

Boutros Boutros-Ghali, 1994[1]

Introduction

International financial flows come in a variety of forms and serve a range of goals. Such financial flows range from government-to-government aid, which can either be bilateral or multilateral when administered through an international financial institution, or private capital flows such as short term portfolio investment and foreign direct investment. This paper examines the multilateral aid programmes administered by the International Monetary Fund (IMF) and the World Bank (IBRD), with the objective of outlining ways of reforming these institutions to better meet the challenges of international development in the post-Cold War international order.

Historically, there has been a linkage between systemic shocks and changes in the priorities and programmes of these institutions. Without a major new financial crisis on the magnitude of those that occurred in the 1970s (the oil crises) and early 1980s (the debt crisis of the Less Developed Countries, LDCs), it is unlikely that either the IMF or the IBRD (and the rich countries that control them) would have enough incentive to make major changes to accommodate poorer countries. Both institutions have been slow to change, and have been reactive rather than proactive. There is no reason to believe that a major shift in their mode of operation would come about quickly.

This pessimistic outlook is not to suggest that reform of these institutions is impossible or undesirable. Instead, it cautions against making reform proposals that are unrealistic or unfeasible. The most feasible avenues for reform must involve changes that can be accommodated within the structure and operation of the IMF and the IBRD as presently constituted. One of the few developments that give cause for some optimism is that a normative and policy convergence appears to be emerging in the form of an acceptance in many LDCs of the importance of the market in economic development, and of political pluralism as a basis of governance.[2] As a result of this apparent convergence, the parameters of the debate on the issue of economic development, and especially on the role of the state, have been narrowed. If properly managed and sustained, this new normative consensus could form the basis of a more effective regime for global development cooperation.

In outlining ways of reforming the IMF and the IBRD, there are two aspects that need to be addressed. The first is to provide an indication of what needs to be changed and for what purpose. The second is to provide an analysis of how that change could be effected. Accordingly, the discussion begins with a brief outline of the context for international development in the 1990s and an assessment of the role of the IMF and the IBRD, and then focuses on alternative ways of reforming them.

The Context of International Development in the 1990s_

An examination of the evolution of the lending practices of the IMF and the IBRD indicates that some changes have occurred. Both institutions have made limited progress towards recognizing the special needs of developing countries as a whole, and the mandate of the IMF has extended beyond what its original *Articles* envisaged. From its original focus on short term balance of payments financing, the IMF today is very much involved in economic development assistance. Yet these changes are hardly sufficient. By the end of 1993, after over a decade of Structural Adjustment reforms undertaken throughout the developing world under the auspices of these two institutions, the record leaves much to be desired.

A comparison of key economic indicators for developing and industrialized countries over the period 1970-1993 reveals a mixed picture. Three aspects are noteworthy. The first is that there was a deceleration in economic growth rates during the 1980s in almost all parts of the world. Between 1980 and 1991, for example, the average annual growth in GDP for industrialized countries was 2.9%, compared with a growth rate of

3.2% in the period 1970-1980. For LDCs, the annual average growth in GDP declined from 5.3% in the period 1970-1980, to 3.3% in the period 1980-1991.[3]

While the economies of LDCs as a whole have consistently grown faster than the economies of the industrialized countries, when population growth rates are included to reveal the growth in per capita incomes the picture changes in two significant ways. First, the higher overall economic growth rates of LDCs is largely cancelled out by their faster population growth rate; and second, the per capita incomes in some regions within the developing world actually declined during the 1980s (see Table 18.1).

The second aspect is the variation in economic performance within the group of countries classified as developing. The LDCs today include the fastest growing economies (China and the Asian Newly Industrializing Countries, NICs) as well as the economies that have suffered the most. The most depressed region is sub-Saharan Africa, where GNP per capita actually declined by an annual average of 1.3% between 1980 and 1990. In addition to sub-Saharan Africa, highly-indebted middle income countries and oil-exporters also experienced declines in the 1980s. Although this variation in economic performance makes it extremely difficult to make meaningful generalizations about such a varied group of countries, what is evident is the harsh reality of poverty for many in the developing world. According to the World Bank's definition of poverty (an income of less than $370 a year), over 20% of the world's population – more than a billion people – were living in poverty in 1990.[4]

Table 18.1
Growth in GNP per capita, Developing Countries, Selected Periods

	Average annual growth of GNP per capita (%)			
	1965-73	1973-80	1980-90	1991
All LDCs	4.3	2.7	1.2	-2.1
Low-Income Economies	2.5	2.6	4.0	2.1
Sub-Saharan Africa	1.7	0.9	-1.3	-2.5
Latin America and the Caribbean	4.6	2.2	-0.4	1.7
East Asia & Pacific	5.0	4.8	6.2	5.0
South Asia	1.2	1.7	3.2	-0.7
Middle East & North Africa	6.0	1.7	-2.5	-1.3
Severely Indebted Economies	5.2	3.4	-0.8	-2.5

Source: World Bank, World Development Report, 1993, Table A.2.

The third major area is the continuing, if not intensifying, LDC debt crisis. Total LDC long term debt increased from $480 billion in 1980 to over $1.4 trillion by the beginning of 1994 (Table 18.2). Debt as a proportion of export earnings increased from 89% in 1980 to 179% in 1993. Debt-service ratios rose from 13.5% in 1980 to a high of 25.9% in 1986 and declined somewhat to 18.5% in 1993. Between 1986 and 1991, the debt-related net transfer was negative. In 1988 alone, $40.9 billion was transferred from LDCs to the North. Between 1980 and 1991, the 15 largest debtors had a net financial outflow of $241 billion, and a decline in per capita income of 10%.[5] Both the Fund and the World Bank became net recipients of financial resources from LDCs. In 1992, for example, gross lending by the World Bank to LDCs totalled $22 billion. If this figure is netted against repayments of loans, LDCs actually transferred $1.7 billion to the World Bank.[6]

Export earnings that could have been used to finance economic development in developing countries are instead being used to service debt. To add insult to injury, export earnings of these countries have also declined, reflecting the instability in commodity prices and the deterioration of their terms of trade. According to World Bank figures, the terms of trade for agricultural and fuel primary exports, which had been favourable for most of the 1970s, declined between 1980 and 1990.[7] For many LDCs, the 1980s were indeed the "lost decade"; and their prospects in the 1990s do not look any brighter.

Proposals for Reform

What changes can the IMF and the IBRD make to alleviate the problems of LDCs? Any discussion of reform of these two International Financial Institutions (IFIs) is complicated by the different ways in which changes might be effected. There are two broad categories of reform that have been put forward by critics and supporters of the IFIs. These include: (1) changes to redress the imbalance that exists between the influence of developed and less developed countries within these institutions; and (2) changes in the priorities and programmes of the institutions.[8]

These two types of reforms undoubtedly are inter-related and overlap to a considerable degree. However, and this is where the complications set in, changes in each of them entail different approaches to reform and have different possibilities of realization. The first would involve dramatic changes which, in the absence of a major international financial crisis, are unlikely to receive support either from the industrialized countries or from

Table 18.2

External Debt Totals and Indicators for Developing Countries, 1980-93

	1980	1986	1988	1990	1991	1992	1993
Total Long term Debt ($ million)	480,848	995,858	1,128,136	1,209,840	1,269,325	1,308,227	1,410,910
Net Transfers on Debt ($ million)	65,441	-35,740	-40,976	-12,772	-8,450	13,057	11,387
External Debt/ Exports of Goods and Services (%)	89.0	201.7	177.7	162.0	1703	174.4	179.5
Total Debt Services/ Exports of Goods and Services (%)	13.5	25.9	23.4	18.8	18.6	18.7	18.5

Source: World Bank, World Debt Tables, 1993-94

within the IMF and the IBRD. Thus, the most feasible avenue for reform must involve changes that can be accommodated within the structure and operation of the IFIs as presently constituted, *i.e.*, changes in the priorities and programmes of the institutions.

For example, proposals to redress the North-South balance in influence might include changes in IMF quota subscriptions and hence voting rights. There are three major problems with such an approach. First, the industrialized countries do not recognize the need for a fundamental revision of the existing monetary system or of the norms, structures and procedures through which the system is implemented.[9] Second, both the IMF and the IBRD are among the most institutionalized international agencies and enjoy a considerable degree of autonomy. These organizations are highly bureaucratized, with organizational routines that influence, and are influenced by, professional norms.[10] Thus, even if IMF quota subscriptions could be changed to redress the North-South imbalance in voting rights, this in itself might not result in any significant changes in the actual policies and priorities of the institution.

The third aspect of the problem focuses on the sources of funding for the institutions. The IMF and the IBRD have different ways of raising finance for their programmes, and the IBRD has more flexibility in this regard than the IMF. The IBRD raises finance for its programmes by borrowing money on international bond markets, which it then lends to needy countries. The sources of funding for the IMF, on the other hand, come from members' quota subscriptions that are proportional to the size of their economies. Hence richer countries pay more, with the USA alone contributing 20% of IMF quotas, about $24 billion. The problem here is that, since quota subscriptions are linked to the size of economies, if the LDCs are granted a greater proportion of quotas, they would have to contribute proportionately more to the IMF. Where would they get the money?

A more feasible avenue for reform is to attempt to bridge the divide that exists in the international framework for development cooperation, between institutions and agencies within the United Nations system on the one hand, and those institutions that are effectively outside this system on the other hand. Currently, although the IMF and the IBRD are nominally part of the UN system, they enjoy a considerable degree of autonomy, and restrict the ability or authority of central UN representative organs such as the General Assembly or the Economic and Social Council (ECOSOC) to supervise their activities or to make recommendations to them. As a general rule, the institutional norms regarding economic development have been closer to the interests and perspective of LDCs the more firmly the institution is within the UN framework, and therefore subject to the supervision or recommendations of the General Assembly or the ECOSOC. Examples in this regard are the United Nations Development Programme (UNDP) and the United Nations Conference on Trade and Development (UNCTAD). Conversely, the institutional norms regarding economic development have been less in tune with the interests and perspective of LDCs, where activities are regulated by an institution that is outside the UN system. The IMF and the IBRD fall into this latter category. The question is, could or should the operations of IMF and the IBRD be brought further within the UN system, and would this make a difference?

The major problems here are normative and political. Historically, there has been quite a divergence between the development norms elaborated within the representative organs of the UN and the norms elaborated by the IFIs following their foundation at Bretton Woods. Within representative organs of the UN system, where LDCs enjoy numerical superiority and where voting procedures based on sovereign equality have allowed them to enhance their political weight, the norms regarding economic development have been explicitly redistributive. This has been the case with UN organs and agencies such as the General Assembly, ECOSOC and UNCTAD, where the LDC bloc – the G-77 – has articulated norms of international redistribution since its formation in the early 1960s. The three General Assembly resolutions in 1974: *Res. 3201 and Res. 3202* (April-May 1974, 6th Special Session), *The Declaration of Action on the Establishment of the NIEO*, and *The Programme of Action on the NIEO*; and *Res. 3281* (December, 1974, 29th General Session) *The Charter of Economic Rights and Duties of States*, as well as the numerous UNCTAD resolutions, gave formal institutional expression to these norms.[11]

In essence, UN development norms have been concerned with achieving a more equitable distribution of wealth, resources and political influence between rich countries and poorer countries, within a state-centric system. At the core has been a concern for the preservation of state sovereignty and a strengthening of the state as the prime agent in the process of economic development. This emphasis on the state as the prime subject and beneficiary of international redistribution was itself a reflection of the state-centrism of the *UN Charter* – specifically, the provisions of *Article 2(4)* and *Article 2(7)*.

In contrast to these statist redistributive norms are the liberal internationalist norms of the IMF and, to a lesser extent, the IBRD.[12] These liberal norms have shown a preference for the market as the prime agent of economic growth, the openness of national economies, non-discrimination between nationals and foreigners, and multilateralism. These norms are a reflection of the interests of the industrialized countries that provide the IMF with the bulk of its resources.[13] Thus, at a fundamental level, the two sets of norms, and the political interests supporting those norms (those elaborated within the UN representative organs and those elaborated by the IFIs), have been incompatible. At the root of this incompatibility has been a disagreement between rich and poor countries about the role of the state and the market in the process of economic development.

The most feasible avenue for reform must attempt to reconcile the divergence between the two positions. Recent developments suggest that such a reconciliation is already under way. LDCs appear to have embraced the market and the idea of political pluralism as a basis for development, while the IMF and IBRD are becoming more aware of the political requirements of economic prescriptions. The analysis below explores how this apparent normative and policy convergence emerged, and how it could form the basis for a new framework for international development cooperation.

Policy Convergence

A certain degree of convergence, both at the normative and at the policy level, in both domestic and foreign economic policy, is required for the creation of an international regime for development cooperation. It is difficult to create regimes and to govern relationships among actors at the international level when their domestic policies, political institutions and norms are radically different.[14]

A high degree of convergence in domestic state-society relations among industrialized countries at the end of World War II was one of the main factors that facilitated the creation of the Liberal International Economic Order at Bretton Woods in 1944.[15] From the end of World War II until the 1980s, there was no truly global framework for development cooperation. There were, instead, at least three frameworks: one centred around the Bretton Woods institutions (the IFIs) and reflecting the interests, priorities and judgements of the Western industrialized countries; one centred around the UN system and reflecting the interests, priorities and judgement of the LDCs; and the third centred around the Communist Bloc and reflecting the interests, priorities and judgements of the USSR and its satellites.

During the 1980s, two significant transformations occurred in the developing world. The first was the retreat of the state, and the second, closely related to the first, was the transformation of economic policy. With respect to the retreat of the state, the 1980s witnessed a weakening of authoritarian governments in many LDCs, especially in Latin America. Beyond changes in forms of government, at a more fundamental level an adjustment occurred in the relationship among state, society and the economy, involving a weakening of the central state machinery within many LDCs and its retreat from society and the economy to varying degrees. There emerged in country after country stronger civil societies, each determined to carve out autonomous spheres of social and economic interaction independent of the state.[16]

With respect to economic policy, the most influential model of economic development in much of the developing world during the 1960s and 1970s emphasized economic nationalism, state intervention and import-substitution industrialization.[17] During the 1980s, however, there was a dramatic shift in economic policy involving a reduction in the forms and extent of state intervention, the liberalization of trade and exchange regimes, and a greater reliance on market forces in the allocation and distribution of resources.[18]

It is clear that the change in economic policy in the LDCs accompanied the widespread adoption of Structural Adjustment Programmes imposed by the IFIs. What is not so clear, however, is whether the IMF and the IBRD, or the constraints of the international economic system, were ultimately responsible for imposing these programmes. The debt crisis of the early 1980s, the collapse in commodity prices, the failure of import-substitution, the need for external finance and the leverage of the international financial institutions, and the deep economic trough into which many LDCs had sunk certainly influenced the adoption of these liberalization policies.

But to focus only on external sources of change ignores the important domestic transformations that were occurring concurrently within many LDCs,[19] and therefore provides an incomplete explanation of the change in economic policy. Indeed, in some LDCs, the retreat of the state preceded the adoption of a Structural Adjustment Program. There is evidence that, in many parts of the developing world, there has been an acceptance, however grudgingly, of the importance of the market. This was given institutional expression at the *UNCTAD VIII Conference* in Cartagena, Colombia (1992), where a resolution passed at a plenary session affirmed the importance of market-oriented economic policies and political pluralism as the basis for development.[20]

At the beginning of the 1990s then, with the convergence described above, there appears to be a basis, for the first time since World War II, for the creation of a truly global regime for development cooperation. This convergence in economic policy may turn out to be more apparent than real. The issue is intimately tied to the question of the continued sustainability of reform in many parts of the developing world, and this in turn hinges on whether or not market-driven reforms can produce economic benefits to halt the decline, and improve living conditions. And here the role of the IMF and the IBRD is critical. Two main areas stand out: the constraints in the international political economy, particularly external debt and commodity prices; and domestic constraints.

Constraints in the International Economy

Since the LDC debt crisis erupted, the burden of adjustments has been disproportionately borne by LDC debtors. The central and serious flaw in the logic of the Structural Adjustment Programmes being assiduously promoted by both the IMF and the IBRD is that they rely on domestic adjustments to respond to external shocks. These programmes do not give equal attention to changes to existing structures and relations in the international political economy. The mounting LDC debt burden and the instability in commodity prices are the two areas that stand out. In the absence of concrete measures to alleviate the crippling debt burden through debt relief and increased finance, and to stabilize commodity prices, it is unlikely that domestic adjustments will achieve economic recovery. This is the real tragedy of Structural Adjustment.

The record of Structural Adjustment points to the importance of financing for adjustment. Adjustment and financing are not to be seen as mutually exclusive, but as two sides of the same coin. Sustaining adjustment requires adequate finance. It is interesting to note that, within the *IMF Articles of Agreement,* is a provision for sharing the burden of adjustment between creditor/surplus countries and deficit countries. This is the *Scarce Currency Clause (Article VII),* which would allow the IMF to declare a particular surplus country's currency to be scarce and thus permit other member countries to impose discriminatory exchange and import controls against the surplus country.[21] To date, this provision has never been invoked, and thus there is little pressure on creditor countries to adjust. In addition, the availability of alternate sources of finance in the international capital markets gives some debtor countries with high credit ratings (*e.g.,* the USA) the option of avoiding adjustment altogether. As a result, it is difficult not to be cynical about the sincerity, or at least the evenhandedness, of IMF advice to LDC debtors.

What options do LDC debtors have? There are essentially three options, none of which are feasible, at least not in the short term. The first is to repudiate external debt altogether and start afresh. While this may have the advantage of freeing up resources for more immediate needs, it would almost certainly have the far more serious disadvantage of closing off access to markets, technology and additional finance. The second option is to seek bilateral assistance only. This is not much of an option, since the bulk of bilateral assistance today is linked to the adoption of IMF and IBRD Structural Adjustment Programmes. The third option would be for LDCs to go it alone – avoid adjustment, by-pass the international financial institutions and seek greater regional and intra-LDC cooperation. This option is available to only very few LDCs. While greater intra-LDC cooperation is appealing, regional integration schemes are only likely to work if they are constructed within a global framework and receive the support of the international financial institutions.[22]

Thus, in reality, most LDCs have few options outside that of seeking the assistance of the IMF and the IBRD. And since the LDCs to a large extent are fulfilling their part of the bargain – by implementing the adjustment programmes – the IMF and the IBRD should in turn take initiatives to ease the burden of adjustments. These initiatives might include an expansion in the scope and number of special LDC facilities to build upon the special facilities already in place, such as the IMF's *Extended Fund Facility* (EFF-1974), *Structural Adjustment Facility* (SAF-1986), the *Enhanced Structural Adjustment Facility* (ESAF-1987) and the new *Compensatory and Contingency Finance Facility* (CCFF-1988); and the World Bank's *Structural Adjustment Loans* (SAL-1982) and the *Special Programme of Assistance* (SPA) that was developed in 1988 to assist debt-distressed African countries.

In addition to the expansion of these facilities, the IMF and the World Bank need to address the flaws inherent in the design of their current adjustment formulas, and the inconsistencies in the phasing and sequencing of particular instruments, targets and conditions. The rigidity in the formula for Structural Adjustment is both unnecessary and misguided. Greater flexibility in the selection of instruments and targets, greater attention to the political requirements of the different phases of adjustment, greater attention to structural and growth-oriented issues, and greater concern for the distributional impact of adjustment on the most vulnerable groups, will reduce many of the negative political and social costs engendered by the current adjustment formula.[23] In effect, there should be a more careful effort to tailor programmes to suit local political and economic circumstances.

The IMF and the IBRD, particularly the latter, have recently begun to emphasize poverty alleviation and the impact of adjustment on the most vulnerable groups. In addition, there is increasing pressure on these institutions from governments of industrialized countries and from non-governmental agencies, to expand the scope of conditionality to include other non-economic criteria such as environmental protection, democratization and human rights. Most recently, a Global Environment Facility has been created to be jointly administered by the UNDP, the UNEP, and the IBRD [see Chapter 16].

The inclusion of such criteria will result in expanded and more intrusive conditionality which could be counterproductive, if it is perceived by LDC recipients as yet another form of Western domination. The main issue here is the conflict between state sovereignty and external intervention. Evidence suggests that a primary factor in the ability and willingness of LDCs to implement reform programmes is the degree of government commitment to the aims and objectives of the programme. And this commitment is in turn based on a recognition and acceptance by the LDC government of the necessity of the reform measures. Thus, commitment – and the learning process on which such commitment is based – begins at the stage where programmes are negotiated between the international financial institution and the recipient government.[24] Expanding the scope of conditionality to include broadened non-economic criteria must be done with sensitivity and with the consent of LDC governments. If the convergence of normatives and policy described above is real, then the prospects of obtaining this consensus are greater now that the ideological and political dimensions of the issues concerning governance and economic development have been reduced.

Some critics have argued that the IMF should abdicate its role in Structural Adjustment in favour of the IBRD.[25] The argument here is that the IMF was never intended to be a development institution and is ill-suited to the task. Its primary mandate is to provide finance for balance of payments adjustments. By involving itself in structural and growth-oriented areas, the IMF's activities have become less finance-oriented. By getting rid of facilities like the EFF, SAF and ESAF, the argument goes, the IMF would have more liquidity available to focus on financing balance of payments disequilibria.

While there may be some merits to this argument, it ignores the reasons why the newer facilities were introduced in the first place – deficiencies in the approach to, and the facilities for, balance of payments financing. Moreover, the issue of the amount of resources the IMF has available to finance its programmes has nothing to do with its role in Structural Adjustment. It has everything to do with the difficulties of reaching agreement among IMF members on increasing quota subscriptions and the operational modalities of the *Special Drawing Rights* (SDRs), the IMFs reserve currency. Like it or not, the IMF today is involved in international development; what is more important is how this role is carried out.

Domestic Constraints

In addition to the external constraints outlined above, there are important domestic constraints that have to be addressed if market-driven reforms are to be sustained and are to produce economic benefits. These constraints centre on the paradoxical relationship between the state and the market in the process of economic development.

The primary thrust of Structural Adjustment is to reduce the role of the state in the economy. The rationale for the restoration or creation of market mechanisms, from the perspective of the IMF and the IBRD, is to increase competition and thus improve efficiency in domestic production. The assumption is that development and growth are best served by sending market-signals to producers and consumers in order to increase total production and rationalize distribution.[26]

But is this really the case? As critics have been quick to point out, this notion rests not only on questionable psychological assumptions, but also on doubtful historical evidence.[27] In the post-World War II era, the few development successes to date – the Asian Newly Industrialized Countries (NICs) – adopted a development model that involved tight state controls over the operation of the market in the areas of finance, foreign investment, and industrial and export development. Aside from the absence of recent historical evidence confirming the ability of the market alone to promote development, the problem of relying solely on market mechanisms is that, in many LDCs, the state is weak, but the market is even weaker.

The transition from a centrally-planned economy, in which key macroeconomic variables are controlled by the government, to a liberalized one, in which the market mechanism is given freer rein, is difficult, both technically and politically. This stems from the fact that the market requires a strong set of normative and institutional underpinnings in order to function effectively. And these normative underpinnings are provided by the state.[28] Sending market-signals through changes in relative prices to self-interested utility maximizers, although necessary, is not sufficient to elicit the desired supply response. Market actors also need to be persuaded, through (political) confidence-building measures, of what the rules of the game are and that these rules are in their interest.[29] In essence, market actors need a measure of political influence – structures of governance and accountability that are accessible to them. Although market mechanisms will reduce the politicization of economic activity, without institutionalized normative underpinnings the market may not serve as an engine of growth.

The most prominent shortcoming of Structural Adjustment, in this respect, has been the failure to examine the political assumptions, requirements and consequences of economic prescriptions, particularly in the relationship between the state and the market in the areas of consumption, distribution, production and investment. There are numerous examples of governments that have embarked on Structural Adjustment and that encountered stiff political opposition. These governments have found themselves with a weak domestic constituency, which threatens the future sustainability of reform. In Africa there are the examples of Ghana and Nigeria; in Latin America there are Brazil, Argentina and Venezuela; and in Asia there are Thailand and Malaysia.

Thus, the greatest problem is the absence of a coherent and systematic development programme. Both the IMF and the IBRD have belatedly begun to recognize the importance of the issue of governance and specifically to incorporate political variables into the design of their programmes.[30] However, after over a decade of Structural Adjustment lending, the IMF and the IBRD are yet to articulate a comprehensive development programme – a long term programme that not only includes specific economic targets and instruments, but also addresses fundamental political constraints. Economic development is not reducible to sending the "right" signals to market actors. The greatest political challenge to LDC governments pursuing structural reforms is the absence of this political component.

These observations raise questions about whether the conditional aid administered by the international financial institutions is the most appropriate instrument for long term development financing. The IMF and the IBRD both acknowledge that accelerated and self-sustaining economic growth in LDCs over the long term is contingent on increased private capital flows and the expansion of private capital markets.[31] Perhaps the financial assistance of the IMF and the IBRD is most relevant and needed between the period when an economy is stabilized and structural reforms have begun and the period when private capital, both foreign and local, begins to flow into an economy. Although significant resource transfers to LDCs from official sources do mitigate many of the negative consequences of adjustment and thus help to ensure its sustainability, in many ways official aid transfers contradict the logic of the market, and in some instances may actually impede the growth of the private sector and private investment over the long term.[32]

Conclusion

Conditional aid of the kind administered by the IMF and the World Bank cannot by itself solve the problems of international development, but it is a necessary ingredient. The patterns of conditional aid administered by these International Financial Institutions have not, in the past, been particularly insensitive to the needs of LDCs. As a result of a fundamental divergence in the norms regarding international development, and of the political differences among the actors that buttressed these norms, a truly global framework for development cooperation did not exist for much of the post-World War II period. At the beginning of the 1990s, however, there appears to be a foundation for the creation of such a global framework which, if properly managed, could provide a more effective multilateral approach to addressing problems of economic development. And this foundation lies in the apparent normative and policy convergence on the role of the market and political pluralism in development.

While it is too early to determine if this convergence is transitory, what is evident is that it is fragile – much depends on whether or not market-driven reforms in LDCs can produce economic benefits. And this in turn hinges on certain changes the IMF and the IBRD, as presently constituted, could make in their programmes and priorities to ease the costs and risks of economic policy reform in LDCs. These changes include:

(1) reducing the intrusiveness of conditionality by creating a truly multilateral framework that involves LDCs in the setting of standards and objectives;

(2) greater efforts to share the burden of adjustments between creditor and deficit countries and an increase in the amounts of financing for adjustment;

(3) the expansion of debt-relief programmes and efforts to ensure access of

LDC exports to markets in industrialized countries;
(4) greater effort to tailor programmes to suit local political and economic circumstances of aid recipients and greater attention to the political requirements of economic prescriptions, and to the phasing and sequencing of reform measures;
(5) more attention to poverty-alleviation and the impact of adjustment on the distribution of income;
(6) greater efforts to encourage increased international private capital flows into those developing countries whose structural and institutional reforms have progressed to the stage where domestic capital markets are emerging to play a key role in economic growth.

With the increasing regionalization of the world economy, for many LDCs that are not fortunate to be part of the emerging regional centres – North America, Europe and Asia centred around Japan – the prospect of marginalization is very great. Regionalization of the world economy would only hurt the majority of LDCs, particularly African countries and the smaller countries of Latin America and Asia. For these countries, institutions such as the IMF and the IBRD will have a critical role to play. In addition, with the emergence of the countries of Eastern Europe and the former Soviet republics, the possibility of a diversion of development assistance away from the poorer countries of Africa, Asia and Latin America to Eastern Europe is great, especially in view of the more immediate political and strategic importance to Western industrialized countries of the consequences of economic catastrophe in their neighbouring countries. Thus, the centrality of institutions such as the IMF and the IBRD will be required to offset the tendency towards regionalization and parochialism, if the possibility of economic growth and stability is to be ensured for all the world's nations, rich and poor.

References

1 Boutros-Ghali, B. "Global Developing Cooperation" *Emory International Law Review* 7 1993 Spring 2.
2 Busumtwi-Sam, James 1993 "Economic Crisis and Policy Adjustment: The Politics of Foreign Economic Policy Making in Ghana, 1982-1990," Ph.D. Thesis, Department of Political Science, University of Toronto; Biersteker, Thomas "The 'Triumph' of Neoclassical Economics in the Developing World: Policy Convergence and Bases of Governance

in the International Economic Order" in Czempiel, Ernst-Otto and James Rosenau eds. 1992 Governance Without Government (Cambridge University Press).

3   World Bank World Development Report 1993 Table 2.

4   World Bank World Development Report 1990 1-29.

5   IMF World Economic Outlook 1992.

6   Comments by Mahbub ul Haq, United Nations Development Advisor, as quoted in the Globe and Mail 14 July 1993 B6.

7   World Bank World Development Report 1990 appendix tables.

8   Ascher, William "New Development Approaches and the Adaptability of International Organizations: The Case of the World Bank" International Organization 37 1983 3; Amuzegar, Jahangir "The IMF Under Fire" Foreign Policy 1986 64.

9   Jahangir, see note 8; Pauly, L.W. "Promoting a Global Economy: The Normative Role of the IMF" in Stubbs, R. and G. Underhill eds. 1994 Political Economy and the Changing Global Order (McClelland & Stewart: Toronto) 206-208.

10 Ascher, see note 8; Naim, Moises "The World Bank: Its Role, Governance and Organizational Culture" Conference on Managing the International Economy of the Future (Institute for International Economies: Washington DC May 1994).

11 Snyder, P. and P. Slynn eds. 1987 The International Law of Development; Charterjee, S.K. "The Charter of Economic Rights and Duties of States: An Evaluation after 15 Years" International and Comparative Law Quarterly 40 3 1991 669-684.

12 Pauly, see note 9, 204-215.

13 Pauly, see note 9, 207.

14 Keohane, Robert 1984 After Hegemony (Princeton University Press) 6-7; Ruggie, John G. "International Regimes, Transactions and Embedded Liberalism in the Postwar Economic Order" International Organization" 36 Spring 1982 393-397.

15 Ruggie, see note 14, 393-397.

16 The extent and significance of this phenomenon varied considerably among LDCs, with African countries such as Ghana and Zaire as extreme examples of state decay and collapse. See, for example, Bratton, Michael "Beyond the State: Civil Society and Associational Life in Africa" World Politics 11 1989 407-430.

17 There were some important exceptions to this general trend, most notably the NICs (South Korea, Singapore, Taiwan, etc.) which, although following the general pattern of state intervention and eco-

nomic nationalism, pursued outward-oriented growth strategies.

18 Busumtwi-Sam, James 1993 Economic Crisis and Policy Adjustment 425-439; Nelson, Joan ed. 1990 Economic Crisis and Policy Choice (Princeton University Press) Chapter 1.

19 Busumtwi-Sam, see note 18; Biersteker, see note 2, 124-25.

20 Marchand, Marianne H. "The Political Economy of North-South Relations" in Stubbs, R. and G. Underhill eds. 1994 Political Economy and the Changing Global Order (McClelland & Stewart: Toronto) 294-295.

21 IMF Articles of Agreement 1988 26-28; MacBean, A.I. and P.N Snowden International Institutions in Trade and Finance 1981 (Allen & Unwin: London) 4-9.

22 There are numerous examples of failed attempts to promote greater intra-LDC cooperation. In Africa, for example, the Lagos Plan of Action and the African Common Market failed to materialize.

23 Busumtwi-Sam, see note 18, Chapters 5 and 6.

24 Nelson, Joan "Beyond Conditionality" Harvard International Review (1992 Fall) 4-7; Busumtwi-Sam, see note 18, Chapters 4 and 5.

25 See, for example, Amuzegar, note 8.

26 Biersteker, Thomas "Reducing the Role of the State: A Conceptual Exploration of IMF and World Bank Prescriptions" International Studies Quarterly 34 1990 485.

27 Biersteker, see note 26; Broad Robin, John Cavanagh and Walden Bello "Development: The Market is not Enough" Foreign Policy 81 Winter 1990-91 144-162.

28 This is an observation made by economic historians. See, for example, Gershenkron, Alexander 1966 Economic Backwardness in Historical Perspective (Harvard University Press: Cambridge); Evans, Peter and Deitrich Reuschemeyer "The State and Economic Transformation" in Evans, P., D. Reuschemeyer and T. Skocpol eds. 1985 Bringing the State Back In, (Cambridge University Press) 44-47.

29 For arguments along a similar vein, see Evans, Peter and Dietriech Reuschemeyer "The State and Economic Transformation" in Evans et al., see note 28; Ardito-Barletta, Nicholas "Managing Development and the Transition" Conference on Managing the World Economy of the Future (Institute for International Economics: Washington DC May 1994); Haggard, Stephen "Alleviating Markets, Poverty and Income Distribution: An Assessment of Neoliberal Claims" Ethics and International Affairs 5 1991.

30 See, for example, "Reflections on Africa" address by Barber B. Conable, President of The World Bank, Washington DC, World Bank 1991;

World Bank 1989 Sub-Saharan Africa: From Crisis to Sustainable Growth.

31 See, for example, IMF World Economic Outlook May 1994 7-9; World Bank World Debt Tables 9-22.

32 See Younger Stephen D. "Aid and the Dutch Disease: Macroeconomic Management When Everybody Loves You" World Development 20 November 1992 1587-1597.

PART VI

INTERNATIONAL LAW

Commentary on Part VI

Ronald St.J. Macdonald

The evolution of the United Nations parallels the evolution of international law in the half-century following the conclusion of the Second World War. The post-colonial states, non-state actors and individuals all have sought recourse to legal norms and principles in international relations in an extraordinarily dynamic period. The challenge is to ensure that international law remains sensitive to the changing international scene and relevant to all those whom it seeks to serve.

The two chapters in Part VI detail in very important ways how this challenge is being answered at the point of the 50th Anniversary of the *United Nations Charter.* Professor Sharon Williams closely scrutinizes the rationale for an international criminal court. In so doing, she undertakes the analysis essential for international law – what interests are sought to be served by the promulgation of international law or an international institution; how legal approaches might provide a sufficient response; and how the application of domestic principles might survive the unique constraints posed by the international arena. Williams reminds us that the problems requiring international legal solutions are regrettably ever-present: the manifestations of violence and indignity in Rwanda and the former Yugoslavia are but recent examples of atrocities which have been so prevalent in human history. The search for legal solutions, though, has also been ever-present, and Williams notes how the progress towards an international criminal tribunal has been on the international agenda since the time of the League of Nations, and is rooted well prior to that time. This is all by way of introduction to an exciting development – the setting aside of the obstacles traditionally standing in the way of an international criminal tribunal empowered sufficiently to address the challenges of such long standing. The detail Williams provides affords an insight both into the birth of an important new legal instrument and also the peculiar nature of the legal dimensions of international affairs that must be addressed in order that international legal documents or instruments can be potent.

Paul Paton engages the challenges facing the international legal order from a broader expanse: the *United Nations Decade of International Law* is, as he discusses, a crucible for considering the nature of and scope of international legal approaches to the changing international order. The *Decade* highlights both the promise and the potential for disappointment inherent in putting international law under close scrutiny for ten years. The tensions underlying the Decade – between those viewing international law as a merely political tool and others who see a means of ensuring an equal and equitable international order – make the choice of title for the 1995 *United Nations Congress on Public International Law* (and Paton's chapter) especially apt: one of the special tasks for the international community as it reshapes itself in the post-Cold War era, is to determine how indeed international law can remain a currency for international relations. Engaging widespread support for principles broadly defined, while at the same time seeking substantive reform, is an ageless, timeless challenge for the international community. Paton's contribution here highlights how the challenges have been framed in light of current concerns, and his straightforward presentation of the pitfalls and the potential grants both the informed and the neophyte reader a point of access to the role law and legal reform can play during the balance of the United Nations' first century.

Both chapters, then, fulfil a critical purpose: to remind the reader that international law is an integral part of the United Nations' history, as well as its promise. They demonstrate how international legal debate is a microcosm of larger political and economic questions about the relationship between states and peoples, and they hold out the promise of UN-led legal solutions to the very real, daily concerns of states and peoples. They stand as a celebration of UN accomplishment, and a challenge to the United Nations and its constituent parts to take up the legal, as well as the political and economic dimensions of answers through the next fifty years.

CHAPTER 19

International Law as a Language for International Relations: Legal Reform and The United Nations

Paul D. Paton

Law and legal institutions lie at the heart of non-violent approaches to conflict resolution in the international arena, and are taking on increased importance in the shaping of the post-Cold War world. The United Nations itself acknowledged this in declaring the period 1990-1999 the *United Nations Decade of International Law*, and in devoting particular attention through the Sixth Committee of the General Assembly during the period to an evaluation of international law and its prospects. The *Decade* affords a ready opportunity for critical assessment of the utility and functioning of international law and international legal institutions, and the debates which have already taken place present a brief glimpse of areas ripe for reform. The International Court of Justice, and the protection of the environment in times of armed conflict, are two topics which have received special scrutiny to date. The *United Nations Congress on Public International Law* proposed for 1995 will be a crucible for consideration of these topics and a test for the future of international legal reform. Coinciding with the mid-point of the *Decade* and the 50th Anniversary of the *United Nations Charter*, the *Congress* will focus further attention on international legal institutions, the work of the *Decade*, and the critical role international law might play in the next century.

The United Nations Decade of International Law

On 17 November 1989, the 45th session of the United Nations General Assembly declared the period 1990-1999 the *United Nations Decade of International Law*.[1] *Resolution 44/23* was adopted by consensus and set out four purposes for the *Decade*:

(1) the promotion of the acceptance of and respect for the principles of international law;

(2) the promotion of means and methods for the peaceful settlement of disputes between states, including resort to and full respect for the International Court of Justice;

(3) the encouragement of the progressive development of international law and its codification; and

(4) the encouragement of the teaching, study, dissemination and wider appreciation of international law.

The *Resolution* also proposed that a third *International Peace Conference*, to take place at the end of the *Decade*, be discussed.[2]

Resolution 44/23 was both the starting point for the work of the international community and the realization of the aspirations of many in the Non-Aligned Movement. The *Hague Declaration*, issued at the conclusion of a meeting of the Non-Aligned States in June 1989, contained the seeds of the four principles outlined above. In addition, it set out a solemn pledge to realise a peaceful world with justice for all, and expressed the aspiration that the *Decade's* purview would include the achievement of complete and general disarmament.

Professor Budislav Vukas of the former Yugoslavia was appointed by the Sixth Committee to be Chairman of a Working Group on the *Decade*. He bore the responsibility for steering the work of the Group in identifying and developing a programme for the first term of the *Decade* (1990 - 1992) which would be generally acceptable to governmental and non-governmental organizations, who were canvassed for their views. The *Vukas Report*[3] was debated by the Sixth Committee of the General Assembly on 13-15 November 1990 and received a favourable response from the delegates. The proposals addressing the peaceful settlement of disputes, and the encouragement of the teaching, study and dissemination of international law were strongly supported, setting the stage for the tenor and direction of future debates in the Sixth Committee. The emphasis in the report's first annex, the programme for 1990-1992, is on consultation and general consideration of how the aims of the *Decade* may be achieved, rather than definitive action. The second annex sets out more comprehensive and ambitious suggestions for the programme for the balance of the *Decade*. These include the formulation of rules for stabilizing the price of raw materials, the elaboration of legal norms to accomplish complete disarmament and the development of specific human rights, including the right to food.[4] The tension between conservative modification and more radical innovation remains the fundamental theme in the work of the *Decade*, and reflects the overarching difficulties in accomplishing substantive and meaningful legal reform.

In the context of the *Decade*, this tension is not surprising. The emergence of the *Decade* from a meeting of the non-aligned nations engendered suspicion from other, particularly Western, states. The primary concern in this regard was the underlying motivation for the *Decade*, and the sentiment that the *Decade* would serve only as a vehicle for the repeated demands of the Third World for a New International Economic Order. There was also concern that the *Decade* should not place international legal reform on the agenda merely to see it frustrated by a lack of substantive accomplishment, disappointing both those who conceive of international law as a useful if not comprehensive tool in interstate relations, and those newer states who look to international law as a critical foundation for their participation in international relations. Anthony Aust, representative of the United Kingdom Mission to the United Nations, expressed rhetorically the most pertinent question in evaluating the *Decade* and international legal reform in his address to the Sixth Committee of the General Assembly on 13 November 1990: how the United Nations and the *United Nations Decade of International Law* can help ensure that international law is "not going to be merely a thing of textbooks and speeches, but ... the means by which the world community can ensure the rule of law." His own response focused on concrete tasks and actions, and on creating the political will requisite to accomplishing change: "Just talking about international law, and how to develop and strengthen it, is not enough. Adopting, and even bringing into force Conventions is not enough. Always there must be the political will to carry out the good intentions ... The *United Nations Decade of International Law* can help in many ways to create the political will."[5]

An informal meeting of the heads of offices responsible for international legal services of the foreign ministries of the United Nations Member States in October 1993 similarly focused on achievable tasks in assessing the proposed 1995 *Congress*. A report of the meeting noted that "formulation of a concrete programme of practical topics was viewed as essential. Many participants urged Legal Advisors to help with preparations for the *Congress*, stressing that their involvement would be essential to its success."[6] The same meeting assessed the proposal of the Non-Aligned States for a *Third Peace Conference* in 1999 as the culmination of the *Decade*, and tensions similarly emerged between aspiration and concrete accomplishment, between developed and developing world. Numerous Legal Advisors questioned even the need for such a conference, given that existing mechanisms for the peaceful settlement of disputes were comprehensive; in their view "the only major component missing was the political will to subscribe to such mechanisms."[6] Another voice, though, suggested that "since existing mechanisms had been formulated primarily by developed countries, developing countries might be more willing to adhere to procedures for the settlement of disputes to which they had contributed."[6] Questions of political will and fundamental understanding of the role, function and legitimacy of international legal norms and institutions will lie at and shake the foundation of any attempts to reform international law in the context of the *Decade* or otherwise.

Debates about the *Decade* in the Sixth Committee have evinced these considerations strongly, pitting the Non-Aligned States against the developed world on these fundamental issues. In 1992, for example, the delegate from Pakistan looked to expand the scope of the *Decade* to include the "resolution of international economic problems, particularly of the developing countries, through such measures as reduction in interest rates, increase in development assistance, curbs on protectionist policies and trade barriers, technology transfer to developing countries" and other similar measures.[7] The delegate from Indonesia saw the *Decade* as a "useful instrument to reiterate faith in the utility of international law," which might be best achieved by accomplishing the "objectives enunciated by the non-aligned countries for a New International Economic Order, a New International and Communication Order and for the democratization of international relations as a whole."[8] Western states, apart from Austria, Australia, the Nordic Countries, Rumania and Mexico, have been largely uninterested in expanding the ambit of the *Decade*, preferring instead to focus on incremental, concrete tasks, such as ensuring the domestic implementation of international obligations, increased recourse to the International Court of Justice for advisory opinions, and educating domestic populations about the utility and importance of international legal instruments.[9]

The statement by the delegate from Malta during debates in the Sixth Committee on the *Report of the Special Committee on the Charter of the United Nations and on the Strengthening of the Role of the Organization*[10] is indicative of the restrained ambition with which the other aspirations are being met by Western States. The delegate expressed support for the enhancement of the role of the International Court of Justice, and for the proposal that the Secretary-General be authorized under *Article 96, Paragraph 2* of the *United Nations Charter* to request advisory opinions from the Court, believing that "more frequent recourse to the Court by States, the General Assembly, the Security Council and international organizations would be beneficial to the development of international law and contribute to its increased observance in international relations." He also stated that "the various proposals and initiatives for reforming and restructuring the United Nations ... should not be evaluated in isolation but as an integral part of a comprehensive exercise so as not to distort the fine balance between the Organization's main organs."[11] This more incremental approach is sensitive to the constraints of reforming international legal norms in an international environment dominated by the political power of States, but is at the same time an obvious impediment to those seeking wholesale changes to the meaning of international law and to its implementation in non-traditional ways.

Two areas of potential change or reform, however, are nonetheless attracting attention as the *Decade* progresses. Both of these will be explored in turn below. The first, facilitating or mandating increased recourse to the International Court of Justice by Member States and by the officers of the United Nations Organization, is on its face a move notable for what would appear to be its lack of ambition. The political tensions underscoring the use of the Court, particularly as a result of recent US interaction with the Court, though, should not be underestimated.[12] These tensions underlie any discussion about recourse to the Court and understanding them is critical for appreciating any efforts for reform. The second issue, the protection of the environment in times of armed conflict, presents opportunities for innovation responding to a new set of problems arising in interstate relations. The topic presents a late 20th century spin on the rules of conflict arising from the *Peace Conferences* of roughly a century ago. Support for reform here has been garnered across the above-noted barriers, and yet here, too, change is slow and grudgingly incremental. Both areas thus serve as examples of the often glacial pace and seemingly uninspired nature of international legal reform, problems apparently endemic in an arena of political as well as legal considerations.

Reforming the International Court of Justice

Increased recourse to the International Court of Justice (ICJ) is a cornerstone purpose of the *Decade,* and the wording of *Resolution 44/23* acknowledges the difficulties the Court has faced in the international arena: the *Resolution* speaks of the need for "resort to and full respect for" the ICJ. Encouraging greater use of the Court for the peaceful resolution of disputes between States is meaningful only if they are willing to refer matters to the Court for its adjudication, willing to respect the decisions of the Court and abide by them. It is trite understanding that the fundamental difficulty for international law, and for the rulings of the ICJ in particular, is that there is no effective enforcement mechanism beyond national self-interest and moral suasion. Suggestions regarding the ICJ during the *Decade* have thus been aiming at the problem both from above and below: increasing the utilization of the Court will give it greater currency and force as it becomes a more recognized and respected tool for the settlement of disputes; increasing understanding of the Court through education aimed at broadening understanding of international law generally can help build the political fortitude needed to give the Court's decisions the force of popular will.

In *An Agenda for Peace, a Report of the Secretary General on Preventive Diplomacy, Peacemaking and Peacekeeping*,[13] the UN Secretary-General Boutros Boutros-Ghali noted that the Court "remains an under-used resource for the peaceful adjudication of disputes." He pointed out the power of the Security Council under *Articles 36* and *37* of the *Charter* to recommend to Member States the submission of a dispute to the Court, arbitration or other dispute-settlement mechanisms, and he also sought authorization for the Secretary-General to take advantage of the advisory competence of the Court, pursuant to *Article 96, Paragraph 2* of the *Charter*. In addition, he set out the following recommendations "to reinforce the role" of the Court: (1) that all Member States accept the general jurisdiction of the Court under *Article 36* of its *Statute* without reservation before the end of the *Decade of International Law* in the year 2000 and that, where domestic structures prevent this, States should agree bilaterally or multilaterally to a comprehensive list of matters they are willing to submit to the Court and should withdraw their reservations to its jurisdiction in the dispute settlement clauses of multilateral treaties; (2) where submission to the full Court is not practical, the Chambers jurisdiction should be used; and (3) that States should support the Trust Fund established to assist countries unable to afford the cost involved in bringing a dispute to the Court, and that such countries should take full advantage of the Fund in order to resolve their disputes. Boutros-Ghali's thrust is thus relatively simple yet substantive: remove the procedural impediments to full utilization of the Court, and encourage lesser developed states to resort to this mechanism by providing a form of international "legal aid" funding to alleviate financial constraints. *An Agenda for Peace* speaks to both developed and developing constituencies, and recognizes the importance of the *Decade of International Law* as a conceptual time-frame and crucible for action in the international political community.[14]

Resolution 44/23 is not the first to encourage more frequent use of the

ICJ. In 1974, the General Assembly adopted *Resolution 3232*, calling for a review of the role of the ICJ and making several recommendations to promote increased recourse to the Court. The experience of the Court thus far, with approximately sixty contentious cases and roughly twenty advisory opinions, has been described as neither "overwhelming," nor "unimpressive."[15] Yet there is grave concern about the withering of the Court from neglect, and underlying worry about the credibility of the Court in the new international order.

In part, the concern about the present approach of States to the Court is validated by their increasing preference for having specialized bodies consider certain types of disputes. The International Criminal Court, is but one innovation of this sort [see Chapter 20]. The *Law of the Sea Convention* establishes an elaborate mechanism for the settlement of disputes under its jurisdiction. The World Trade Organization, emerging in 1994 from the *Uruguay Round* of discussions on international trade and the *General Agreement on Tariffs and Trade*, holds out the promise of streamlined and specialized means for the resolution of such disagreements.[16] There are other examples receiving substantial attention. For instance, during the debates of the Sixth Committee in November 1993, the Australian delegate emphasized that the Permanent Court of Arbitration could serve as a valuable complement to the ICJ, and that because of its institutional flexibility, the Permanent Court of Arbitration was possibly "of greater value in the peaceful settlement of disputes in cases in which political considerations were the determining factors."[17] Having a plethora of tribunals and panels under bilateral and multilateral treaties[18] makes sense as providing an accessible and potentially more immediate response to the concerns of the contracting parties, and also holds out the promise that the tribunals will be utilised by those who have had a hand in fashioning their creation.

It is important to understand that the decisions of the Court are not necessarily binding upon States in the manner of decisions of domestic courts, either as precedent for future events or for actors not party to a dispute being decided by the Court. Further, States are not automatically under the jurisdiction of the Court and do not therefore have to appear before it or refer disputes to it. The impact and legitimacy of the Court is therefore a nagging and critically important concern. *Article 94(1)* of the *United Nations Charter* provides that each member of the United Nations undertakes to comply with the decision of the Court "in any case to which it is a party." The constituting Statute of the International Court of Justice sets out, in *Article 59*, that the decision of the Court "has no binding force except between the parties and in respect of that particular case." The *ICJ Statute* also contains what is commonly known as the "*Optional Clause*," *Article 36(2)*, which makes the acceptance of the compulsory jurisdiction of the Court contingent upon a declaration of a State: a State "may at any time declare that they recognize as compulsory *ipso facto* and without special agreement, in relation to any other State accepting the same obligation, the jurisdiction of the Court in all legal disputes" in respect of categories of cases enumerated within *Article 36(2)* itself. The accession to the compulsory jurisdiction of the Court encouraged by Boutros Boutros-Ghali in *An Agenda for Peace*, and the willingness to effect the Court's decisions, is a decision of tremendous political import. The issue highlights further the tension between the political and the legal in international affairs, and underscores the continuing importance of the concept of national interest and state sovereignty in what continues to be a state-centred international order.

The Protection of the Environment in Times of Armed Conflict

The 1992 *United Nations Conference on Environment and Development* (UNCED) held in Brazil, focused attention on the sharp increase in political conflicts with potentially explosive environmental implications in recent years. *Chapter 39* of *Agenda 21*, adopted by UNCED, emphasized that, in the area of avoidance and settlement of disputes with environmental implications, States should study and consider methods to broaden and make more effective the range of techniques presently available.[19] The topic thus has the potential to both address an area ripe for substantive response, and to provide a vibrant example of reform of international legal rules and instruments.

The Secretary-General was requested by the General Assembly in *Resolution 47/37* to invite the International Committee of the Red Cross (ICRC) to report on its activities and those of other relevant bodies with respect to the protection of the environment in times of armed conflict and to submit a report on the matter to the General Assembly.[20] The ICRC convened three meetings of experts, and on the basis of the considerations canvassed therein prepared a comprehensive report incorporating draft guidelines for military manuals and instructions on protecting the environment during hostilities. In introducing the report to the Sixth Committee, the representative of the ICRC noted that, "as a rule, international humanitarian law prohibited the destruction of civilian objects, thus implying a general protection of the natural environment, which did not, *a priori,* constitute a military objective." The ICRC experts had highlighted the duty of States derived from their "general obligation to respect and ensure respect for international humanitarian law," to "disseminate knowledge of that law, and to put an end to violations and repress grave breaches thereof."[21] The ICRC determined that no general codification of the rules protecting the environment in times of armed conflict should be undertaken at this point, and that emphasis should be placed instead on increasing compliance with, and disseminating, the rules. The draft guidelines for military manuals appended to the report were aimed towards this end.

Comments made during the debates of the Sixth Committee on the report reflect the general preference for an incremental approach, even in an area such as this where there had been widespread accord on the importance of protecting the environment generally.[22] The delegate from Belgium, speaking on behalf of the European Union, emphasized the EU's agreement with the "balanced approach" of the ICRC report, noting the ICRC's reservations about proposals for a new process of codification of the rules protecting the environment in times of armed conflict and its belief that such a process "would be of dubious value and could even be counter-productive." The EU stressed its agreement with the ICRC conclusion that, if several aspects of the existing law were elaborated upon and if the law were more fully implemented, adequate protection would be ensured. The delegate from Myanmar (Burma) took another tack, reflecting upon the proliferation of weapons of mass destruction and the threat they posed to the environment. In this respect, it was important to comply strictly with existing norms and to accede to the relevant international instruments, including the *Convention on the Prohibition of the Development, Production, Stockpiling and Use of Chemical Weapons and on Their Destruction.*[23] Like the EU, Nepal endorsed the ICRC view that the general codification of the rules pertaining to environmental protection might not be feasible at this point. However, Nepal hoped that the conclusion of a treaty establishing an international criminal jurisdiction might ensure that the rules pertaining to the protection of the environment in times of armed conflict were respected, and looked to the simultaneous application of the rules of environmental and humanitarian law towards this end.[24] Canada pointed to the final declaration of the *Conference* on the protection of victims of war held in Geneva on 1 September 1993, which urged reaffirmation of respect for the rules of international law protecting the natural environment, as inspiration for the refining and review of the guidelines proposed by the ICRC.[25]

The ICRC report and the responses to it are far from dramatic, but in this respect may reflect the likely tone and approach for the balance of the *Decade* and for international legal reform generally. The recognition and acknowledgement of a problematic topic area encourages a consensus that a legal response is required. Opportunity exists for creative and innovative development. This opportunity is not foreclosed by in-depth examination by experts, but rather is pursued in a different direction as a result of widespread accord that the problems which arise legally result not from an absence of rules, but rather the lack of widespread dissemination, understanding, and commitment to those rules. In this case, the innovation in the draft guidelines for military manuals is before national governments for their review and comment, and substantive work by the ICRC continues in areas of the relevant law requiring clarification, particularly the law applicable to armed conflicts that are non-international in nature. Further discussion and development will determine whether changes are incremental, widespread, or quietly buried. This will provide a marker to the substantive progress and potential for international legal reform during the *Decade*, and some indication of the potential for reform in other areas.

The United Nations Congress on Public International Law

Just as the substantive area of the law pertaining to the protection of the environment in times of armed conflict is watched closely, the *Congress on Public International Law* proposed for 1995 will come under close scrutiny for its contribution to international legal reform and to the *Decade* of *International Law*. The *Congress* was first proposed by Iran and Mexico[26] in 1992 during the drafting of the programme for the second term of the *Decade* by the Working Group struck by the Sixth Committee in 1991. The *Report of the Working Group* in which the proposal crystallized noted that a week-long *Congress* would present an opportunity to "take some practical measures to uphold the aims of the *Decade*."[27] The *Congress* also neatly coincides with the celebrations of the 50th Anniversary of the United Nations, and so puts international law on centre stage at a time when the attention of the international community is drawn towards the UN as an organization preparing for the next century.

Support for the *Congress* has been widespread and generally enthusiastic, but with cautious notes indicative of the manner in which international legal reform is generally approached. Reservations were expressed even in the Working Group where the *Congress* was proposed as to whether such an event "could address all the issues before the *Decade* in a responsible, non-politicized manner."[28] During the November 1992 meeting of the

Sixth Committee, the representative from the Netherlands commented that careful planning was necessary "in order not to end up with having a congress for the sake of having a congress."[29] Questions as to the purpose, structure, participants and funding of the *Congress* have generated considerable debate, which reflects both the high profile that the event is expected to generate, and the extreme concern that the opportunity not be frittered away. The intricacy of the efforts and the planning only scratch the surface of the diplomatic, political and legal complexities entailed in any endeavour to reform international legal institutions and instruments.

The draft programme for the *Congress* set out by the 1993 Working Group on the *Decade*[30] suggests that it will be convened at United Nations Headquarters in New York in 1995, immediately after the end of the second week of the 1995 Session of the Special Committee on the Charter of the United Nations and on the Strengthening of the Role of the Organization. The general theme proposed is, "Towards the twenty-first century: International Law as a Language for International Relations." It is expected that the *Congress* will last for five days. The 1993 *Working Group Report* suggests that a day be devoted to each of the four principal purposes enumerated for the *Decade*, with the final day set aside for reflection on and consideration of new challenges and expectations for international law in the twenty-first century. The *Report* also stresses that the aim of the *Congress* should not be the adoption of a declaration or any other kind of formal or binding document. Further, it is explicit in the summary of the Working Groups discussions that "the congress should not become another meeting of government representatives, but should rather be as informal and non-governmental as possible."[31]

This approach, seeking not immediate and substantive reform from government representatives but instead looking to deepen the understanding and appreciation of international law of representatives from across a range of constituencies, is bold in conception if fraught with risk that the gathering will generate merely more discussion and provide no impetus to substantive consideration of reform.

The tension between broad conception and a practical emphasis on substantive legal advice and implementation runs through the November 1993 Sixth Committee debates about the proposal for a *Congress*.[32] Nepal urged that the *Congress* "should not become another forum for a debate on topics traditionally discussed in the context of the *Decade*. On the contrary, it should be an academic forum to give free flow to an exchange of ideas on the role of international law in international relations."[33] Japan suggested that the primary purpose of the *Congress* should be "the dissemination of public international law through a free exchange of views among the various participants."[34] In contrast, Chile noted that "it was necessary to be realistic. The effects desired would not be achieved by the meeting alone, but would require further stages and further commitments to bring the initiatives of the *Congress* into effect."[35] In this same vein, Finland proposed that the *Congress* concentrate on "specific and well-defined topics and seek to make specific proposals for the further development of international law in particular fields," stressing as a possible topic the role of the International Court of Justice in the settlement of environmental disputes.[36] Ukraine and Belarus stressed even more forcefully the need for substantive consideration, expressing a desire that topics such as the dissolution of states and the rights and obligations of newly independent states, the legal implications of federation, the territorial integrity of states, regional security guarantees and "priority aspects of international law with regard to ecological security" all be addressed.[37]

The *Report* affords room for the Secretary-General, who is entrusted with the task of organizing the meeting, to be flexible in designing the agenda for the *Congress*. China has signalled that it wishes to discuss this matter further, stating that more time is needed to select the themes for the *Congress*, as no consensus on that has yet been reached.[38] As the time for the meeting draws near, the tensions briefly explored above will no doubt be played out and will determine the likely course of the meeting. It appears that, whatever the eventual substance of the agenda, the focus on exchange and dialogue between individuals outside the ordinary cadre of official representatives expected at such meetings has the potential to revolutionize the debates about the substance and direction of international legal reform. Merely talking about international law is of itself insufficient, but if the net of those informed and interested in international legal instruments is cast more broadly, chances are that the pressure which might be brought to bear on international legal instruments and institutions will not so easily be resisted; further, the opportunities for new insight and innovation will be multiplied exponentially. The caution about the Congress expressed in the Sixth Committee debates is well founded, as the *Congress* will bring matters under the spotlight; creating an ambitious agenda, fostering productive exchange, and following up the meeting with substantive assessment will be important both for the success of the *Decade* and for determining the reception and implementation of international law in the next century.

Towards International Legal Reform

The proposed theme of the 1995 *Congress on Public International Law* – "Towards the twenty-first century: International Law as a Language for International Relations" – is truly apt. The interplay between international legal instruments and institutions, and the political background against which they are cast and implemented, is fluid. Using international law to govern, or at least guide, interstate relations requires a sensitivity to multitude of demands and interests from state and non-state actors, and to their broad policy goals and aspirations.[39] The difficulties experienced by the International Court of Justice merely highlight the fact that international law and international legal institutions are subject to demands not readily paralleled in domestic legal systems. Equally, however, the fact that international accord is a prerequisite to the creation and proper functioning of any international legal instrument makes international law a powerful currency in assessing the new international order. The promise of international law is great, and its potential for ready adaptation to the demands of the twenty-first century is inspiring.

The challenge of protecting the environment in times of armed conflict, as a topical example, is being met both by the creation of new legal rules and by suggestions for more creative and effective use of existing international legal instruments.

As a foundational legal instrument in the United Nations era, the International Court of Justice is both a focus of concern and a tool ready for utilization. The close attention being paid to the ICJ during the course of the *Decade of International Law* is both a reflection of the faith of the international community in the rule of law and the manifestation of disappointment in the fact that the Court has not been used by states in the international community to greater effect. Turning to international law as a guide to conflict resolution and avoidance in the international community is an important and complex step. Understanding the potential and the pitfalls, which the 1995 *Congress* aims to do, will be critical to reforming and recasting the law and the institutions through which the law is promulgated, and so to ensuring that this pillar of the United Nations system, and the complex web of law and legal institutions at the symbolic head of which the ICJ sits, remains ready and able through the rest of this century and into the next.

Notes

1   G/A Res. 44/23, United Nations General Assembly Official Records, 44th Session, Supplement No. 49, UN Doc. A/44/49 1989.

2   For further consideration of the origins of the *Decade* generally, see Hopkins, Tamra and Paul Paton "The United Nations Decade of International Law" *Canadian Council on International Law Bulletin* 1991 2; Macdonald, R. St. J. "The United Nations Decade of International Law" *Canadian Yearbook of International Law* 28 1990 417; Thomas, Jeremy "The United Nations Decade of International Law – Insights into an Asian Perspective of International Law" *Dalhousie Law Journal* 14 1991 266.

3   UN Doc. A/C.6/45/L.5.

4   Thomas, Jeremy "New Opportunities for the United Nations Decade of International Law – The Views of a City Corporate Lawyer" unpublished paper presented at the *Annual Conference of the American Society of International Law* Washington DC 6-9 April 1994 .

5   Statement by Aust, Anthony, representative of the United Kingdom Mission to the United Nations, to the Sixth Committee of the 45th Session of the General Assembly, Press Release, 13 November 1990.

6   Mawhinney, Barry and Kim Girtel, "Fourth Legal Advisors' Meeting at UN Headquarters in New York" *American Journal of International Law* 88 1994 379.

7   "Statement by Justice Akhtar Ali Kazi, Pakistan Delegate at the Sixth Committee of the Forty-Seventh United Nations General Assembly on Agenda Item 128: United Nations Decade of International Law" Press Release, Pakistan Permanent Mission to the United Nations, New York, 16 November 1992.

8   "Statement by Mr. Sadewo Joedo before the Sixth Committee on Agenda Item 128: United Nations Decade of International Law," Press Release, Permanent Mission of the Republic of Indonesia to the United Nations, New York, 16 November 1992.

9   Review, for example, the debates in UN Docs. A/C.6/47/SR.34 and 36 and in particular the statements of delegates from Japan, Singapore, Canada and Sweden.

10 See UN Docs. A/48/33 and Corr.1, A/48/140-S/25597, A/48/205-S/25923, A/48/209-S/25937, A/48/379-S/26411, A/48/398 and A/48/445-S/26501.

11 UN Doc. A/C.6/48/SR.8 6.

12 On 18 January 1985 the United States announced that it would no

longer participate in proceedings initiated by Nicaragua in the International Court of Justice [*Military and Paramilitary Activities In and Against Nicaragua (Nicaragua vs. United States)*]. [See 1986 ICJ 14; 1984 ICJ 169; 1984 ICJ 215; and 1984 ICJ 392 for decisions prior to the withdrawal announcement]. Nicaragua claimed $375 million as compensation for alleged American involvement with the contra insurgency. The decision to withdraw was made in spite of the fact that the case would continue, undefended, and in spite of the perceived strength of the legal and political arguments with which the United States might have continued the case. The US Statement announcing the decision accused Nicaragua of using the proceedings "merely to score propaganda points in a dispute which is not "legal" but "inherently political" and thus "not appropriate for judicial resolution." See US Dept. of State "Statement: US Withdrawal from the Proceedings Initiated by Nicaragua in the International Court of Justice" 1985 24 ILM 246; and Franck, Thomas M. and Jerome M. Lehrman, "Messianism and Chauvinism in America's Commitment to Peace Through Law" in Damrosch, Lori F. 1987 *The International Court of Justice at a Crossroads* (New York) 3. On 7 October 1985 the United States terminated, effective April 1986, its 1946 instrument of acceptance of the compulsory jurisdiction for the Court under the Optional Clause, *Article 36(2)* of the ICJ Statue. Damrosch has noted, at pp. xvii-xviii, that while the United States remained subject to compulsory jurisdiction under numerous bilateral and multilateral treaties in force, and while the United States announced that it would "continue to make use of the Court to resolve disputes whenever appropriate and will encourage others to do likewise," the decision to withdraw marked a major reconsideration by the United States of its policies towards international adjudication. See the Damrosch volume generally, and also Mullerson, Rein "Self-Defense in the Contemporary World" in Fisler, Lori Damrosch Fisler and David J. Scheffer 1991 *Law and Force in the New International Order* (Boulder) 113.

13 UN Doc. A/47/277-S/24111.

14 See the Report of the Working Group of the Sixth Committee on the *Decade of International Law* at A/C.6/47/L.12, annex, for a reflection of *An Agenda for Peace* recommendations with respect to the ICJ in the suggestions for the programme (in Sections II and III of the Report) for the second term of the *Decade*. See also the debates at A/C.6/47/SR.34 for discussion of this point.

15 Hughes, Valerie "United Nations Decade of International Law: The Promotion of Means and Methods for the Peaceful Settlement of

Disputes Between States, Including Resort to and Full Respect for the International Court of Justice" *Canadian Council on International Law Annual Proceedings* 21 1992 199.

16 "Trading in a Post-Uruguay World: The New law of the GATT/World Trade Organization" *American Society of International Law Proceedings* 1994 [to follow].

17 UN Doc. A/C.6/48/SR.32 at 19; see also the statement of the Observer for the Permanent Court of Arbitration to the Sixth Committee at A/C.6/48/SR.31.

18 For other mechanisms, see Carter, Barry "Commentary on Formal Dispute Mechanisms Other than the International Court of Justice" Damrosch, Lori F., and David J. Scheffer 1991 *Law and Force in the New International Order* (Boulder) 308.

19 Comments of the Austrian delegate to the Sixth Committee at A/C.6/47/SR.34 12.

20 Report of the Secretary-General at UN Doc. A/48/269.

21 A/C.6/48/SR.31 3.

22 Report of the Working Group of the *Decade* at A/C.6/48/L.9 noting this consensus.

23 A/C.6/48/SR.32 2-3.

24 A/C.6/48/SR.32 4.

25 *Ibid.*, 9.

26 The *Congress* was proposed by the two independently, in separate notes. See A/C.6/48/SR.32 15.

27 A/47/384 (1992) 19.

28 *Ibid.*, 7.

29 "Statement by the Representative of the Kingdom of the Netherlands, Mr. Teunis Halff, in the Sixth Committee on Monday, 16 November 1992" Press Release, Permanent Mission of the Kingdom of the Netherlands to the United Nations, New York, 16 November 1992.

30 The report of the Working Group is found at A/C.6/48/L.9; see also the report of the Secretary-General on a preliminary operational plan for the congress at A/48/435

31 A/C.6/48/L.9 8.

32 See Morris, Virginia and M.-Christiane Bourloyannis-Vrailas "The Work of the Sixth Committee at the Forty-Eighth Session of the UN General Assembly" 88 *American Journal of International Law* 1 1994 343 for a summary of the 1993 debates on the *United Nations Decade of International Law* and the proposed congress.

33 A/C.6/48/SR.32 4.

34 *Ibid.*, 5.

35 *Ibid.*, 16.

36 *Ibid.*, 7.

37 *Ibid.*, 8-9 and 14.

38 A/C.6/48/SR. 31 7.

39 See the "architectural metaphor" proposed for understanding the UN legal order proposed by Schachter, Oscar in "United Nations Law" 88 *American Journal of International Law* 1 1994 22-23 for a useful methodology with which to assess the competing demands and influences on international legal instruments and institutions.

CHAPTER 20

The Establishment of an International Criminal Tribunal: Is the Time Ripe?

Sharon A. Williams

If there were no national crimes we would not be in need of national criminal courts. If there were no international crimes abhorrent to all peoples the thrust for an international criminal tribunal would be unnecessary. We do not, however, exist in that happy situation. On a national level, regardless of the country under consideration, criminal law and a scheme of prosecution is necessary. On the international level, to deal with international crimes proscribed by international conventional and customary international law, in the absence of an international criminal tribunal,[1] reliance has had to be placed on an indirect scheme of prosecution through national courts. International conventions dealing with international crimes *stricto sensu,* such as, for example, hijacking and other forms of terrorism against civil aviation,[2] obligate states parties to amend their domestic criminal laws to enable prosecution before their courts on a wide variety of jurisdictional bases, including presence within the territory, which is based on the principle of universal jurisdiction; that is, because of the nature of the crime as one affecting the international community, any state may prosecute that attains custody over the alleged offender.[3] The other provision of fundamental importance in these conventions is based on the maxim *aut dedere, aut judicare,* that obligates a state party, without exception whatsoever, to extradite alleged offenders found within its territory to another state with jurisdiction based on the locus of the crime within its territory, on aircraft or maritime vessels registered in the state, on the nationality of the offenders or victims, or to submit the case to its own competent authorities for the purposes of prosecution. This obligation is central to the efficacy of the scheme. However, in this area of international criminal law there are three perceived problems in the treaty approach. First, there may be third party frustration of the agreements by non-party states; second, some states parties may not fulfil their obligations in good faith; and third, the impact of the ideologically motivated offender, who has little or no regard for her or his own safety, may well call into question the deterrent value of such an approach.

The sophisticated and even notorious international criminal may well be able to use the jurisdictional gaps or other deficiencies in international cooperation to escape justice. In many instances, crimes against peace and crimes against humanity have allegedly been committed by persons who at the time were government officials. The International Law Commission has pointed out that it discredits the norms of international law if they are not enforced.[4] It cites the example of the 1948 *Genocide Convention*, which provides for prosecution of persons committing crimes of genocide whether they are constitutionally responsible rulers, public officials or private individuals.[5] However, with respect to enforcement it is extremely weak, providing that persons so charged shall be tried by a competent tribunal of the state in the territory in which the act was committed, or by such international penal tribunal as may have jurisdiction. There is, however, no such tribunal and universal jurisdiction is not provided for. There has never been a prosecution under this *Convention*, despite the fact that notorious cases of genocide have occurred since 1948.[6] It is of ever-increasing importance to have an international tribunal with the mandate to adjudicate on complex international crimes, and the official position of an accused person as head of state or member of government should not be a defence. Collective action to benefit all peoples of the world is the keynote.[7] In particular, four different situations have presented to the world the important role that an international criminal tribunal could play in adjudicating, in a neutral forum crimes of international concern. First, there is the scenario where several states are contesting for the right to prosecute and perhaps, in addition, the state of nationality of the offenders refuses to extradite its own nationals. As well, the state of nationality might itself be implicated in the crime. Here, trial before an international criminal tribunal would be the only forum to which in all likelihood all the involved states would agree. A case in point is the impasse created by the refusal of Libya to extradite the alleged offenders connected with the bombing of Pan Am flight 103 over Lockerbie, Scotland, in which 270 people were killed, and the refusal by the United Kingdom and the United States to accede to prosecution in Libya, albeit that this would fulfil the requirements *aut dedere, aut judicare* of the *Montreal Convention*.[8] Second, the facility presented by an international criminal tribunal for the prosecution of mega-drug traffickers or terrorists would be instrumental in eradicating these scourges of international society, in that some states that wish offenders to be prosecuted fear the violent repercussions if done domestically. Third, there are the cases of crimes committed by government officials, where the successor government is unwilling or unable to prosecute and would prefer to turn the cases over to an international tribunal.[9] Fourth, the violations of international humanitarian law committed in the territory of the former Yugoslavia and the acts of genocide in Rwanda present on a day-to-day basis atrocities that must be brought to trial, in a setting that safeguards the victims' rights, but also those of the accused.

Deterrence must play a role in international criminal law. It was stated above that the ideologically motivated terrorist may not care one jot for personal safety or prosecution or punishment. In fact, the latter may be viewed as giving added publicity to the cause. However, with respect to other potential offenders, in cases of armed conflicts or other situations with an international dimension, this may not be the case. If the will of the international community to prosecute before an impartial international tribunal is clear, and if the process and procedure is laid down, then would this not discourage war crimes, crimes against humanity and other international crimes? Would a real threat of prosecution perhaps have deterred leaders such as Adolf Hitler, Pol Pot, Saddam Hussein, the Bosnian Serb leaders in the former Yugoslavia or the leaders of the Hutu army in Rwanda from undertaking the actions they did in violation of international law, or was their underlying philosophy that they would be able to get away with it? In answer to this question, in a 1936 speech given at a Nuremberg rally, Hitler addressed this ineptitude on the part of the world community to get together to take effective sanctions when he asked, "And now who remembers the Armenians?"[10] One may ask whether the failure by the international community in that case encouraged the policies of genocide and extermination carried out by the Nazi regime.

The establishment of an international criminal tribunal has been on the agenda of the international community since at least the time of the League of Nations. At the outset it should be emphasized that, although the precedents of the war crimes trials to be discussed below are important in connection with the subject matter jurisdiction of any international tribunal to be established, they do not tell the whole story. Any permanent international criminal tribunal should have a wider mandate, including international crimes of terror or violence and international drug offences as but two examples, as well as jurisdictional disputes between states.

Although examples of prosecutions of war crimes and crimes against peace may be found stemming from the thirteenth century in Europe,[11] the contemporary idea of establishing an international tribunal may be said to have stemmed from the *First Hague Convention for the Pacific Settlement of International Disputes.*[12] It was, however, the *Versailles Treaty* of 1919[13] at the culmination of the First World War that saw for the first time an allied attempt at the prosecution of war crimes. Nevertheless, even though *Articles 227-229* provided for the prosecution of the Kaiser Wilhelm II and other German members of the armed forces who had committed war crimes, none were turned over to the allies for prosecution. Instead, the Kaiser remained in the Netherlands, where he had sought asylum, and other prosecutions were eventually entertained, by agreement with the allies, by the German Supreme Court sitting in Leipzig.[14] These trials have been recorded as infamous in that only twenty-one persons were prosecuted,[15] and of these six were acquitted. The heaviest sentence imposed was four years. All this being said, this effort can be regarded as at the very least an attempt to prosecute international criminals through international means, albeit before domestic courts.

In 1937 there was an attempt by the League of Nations to bring into operation a multilateral *Convention for the Prevention and Punishment of Terrorism*, and an annexed *Protocol* on the establishment of an international criminal court to deal with such offences.[16] The *Convention* and *Protocol* never came into force. The only state to ratify was India.

Following the end of the Second World War, the *London Charter* in 1945 set up the International Military Tribunal which sat at Nuremberg.[17] It provided a forum for the prosecution of the major war criminals of the Axis powers, whose crimes had no particular geographical location. A similar tribunal was set up for the Far East theatre of war in Tokyo.[18] These courts were *ad hoc* tribunals for the trial of specific persons within a determined time frame. As well they were not truly "international," given the composition of the bench. At Nuremberg the Tribunal, as well as the prosecutors, were composed of nationals of France, the United Kingdom, the United States and the USSR. As precedents, therefore, they have limited value in terms of the composition of the court and the separation of the prosecutor's office from the bench. Nevertheless, the *Nuremberg Charter*, the judgment of the Tribunal and the *Nuremberg Principles* extrapolated therefrom by the International Law Commission and accepted by the United Nations General Assembly, are extremely pertinent in terms of the definition of the offences of crimes against peace, war crimes and crimes against humanity, as well as on other issues such as individual criminal responsibility, superior orders and command responsibility.

In 1947 the International Law Commission was set up by the United Nations General Assembly. It was given the initial mandate to formulate the *Nuremberg Principles*[19] and then to formulate a *Draft Code of Offences* (today entitled *Crimes*) *against the Peace and Security of Mankind*. The work on the *Draft Code* is still in progress,[20] but the *Reports* of the

Commission in 1992[21] and 1993[22] focused on the establishment of an international criminal tribunal. It is not necessary that the *Draft Code* be adopted simultaneously with a statute for the international criminal tribunal. Each may exist independently. Standing alone, the *Draft Code* would act as a composite codification of existing multilateral international criminal obligations, harmonizing inconsistencies of language and adding new crimes. The Tribunal once in operation would, in terms of its subject matter jurisdiction, have competence over crimes contained in existing multilateral conventions in force, including the *Draft Code* once adopted and in force.

During the period that the International Law Commission's project was lying dormant, the 1973 *Convention on the Suppression and Punishment of the Crime of Apartheid* was adopted.[23] *Article* V provided for prosecution by courts of any state party, thus relying on the principle of universal jurisdiction or by an international penal tribunal. It came into force in 1976, but no international penal tribunal was ever set up under this article.[24] Also no Western state ratified it.

Another attempt to deal with a specific international crime occurred at the 1989 United Nations General Assembly concerning the illicit traffic in narcotic drugs. With Trinidad and Tobago assuming a leadership role, fifteen Caribbean and Latin American states supported the establishment of an international criminal court during the Fall General Assembly and at a Special Session on the topic in 1990.[25] However, the majority of Western states were opposed at that time and consequently the only result was, as one commentator has put it, "a cautious and … ambiguous mandate given by the General Assembly to the International Law Commission to continue its study of the question."[26]

There are many reasons why it has taken so long for the international community to agree on the need to produce an international criminal tribunal. Amongst the apparent obstacles have been a reluctance to yield up any element of sovereignty to an international tribunal, nationalistic pride in the superiority of a state's domestic criminal law, reticence to participate in establishing another international institution, problems of obtaining consensus on subject matter jurisdiction, applicable substantive and procedural criminal law rules, issues relating to recognition and enforcement of judgments and, lastly, the cost.

Putting these difficulties to one side, there are a number of possibilities for the structure of such a tribunal. It could be a special chamber of the existing International Court of Justice at the Hague; it could be set up as a separate judicial organ under the *Charter*; it could be constituted by way of a plenipotentiary conference and a multilateral convention; or it could be established by the United Nations Security Council acting under *Chapter VII* of the *UN Charter*. In any of these modes, the tribunal could be permanent or *ad hoc*. Based on the work to date of the International Law Commission and on the views of states and of groups of experts, it seems that in all likelihood the tribunal will be permanent, but not full time, at least at its inception. It should be a permanent institution that sits when required. It would appear that such a tribunal would be best served by being adopted by a plenipotentiary conference, if wholesale support is to be achieved in the long run. It would also avoid any need to amend the *UN Charter*. The case for a permanent international criminal tribunal that is to have a global jurisdiction with crimes going beyond those crimes associated with armed conflicts, should be so endowed.

This is to be contrasted with the urgency of the situation in the territory of the former Yugoslavia, where the widespread and flagrant crimes being committed in the face of the world community, in particular in the Republic of Bosnia-Herzegovina, including reports of mass killings, systematic detention and rape of women, and "ethnic cleansing," necessitated immediate action. On 22 February 1993, in *Resolution 808*, the United Nations Security Council decided that an international tribunal should be established for the prosecution of persons allegedly responsible for such crimes committed since January 1991. The Secretary-General Dr. Boutros Boutros-Ghali was requested to submit a report on all aspects of the matter, including specific proposals, as well as options for the effective and expeditious implementation of such a tribunal. His *Report* of 3 May 1993 recommended that immediate action on an *ad hoc* basis was called for and that the tribunal should therefore be established on the basis of a decision under *Chapter VII* of the *Charter*. It is important to note that such an action under *Chapter VII* would constitute a measure to maintain or restore international peace or security, following the determination of the existence of a threat to the peace, breach of the peace or act of aggression and would be therefore effective immediately. It binds Member States to take whatever action is required. On 25 May 1993, by *Resolution 827*,[27] the Security Council decided to establish the tribunal and endorsed the thirty-four-Article *Statute* annexed to the *Report of the Secretary-General*.

Many of the issues under consideration by the International Law Commission for the future permanent international criminal tribunal will have a testing ground in the *Ad Hoc* Tribunal for the former Yugoslavia. Even though the Tribunal's jurisdiction is limited to the war torn area of that former federal state, and the crimes as laid out in the statute for the purposes of prosecution are likewise limited to war crimes and crimes against humanity, it is clearly going to be the place where the credibility of the international community, as prosecutor, judge and the conscience of humankind, is under scrutiny. It is imperative that the Tribunal have serious cases brought before it and that, in the peace process, the so-called "leaders" of factions accused of atrocities not be given amnesty, with only the "foot-soldiers" coming to trial, possibly in small numbers. All must be done to ensure that the Tribunal functions independently, respects basic human rights and guarantees fairness to both the accused and the victims.

If the *Ad Hoc* Tribunal fails to be seen as an effective mechanism in doing justice in either of those respects, any hope for a permanent tribunal with a wider criminal mandate is probably a pipe-dream. The combined *Statute* and the *Rules of Procedure and Evidence* produced by the eleven elected judges on 11 February 1994[28] offer hope in this regard, in having detailed rules on investigation and rights of suspects and rights of the accused; the right to be informed promptly, in detail and in a language that he or she understands, of the nature and cause of the charge; the right to counsel of choice; the right to be tried without due delay; the right to examine or have witnesses; the right not to be compelled to testify against himself or herself or to confess guilt; the right not to be found guilty unless proved beyond a reasonable doubt and the non-admissibility of evidence obtained directly or indirectly by means that could constitute a violation of international human rights law. Also contained therein are rules on the protection of victims and witnesses. Penalties under the *Ad Hoc* Tribunal are limited to imprisonment for a term up to and including the remainder of life. The Working Group of the International Law Commission has gone a similar route, but has also recommended fines of any amount.

In discussions about the permanent tribunal, as with the *Ad Hoc* Tribunal, there have been considerations of where it will sit. The statute of the *Ad Hoc* Tribunal provides for the Hague, although if necessary the Tribunal may sit elsewhere, if the President of the Tribunal so authorizes in the interests of justice.[29] The International Law Commission does not specify a locale. In both cases the working languages are English and French. However, *Article 18(3)* of the *Ad Hoc* Tribunal's statute provides that the accused has the right to necessary translation into and from a language that he or she understands. *Article 12* of the *Ad Hoc* Tribunal's statute provides for a total of eleven judges, no two of whom may be nationals of the same state. Six judges will serve on the two three-person trial panels and the remaining five on the Appeals Chamber. Apart from the usual expected qualifications of judges, such as high moral character, impartiality and integrity, the provision is noteworthy in that due account be taken of the experience of judges in criminal law, international law, including international humanitarian law and human rights law. This is also found in the 1993 *Report* of the International Law Commission's Working Group on a statute for an international criminal court.[30] In September 1993, the eleven judges were elected pursuant to *Article 13(2)* by the UN General Assembly from a list submitted by the Security Council.[31] The eleven judges so elected include two from North America (Canada and USA), three from other developed states (Australia, France and Italy), three from Asian states (China, Malaysia and Pakistan), two from African states (one Sub-Saharan, Egypt and Nigeria) and one Latin American (Costa-Rica). The representation in terms of legal systems is positive, with presence of common law, civil law and Islamic law jurists. On account of the use in the former Yugoslavia of rape as a weapon of war, it is also important that there are two women judges on the Tribunal.

Both the permanent tribunal proposal and the *Ad Hoc* Tribunal detail a Prosecutor's Office that is independent. Under the statute of the *Ad Hoc* Tribunal the Chief Prosecutor shall be appointed by the Security Council on nomination by the Secretary-General. As of April 1994, the Chief Prosecutor was not in place. There is also provision for a Registrar's office. Other key features, following essentially the *Nuremberg Principles*, are individual criminal responsibility, no act of state defence, superior orders and command responsibility. Under both schemes the judges shall adopt the rules of procedure and evidence for the functioning of the Tribunals. In the case of the *Ad Hoc* Tribunal, this was accomplished on 11 February 1994.[32]

With regard to the *Ad Hoc* Tribunal, as indicated above, eleven judges have been elected by the United Nations. Nominations could have been made by any member state of the United Nations, or by non-Member States with permanent observer missions at the United Nations. This is in keeping with the fact that the Tribunal has been set up under *Chapter VII* and that, in *Resolution 827*, the Security Council decided that all states shall cooperate fully with the Tribunal and take any measures necessary under their domestic law to implement the provisions of the resolution and the statute, including the obligation to comply with requests for assistance or orders issued by a trial chamber under the statute. Concerning the permanent tribunal, it may be questioned whether similarly election should be open to nationals of all United Nations Member States and permanent observer states and be conducted in the United Nations, or whether it should be limited to nationals of states who ratify or accede to the convention setting up the permanent tribunal. The International Law Commission, in its *Working Group Report* of 1993, has suggested that it should be restricted to parties to the statute.[33]

A major issue is how the accused will be brought before the Tribunal. Under the *Statute* of the *Ad Hoc* Tribunal, Member States of the United Nations are obliged to cooperate with the International Tribunal in the investigation and prosecution of accused persons. They also shall comply without undue delay with requests for judicial assistance, including the identification and location of persons, taking of testimony and evidence, service of documents, arrest and detention of persons, and the surrender or the transfer of the accused to the Tribunal. One issue to be addressed is whether Serbia-Montenegro is so bound. After the demise of the former Yugoslavia, Bosnia-Herzegovina, Croatia, Slovenia and eventually Macedonia were accepted as new Member States into the United Nations. Serbia wished to succeed to the place of the former Yugoslavia, but this appears to have been denied. However, representatives of Serbia have been allowed to attend certain UN committee meetings. Clarification from the Secretary-General and the Security Council is needed on this important point. The International Law Commission's proposal is more limited, in that the *Working Group's Report*[34] deals only with the mandatory obligation of international cooperation and judicial assistance by states parties to the statute. It does refer to cooperation by non-parties with the Tribunal, but only on the basis of "comity, a unilateral decision, an *ad hoc* agreement or other agreement with the Court."[35]

With regard to enforcement of sentences, the *Rules of Procedure* of the *Ad Hoc* Tribunal provide that imprisonment shall be served in a state designated by the Tribunal from a list of states which have indicated their willingness to accept convicted persons.[36] The Working Group of the International Law Commission is proposing that states parties to the statute of the permanent court be requested to offer facilities, or in the absence of such a designation, they be located in the state where the Tribunal has its seat.[37]

In conclusion, the post-Cold-War period with the new-found consensus ability among Member States in the United Nations has presented the international community with an historic opportunity and challenge to establish immediately the *Ad Hoc* Tribunal for the former Yugoslavia and for the long term a permanent international criminal tribunal. The permanent tribunal would act as a deterrent as well as a forum for prosecution of those offenders who breach the rules of conventional and customary international criminal law and thereby impact on the peace and security of humankind. It would contribute thereby to the aims of the United Nations in preserving and keeping the peace.

Notes

AUTHOR'S NOTE: Since the writing of this chapter, the United Nations Security Council, acting under *Chapter VII* of the *United Nations Charter*, has established the *Ad Hoc* Tribunal for the purposes of prosecuting persons responsible for genocide and other serious violations of international humanitarian law allegedly committed in the territory of Rwanda and Rwandan citizens allegedly responsible for such crimes in the territory of neighbouring states between January 1 and December 31, 1994. See UN Doc. S/Res/955, adopted November 8, 1994. It should also be noted that the International Law Commission adopted in its 46th Session in 1994 a Draft Statute for an International Criminal Court and recommended that an international conference of plenipotentiaries be convened to study it and conclude a convention on that topic. See UN GAOR, 49th Sess. Supp. No. 10; UN Doc A/46/10 (1994).

1   The International Court of Justice at the Hague, the judicial organ of the United Nations system, does not have jurisdiction to hear criminal prosecutions of individuals. Under its Statute, which is annexed to the *United Nations Charter*, it has competence to hear contentious cases between states (*Arts* 34-40) and to give advisory opinions on legal questions (*Arts* 65-68).

2   See the *Tokyo Convention on Offences and Certain Other Acts Against Aircraft* 1963, 704 UNTS 219 1970 Can. T.S. No. 5; *Hague Convention for the Suppression of Unlawful Seizure of Aircraft* 1970 860 UNTS 105; 1972 Can. T.S. No. 23; *Montreal Convention for the Suppression of Unlawful Acts Against the Safety of Civil Aviation* 1971 974 UNTS 177 1973 Can. T.S. No. 6; *Montreal Protocol for the Suppression of Unlawful Acts of Violence at Airports Serving International Civil Aviation* Int. Leg. Mat. 27 1988 627. See Williams, S.A. "International Law and Terrorism: Age-Old Problems, Different Targets" *Can. Y. B. Int. L.* 26 1988 87.

3   On the use of the universal principle see the *Eichmann case* 1961 36 I.L.R. 5 (Dist. Ct Jerusalem), aff'd 1961 36 I.L.R. 277 (Israel Sup. Ct) and *Demjanjuk* v. *Petrovsky* 776 F. 2d 571 (6th Cir.) 1985.

4   Report of the International Law Commission on the Work of its Forty-

Fourth Session, UN GAOR, 47th Sess., Supp. No. 10 (A/47/10) 1992 155-56.

5 *Convention on the Prevention and Punishment of the Crime of Genocide* 78 UNTS 277.

6 See note 4, 156.

7 A vast amount has been written on an international criminal tribunal. For recent material see Bassiouni, M.C. *Draft Statute International Tribunal, Nouvelles Etudes Penalés,* Ass'n Int. de Dr. Penal 1993; Report, International Meeting of Experts on the Establishment of an International Criminal Tribunal (Vancouver, 22-26 March 1993) and Bassiouni, M.C. and C.L. Blakesley "The Need for an International Criminal Court in the New International World Order" Vanderbilt and *J. Trans. L.* 25 1992 151.

8 See note 2. Note that on 21 January 1992 the UN Security Council adopted Res. 731 unanimously condemning the destruction of the Lockerbie flight and also the destruction of UTA flight 772 over Chad and deplored the fact that Libya had not responded effectively to requests to cooperate fully in establishing responsibility for the terrorists acts. It urged Libya to provide an effective response to the requests. The term extradition was never used, but that clearly was the intent. A decision to impose sanctions was taken unanimously in Res. 748 of 31 March 1992, under *Chapter VII* of the *Charter.* This was a controversial step as the use of sanctions in such a circumstance was unprecedented. In its decision *Aerial Incident at Lockerbie Case: Case Concerning Questions of Interpretation and Application of the 1971 Montreal Convention Arising from the Incident at Lockerbie (Libya v. United States; Libya v. United Kingdom)* 1992 ICJ Rep. 3, the International Court of Justice held, *inter alia,* that Res. 748 adopted under *Chapter VII* took priority over any other treaty commitment of Member States in accordance with *Article 103* of the *UN Charter.*

9 See note 4, 156.

10 Willis, J.F. 1982 *Prologue to Nuremberg* 173; Woodward, E.L. *et al. Documents on British Foreign Policy* 1919-1939 (3rd ser. 9 vols., 1949-55). See note 13 below concerning the Armenians.

11 Note the trial and execution of Conradin von Hohenstaufen in Naples in 1262 for initiating an unjust war, and the trial in 1474 of Peter of Hagenbach at Breisach for "tramp[ling] under foot the laws of God and man." See Schwarzenberger, G. 1968 *International Law as Applied by International Courts and Tribunals* 462; Keen, M. 1965 *The Laws of War in the Late Middle Ages* 23-59; Bassiouni, see note 21; Bassiouni, M.C.,

and C.L. Blakesley "The Need for an International Criminal Court in the New International World Order" Vanderbilt J. Trans. 25 1992 L. 151 and Green, L.C. "Group Rights, War Crimes and Crimes Against Humanity" *Int. J. Group Rights* 1 1993 107.

12 19 July 1899, 26 *Martens Nouveau Recueil* (2d) 720.

13 28 June 1919, 11 *Martens Nouveau Recueil* (3d) 323. Note also that in 1919 a special commission was set up by the allies to address, *inter alia*, crimes against humanity. This was of especial significance to the 1,000,000 Armenians annihilated by Turkey. Due to United States opposition this crime was omitted from a list of offences that an international tribunal would be given jurisdiction to prosecute. However, although the *Treaty of Sèvres*, between the allied powers and Turkey, 10 August 1920 15 *AJIL* 179 (Supp. 1921), provided for the surrender by Turkey of such accused persons, the subsequent *Treaty of Lausanne* between the same parties, 24 July 1923, 28 LNTS 11, gave them amnesty.

14 Mullins, C. 1921 *The Leipzig Trials* and Bassiouni, see note 7, 21.

15 Bassiouni, see note 7, 21

16 Hudson *International Legislation* 7 862.

17 82 UNTS 279. See also the earlier Moscow Declaration of 1943 *Dept. of State Bull.* 1943 311.

18 1948 15 *Ann. Dig.* 356.

19 UNGA Res. 174(II), UN GAOR., 2nd Sess. UN, A/519, at 105-10 1947.

20 See UN GAOR, 46th Sess. Supp. No. 10; UN Doc A/46/10 1991. Note that the International Law Commission produced a Draft Code in 1954 but it was tabled by the UN General Assembly. The political will to adopt the Code appeared to be lacking. Another reason given was that there was no agreed definition of aggression. However, even though the UN General Assembly adopted by consensus a resolution in 1974 defining aggression, UNGA Res. 3314 (XXIX), 29 UN GAOR, Supp. 31 at 142; UN Doc. A/9631 1974, the International Law Commission did not resume its work on the Draft Code until 1982. The Special Rapporteur continues to work on the topic, and the comments of states following his report in 1991, UN GAOR, 46th Sess., Supp. No. 10; UN Doc. A/46/10 1991 are being taken into consideration.

21 UN GAOR, 47th Sess., Supp. No. 10; UN Doc. A/47/10 1992.

22 UN GAOR, 48th Sess., Supp. No. 10; UN Doc. A/48/10 1993.

23 GA Res. 3068 (XXVII), 28 UN GAOR, Supp. (No. 30), 75, UN Doc. A/9030 1973.

24 See the interesting account by Bassiouni, M.C. *Draft Statute*

International Tribunal, note 7-8, of the attempt to establish an international criminal tribunal to prosecute for the crime of apartheid and the lack of political will to do so on the part of the "Western Bloc" resulting in no United Nations action.

25 GA Res. 43/164 1988 and 44/39 1989.

26 Bassiouni, see note 7, 11.

27 UN Doc. S/Res/827 1993.

28 UN Doc. IT/32, 14 March 1994.

29 Rules of Procedure and Evidence, of the International Tribunal for the Prosecution of Persons Responsible for Serious Violations of International Humanitarian Law Committed in the Territory of the former Yugoslavia since 1991, adopted 11 February 1994, UN Doc. IT/32, 14 March 1994.

30 See note 22, Annex, 255, at 261, *Art.* 6.

31 The UN Security Council had established this list from a previous list supplied by Member States *via* the Secretary-General. The list established by the Security Council was mandated to have not less than 22 and not more than 33 candidates, taking into consideration adequate representation of the world legal systems.

32 See also the ILC Working Group Report in note 22.

33 See note 22, *Art.* 58.

34 See note 22, *Art.* 58.

35 See note 22, *Art* 59.

36 See note 29, Rule 103(A).

37 See note 22, *Art.* 66(1) and (3).

PART VII

RECOMMENDATIONS

CHAPTER 21

Recommendations to the Commission on Global Governance

Science for Peace Workshop on United Nations Reform

The *Workshop on United Nations Reform,* organized by Science for Peace for 23 and 24 November 1993, operated with the express mandate, "to make recommendations on United Nations Reform relevant to the mandate of the Commission on Global Governance" [see Bibliography].

The following Recommendations were developed from papers presented at the Workshop, and from their subsequent discussion in each of the three sessions scheduled. Speakers at the Workshop (all but one of whose papers are reproduced in the present book), as listed below, indicated their approval of the recommendations.

Newton Bowles
Professor David Cox
Professor Dietrich Fischer
Dieter Heinrich
Dr. Hanna Newcombe
Peter Padbury
Geoffrey Pearson
Professor Robert Matthews
Professor K. Venkata Raman

(1) The UN should have two Assemblies: one of them, the present General Assembly, in which states are represented; the other, the UN Parliamentary Assembly, comprising parliamentarians selected by their peers, supplemented in countries that do not have a parliamentary system by members elected by a process still to be worked out, but involving Non-Governmental Organizations (NGOs) to a considerable degree. The UN Parliamentary Assembly should act initially in an advisory capacity to the General Assembly, but its powers should widen in due course, as happened in the European Parliament.

(2)   The UN Security Council should be reformed to represent continental or subcontinental regions, rather than selected and elected particular states as at present. Since the UN Security Council now has a great deal of power and is not truly representative of the world community of nations, it should have an Advisory Body chosen by the General Assembly, which could help the Security Council become more representative of the world community.

(3)   The veto in the Security Council may be modified: by requiring at least two regions to vote "No" before a resolution is defeated; by waiving the veto rule for some classes of resolutions; and by allowing the General Assembly to overrule the Security Council in certain cases. The International Court of Justice should serve as an appeals court for decisions made by the UN Security Council.

(4)   In all UN interventions, we should ensure UN leadership and authority, and should not delegate these to any individual state(s). Traditional collective security measures, *i.e.*, wars to repel or punish aggressors, should be considered only as a last resort, because they kill too many innocent people and sometimes leave the guilty ruler still in power. There should be a shift from military interventions, which endanger UN impartiality and lead to war casualties, to protection of civil order and delivery of needed supplies. Besides official diplomacy aimed at resolving conflicts, second-track or unofficial (citizen) diplomacy should be increasingly utilized, both being preventive in nature.

(5)   A volunteer UN force of about 5,000 to 10,000 should be created, responsible to the UN Secretary-General, with some component ready to act at 24-hours' notice. Women should constitute a considerable part of this force. Members of the UN force should receive anti-racist and anti-discrimination training, and be instructed to respect local cultures and customs.

(6)   The UN should have at its disposal an International Satellite Monitoring Agency (ISMA), as originally proposed by France, in order to be able to monitor danger zones around the world and predict impending crises or wars, so that the UN can take appropriate preventive actions.

(7)   A very urgent matter is to formulate new rules for UN humanitarian intervention in countries suffering from chaotic internal war, widespread famine, or gross violations of human rights. When and how UN forces become involved should be carefully considered in each specific case.

(8)   There should be an International Criminal Court to conduct trials of

persons (including national leaders) or corporations accused of crimes against humanity, as defined in the War Crimes trials after World War II.

(9) The NGO consensus-building process on seeking solutions to the great global problems, which was used successfully at the *UNCED Conference* in Rio de Janeiro (the people's treaties process), should be supported and further developed, to be included in global institutional decision making. Women should increasingly be included in the NGO process. The number of women participating in UN decision making in general should be increased with the aim of soon achieving roughly equal gender representation.

(10) The Global Environmental Facility, which provides financial aid from rich industrialized countries to developing countries to help them avoid environmentally destructive practices in their development, should be supported and further developed.

(11) The UN needs an independent source of revenue. This should come from taxes on seabed mineral mining or international flights or international money transactions, or from a combination of such taxes.

(12) The UN should have an International Democratic Elections Agency to supervise and monitor national elections, plebiscites or referenda, when so requested or when this is required to ensure fair election practices.

Professor Eric Fawcett
Chairman of the Workshop

Professor Derek Paul
President of Science for Peace

December 20, 1993

Commentary on Recommendations to the Commission on Global Governance

William H. Barton

Since the founding of the United Nations, Canadians have been enthusiastic supporters of the Organization and of the *Charter* that it was established to implement, which is not to say that they have been oblivious to its problems and shortcomings. Thus it is that both the Government and the public, over the years, have been advocates of reform, both in major policy areas and in administrative efficiency and effectiveness.

As the UN approaches its 50th Anniversary, it is being called upon to respond to unprecedented challenges and responsibilities. This, combined with the natural desire to make the occasion of celebrating a significant anniversary an opportunity for change, has sparked a rash of studies, for both official and non-governmental sources, on what should be done.

Successful politics is sometimes described as a judicious exercise of the art of the possible, and this inevitably influences governments in the way they approach the measures they advocate. But those working outside official channels are under no such limitations. They are free to advocate ideas that ignore traditional barriers and hopefully will spark new approaches that may ultimately influence the path of history.

For this reason, I urge the sponsors of recommendations, about which I have expressed doubts, not to conclude that their continued advocacy will serve no useful purpose. Ideas are like seeds – they may fall on stony ground, but that is not to say they will not ultimately flower.

The following Commentary refers to the twelve recommendations made to the Commission on Global Governance made by the participants in the 1993 Workshop on United Nations Reform and listed above.

(1) Two Assemblies

As I see it, this recommendation is based on the assumption that the member governments of the UN are members of a Union, somewhat like the European Community. I do not believe that any government today would be prepared to convert its membership in the UN to such a relationship. Put in its bluntest terms, the UN is a Standing Diplomatic Conference, with a Secretariat to carry out activities approved by the Members, each of which exercises a sovereign right, subject to the limitation of the powers vested in the Security Council, to conform or not.

(2) Reform of the Security Council

Pressure for reform of the Security Council is strong, and no doubt efforts will be made to achieve agreement at the Fiftieth Session of the General Assembly, but I for one will be surprised to see an early solution to this issue. I believe there is general recognition that the Security Council must not be expanded to the point where its membership becomes unwieldy. This being the case, every proposal for awarding permanent seats, *e.g.*, to Brazil, Germany, India, Japan or Nigeria, means fewer seats for other members. Up to now, Germany and Japan have had both constitutional and political reasons for staying on the sidelines with respect to peacekeeping operations. Is this consistent with permanent membership? Governments in many parts of the world will find it hard to contemplate a solid phalanx of Northern European states enjoying permanent membership, but both Britain and France can protect their positions with their veto, so whatever the final solution it will have to be acceptable to them.

The recommendation talks about representation from continental or sub-continental regions, but this would mean that Canada would in effect have a permanent seat, or no seat at all, and where do Australia and New Zealand fit in?

I think that Security Council reform will ultimately come, but it will be as a result of complex and devious political negotiations, the result of which is difficult to foresee.

(3) Security Council Veto

The question of the veto will inevitably form a part of the negotiations on reform of the Security Council, but my guess is that it will be a frosty Friday before any of the Permanent Members will be willing to give it up. We should not lose sight of the fact that the governments with veto power have to pick up almost all the cost of actions initiated by the Security Council, and it has been demonstrated time and time again that they will not do so if the Security Council calls for an operation with which they do not agree. The refusal of the former USSR and France to pay the costs of the peacekeeping operations in the Congo, and the subsequent financial crisis of 1965, is indicative of what might be expected.

(4) UN Intervention

This recommendation sets out a policy that should be endorsed by all supporters of the UN. The catch is that the US government, and Congress in particular, are slow learners. There are signs from time to time that they are beginning to see the light. We must do all that we can to encourage them.

(5) UN Volunteer Force

The day may come when the membership of the UN would be prepared to authorize (and pay for) a sort of UN Foreign Legion, but I think agreement will have to be reached on a number of issues before that happens. I expect that the Security Council would not wish to see such a force deployed without its approval. Under what circumstances could it be deployed? It is one thing to intervene between the forces of Member States with their consent, but what about the much more ambiguous situations of internal conflict that seem to be arising with increasing frequency? These are most insuperable problems, provided that enough governments are convinced of the desirability of action, but judging from the desultory efforts to follow up on the recommendations in *An Agenda for Peace*, governments are going to need to be pushed. Maybe that will happen during the 50th Anniversary, but my guess is that the time has not yet come.

(6) International Satellite Monitoring Agency

The UN would no doubt find it useful to have an independent monitoring service at its disposal, but as I understand it the cost of operating such a system and maintaining the data analysis facilities that would have to accompany it would be very high. The question then to be answered is whether this would be justified in the face of limited resources.

(7) Humanitarian Intervention

This is an important recommendation that should be pursued vigorously, governmentally and by NGOs.

8) International Criminal Court

I am not up-to-date on what has been going on in this area, but I suppose that the tribunal to which Mr. Justice Deschenes has been appointed regarding atrocities in the former Yugoslavia is relevant. My only concern with moves in this direction is that there should be consistency. What applies to one should apply to all, and I can foresee problems in ensuring that this is attainable.

(9) NGO Consensus-building

Looking back over the past forty years of my experience, the role of NGOs in influencing UN decision making has strengthened enormously. I cannot conceive of a UN Conference today that would not have a parallel NGO Conference to act as a ginger group and to inspire progress. I am sure this process will continue to develop and improve in effectiveness in the years ahead. The recommendation is right in pointing out the need for greater participation by women, both in the Secretariats of UN bodies and in governmental delegations. By UN standards, Canada is among the leaders in pressing for reform, but we have lots of room for reform ourselves.

(10) Global Environmental Facility

This is an important recommendation. Canada has played a leading role in this area, and the head of the UN environmental agency is a Canadian. We should do all within our power to enhance its effectiveness.

(11) UN Financing

The idea that the UN should have an independent source of revenue has a superficial attraction. But governments would not want the UN to be completely independent of their power to exercise control by way of the power of the purse. It is often argued that the provision of a partial source of revenue, independent of assessments against member governments, would be useful to help provide adequate financing of peacekeeping operations. But to the extent that such a flat levy did exist, I am afraid that all that would happen is that governments would reduce their contributions accordingly.

(12) International Democratic Elections Agency

It is my understanding that the UN has a mechanism for providing election observers and to give advice on the conduct of elections. But if this would be improved by the formal establishment of an Elections Agency, then by all means establish one.

CHAPTER 22

Canadian Priorities for United Nations Reform

Canadian Committee for the
Fiftieth Anniversary of the United Nations

This summary concentrates on six key areas of action chosen from among the 52 recommendations for policy changes by the United Nations and the Government of Canada appearing in a document released in June 1994 that was prepared by the Canadian Committee for the Fiftieth Anniversary of the United Nations [see Bibliography].

The human race is currently undergoing the most fundamental and rapid revolution in its history. Its origin and driving force are the enormous and accelerating discovery, spread and use of knowledge, the momentum of which cannot be stopped or its general direction changed. Indeed, it can barely be influenced, even when it produces obvious and avoidable threats like nuclear weapons, unsustainable use of resources, and obscene human inequities, all of which add to the complexity, distortions, pressures and, ultimately, the instability of the international system.

To meet these challenges and to become the main instrument for building a peaceful and more equitable world, the United Nations must command belief in its effectiveness. As its functions expand, its form must be equal to the new or more intensified tasks it is asked to undertake.

(1) Reform of the Security Council
In particular, reform of the Security Council is pressing for two reasons: first, its permanent membership no longer reflects the reality of global power; secondly, its credibility as an impartial intervenor in situations that threaten common security is undermined by the disproportionate influence within it of Northern, and especially North Atlantic states. The significance of these shortcomings in the Security Council is magnified by the fact that, alone among UN bodies, its decisions are binding on all Member States.

At some future time, the distinctions between permanent and non-permanent members, members with and without a veto, deserve to be eliminated. That time, it is generally agreed, is not yet. If, as the Secretary-

General hopes, a partial reform of the Security Council is still possible for the 50th Anniversary, intensive negotiations will take place, and compromises will have to be reached. Canada, as an active member of the Open-ended Working Group on the Reform of the Council, will have a vital role to play in these negotiations. Rather than adopting a fixed position, it is recommended that Canada should follow these guidelines:

- Support an increase in the number of Security Council members up to 21 members (from the current 15).
- Agree to an increase in the number of permanent seats for developed countries only if permanent seats are added for three states from the South.
- Work for reduction in the significance of the veto power by such means as: (a) denying the veto power to new members of the Security Council; or (b) making the veto valid only if exercised by three permanent members rather than, as at present, any one permanent member; (c) and/or limiting the kinds of issues on which the veto can be exercised (at a minimum, the veto over amendments to the Charter and the appointment of the Secretary-General should go); and/or (d) establishing new majorities for passage of categories of Security Council resolutions to replace the general veto for permanent members.
- Support the principle of a fixed proportion of the seats on the Security Council coming from the South. (See Recommendations 2-5 in the June 1994 report Canadian Priorities for United Nations Reform of the Canadian Committee for the 50th Anniversary of the United Nations.)

(2) Finances

Both the revenues and expenditures of the UN need attention. It is gratifying that Canada has never been in arrears in either its regular or peacekeeping payments to the UN. Unfortunately, the record of many other states is quite different.

The expenditures of the United Nations are undoubtedly made with the same level of control and effective management as most of the better-run Member States. That does not mean that they are not in need of improvement – far from it.

- Canada should renew its support, first given in 1979, for value-for-money auditing; for the appointment of an Auditor-General for the UN, with a five-year contract, appointed by and accountable to the

General Assembly; and for the parallel creation of an internal management review system accountable to the Secretary-General. (See Recommendation 16.)

(3) An Agenda for Peace

There are a number of questions that must be posed about the capacity of the United Nations to maintain international peace and security. Among them are following:

- What is the responsibility of United Nations members for disasters like Rwanda and Bosnia that do not directly affect their national security and other interests? In fact, is there an international responsibility that arises from membership in the UN?
- Under what legal authority can an international organization assume quasi-government responsibilities in failed states, of which there is a lengthening list?
- Except when there is a clear case of aggression, are there any circumstances in which an international force should take sides or fight in a civil war? If so, who is to do the fighting?

The UN faces a dilemma. The expectations of the public for the world body grow with every fresh disaster, but the Member States of the UN still have not committed themselves to the fundamental concept of common security. The UN's capacity to respond effectively is constrained by a hundred practical shortcomings and by the reluctance and hesitations of the Member States which comprise the organization and which appear not to support a more effective role.

Partly in an effort to break through this impasse, the Secretary-General of the United Nations issued *An Agenda for Peace* in 1992, pursuant to a request from the first and only *Summit Meeting* of the Security Council for an analysis of potential international capabilities in the fields of preventive diplomacy, peacemaking and peacekeeping. This document has set off a worldwide round of reflection and debate. Canadians in particular, however, have been keen to do their part to move the organization beyond debate to action that would dramatically improve UN capacities.

Among the many suggestions that *An Agenda for Peace* made was a proposal that special forces – peace enforcement units – be constituted in situations of high risk. Peace enforcement units, therefore, would be a mid-point between traditional UN peacekeeping and *Chapter VII* style enforcement actions. The Secretary-General has since clarified that he had in mind a standby quick reaction force composed of national elements, which in turn would be based on volunteers from the regular units of national military forces.

Even though the political climate is not currently receptive, it is important for Canada to examine this concept. The proposal for a UN standby force able to deploy quickly is closely linked to both early warning and preventive deployments whereby a potential conflict is deterred or contained through an early UN presence in the field.

Official Canadian statements have invariably emphasized the need for international action prior to the point where bloodshed hardens the attitudes of the parties. The exploration of the requirements for a UN quick reaction force and possible Canadian commitments thereto is a logical extension of the Canadian approach.

• The Government of Canada should press for the creation of international peace enforcement units to be deployed either as a quick reaction force or in other situations of high risk. It should immediately offer a Canadian contribution to such units. These troops, to be drawn on a volunteer basis from among both regular and reserve personnel of the Canadian Forces, would be more heavily armed and could undertake a variety of tasks from providing protection for humanitarian relief work to securing ceasefire lines. (See Recommendation 25.)

(4) Arms Proliferation

In today's strategic climate, there is a consensus among the former Cold War adversaries on the need for a more systematic, international approach to restrictions on arms sales so as to prevent regional arms races and limit the consequences of regional instability. Unfortunately, agreeing on the principle of arms export restraint is far easier than putting it into practice.

Late in 1991 the UN General Assembly adopted a resolution which formally established the *United Nations Register of Conventional Arms.* This requested member nations to provide data regarding certain categories of arms exports and imports. The *Register* is viewed as an "early warning device" which will provide advanced notice of nations and regions where a potentially destabilizing build-up of armaments is taking place. It is intended to establish a universal and non-discriminating repository of data and information. No verification provisions are included in the *Register* but entries can be cross-checked to see if declared imports by one nation tally with exports from others.

Nevertheless, the *Register* has been criticised for being far too general in that it does not require specific types of weapons to be identified. Genuine transparency requires knowing what a state is holding and acquiring, not merely what it is importing. The best estimate is that only between 20-25 percent of arms production is traded internationally; the rest is procured by their producer.

- There are three ways in which Canada should seek to improve the UN's Register of Conventional Arms:
    a) universal reporting by all Member States should be strongly encouraged;
    b) other arms-supplying countries should be encouraged to prohibit sales to countries which do not report to the UN Register;
    c) definitions should be improved and the scope of the Register enlarged to include domestic procurement and national holdings so as to give a true picture of military capabilities; and
    d) Canada should prohibit arms sales to countries which do not report fully to the UN Register, or which are subject to UN embargoes. (See Recommendation 33.)

The fundamental problem with respect to weapons proliferation is that export controls are not the solution to solving regional conflicts. Export controls can slow down regional arms races and delay or even prevent the acquisition of some of the most threatening weaponry. Yet if nations feel threatened militarily, they will seek to enhance their security by acquiring whatever armaments they can. The most effective means of curbing the trade in arms will be by seeking political settlements and agreements on arms control at both the regional and global levels.

(5) An Agenda for Development

As we approach the 50th Anniversary, we find that the UN's accomplishments in the economic and social sphere receive very mixed reviews. Individual specialized agencies are credited with solid achievements, but dissatisfaction with the system of international development runs deep. A Nordic study found that the UN's development work was marked by "overlapping and duplication of work, limited responsiveness as well as lack of transparency and accountability."

In order to change the system, there must be a sense of urgency about reform. The facts on poverty and inequity should be stimulus enough in themselves: for example, that the income gap between the top 20 percent and the bottom 20 percent of the world's population has doubled between 1960 and 1990; or that 50 percent of Africa's children suffer from chronic malnutrition; or that the net financial flow from the South to the North in the 1980s was as great as the North to South flow in the 1970s.

The gap between Northern and Southern thinking on development may be narrowing; there is increasing evidence of a "pragmatic and non-confrontational approach" taken to reforms. In addition we must take into account the concern for sustainable development, the enhanced awareness of the environmental catastrophes risked by unsustainable development policies in North or South. The impact of expanded international trade on development is profound and the successful conclusion of the Uruguay Round of GATT negotiations opens the door to development strategies based upon larger flows of capital, goods and services. Finally, the very concept of development has evolved away from a preoccupation with capital accumulation and towards a view that gives more place to good governance and sustainable human development, and which looks to civil society as much as to the state for initiatives that promote development.

Coordination is the most difficult task faced by any UN reformer in the field of international development. On the surface, the problem seems straightforward. The *UN Charter* locates responsibility for economic and social matters in ECOSOC which, as we have seen, is described in *Chapter X* of the *Charter*. That body, however, has never been as effective as either the General Assembly or the Security Council. While *Article 63* gives ECOSOC the right to coordinate the activities of the specialized agencies, it specifies that it must do so "through consultation with and recommendations to such agencies and through recommendations to the General Assembly and to the Members of the United Nations." In practice, the independence of the specialized agencies from both ECOSOC and the Secretary-General/Secretariat has been wide indeed. Moreover, any blunt attempt to bring them under a single, central control would undoubtedly fail, for some of the specialized agencies enjoy more support from UN Member States than does the UN itself. On the other hand, leaving things as they are means perpetuating the disarray we have already noted.

The Canadian Government should therefore in cooperation with like-minded governments:

- Strongly urge the creation within the UN of a Sustainable Development Security Council, a high-level decision-making body with full coordination powers over specialized agencies. It should consult widely, especially with NGOs, on the details of the structure and mandate of such a body. The Canadian Government should present proposals on such a body to the World Social Summit as well as to the appropriate fora of the UN itself. (See Recommendations 40, 41.)

It was also felt that the Canadian Government would be in a much stronger position to press UN reforms in development if it were also to:

• Establish an International Development Advisory Council composed of individuals with experience and knowledge relevant to the effective pursuit of CIDA's humanitarian and development goals. The Council would assist the Government of Canada in formulating development policy; suggest ways of eliminating any discrepancies between commercial and international development policies; and submit an annual report to a parliamentary committee on CIDA's pursuit of its Charter objectives. The Council should also seek to relate humanitarian and development objectives to other aspects of post-conflict peacebuilding as elaborated in An Agenda for Peace. (See Recommendation 39.)

(6) An Agenda for Human Rights

The United Nations was born with an internal contradiction that has never been resolved: its members are states, but its goals are human values. In the light of such divergent pressures, the accomplishments of the 1993 *Vienna World Conference on Human Rights* are all the more impressive. The *Vienna Declaration* stands as a strong endorsement of the basic premises that have underpinned the UN's human rights activities since 1948: "the universal nature of [established international human rights principles] is beyond question"; "the promotion and protection of all human rights is a legitimate concern of the international community"; and "it is the duty of States … to promote and protect all human rights and fundamental freedoms."

The *Vienna Declaration* was subsequently approved at the Fall 1993 session of the UN General Assembly, which also adopted a *Declaration on Violence Against Women* and, most significantly, created the post of UN High Commissioner for Human Rights. The mandate of this Commissioner needs to be carefully scrutinized to see how it unfolds because, although the office has considerable potential, the obstacles to its effectiveness are no less substantial.

An important challenge for the High Commissioner will be to encourage basic administrative coherence and efficiency. The UN human rights organs have evolved in *ad hoc*, spasmodic and politically pragmatic ways such that the High Commissioner has inherited what might be described as the antithesis of a system – one that is characterized by lack of coordination, of a national division of labour, or of any clear institutional blueprint.

• In developing proposals for an international early warning system for the United Nations, the Government should encourage efforts to coordinate with highly relevant UN agencies such as the High Commissioner for Human Rights and the High Commissioner for Refugees. At this point, the High Commissioner for Human Rights has no information system and needs one.

Canada should press for greater coordination between UN specialized agencies and Secretariat functions over human rights questions. It should urge that the Secretary-General create a high-level task force charged with recommending a series of steps that could be taken across the UN system, plus suggestions as to implementation. The High Commissioner for Human Rights should convene annually a meeting of representatives of all relevant UN specialized agencies to facilitate coordination and the exchange of information. The Government of Canada should press for the rapid implementation of a programme of action for the newly created High Commissioner for Human Rights to ensure an effective UN field presence when human rights are violated or are in jeopardy, including maximizing the use of existing field offices of such agencies as the UNDP and the UN High Commissioner for Refugees. (See Recommendation 49.)

PART VIII

UNITED NATIONS REFORM: EPILOGUE

CHAPTER 23

The United Nations of the Future

Douglas Roche

After the hopes and heartbreaks of fifty years of United Nations activity, after the Cold War and the monstrous buildup of nuclear weapons, after the suffering of billions of the most vulnerable people, so often children, never able to escape the ravages of poverty, after the wars, inter-state and intra-state, with their horrifying and senseless killings, after the countless resolutions, vetoes, conferences and reports on every subject from deep sea to outer space, after the peacekeeping missions, the development programmes, the environmental protection, the advances in human rights and international law – after the rhetoric and programmes, the successes and failures of the only international institution where the world's peoples come to sort out their problems, is there now a basis for hope that the diverse human family can at last find a way to live in peaceful community?

One minute I want to answer with a resounding "Yes." We are clearly maturing in our civilization. We understand the planet and its inter-linkages as no generation before us. Medicine, science, education, communications and transportation have all made quantum leaps in the past fifty years. More people live at a higher standard than ever before. The pragmatics of global security are forcing new systems of cooperation.

The next minute I am filled with doubt. Violence spreads. Refugees mount. Weapons multiply. The gap between the rich and poor – everywhere, not just between North and South – is widening. The arms trade, driven by the most powerful nations, sweeps through the South. Populations swell in the most disadvantaged States. Economic success, where it occurs, is identified with escalating consumer consumption, which exacerbates resource depletion and environmental pollution, drawing the planet ever closer to the primal and as yet unanswered question about its carrying capacity. Sustainable development, on present trend lines, seems unattainable. The forces of greed, which have driven economic development since the Industrial Revolution, appear unassailable. The age-old struggle between the powerful and the weak is now played out in global terms.

A wondrous dawn or a dark night?

No one, of course, can predict the future. Who, five years ago, could have predicted the fall of the Berlin Wall, the disintegration of Communism as an international force, the dissolution of the Soviet Union and sweep of democracy through the East European States, a Middle East accord between Israel and some Arab States, the ending of apartheid and election of Nelson Mandela as President of South Africa?

The present is too volatile. The transition from the Cold War into the post-Cold War era is jolting, almost raw in its visceral effects. No planning was done beforehand. The international system was paralyzed by the Cold War polarity. There is certainly not a shared system of values that transcends the North-South divide, or even the racial, cultural or religious divisions. The human curve may indeed turn upward; or it may collapse under the weight of uncontrolled events.

Caught in this whirling mixmaster, the United Nations enters its second half-century.

The UN was designed for a world that is over. It is unable to respond adequately to the crises of the present. Without reform, it will lack both credibility and capacity to meet the challenges of the kind of imbalanced and alienated world whose outline is now on the horizon of the 21st century.

The UN is not devoid of ideas. It is not short of plans or projections. Disarmament, equitable and sustainable development, protection of the environment, and advancement of human rights have all been intensely studied and charted. The compass to the future is available. There is a scandalous shortage of money, of course, but that is not the UN's most serious deficiency.

What must be overcome if the UN is to play its rightful role in assuring stability and security in the next fifty years, is the resistance of the powerful to change. Will the powerful on the Security Council genuinely share their power with a more representative selection of permanent members? Will the powerful, who dominate the international financial institutions, share their power with the less developed states? Will the powerful accept the inevitability that they must eliminate all their nuclear weapons to prevent horizontal proliferation? Will the powerful, in short, bring to the international system the tenets of democracy that they espouse for the conduct of the nation states themselves?

At this turning point in UN history, the answers to the above questions, in every case, appear to be negative. The spirit that created the UN, perhaps motivated out of fear of a repetition of the World War II ashes, is not alive today. It is, in fact, the powerful who have to be dragged, pushed, cajoled into the most modest of advances.

A comprehensive nuclear test ban is delayed and delayed again. The sharing of resources with the disadvantaged is blocked. The cleaning of the environment is set aside. The World Court is left in ambiguity. A permanent UN police force is denied. The UN, the repository of hope for the strengthening of the international system, is starved of funds.

Yet with all the obfuscation put in the way by the powerful, who have the resources to dominate and manipulate the international system, there remains a great counter-force. The synergy of energy of caring, committed and competent people working in the myriad of non governmental organizations has the potential to overcome the political and bureaucratic machinations that prevent genuine human progress.

The dismantled Berlin Wall is itself testimony to the power of people once aroused. The networks of NGOs, visible at the UN *Conference on Environment and Development* in Rio de Janeiro, the Cairo *Conference on Population and Development*, and especially the energetic preparations for the Beijing *Conference on Women* are starting to make an imprint on international decisions. This work, as can be said of the United Nations itself, is still in its early stages. NGO future effectiveness will depend on two things: their numbers and their mastery of the decision-making process.

Left to themselves, the politicians and bureaucrats will never change the present systems to the degree required for true human security. The influence of the financially powerful, who would have to pay a price for equitability, will protect the *status quo*. But only up to a point. When the force of public opinion becomes a gale that affects all the media decisions about what to publicize, business and politics will move. The ethic for change must come from the people. There is no other hope.

This populist desire for change is already feeding the desire for a Parliamentary Assembly of the UN. Major governments will resist this broadening of the base of ideas brought into global discourse, but they will not be able to stop it once the fire of human solidarity for change ignites. A Parliamentary Assembly is not the sole salvation of the UN – or of the world. Neither is the successful extension of the *Non-Proliferation Treaty*, a new Security Council for Development, a world-wide Verification Agency to enforce disarmament, or a Global Watch Office to prevent conflicts from breaking out. But together these advances in institutional arrangements to provide the kind of global protection that we look for in our own communities would be a mighty force, not only for planetary survival but for enduring peace.

The drafters of the *UN Charter* showed a prescience when they opened the document with these words: "We the Peoples of the United Nations ..." Governments, greed and wars, cold and hot, trampled over those words in the UN's first fifty years. Now, at this transformation moment, people everywhere are challenged to give life to those words. If they do, the United Nations of the future will create, rather than respond to, history.

GLOSSARY OF ACRONYMS
(see also Table 3.1 on page 64 for UN institutions)

ACC	Administrative Coordinating Committee (on sustainable development)
ACHR	American Convention on Human Rights
ACUNS	Academic Council on the UN System
ASEAN	Association of South-East Asian Nations
CAMDUN	Conferences on a More Democratic United Nations
CD	Geneva Committee on Disarmament
CEDAW	Convention on the Elimination of All Forms of Discrimination Against Women
CFE	Conventional Armed Forces Treaty
CONGO	Congress of Non-Governmental Organizations
CSCE	Conference on Security and Cooperation in Europe
CSD	Commission on Sustainable Development
CTBT	Comprehensive Test Ban Treaty
CWC	Chemical Weapons Convention
EC (EU)	European Community (now European Union)
ECOSOC	Economic and Social Council
GA	General Assembly
GEF	Global Environment Facility
GEMS	Global Environmental Monitoring System
HCHR	High Commissions for Human Rights
HDI	Human Development Index
ICCPR	International Covenant on Civil and Political Rights
ICESCR	International Covenant on Economic, Social and Cultural Rights
ICRC	International Committee of the Red Cross
INGO	International Non-Governmental Organizations
IPA	International Peace Academy
NAFTA	North American Free Trade Agreement
NATO	North Atlantic Treaty Organization
NGO	Non-Governmental Organization
NPT	Non-Proliferation of Nuclear Weapons Treaty
OAS	Organization of American States
OAU	Organization of African Unity
ORCI	Office of Research and Collection of Information
UNCED	UN Conference on the Environment and Development
UNEF	UN Emergency Force
UNIFEM	UN Fund for Women
UNPA	UN People's Assembly (proposed)
UNPROFOR	UN Protection Force
UNRRA	UN Refugee Rehabilitation Agency
WEOG	Western and Other Group Countries
WTO	World Trade Organization

BIBLIOGRAPHY ON
UNITED NATIONS REFORM

Bakwesegha, Christopher "The Need to Strengthen Regional Organizations: A Rejoinder" *Security Dialogue* 24 (4) December 1993.

Baratta, Joseph Preston "The Veto: Abolition, Modification or Preservation?" in Hoffmann, Walter ed. 1991 *A New World Order* (World Federalist Association).

Barnaby, Frank ed. 1991 *Building a More Democratic United Nations* (Frank Cass: Portland OR).

Bartos, Adam, and Christopher Hitchens 1994 *International Territory: The United Nations 1945-95* (Verso: London).

Bertrand, Maurice 1985 *Some Reflections on Reform of the United Nations* Joint Inspection Unit JIU/REP/85 (United Nations: Geneva).

Biesecker-Mast, Gerald "The World Court: How Do We Achieve Universal Acceptance?" in Hoffmann, Walter ed. 1991 *A New World Order* (World Federalist Association).

Boutros-Ghali, Boutros 1994 *Building Peace and Development* Annual Report of the UN Secretary General on the Work of the Organization (United Nations: New York).

Boutros-Ghali, Boutros 1992 *Report on the Work of the Organization from the Forty-sixth to the Forty-seventh Session of the General Assembly* (United Nations: New York).

Bozickovic, Mile "The Urquhart Debate: Pros and Cons of the UN Military Force" *Peace Magazine* Nov/Dec 1993: 10-11.

Canadian Committee for the 50th Anniversary of the United Nations *Canadian Priorities for United Nations Reform* June 1994 (808-63 Sparks St., Ottawa K1P 5A6) 47 p.

Canadian Department of Foreign Affairs and International Trade December 1994 *Canadian Reference Guide to the United Nations.*

Centre for International Studies 1994 *Canada 21: Canada and Common Security in the Twenty-First Century* (University of Toronto) 93 p.

Centre for International and Strategic Studies *Peacekeeping: Norms, Policy and Process, 1993 Peacekeeping Symposium* (York University: Toronto) 148 p.

Childers, Erskine B. "The Future of the United Nations: The Challenge of the 1990s" *Bulletin of Peace Proposals* 21 (2) June 1990 143-152.

Childers, Erskine, and Brian Urquhart 1994 *Renewing the United Nations System* (Hammarskjold Foundation: Uppsala, Sweden).

Commission on Global Governance (chaired by Ingvar Carlsson and Shridath Ramphal) 1995 *Our Global Neighbourhood* (Oxford University Press).

Damm, Kathryn "Global Security: Should There be a Standing UN Police Force?" in Hoffmann, Walter ed. 1991 *A New World Order* (World Federalist Association).

Damm, Kathryn "Human Rights – How Can the Conventions Be Promoted and

Enforced?" in Hoffmann, Walter 1991 *A New World Order* (World Federalist Association).

Dewitt, David B. "Canadian Defence Policy: Regional Conflicts, Peacekeeping, and Stability Operations" *Canadian Defence Quarterly* 21 (1) 1991.

Dobell, Graeme "The Media's Perspective on Peacekeeping" in Smith, Hugh ed. 1993 Peacekeeping – *Challenges for the Future* (Australian Defence Academy).

Dorn, Walter "UN Should Verify Treaties" *Bulletin of the Atomic Scientists* 46 July-August 1990 12.

Dorn, Walter A. "The Case for a UN Verification Agency" *IEEE Technology and Society Magazine* 9 No. 4 January 1991 16-27.

Doyle, Michael W., and Nishkala Suntheralingam "The UN in Cambodia: Lessons for Complex Peacekeeping" *International Peacekeeping* 1 No. 2 Summer 1994.

Earth Summit *Agenda 21: The United Nations* Programme of Action from Rio de Janeiro 1992 (United Nations: New York).

Eisler, Riane 1988 *The Chalice and the Blade* (Harper-Collins).

Evans, Gareth 1994 *Cooperating for Peace: The Global Agenda for the 1990s and Beyond* (Allen & Unwin).

Fischer, Dietrich "An Active Peace Policy" in Shuman, Michael, and Julia Sweig eds. 1991 Conditions *of Peace: An Inquiry* (Exploratory Project on the Conditions of Peace: Washington DC).

Fischer, Dietrich 1993 *Nonmilitary Aspects of Security: A Systems Approach* (Dartmouth Publishers: VT).

Fischer, Dietrich 1984 *Preventing War in the Nuclear Age* (Rowman & Allanheld: Totowa, NJ).

Fisher, Roger, and William Ury 1981 *Getting to Yes: Negotiating Agreement Without Giving In* (Houghton Mifflin: Boston).

Forsythe, David P. "The Politics of Efficacy: The UN and Human Rights" in Finkelstein, Lawrence S. ed. 1988 Politics *in the UN System* (Duke University Press: Durham, NC).

Franck, Thomas 1985 *Nation Against Nation* (Oxford University Press).

Fromuth, Peter ed. 1988 *A Successor Vision – The United Nations of Tomorrow:* First *Final Report to the United Nations Association of the United States of America* (University Press of America: Lanham, MD).

Galtung, Johan 1984 *There Are Alternatives! Four Roads to Peace and Security* (Spokesman: Nottingham, UK).

Gordenker, J. "The Security Council I" in Holmes, J. ed. 1983 *No Other Way: Canada and International Security Institutions* (Centre for International Studies: University of Toronto).

Heinrich, Dieter 1992 *UN Parliamentary Assembly* (World Federalist Movement: 777 UN Plaza, New York 10017).

Holmes, John W. 1986 *No Other Way: Canada and International Security Institutions* (Centre for International Studies: University of Toronto).

Hunt, B.D., and R.G. Haycock eds. *Canada's Defence* 1993 (Copp Clark: Toronto).

Independent Commission on Disarmament and Security Issues (chaired by Olof Palme) 1982 *Common Security: A Blueprint for Survival* (Simon & Schuster: New York).

Independent Commission on the Future of the United Nations 1993 *Toward Common Goals: Conference Report* (World Federalists of Canada: 145-207 Spruce St., Ottawa K1R 6P1) 30 p.

Independent Commission on International Development Issues (chaired by Willy Brandt) 1980 *North-South: A Programme for Survival* (Pan Books: London).

James, Alan 1990 *Peacekeeping in International Politics* (St. Martin's Press: New York).

James, Alan "Internal Peacekeeping: A Dead End for the UN?" *Security Dialogue* 24 (4) December 1993.

Johnstone, Ian 1994 *Aftermath of the Gulf War: Assessment of UN Action* (International Peace Academy: New York).

Jonah, James O.C. "The Management of UN Peacekeeping" in Rikhye, J., and K. Skjelsbaek eds. 1991 *The United Nations and Peacekeeping* (St. Martin's Press: New York).

Jones, Amy Janello, and Brenman Jones 1995 *A Global Affair: an inside look at the United Nations and its history* (to be published).

Keohane, Robert 1984 *After Hegemony* (Princeton University Press).

Kieseker, Peter "Relationships between Non-Government Organizations and Multinational Forces in the Field" in Smith, Hugh ed. 1993 *Peacekeeping – Challenges for the Future* (Australian Defence Academy).

Lambourne, Wendy "Humanitarian Intervention – Has Anything Changed?" *Pacific Research* 7 (1) February 1994 13.

Lautensach, Sabina "United Nations and Peacekeeping: An Evolving Concept" *Peace Research Reviews* 13 No. 2 1994.

Leontief, Wassily, and Faye Duchin 1983 *Military Spending: Facts and Figures: Worldwide Implications and Future Outlook* (Oxford University Press).

Liu, F.T. 1990 *United Nations Peacekeeping: Management and Operations* (International Peace Academy: New York).

Lunn, Jon "The Need for Regional Security Commissions within the UN" *Security Dialogue* 24 (4) December 1993.

MacNeill, Jim, Pieter Winsemius and Taizo Yukushiji 1991 *Beyond Interdependence – The Meshing of the World Economy and the Earth's Ecology* (Oxford University Press).

MacPherson, Brian F. "An International Criminal Court: Should World Law be Applied to Individuals?" in Hoffmann, Walter ed. 1991 *A New World Order* (World Federalist Association).

Marchand, Marianne H. "The Political Economy of North-South Relations" in Stubbs, R. and G. Underhill eds. 1994 *Political Economy and the Changing World Order* (McClelland & Stewart: Toronto) 294.

Matthews, Robert O. "United Nations Reform in the 1990s: North-South Dimension" *ACUNS Reports and Papers* No. 5 1993 15-42.

Mische, Patricia, and Gerald Mische 1977 *Toward a Human World Order* (Paulist Press: New York).

Muller, Robert 1991 *The Birth of a Global Civilization* (World Happiness and Cooperation: Anacortes WA).

Newcombe, Hanna 1983 *Design for a Better World* (University Press of America: Lanham, MD).

Newcombe, Hanna 1991 *Hopes and Fears: The Human Future* (Science for Peace Series, Samuel Stevens: Toronto).

Protheroe, David 1988 *The UN and Its Finances: A Test for Middle Powers* (North-South Institute: Ottawa).

Reed, David 1991 *The Global Environment Facility: Sharing Responsibility for the Biosphere* (WWF International No. 13).

Reich, Robert R. 1991 *The Work of Nations – Preparing Ourselves for 21st Century Capitalism* (Vintage Books: New York).

Russett, Bruce 1993 *Grasping the Democratic Peace: Principles for a Post-Cold War World* (Princeton University Press).

Scott, Douglas, and Markland Policy Group 1990 *Disarmament's Missing Dimension* (Science for Peace Series, Samuel Stevens: Toronto).

Segall, Jeffrey J., and Harry H. Lerner eds. 1992 *CAMDUN-2: The United Nations and a New World Order for Peace and Justice: Report of the Second International Conference on a More Democratic United Nations (Vienna 1991)* (CAMDUN Project: London and New York).

Sherif, Muzafer *et al.* 1961 *Intergroup Conflict and Cooperation: The Robbers' Cave Experiment* (University of Oklahoma Press: Norman, OK).

Simoni, Arnold 1992 *Regional Security Associations* (Peace Research Institute-Dundas: 25 Dundana Ave., Dundas L9H 4E5, Canada).

Sivard, Ruth Leger 1993 *World Military and Social Expenditures* (World Priorities: Leesburg, VA).

Soedibyo, Brigadier General "Regional Associations and Peacekeeping in the Asia Pacific Region" in Smith, Hugh ed. 1993 *Peacekeeping – Challenges for the Future* (Australian Defence Academy).

South Commission (chaired by Julius Nyerere) 1990 *Challenge to the South. Report of the South Commission* (Oxford University Press).

Stanley Foundation 1993 *The Role and Composition of the Security Council: Report of Vantage Conference* (Stanley Foundation: Muscatine, IO).

Starke, Linda 1990 *Signs of Hope – Working Towards Our Common Future* (Oxford University Press).

Stiles, K., and M. MacDonald "After Consensus, What? Performance Criteria for the UN the Post-Cold War Era" *Journal of Peace Research* 25 1992.

Tessitore, John, and Susan Woolfson eds. 1994 *A Global Agenda: Issues before the 49th General Assembly of the United Nations* (University Press of America for UNA-USA).

Tinbergen, Jan 1991 "Supranational Decision Making: A More Effective United Nations" Booklet 29 in *Waging Peace Series* (Nuclear Age Peace Foundation: Santa Barbara, CA).

UN Association for the USA 1987 *A Successor Vision: The UN of Tomorrow* (United Nations: New York).

UNICEF 1990 *The State of the World's Children* (Oxford University Press).

US Commission on Improving the Effectiveness of the United Nations 1993 *Defining Purpose: The UN and the Health of Nations* 116 p.

Urquhart, Brian E. "Reflections by the Chairman" in Rikhye, J., and K. Skjelsbaek eds. 1991 *The UN and Peacekeeping* (St. Martin's Press: New York).

Urquhart, Brian E. "United Nations Reform" *New York Review* 41 (9) 12 May 1994 29.

Urquhart, Brian, and Erskine Childers 1990 *A World in Need of Leadership: Tomorrow's United Nations* (Dag Hammarskjold Foundation: Uppsala, Sweden).

Urquhart, Brian, and Erskine Childers 1992 *Towards a More Effective United Nations* (Dag Hammarskjold Foundation: Uppsala, Sweden).

Wainhouse, David 1966 *International Peace Observation* (Johns Hopkins Press: Baltimore, MD).

Wallersteen, Peter "Representing the World: A Security Council for the 21st Century" *Security Dialogue* 25 (1) March 1994.

Warren, A. "What Went Right and What Went Wrong? A Canadian Perspective" in Holmes, J. ed. 1986 *No Other Way: Canada and International Security Institutions* 1986 (Centre for International Studies: University of Toronto).

Whitman, J., and L. Bartholomew "Collective Control of UN Peace Support Operations: A Policy Proposal" *Security Dialogue* 25 (1) March 1994.

Wiseman, Henry ed. 1987 *Peacekeeping: Appraisals and Proposals* (Pergamon Press: New York).

World Commission on Environment and Development (chaired by Gro Harlem Brundtland) 1987 *Our Common Future* (Oxford University Press).

World Federalist Association *A New World Order: Can It Bring Security to the World's People?* Hoffmann, Walter ed. 1991 (WFA: Washington DC).

Yakich, Mark "UN Funding: Supplemental or Direct Taxation?" in Hoffmann, Walter ed. 1991 *A New World Order* (World Federalist Association).

Yost, Jack "The Secretary-General: Should His Role be Enhanced?" in Hoffmann, Walter ed. 1991 *A New World Order* (World Federalist Association).

ABOUT THE CONTRIBUTORS

WILLIAM H. BARTON was born in Winnipeg and graduated from the University of British Columbia in 1940. After service in the Canadian army during World War II, he joined the Defence Research Board, transferring to the Department of External Affairs in 1952. He served abroad as representative to the International Atomic Energy Agency in Vienna, 1956-60; as Minister at the Canadian Mission to the UN in New York, 1961-64; as Head of the United Nation Division, and subsequently Assistant Under-Secretary of External Affairs in Ottawa, 1964-72; as Ambassador to the UN in Geneva and Canadian representative on the Conference of the Committee on Disarmament, 1972-76; as Ambassador and Permanent Representative of Canada to the UN in New York, 1976-80; and as President of UN Security Council, 1977 and 1978. After retirement he was appointed Chairman of the Board of Directors of the Canadian Institute for International Peace and Security, 1984-89. He was awarded the honorary degree of LL.D. by Mount Allison University in 1978, and was appointed a Member of the Order of Canada in 1994.

NEWTON R. BOWLES, a Canadian of China Missionary heritage, began his UN career in 1945, when he was responsible for UNRRA humanitarian aid during China's civil war. He then joined UNICEF, where he eventually became Programme Director. He participated in the elaboration of UNICEF policies over the years, from emergency aid to the long-range approach that sets children at the core of national development. His responsibilities took him to all regions of the world and involved formal networking throughout the UN system, including the Specialized Agencies, the World Bank and major bilateral organizations. He has been a member of the UN Inter-Agency Task Force on Child Survival and Development and, since retirement, has been an adviser to UNICEF on Children and War. He is on the Board of the UN NGO Committee on Disarmament and represents Canada's Group of 78 at the UN. His recent articles include *Policies and People*, an address at the 1994 Victoria University Conference celebrating Lester B. Pearson; and *Are Children People?*, a discussion of the *UN Convention on the Rights of the Child.*

JAMES BUSUMTWI-SAM was born in Ghana and received his doctorate from the University of Toronto in 1993. He is currently a visiting Assistant Professor at the Department of Political Science, University of Toronto, where he teaches international politics, international law and international organizations. He is currently working on a book-length manuscript on the domestic and international dimensions of governance, political learning and economic development in Africa.

A. WALTER DORN is a research associate at Trinity College and the principal researcher for the project on *UN fact-finding/intelligence for peace* of the International Relations Programme (University of Toronto). He is a scientist by training with a Ph.D. in chemistry from the University of Toronto, and has specialized in lipid membranes. Since 1983, he has served as the UN Representative of Science for Peace. In 1992/93, he was a Programme Coordinator with Parliamentarians for Global Action, responsible for promoting arms control verification and the Chemical Weapons Convention. He wrote the Index to the Chemical Weapons Convention for the United Nations Institute for Disarmament Research and has published widely on arms control.

SHIRLEY FARLINGER is a journalist specializing in peace, environment and women's issues. A graduate of Ryerson Polytechnical Institute in Journalism, 1980, she is the author of a forthcoming book *A Million for Peace: The Story of the Peacemaking Fund of the United Church of Canada*. She is a contributor to, and a member of the editorial board of *Peace Magazine*. As a member of the United Nations Circle of Voice of Women for Peace, she has participated in several UN orientation trips and one to the conference on disarmament in Geneva. She has also reported to the *UN Children's Summit*, the elections in Nicaragua and the *International Celebration of Partnership* in Crete.

ERIC FAWCETT is Professor Emeritus of Physics at the University of Toronto. He was educated in England and came to Canada in 1970 after ten years as research scientist at Bell Telephone Laboratories. In 1981 he became founding President of Science for Peace, which he has served since then in many capacities. In 1980 he was the first Chair of the Canadian Committee of Scientists and Scholars, of which he is now Secretary.

DIETRICH FISCHER, born 1941 in Switzerland, is Professor of Computer Science at Pace University in White Plains, New York. From 1986-88 he was a MacArthur Fellow in International Peace and Security Studies at Princeton University. From 1976-86 he taught economics at New York University. He is author of *Preventing War in the Nuclear Age* (1984) and *No-Military Aspects of Security: A Systems Approach* (1993), and co-author of *Warfare and Welfare* (1987, with Jan Tinbergen), *Winning Peace* (1989, with Wilhelm Nolte and Jan Oberg), and *Conditions of Peace* (1991, with Grace Boggs *et al.*). He has also lectured widely and published many articles on peace and security. He has been a consultant to several United Nations agencies on questions of disarmament and development.

GEOFFREY GRENVILLE-WOOD was born in Cairo, Egypt, in 1943, attended primary schools in Egypt, England and South Africa, secondary schools in South Africa and, from September 1959, in Canada. He was the Executive Director of the United Nations Association in Canada from 1974 to 1977. He is a Barrister and Solicitor in private practice in Ottawa with the firm Shepherd, Grenville-Wood. Particular areas of his practice include labour law, domestic and international environmental law and civil litigation. In 1989 he became Honorary Legal Counsel of the UNA/Canada and was National President from 1990 to 1993. In 1991 he was elected Chairman of the Executive Committee of the World Federation of United Nations Associations, which is based in Geneva and New York, a position he still holds. Mr. Grenville-Wood is married to Jacqueline Léger. They have two children, Emma and Simon.

DIETER HEINRICH has worked as a writer, speaker and organizer on behalf of global justice and security issues for almost 15 years. He is a member of the Executive Committee of the World Federalist Movement. The organization works to achieve closer cooperation among the world's peoples and governments leading toward a federal system for a supranational decision-making. He is a past president of the World Federalists of Canada. He has a degree in journalism and is author of numerous articles and much of the literature of the World Federalist Movement. He has worked as a consultant on global security for Parliamentarians for Global Action in New York.

RONALD ST.J. MACDONALD is a judge at the European Court of Human Rights in Strasbourg, and Senior Scholar in Residence at the University of Toronto. He is Honorary Professor in the Law Department of Peking University, Beijing.

ROBERT O. MATTHEWS is Professor and Chair of the Department of Political Science at the University of Toronto. He has recently completed a study of UN reform from a North-South perspective that was published in the Academic Council on the UN System (ACUNS) annual series. In addition to environmental concerns his interests include human rights and conflict resolution on which subjects he has authored many journal articles.

ROBERT I. MCLAREN is Professor in the Faculty of Administration at the University of Regina, Saskatchewan. His teaching and research areas are public administration, public sector management and administration of international organizations. He has long been deeply involved with the Institute of Public Administration in Canada (IPAC) and has worked with UNICEF.

HANNA NEWCOMBE was born in Prague, Czechoslovakia, but has been in Canada since 1939. With a Ph.D. in chemistry, she switched to peace research in 1962 and has been the editor of *Peace Research Abstracts Journal* from 1964 to the present. She is a co-founder of the Canadian Peace Research and Education Association, and is a former President of the World Federalists of Canada and current President of the World Federal Authority Committee. She teaches a peace course at York University (Toronto), and is the author of *Design for a Better World* and many articles and book chapters. She is the recipient of the Lentz International Peace Research Award and an Honorary LLD from McMaster University, Hamilton, Ontario.

MICHAEL OLIVER is the National President of the United Nations Association in Canada and Chair of the United Nations Reform Satellite Committee of the Canadian Committee for the 50th Anniversary of the United Nations. He was formerly President and Vice Chancellor of Carleton University (1972-78) and Vice Principal (Academic) at McGill University (1967-72). He has been Professor of Political Science at McGill, Carleton, and the University of Papua New Guinea and a Visiting Fellow at IDS, Sussex (1984) and at ANU, Canberra (1989). At various times he has been founding Federal President of the New Democratic Party, Research Director for the Royal Commission on Bilingualism and Biculturalism, Chairman of the Board of Canada World Youth and the World University Service of Canada, and the founding Director, International Development Office, Association of Universities and Colleges of Canada (1978-83). He lives at present near Magog, Quebec, and is Visiting Professor at Bishop's University.

PETER PADBURY has a Master of Science in Future Studies from the University of Houston and a Bachelor of Independent Studies from the University of Waterloo. Peter is interested in processes for developing vision and strategy and tries to weave these themes into most of his work. He has seventeen years experience doing policy studies, strategic planning, future studies, project management and programme evaluation. He has worked in Indonesia and Thailand. His career has crossed back and forth between environment and development many times. Over the last four years Peter has worked as the Coordinator for the Sustainability Programme at the Canadian Council for International Cooperation, where his primary responsibility was the NGO policy dialogue and policy advocacy, particularly around the UN Conference on Environment and Development and the UN Commission on Sustainable Development and related follow-up activities. He is currently Co-chair of the International NGO Fora, which is an attempt to build new mechanisms for NGO cooperation in the search for alternative development policies and strategies. He is also actively involved in designing a multi-stakeholder process to involve thousands of Canadians in preparing a sustainability plan for Canada.

PAUL D. PATON, B.A. (Toronto), M. Phil. (Cambridge), LL.B. (Toronto), of the Bar of Ontario, is an associate lawyer with Davies, Ward & Beck in Toronto, practising in the area of civil litigation. He is also Associate Director of the Canadian Studies Programme at the University of Toronto. He interned in the Office of the Director of the Political and Security Council Affairs Division at UN Headquarters in 1990. Paton and a colleague organized a series of *Round-Table Conferences on the United Nations Decade of International Law* held across Canada between 1991 and 1993, and co-authored numerous articles as a result of this work, including publications in the 1993 *Canadian Yearbook of International Law* and the 1992 *Proceedings of the Canadian Council on International Law.*

GEOFFREY A.H. PEARSON was educated at the University of Toronto and Oxford University. He joined the Department of External Affairs of Canada in 1952. In Ottawa, Mr. Pearson served in a range of senior assignments in the Department, including Chairman of the Policy Analysis Group, Director General of the Bureau of the United Nations Affairs, and Advisor on Disarmament and Arms Control Affairs. He held diplomatic appointments at Canadian Embassies in Paris, Mexico City, and at the High Commission in New Delhi. From 1980 to 1983 he served as Canada's Ambassador to the USSR. In late 1983, Mr. Pearson was appointed to a Special Representative of the Prime Minister for Arms Control. He was the first Executive Director of the Canadian Institute for International Peace and Security from 1985 to 1989. He is the author of *Seize the Day; Lester B. Pearson and Crisis Diplomacy* published by Carleton University Press in 1993.

JOHN C. POLANYI was educated at Manchester University in England, and joined the University of Toronto in 1956. His research is on the molecular motions in chemical reactions. He is a Fellow of the Royal Societies of Canada, of London, and of Edinburgh, also of the American Academy of Arts and Sciences, the US National Academy of Sciences and the Pontifical Academy of Rome. His awards include the 1986 Nobel Prize in Chemistry (shared) and the Royal Medal of the Royal Society of London. He served on the Prime Minister of Canada's Advisory Board of Science and Technology, as Honorary Advisor to the Max Planck Institute for Quantum Optics, Germany, as Board Member of the Steacie Institute for Molecular Science, Canada, and as Foreign Honorary Advisor to the Institute of Molecular Sciences, Japan. He was the founding Chairman of the Canadian Pugwash Group in 1960, has written over one hundred articles on science policy and on the control of armaments, and has co-edited a book *The Dangers of Nuclear War.*

K. VENKATA RAMAN is Professor of Law at the Faculty of Law, Queen's University, author of *The Ways of the Peacemaker* and editor of *Dispute Settlement Through the United Nations*. Prior to an LLD from Yale, he studied international law at Stanford, The Hague Academy and Andhra University and was a Fellow at the United Nations Institute for Training and Research, United Nations, New York, 1971-78.

ANATOL RAPOPORT was born in Russia in 1911 and received a Ph.D. degree in mathematics from the University of Chicago in 1941. He joined the faculty of the University of Toronto as Professor of Psychology and Mathematics in 1970 and was president of Science for Peace from 1984 to 1986. His books on peace and conflict include *Fights, Games and Debates* (1960), *Strategy and Conscience* (1964), *Conflict in Man-Made Environment* (1974), *The Origins of Violence* (1989), and *Peace, An Idea Whose Time Has Come* (1992).

DOUGLAS ROCHE was the Canadian Ambassador for Disarmament from 1984 to 1989 and Member of Parliament from 1972 to 1984. He is currently Visiting Professor at the University of Alberta, which awarded him an Honorary Doctor of Laws in 1986. He was elected Chairman of the United Nations Disarmament Committee at the 43rd General Assembly in 1988. An Officer of the Order of Canada, Mr. Roche is Chairman of the Canadian Committee for the Fiftieth Anniversary of the United Nations. His latest book is A Bargain for Humanity: Global Security by 2000 (University of Alberta Press, 1993).

DAVID RUNNALLS is the President of Runnalls Research Associates and Senior Advisor to the President of the International Development Research Centre. He is a Senior Fellow of the International Institute for Sustainable Development and an Associate Advisor to the Administrator of UNDP. Active in the field of environment and development for more than twenty years, serving as Research Director for Barbara Ward's book *Only One Earth,* prepared for the original UN Conference on the Human Environment, he remained with Barbara Ward as Director of the London and North American offices of the International Institute for Environment and Development. He is the Board Member for Canada of the World Conservation Union and a member of the Trade Policy Committee, which advises the Minister of International Trade, the Premier of Ontario's Council, and the Ontario Round Table on Environment and Economy. A writer and broadcaster, he served as the Issues Editor of the *Earth Summit Times,* the official newspaper of the Rio Summit, and is a member of the weekly Environment panel for the new Discovery channel.

CRAIG SCOTT is Associate Professor of Law at the University of Toronto. His main area of teaching and research is human rights, as a matter of legal and moral theory, international law, and comparative constitutional law. He has been particularly interested in the legal status and protection to date of "economic and social rights" (and especially their interdependent relationship with "civil and political rights"), the rights of aboriginal peoples, and the rights of local communities to sustainable development. He is currently writing a book, solicited by Oxford University Press for its Clarendon Law Series, which will be a critical theory of international human rights law and politics that emphasizes both the strategic rhetoric and the dialogical potential of international human rights.

ARNOLD SIMONI has been an engineer and head of his own manufacturing company (electronic equipment) in Toronto. In 1964 he participated with Dr. Norman Alcock (a physicist) in founding the Canadian Peace Research Institute. He produced two books, *Beyond Repair* (1972) and *Crisis and Opportunity* (1983), and several booklets and articles. He now works with the Centre for Strategic Studies at York University, Toronto, on disarmament issues.

URS P. THOMAS, born 1944 in Switzerland, has recently completed a Ph.D. in political science on the UN Environment Programme. He previously did an M.B.A., and is now focusing his research on the interaction between the trade-environment and the North-South relationships. He has taught international affairs and business administration at several universities in Quebec and Ontario, and was the Canadian representative for the International Studies Association at the *Earth Summit*. He is presently a research associate at the Institut des sciences de l'environnement de l'Université du Québec à Montréal.

SHARON A. WILLIAMS is Professor of International Law and International Criminal Law at Osgoode Hall Law School, York University, Toronto. She is a Canadian Member of the Permanent Court of Arbitration, the Hague (1991-97) and since 1993 a Fellow of the Royal Society of Canada. She has been an advisor with the Canadian delegation at the United Nations, in the Sixth Committee of the General Assembly and has acted as a consultant to the Canadian Department of Justice on international criminal law matters including extradition, the establishment of a permanent international criminal tribunal and a draft code of crimes against the peace and security of humankind, and to the 1985 Deschenes Commission on War Criminals in Canada. She has presented at conferences and meetings of experts on these matters in several countries. She has authored, co-authored and contributed to several books in the fields of public international law and international criminal law, as well as many journal articles in these areas. She has also written on international environmental law and the international and national protection of cultural property.

LAURIE S. WISEBERG is the Executive Director and co-founder of the Human Rights Internet, an international human rights data bank. Internet was started in 1976 in Washington, then moved to Harvard Law School and is now based at the University of Ottawa. Dr. Wiseberg was educated at McGill University, University of London and UCLA. She has taught Political Science at Ahmadu Bello University in Nigeria, the University of Wales, and the University of Illinois, Chicago. Dr. Wiseberg has published widely on human rights in such journals as *Human Rights Quarterly.*

HENRY WISEMAN, University Professor Emeritus at the University of Guelph, began his academic career in mid-life after twenty years in the business world. Always interested in international affairs, he soon began a study of United Nations peacekeeping and became a founding member of the International Peace Academy, New York, where he later was appointed as Director of Peacekeeping Programs. He has published widely, conducted seminars and lectured on peacekeeping issues in many parts of the world, and served as Special Observer of the cease-fire and elections in Rhodesia/Zimbabwe and as Elections Supervisor with UNTAC in Cambodia. Other interests include publication and production of a set of television documentary programs on the relationship between ethics and technology. He is currently teaching at the University of Guelph and conducting research on contemporary issues of peacekeeping.

OTHER BOOKS FROM SCIENCE FOR PEACE

World Security: The New Challenge, edited by Carl G. Jacobsen, Morris Miller, Metta Spencer, and Eric L. Tollefson. Dundurn Press, 1994. 282 p.

Arctic Alternatives: Civility or Militarism in the Circumpolar North, edited by Franklyn Griffiths. Samuel Stevens, 1992. 313 p.

Hopes and Fears: The Human Future, edited by Hanna Newcombe. Samuel Stevens, 1992. 195 p.

Unarmed Forces, edited by Graeme MacQueen. Samuel Stevens, 1992. 129 p.

Disarmament's Missing Dimension: A UN Agency to Administer Multilateral Treaties, The Markland Policy Group. Samuel Stevens, 1990. 150 p.

Accidental Nuclear War: Proceedings of the Eighteenth Pugwash Workshop on Nuclear Forces, edited by Derek Paul, Michael D. Intriligator, and Paul Smoker. Samuel Stevens, 1990. 169 p.

Militarism and the Quality of Life, by Alex C. Michalos. Samuel Stevens, 1989. 56 p.

Understanding War, by John McMurtry, with a foreword by Anatol Rapoport. Samuel Stevens, 1989. 68 p.

The Name of the Chamber Was Peace, edited by Janis Alton, Eric Fawcett, and L. Terrell Gardner. Samuel Stevens, 1988. 172 p.